Remaking Rwanda

Critical Human Rights

Series Editors

Steve J. Stern ❦ Scott Straus

Books in the series **Critical Human Rights** emphasize research that opens new ways to think about and understand human rights. The series values in particular empirically grounded and intellectually open research that eschews simplified accounts of human rights events and processes.

Since the civil war and genocide of the 1990s, Rwanda's new regime, led by the Rwandan Patriotic Front, has attempted to re-engineer the nation's politics, economics, and society. Cultivating an image of post-conflict Rwanda as a model of stability and growth, the Rwandan state has restricted political parties, civil society, and the media while claiming this was necessary to prevent future ethnic violence. *Remaking Rwanda* probes the mechanisms of the country's recovery and the durability of its success. Resisting simplified, triumphalist accounts of Rwanda's resurgence, this book asks what this experience of top-down, donor-supported, transformative authoritarianism teaches us about the relationship between post-conflict reconstruction and human rights in Central Africa and beyond.

Remaking Rwanda

*State Building and Human Rights
after Mass Violence*

Edited by
Scott Straus and
Lars Waldorf

The University of Wisconsin Press

The University of Wisconsin Press
1930 Monroe Street, 3rd Floor
Madison, Wisconsin 53711-2059
uwpress.wisc.edu

3 Henrietta Street
London WCE 8LU, England
eurospanbookstore.com

Printed in the United States of America

Library of Congress Cataloging-in-Publication Data
Remaking Rwanda: state building and human rights after mass violence / edited by Scott Straus and
Lars Waldorf.
    p.   cm. — (Critical human rights)
  Includes bibliographical references and index.
  ISBN 978-0-299-28264-6 (pbk.: alk. paper)—ISBN 978-0-299-28263-9 (e-book)
  1. Rwanda—History—1994– 2. Rwanda—Politics and government—1994– 3. Human rights—
Rwanda. I. Straus, Scott, 1970– II. Waldorf, Lars. III. Series: Critical human rights.
  DT450.44.R46   2011
  967.57104'3—dc22
2010038912

In honor of
ALISON DES FORGES,
1942–2009

Contents

Preface

SCOTT STRAUS and LARS WALDORF

Remaking Rwanda is dedicated to the memory of Alison Des Forges, who died in a plane crash in Buffalo, New York, on February 12, 2009. Alison was the most vocal and knowledgeable champion for human rights in Rwanda, and her untimely death has been a tremendous loss. She arguably did more than anyone to prevent, publicize, and document the 1994 genocide, one of the worst human rights crimes of the twentieth century, and to ensure justice in its aftermath. Yet she was also able to see past the genocide thanks to her early career as a historian of colonial Rwanda and her late career as a human rights advocate in post-genocide Rwanda. Her historical scholarship, genocide documentation, and human rights reporting were all infused with intellectual rigor, nuanced understandings, and a generous attention to those sidelined by history, historiography, and politics. As a scholar-activist and public intellectual, she mentored, inspired, and influenced several generations of Rwanda scholars, genocide scholars, and human rights advocates.

Most of the chapters in this volume emerged from conferences that we held in Alison's honor in London and Madison.[1] Alison influenced (directly or indirectly) all the contributors, and many of us feel a need to speak up in the wake of her death. A collected volume cannot begin to substitute for her loss, but we wanted to help advance some of Alison's priorities—in particular her concern with the trajectory of post-genocide Rwanda. We also hope the book reflects some of her intellectual qualities: her ability to marry human rights work with deep scholarly knowledge, her attention to the marginalized and dispossessed, her commitment to field and empirical research, and her understanding of historical continuities and legacies.

For those unfamiliar with Alison and her work, an overview is in order.[2] She began her forty-five-year engagement with Rwanda when, as an undergraduate at Radcliffe College in the early 1960s, she worked with Rwandans in refugee camps in Tanzania who had fled violence in the late 1950s and early 1960s. That experience subsequently prompted her to conduct oral history on Rwanda's hills for her PhD in History at Yale University. Her doctoral dissertation, "Defeat Is the Only Bad News: Rwanda under Musiinga, 1896–1931" (1972), presents a trenchant analysis of the Rwandan kingdom before and during the early colonial period—an analysis that still resonates today (and that David Newbury explores in chap. 2, this volume).[3]

After several years of teaching, community activism, and raising children in Buffalo, Alison became re-engaged with Rwanda as a human rights advocate and contemporary historian in the late 1980s. She joined Human Rights Watch (HRW) in 1988 and worked for that organization until her death, first as a board member, then as a researcher and consultant, and finally, from 2001 on, as a senior adviser. In the early 1990s, Alison contributed to three HRW reports, which warned of the potential for a major catastrophe in Rwanda (HRW 1992, 1993, 1994). In 1992 and 1993 she co-chaired the International Commission of Investigation on Human Rights Violations in Rwanda, composed of four human rights organizations, which issued a report in March 1993 detailing government involvement in systematic violence against Tutsi (FIDH 1993).

When the genocide broke out on April 6, 1994, Alison was well-placed to draw the international community's attention to the unfolding horrors and to counter simplistic portrayals of "ancient tribal hatreds."[4] While policymakers dithered, Alison and HRW quickly called the systematic slaughter by its rightful name—genocide. She tirelessly lobbied U.S., European, and UN officials, including members of the Security Council, to describe the violence as "genocide" and to intervene to stop the killing (Power 2002, 329–89). As Roméo Dallaire, the commander of the beleaguered UN peacekeeping mission in Rwanda, remembered: "[she] was one of our greatest allies in trying to encourage the international community to intervene in Rwanda and to expose the genocide for what it was" (Dallaire 2003, 546).

Shortly after the genocide ended, Alison set about a detailed examination of its local, national, and international contours. This ambitious project took five years to complete and produced a comprehensive, 789-page account titled *Leave None to Tell the Story: Genocide in Rwanda* (1999). The book contributed to her earning a MacArthur Foundation "Genius" Grant award. Twelve years after its publication, *Leave None* remains a landmark account of how state actors orchestrated the 1994 genocide. The main argument is that the genocide was a centrally planned, highly organized campaign directed by a small but powerful group of Rwandans. Facing twin threats from the predominantly Tutsi rebels (the Rwandan Patriotic Front, RPF) and a newly formed domestic opposition, this group chose genocide as a deliberate strategy to retain power. In addition to focusing on national-level actors, the book also provides an in-depth discussion of the genocide in two prefectures, Butare and Gikongoro. It also documents international responses to the genocide. Attentive to detail, focused on establishing high-level responsibility, and written in clear prose, the book filled major gaps in what had been previously known about the genocide. Alison characteristically combined the knowledge of a scholar who had studied Rwanda for decades with the ethics and precision of a human rights investigator.

Alison was not content with merely documenting the genocide. She also played a crucial role in bringing *génocidaires* to justice not only as an unpaid expert witness but also as a key prosecution strategist behind the scenes. Between 1995 and 2009 she testified for the prosecution in eleven genocide trials at the International Criminal Tribunal for Rwanda (ICTR) in Arusha, two genocide trials at the Cour d'Assizes in Belgium, and a genocide trial in a Swiss military court, as well as deportation proceedings in Belgium, Canada, and the United States. On the witness stand, her prodigious grasp of Rwandan history, her implacable commitment to the truth, and her calm assertiveness made her invaluable to prosecution teams. The most important ICTR judgments— from an international tribunal's first-ever genocide conviction in 1998 through the conviction of three top military leaders in 2008—all bear her stamp: over and over again, the judges invoke and rely on her expert testimony.

While Alison is best known for her work on the genocide and genocide prosecutions, she also fought for those who were falsely accused of genocide by the current Rwandan regime. For example, after General Léonidas Rusatira was arrested in mid-2002 on an ICTR warrant (encouraged by Rwanda), Alison conducted an investigation that helped convince the ICTR prosecutor to drop the charges.[5] A few years later, in September 2005, Alison was the only person to testify publicly in defense of Guy Theunis, a Belgian priest and former human rights advocate, at a *gacaca* show-trial staged by the government.[6]

Beyond specific cases, Alison repeatedly voiced concern over Rwandan government policies that (intentionally or not) impose collective guilt on the Hutu majority. She criticized *gacaca* courts for opening the floodgates to false genocide accusations. Starting in 2003, she spoke out against the vague and sweeping allegations of "genocide ideology" that have been used to suppress free speech, repress political dissent, and stifle independent civil society (HRW 2003, 2008; see Waldorf, chap. 3, this volume).

Alison's work on genocide justice (and injustice) did not blind her to the crimes against humanity, war crimes, and human rights abuses committed by the current regime. *Leave None* documented the RPF's killings of at least twenty-five thousand to thirty thousand civilians in 1994, the UN's attempt to suppress that information, the "mere pretence of justice" for those crimes, and the international community's indifference (Des Forges 1999, 735). As she eloquently wrote in her last report for Human Rights Watch:

To insist on the right to justice for all victims, as did the [1994] UN Commission of Experts, is not to deny the genocide, nor does such an insistence equate war crimes with genocide; it simply asserts that all victims, regardless of their affiliation, regardless of the nature of the crime committed against them, and regardless of the affiliation of the perpetrator, must have equal opportunity to seek redress for the wrongs done them. (HRW 2008, 90)

Alison consistently pressed the ICTR and its international backers to prosecute those RPF crimes. While Alison will always remain best known for her work on the Rwandan genocide, it should never be forgotten that her overarching commitment was to impartial justice for all of Rwanda's victims.

Notes

1. The proceedings from the London conference are available at http://www.sas.ac .uk/643.html.
2. For a more in-depth discussion of Alison's work, see Newbury and Reyntjens 2010.
3. Alison's dissertation is being published by the University of Wisconsin Press in 2011.
4. See for example the three newspaper op-eds Alison Des Forges wrote for the *Washington Post* in April 1994: "Take Care of My Children," "The Method in Rwanda's Madness; Politics, Not Tribalism, Is the Root of the Bloodletting," and "A Life Saved."
5. For more details of the Rusatira case, see Cruvellier 2010, 145–50.
6. For more on the Theunis trial, see HRW 2008, 60–62.

References

Cruvellier, Thierry. 2010. *Court of Remorse: Inside the International Criminal Tribunal for Rwanda*. Translated by Chari Voss. Madison: University of Wisconsin Press.
Dallaire, Roméo (with Brent Beardsley). 2003. *Shake Hands with the Devil: The Failure of Humanity in Rwanda*. Toronto: Random House.
Des Forges, Alison. 1972. "Defeat Is the Only Bad News: Rwanda under Musiinga, 1896–1931." PhD diss., Yale University.

———. 1994a. "Take Care of My Children." *Washington Post*, April 8, A21.

———. 1994b. "The Method in Rwanda's Madness; Politics, Not Tribalism, Is the Root of the Bloodletting." *Washington Post*, April 17, C2.

———. 1994c. "A Life Saved." *Washington Post*, April 19, A15.

———. 1999. *Leave None to Tell the Story: Genocide in Rwanda.* New York: Human Rights Watch.

Fédération internationale des ligues des droits de l'homme (FIDH). 1993. "Rapport de la Commission Internationale d'Enquete Sur Les Violations Des Droits De l'Homme au Rwanda Depuis Le 1er Octobre 1990." Paris, March 8. http://cec.rwanda.free.fr/documents/doc/RapportMars93/ComIntMars93.pdf.

Human Rights Watch (HRW). 1992. "Rwanda: Talking Peace and Waging War, Human Rights since the October 1990 Invasion." February 27. http://www.grandslacs.net/doc/2523.pdf.

———. 1993. "Beyond the Rhetoric: Continuing Human Rights Abuses in Rwanda." June 1. http://www.unhcr.org/refworld/docid/3ae6a8017.html.

———. 1994. "Arming Rwanda: The Arms Trade and Human Rights Abuses in the Rwandan War." January 1. http://www.unhcr.org/refworld/docid/3ac6a7fc8.html.

———. 2003. "Preparing for Elections: Tightening Control in the Name of Unity." May 8. http://www.hrw.org/en/node/77843.

———. 2008. "Law and Reality: Progress in Judicial Reform in Rwanda." July 25. http://www.hrw.org/node/62098.

Newbury, David, and Filip Reyntjens. 2010. "Alison Des Forges and Rwanda: From Engaged Scholarship to Informed Activism." *Canadian Journal of African Studies* 44, no. 1: 35–74.

Power, Samantha. 2002. *A Problem from Hell: America and the Age of Genocide.* New York: Basic Books.

Abbreviations

ADL	Association rwandaise pour la défense des droits de la personne et des libertés publiques (Rwandan Association for the Defense of Human Rights and Civic Liberties)
AFDL	Alliance des forces démocratiques pour la libération du Congo-Zaïre (Alliance of Democratic Forces for the Liberation of Congo-Zaire)
APRM	African Peer Review Mechanism
ARDHO	Association rwandaise pour la défense des droits de l'homme (Rwandan Association for the Defense of Human Rights)
ASF	Avocats sans frontières (Lawyers without Borders)
AVEGA-AGAHOZA	Association des veuves du génocide (Association of Genocide Widows)
CLADHO	Collectif des ligues et associations de défense des droits de l'homme au Rwanda (Collective of Alliances and Leagues for the Defense of Human Rights in Rwanda)
CNDH	Commission nationale des droits de l'homme (National Human Rights Commission)
CNDP	Congrès national pour la défense du peuple (National Congress for the Defense of the People)
DFID	Department for International Development
DGPR	Democratic Green Party of Rwanda
DRC	Democratic Republic of Congo
EDPRS	Economic Development and Poverty Reduction Strategy
EU EOM	European Union Election Observation Mission
FAR	Forces armées rwandaises (Rwandan Armed Forces)
FARDC	Forces armées de la république démocratique du Congo (Armed Forces of the Democratic Republic of the Congo)

FARG	Fonds d'assistance aux rescapés du génocide (National Fund for the Assistance of Genocide Survivors)
FAZ	Forces armées zaïroises (Zairean Armed Forces)
FDLR	Forces démocratiques de libération du Rwanda (Democratic Forces for the Liberation of Rwanda)
FDU-Inkingi	Forces démocratiques unifiées-Inkingi (United Democratic Forces)
GBS	general budget support
GoR	Government of Rwanda
HRW	Human Rights Watch
IBUKA	"Remember" (survivors' umbrella organization in Rwanda)
ICC	International Criminal Court
ICRC	International Committee of the Red Cross
ICTR	International Criminal Tribunal for Rwanda
IMF	International Monetary Fund
INGO	international nongovernmental organization
IRDP	Institut de recherche et de dialogue pour la paix (Institute of Research and Dialogue for Peace)
IRIN	Integrated Regional Information Networks
JGA	Joint Governance Assessment
LDGL	Ligue des droits de la personne dans la région des Grands Lacs (League for Human Rights in the Great Lakes Region)
LIPRODHOR	Ligue rwandaise pour la promotion et la défense des droits de l'homme (Rwandan League for the Promotion and Defense of Human Rights)
MDR	Mouvement démocratique républicain (Democratic Republican Movement)
MIGEPROF	Ministry of Gender and Promotion of Child and Family Rights
MINAGRI	Ministry of Agriculture and Animal Resources
MINADEF	Ministry of Defence
MINALOC	Ministry of Local Government
MINECOFIN	Ministry of Finance and Economic Planning
MINEDUC	Ministry of Education
MINIJUST	Ministry of Justice
MINITERE	Ministry of Land
MONUC	Mission des Nations Unies en république démocratique du Congo (United Nations Mission in the Democratic Republic of the Congo)

MRND	Mouvement républicain national pour la démocratie et le développement (National Republican Movement for Democracy and Development)
MSF	Médecins sans frontières (Doctors without Borders)
NCHR	National Commission for Human Rights
NEC	National Electoral Commission
NGO	nongovernmental organization
NPA	Norwegian People's Aid
NUR	National University of Rwanda
NURC	National Unity and Reconciliation Commission
OECD	Organisation for Economic Co-operation and Development
PDR	Parti pour la democratie et le renouveau-Ubuyanja (Party for Democratic Renewal-Ubuyanja; PDR-Ubuyanja)
PL	Parti libéral (Liberal Party)
PRI	Penal Reform International
PRSP	Poverty Reduction Strategy Paper
PSD	Parti social démocrate (Social Democratic Party)
PSI	Parti social Imberakuri (Imberakuri Social Party)
RCD	Rassemblement Congolais pour la Démocratie (Congolese Rally for Democracy)
RDF	Rwanda Defense Forces
RISD	Rwanda Initiative for Sustainable Development
RoR	Republic of Rwanda
RPA	Rwandan Patriotic Army
RPF	Rwandan Patriotic Front
RSF	Reporters sans frontières (Reporters without Borders)
RTLM	Radio télévision libre des Mille Collines
SBS	sector budget support
SNJG	Service national des juridictions gacaca (National Service of Gacaca Jurisdictions)
TIG	Travaux d'intérêt général
TRC	Truth and Reconciliation Commission
UNCHR	United Nations Commission on Human Rights
UNDP	United Nations Development Programme
UNHCHR	United Nations High Commissioner for Human Rights
UNHCR	United Nations High Commissioner for Refugees
USAID	U.S. Agency for International Development

Alison Des Forges

Remembering a Human Rights Hero

KENNETH ROTH

I was privileged to work with Alison for nearly two decades. No one matched her dedication, passion, and sense of personal responsibility to the victims of human rights abuse.

I will never forget my visit to Rwanda with her two years after the 1994 genocide, when the wounds were still raw and tensions high. Hearing of a new massacre in a remote part of the country, we dropped everything—which was typical for Alison—and drove there to investigate what had happened. We found a few survivors and interviewed them, but as we started to leave we bumped into the military patrol that had probably committed the massacre. Needless to say, the soldiers were not eager for us to be snooping around. During a tense two-hour standoff on a hilltop in the middle of nowhere, Alison calmly and persistently negotiated our exit. The episode was vintage Alison— determined to get at the truth and deeply devoted to the Rwandan victims of atrocities.

Alison joined Human Rights Watch as a founding member of our Africa advisory committee, a volunteer board. Before I knew it, she was working full time covering Rwanda, but without a salary. I finally had to insist that she let us pay her, and formally made her a member of our staff. In advance of the genocide, she saw the dark omens and tried to sound the alarm. Her long experience in the country let her see things that others could not.

When the genocide began, she worked all-out to stop it. She was on the phone with friends in Rwanda trying to save them. One was Monique Mu-jawamariya, a Rwandan human rights activist and a close friend of Alison. Monique was hiding in her attic, on the phone to Alison, as the *génocidaires* came working their way down her street, hacking people to death. Monique told Alison to take care of her children and hung up the phone. Alison was certain she had been killed, but a couple of days later learned that Monique had successfully hidden herself. To spirit Monique out of the country, Alison then used every connection she had, including President Clinton, whom Alison had introduced Monique to a few months earlier.

During the genocide, Alison spent most of the time alerting the world to the horror that was unfolding and trying to mobilize action. It wasn't easy. Most people in the West knew nothing of Rwanda. Many didn't even know the difference between Hutu and Tutsi. And after the U.S. government's debacle in Somalia the year before, few wanted to get involved in another military venture to stop more slaughter in Africa. They were too willing to dismiss the genocide as a manifestation of "ancient tribal hatreds" about which nothing could be done—a cheap excuse for inaction. Alison refuted that false history of convenience. She proved that the killing was organized, calculated, and directed by a small group.

As she later showed in her book, the *génocidaires* at first tested the waters. They were worried about the international reaction, the possible loss of aid on which Rwanda depended. But when the international community seemed not to care, the genocide proceeded at a horrific pace. Alison showed that the world could have stopped the genocide, but to its shame, it did not.

During the genocide, Alison met with Anthony Lake, the U.S. National Security Advisor, President Clinton's chief foreign policy advisor. She pressed him to commit U.S. troops, or allow UN peacekeeping forces to act, or at least to jam the radio stations that were giving instructions to the killers. But Lake and the U.S. government wouldn't act. He told her to "make more noise," as if the duty to stop mass murder depended on the whim of public opinion.

When the genocide ended, Alison was determined not to forget. She sought to pay respect to the victims by bringing the murderers to justice. She spent months roaming the Rwandan countryside, interviewing survivors, reconstructing events, turning the apparent chaos into a series of impeccably researched events that could form the basis of prosecutions. The result was her eight-hundred-page manuscript for *Leave None to Tell the Story*, the most important historical record there is of the genocide and a virtual guidebook for prosecutors.

Alison was never formally on the staff of the International Criminal Tribunal for Rwanda (ICTR), but she may as well have been. There was probably no more important contributor to its work. Publicly, she was an expert witness in eleven separate prosecutions. She spent days on the witness stand, sometimes facing grueling cross-examination by defense attorneys trying to discredit her. It wasn't easy for her, but Alison had on her side patience, facts, and a quiet, palpable commitment to truth.

Behind the scenes, Alison's role was even more important. No prosecutor had her knowledge of the genocide. She was their personal guide to understanding the genocide and making sense of how to proceed against its authors. That so many *génocidaires* have been brought to justice was due in very large part to Alison's passion and commitment.

With that record, you would think that the Rwandan government would lionize her—that it would sponsor memorials, speak out in praise of her, mourn her loss, recognize her as a dedicated ally. In fact, the opposite occurred. In the last few months of her life, the Rwandan government twice barred her from the country she loved. Why? Because Alison challenged the Rwandan government with her commitment to impartial justice—not victor's justice, not selective justice. Just justice.

Yes, the genocide was the big crime. But genocide victims weren't the only Rwandan victims in 1994. The Rwandan Patriotic Front (RPF), the rebel group that went on to become the current Rwandan government under President Paul Kagame, also murdered some thirty thousand people. She urged the prosecutor of the ICTR to abide by the principle that all victims deserve justice. The prosecutor still hasn't agreed, as he seems reluctant to take on so powerful a figure as the Rwandan president. But it is safe to say that if it were not for Alison's persistence, the issue would not even be on the table. Her principles made her unpopular with the Rwandan government, but they made her deeply respected among the Rwandan people, and among people worldwide.

Technically, I was Alison's boss, as if that were possible, but she was my mentor. I miss her deeply.

The Historian as Human Rights Activist

DAVID NEWBURY

There is no linear relationship between the historical past and the complex present. Contemporary events emerge from the conjunction of many factors of the past—some evident, some obscure. Together, in indeterminate ways, these mold the way people choose to act in the present. Nonetheless, in making sense of the present there are lessons to be learned from the careful study of history in a manner that is methodologically sound. By allowing us to see more clearly the cultural resources and deeper structures that influence how people choose to act, the study of history brings greater understanding of the logic of people's actions—even when we might be repelled by such actions in themselves. Only by understanding why people act as they do can we hope to address the underlying causes of current social processes.

That is why it is important to understand Alison Des Forges as a historian before she was a human rights activist. Her careful work analyzing contemporary processes was marked by a refined sense of historical method, and that training gave her unusual insight into the reasons people either promoted or denied social justice. Far beyond seeing the past as simply a collection of miscellaneous facts separated from any larger context, she sought patterns of relationships among events in her search for explanations. Trained to distinguish between simplified appearances and deeper causal factors, she was quick to note that while the Rwanda genocide took the form of ethnic killings, its causes were far more complex.

In *Leave None to Tell the Story* she traced out the causes of that cataclysm in a manner that was both comprehensive and clear. Much attention has been given to that magisterial work—for good and obvious reasons. But less attention has been given to Des Forges's earlier work, which provided the intellectual foundations for her insightful analysis of the genocide. Indeed, perhaps because it was never published during her lifetime, her 1972 Yale University dissertation has been largely ignored. Yet contained within that work were many elements of both method and substance that, almost thirty years later, contributed significantly to her fine-grained analysis of the genocide. Furthermore, having conducted over one hundred interviews in Rwanda as part of her dissertation research, Des Forges had become adept at identifying the ways in which words could be used as tools in this culture. At the same time, as part of her historical training she learned to assess issues fully conscious of the changing character of human society. That principle was central in drawing her to human rights work, for if history is created by human agency then it follows that humans can equally act to prevent the patterns of the past from being repeated in the future. We can prevent catastrophe if we wish to do so: that was a constant message in her later years as a human rights activist, and it is a core lesson to derive from her historical understanding.

For Des Forges the historical craft was not just an analytic approach; it also consisted of the communication of a worldview. Two hallmarks of her writing style were her sensitivity in identifying relevant issues and her ability to present them in lucid, transcendent language. Explicating complex events with consummate clarity made her writing fully accessible to lay people as well as academics. Nowhere are these skills more evident than in her dissertation—a pellucid account of the politics of Rwanda's royal court during the early years of colonial rule. For the political elite of Rwanda this was a turbulent time, as shown by the constant calculation, deception, betrayal, and (sometimes) murder that characterized the culture of the court. But this was not only a historical drama; for all the differences in context and characters it can also be seen as instructive of Rwanda's more recent political culture, for, as everywhere, there were continuities that characterized certain components of political behavior in Rwanda. With Des Forges's careful assessment of the culture of politics in the early twentieth century, she was well equipped to decipher the politics of a later period, and to interpret elements of more recent political culture in Rwanda that others, operating within a more narrow cultural logic, might have missed.

What interests me here is how her historical training came to have a bearing on her human rights work, and how it helped her penetrate the cultural veil that filters all intercultural encounters, not least in a period of post-genocide Rwanda where emotions remain raw and political legitimacy remains fragile.

In tracing the influences of historical praxis on her more recent work, this chapter draws on four themes from Des Forges's earlier dissertation to assess their relevance to her analysis of events in Rwanda in the 1990s and after. One theme explores the calculations of Rwanda's central court actors at the time of European arrival, at three levels: the relations of the court to colonial power, the effect of this encounter on the court's relations to the common people, and the kaleidoscopic changes in internal confrontations between different factions within the court. A second theme relates to one of the most fundamental issues in Rwandan political history: the continuing strength of regional differences within the political domain, at two levels. The first was reflected in the cultural oppositions so prominent in the enduring distinctions between the northern regions (which remained largely autonomous of central court power until well into colonial rule), and the central and southern regions (more deeply affected by court culture). A second way that regionalism became important emerged with the 1916 Belgian plan to divide the royal domains into two separate administrative regions under two different administrative authorities—a proposal that both exacerbated internal court factions and threatened the court's relations with common people. A third theme relates to the diverse nature of outside power—not only in competing colonial overlords (Germany, Belgium, and, for a while, Britain) but also in the distinctions among institutions operating within the same colonial matrix, particularly the distinctions between the Roman Catholic Church and the Belgian colonial administration. Finally, a fourth element to highlight is the domain of words and power—something Des Forges was very attentive to. As she noted in "Defeat is the Only Bad News," for Rwandans "armed confrontation was not the only way to fight" in a culture where ambiguous language and the employment of ruse represented (in the phrase of one Catholic priest) "a not ignoble contest between two intelligences" (Des Forges 1972, 16–17).

This chapter relates each of these themes to the broader analytic continuity linking "history" and "contemporary history" that so strongly marked Des Forges's human rights work.

The Three-Way Confrontation Facing the Court

For the central court of Rwanda, the major new element of the early twentieth century was the presence of powerful external actors—not simply those stationed on the kingdom's borders but those inserted directly into their society. An early encounter with European-led forces occurred in 1895, when some of Rwanda's elite armies confronted an intruding Belgian force. In a disastrous defeat for the court armies, several of Rwanda's most celebrated warriors were killed. The Rwandan court quickly realized that it was in their interests to find another way to avoid the bad news of "defeat"—a term that in Rwandan concepts refers to a permanent condition, different from the on-going political game of wit, tactics, and perpetual parrying.

In the wake of these changed circumstances, the court met German en-croachments (from 1898) with a different strategy. Des Forges's dissertation deftly presents the court's view of the new external power as a multiple threat to Rwandan political culture—both as a source of imperious military power and as an ideological alternative to Rwandan norms. Furthermore, it was clear that these new intruders commanded substantial economic resources outside the control of the court and military resources they could not match in di-rect confrontation. The court sought to control each of those threats by in-corporating them—channeling each element through the corridors of court politics—with two objectives. One was to co-opt German military resources to protect themselves against the Belgians (who had been responsible for the earlier military setback). The second was to advance their own internal agenda, using German troops to expand the domain of court administrative presence to the north—to areas that had always resisted court rule. As Des Forges notes (1972, 24):

The promise of German defense against the Belgians and their Congolese troops and against any internal threat must have encouraged the court to accept gra-ciously an arrangement which it could not have refused. That the German officer required nothing concrete in return and that he seemed so easy to manage with a combination of courtesy and deception most likely reinforced the Court's willing-ness to enter into the agreement.

In short, co-opting military power was an essential strategy of the early twentieth-century Rwandan court. With this background it is no wonder that Des Forges was quick to see the importance of military force as also a founda-tion for political power in early twenty-first-century Rwanda as well. And no surprise that she was aware of the supple nature of the linguistic contests of post-genocide Rwanda, having been sensitized to the gracious language that sold the court's strategy to the Germans a century ago.

A second form of novel power entering Rwanda consisted of a new set of conceptual tools introduced by the newcomers, including both the teachings of the Roman Catholic Church and the administrative structures of the emergent colonial state. The Rwandan court was slow to understand the ramifications of each of these—or to see these as alternatives to court cultural hegemony;

indeed at first the political elite rather scorned the Europeans for their lack of finesse. Consequently, the first Rwandans to welcome the priests were the subservient classes, who took the opportunities available to them to present their own grievances. For example, as Richard Kandt, one of the earliest Germans to live for any significant time in Rwanda (and who eventually became the first civilian colonial administrator), made his way with a small caravan to the king's court, he noted: "As soon as the Tutsi had turned their backs on our camp [the Hutu] were willing to tell us everything . . . their numerous grievances, . . . their lack of rights, the oppression" (Kandt 1921, 239, quoted in Des Forges 1972, 36). Early missionary caravans reported similar experiences.

At the outset, the Catholic priests far outnumbered the German administrators, and their missions were scattered across the landscape; as religious authorities, they carried moral force as well. Only belatedly aware of the divisive threat as well as the inclusive potential of this new exotic power, the court eventually responded to the missionaries with three strategies. One sought to establish mission stations among communities claiming autonomy from the court, both to remove them from direct influence on court proceedings and, by their very presence in distant areas, implicitly to expand the territorial claims of the court. In three years, five missions were founded, four of them in peripheral areas—and all in areas of weak royal control. A second strategy saw the aristocratic classes turning (if only belatedly) to the Church for education and for alliance; by the late 1920s, they had created what the missionaries termed a "tornado" of catechumens—a flood of postulants that the church was utterly unprepared for. The third strategy was that of encapsulation, shown by the manner in which members of the court were assigned to serve as official hosts for the European visitors, "supposedly to see that their needs were met" (Des Forges 1972, 34) but in fact in order to minimize (or reduce) any effective contact between the powerful new outsiders and the common people. Yet even as they sought to co-opt their visitors, Tutsi aristocrats were also constantly testing the Europeans in an eternal "contest between two intelligences." For example, sensing that Kandt's caravan was poorly armed and—even more important—noting that it was composed entirely of commoners, they offered him only old potatoes and rotten bananas as provisions (ibid., 35). Indeed, they showed nothing but contempt for these Europeans who did not follow the cultured protocol of the court.

Given this background, it was not difficult to find parallels to these early external encounters with more recent forms of interaction: the assignment of escorts (especially for Anglophone visitors); the occasional scorn for outsiders (though well veiled); the deft military alliances, which served more than military purposes but as a means of gleaning information or attempting indoctrination as well. They made a quick turn from overt opposition to incorporating the intellectual (as well as material) resources of the intruders and turning them to useful political effect. In short, Des Forges's early historical work prepared her well to spot the proclivities and policies of later regimes, before 1994 in playing on regional consciousness within the country and, since then, in welcoming powerful newcomers—whether government officials, missionaries, aid agencies, or casual visitors—and in channeling the resources associated with them to serve the political interests of the powerholders, controlling the effects of outsiders' presence in the guise of welcoming them.

Beyond the relations of the court to the outsiders, two new forms of intellectual resources—one associated with the Church, the other with the civil administration—affected colonial relations with the people as well. Indeed, the initial effects of both the Church and the civil administration were greatest on the commoners; only later did the court turn to the European arrivals, seeking to control the new administrative and material resources associated with them. (And when they did, the relationship was symbiotic, as both priests and civil administrators also sought to work through the elites. Thus each of the three parties—the court, the Church, and the colonial state—sought willing conduits through the other two for expanding their influence.) Nonetheless, in the early years only the common people turned to the missionaries, further accentuating the differences of aristocratic culture from commoner culture. It was only the next generation, after the Belgian administration had deposed the king in 1931, and when the power of the Church had been made apparent, that the elites most ardently sought the Church's support. The same trajectory occurred within administrative structures: as colonial rule became more established, the colonial administration came to operate more exclusively through the court/Tutsi personnel, replacing non-Tutsi in many areas—and ultimately in all areas.[1] Again there were parallels with later times, reflected in the decade to follow the genocide in a dramatic narrowing of the political field of political powerholders within the post-genocide government.

The third level of confrontation was reflected in competing factions at the court. Europeans arrived at a time of cataclysmic struggle within the Rwandan court associated with a monumental succession dispute to determine the configuration of power after the death in 1895 of Rwabugiri, one of Rwanda's most ruthless military rulers.[2] The sequel to Rwabugiri's death brought murderous violence, carried out on such a massive scale that the principal historian of the time described it as "a holocaust" (de Lacger 1961 [1939], 367).[3] This factional conflict pit the members of the Abega clan, the ascendant political force at the court, against the royal lineage of the Abanyiginya clan. In some ways the struggle was to last a decade, and resulted in the near-destruction of the royal line; many observers—including Rwandan historians—have asserted that were it not for European arrival the royal descent line would have been wiped out entirely.[4] With both delicate subtlety and brutal clarity, this enduring confrontation between factions at the court emerges as the principal focus of Des Forges's thesis. And just as the various forms of competition among factions were essential to understanding court history in the early 1900s, understanding analogous factions was key to Des Forges's insights on Rwandan political machinations of the 1990s—both before and after the genocide. This is not to say that there was anything deterministic about the events of the later twentieth century; they were sui generis. But Des Forges's careful study of the political patterns of a century earlier undoubtedly attuned her to elements of the Rwandan political culture that others could easily overlook.

The Supple Strength of Regional Identities

Beyond these three layers of confrontation—illustrated in the relations between the court and external actors, between the court and various commoner lineages, and (most visibly) between the multiple, evolving (even evanescent) factions at the court itself—lay a second level of divisions in Des Forges's historical work, this time privileging the role of regional identities that marked (and continue to mark) Rwandan society. She was not the first to note this, for such awareness goes back to the very first arrival of Europeans, and of course these were well-apparent to Rwandans long before that. But the fact that this quality emerged as such a central feature to her historical analysis undoubtedly lay the foundations for her acute sense of their significance in more recent events.

There were two levels at which regional identities operated. The first was in the cultural differences within Rwanda itself. Although "Defeat" is primarily a study of the central court, not a regional (or community-level) study, Des Forges was nonetheless very sensitive to local factors involved in regional relations with the court.[5] Here too, many levels came into play: Catholic priests, court administrators, German soldiers, and multiple local actors—including religious leaders, various claimants to the throne of Rwanda (claiming, for example, to be the legitimate heir deprived of succession by the Bega coup d'état of 1897), and a few independent warlords (the court and the Belgians referred to them as "bandits"). Eventually, superior firepower and a little hypocrisy on the part of the colonial-court alliance prevailed over the persistence and local knowledge of the northern inhabitants. In the end, the northern societies were incorporated into the colonial administrative grid by military force. Given this history, it is not entirely surprising that only seventy years later the core of those who planned and organized the genocide derived from those very areas incorporated by conquest into the court-administered colonial state.

A subtle historical sense of regional distinctions and cultural pluralities permeates the narrative in "Defeat Is the Only Bad News"—qualities pervasive in Des Forges's other writings on Rwanda as well. And as with other historical features, these elements, too, had relevance for the 1990s. One emerges in the hardening rigidities of ethnic perceptions. Indeed one can see the genocide as an attempt by a small faction at the center of political power, challenged from many angles in the early 1990s, to impose a single set of cultural perceptions of social categories (i.e., of ethnic labels) on a population that had retained very diverse cultural perceptions of ethnic salience: for some, ethnicity was important; for others, it was insignificant. (And for still others, it could be significant at some times and meaningless at others.) As Des Forges makes clear, the concept of ethnic divisions for people in the north was heavily influenced by the process of court conquest of the region. Understanding this history undoubtedly made Des Forges sensitive to the manipulation of ethnicity in later times.

But the sense of competing local identities is only part of the presentation of regional issues in this work. Europeans too had their own regional schemes. Having driven out the Germans during World War I, Belgian forces marched imperiously into the royal compound and, speaking in Swahili, demanded to see the king. When the courtiers sent to receive them responded in Kinyarwanda (explaining that they didn't understand Kiswahili), they were shot on the spot (Des Forges 1972, 205). Relations deteriorated from there, as Belgian military power essentially divided the territory into an eastern zone (with an administrative capital in Kigali) and a western zone (with an administrative capital in Gisenyi). According to Des Forges (ibid., 206), two elements about this policy most concerned the actors at the court. The first was their concern that the court would be "eliminated from its position as intermediary between the Europeans and its subjects." The second was their concern that in the new colonial arrangements the court would lose its control over nominating (and dismissing) the administrative cadre of the kingdom—that it would lose its power to reward or to discipline, and hence to control, its own delegated chiefs. Their concern for the second was well placed, but their first concern proved unfounded: as the colonial administration increasingly took over the power to appoint or dismiss administrative chiefs, the court's role as a colonial intermediary was reinforced, not diminished. "Dual administration" flourished.[6]

The Competing Forms of External Power

During the first twenty years of the twentieth century, the Rwandan court confronted multiple forms of external force. In addition to several different colonial powers, the court had to deal with many other forms of external power involving state agents, missionaries, and a motley variety of private armed intruders (traders, raiders, and cattle rustlers among them). These "independent actors" were removed by German power before World War I; however, court relations with state power and with the Church became only more complicated over time. After World War I, while one colonial power (Germany) was removed, two others entered (Belgium and Britain). The British occupied the southeastern quadrant of the country, justifying the annexation by noting that this area had formerly been a political arena autonomous from the Rwandan royal court, ruled by its own royal family (the Abagesera), and conquered by Rwanda only in the late nineteenth century. (Even then it had been administered only superficially.) Ultimately, by a decision of the League of Nations—a decision vigorously lobbied for by the Catholic Church—the British were forced to cede the terrain to the Belgians (and to the Nyiginya royal court).

But in the wake of World War I, British state power was not the only new issue to emerge in the region. British occupying forces had been followed by missionaries of the powerful Church Missionary Society (CMS), an offshoot of the Anglican missionary order based in Uganda and which had competed with the Catholic White Fathers there from the late 1870s. Indeed, only with the rejection of the Catholic faction in the Buganda civil wars of the 1880s had the White Fathers laid plans to evangelize in Rwanda. Now, in the 1920s, they found themselves followed there by an offshoot of the same CMS missionary order. Furthermore, this was only one example of a number of factors and actors to emerge in the 1920s. Policy disputes emerged from differences both within the Catholic clergy and among state Belgian personnel; investors arrived seeking land and labor; new economic sectors emerged; and (sometimes on Rwandans' initiative) new forms of labor and labor migration took shape. Once again, as with the earlier themes, the presence of a changing field of multiple actors was also a factor in the 1990s, as refugees entering Rwanda brought new cultural norms with them and introduced new laws, and as many outsiders, eager to help with the post-genocide reconstruction efforts, flooded into the country. Des Forges's later writings were distinguished by her ability to do justice to this cacophony of diverse actors, discerning clearly their different goals and methods (and levels of cultural awareness) while not losing sight of the ongoing themes within the shifting patterns of power.

David Newbury

Words and Power in Rwandan Culture

By their very nature, factional disputes at the court frequently evoked rich rhetoric as justification for the diverse positions taken. As Des Forges frequently noted, an elegant command of language skills is the quintessential art form of Rwanda. Court eloquence was also in evidence in the relation of the court to Europeans at many levels (and often remarked on by the White Fathers in their diaries and correspondence). The exquisite subtlety of Kinyarwanda and the cultural value placed on its manipulation, from poetry to politics, lent themselves to the same end: at the court, the artistry of words was part of the craft of power. Indeed, part of the power of her analysis resides in the acuity with which Des Forges saw through the language and its subtle manipulative nature. In "Defeat is the Only Bad News" she never lost sight of the politics of words, even while fully appreciating them as elements of artistry; for Des Forges (as for many Rwandans) the politics and poetics of the court were mutually reinforcing. Perhaps no study of Rwanda better illustrates this isometric quality of words and power at the court.

This is particularly apparent in the earlier sections of the work, on the struggles following the death of Rwabugiri, where the official German representative is artfully deceived by introducing him to a stand-in for the king shortly after the installation of the young king Musinga at the court (Des Forges 1972, 23–25). The surrogate sovereign leads the gullible German into a parody of blood brotherhood, with each simply tying a strand of grass around the waist of the other and declaring themselves blood brothers. The German left happy in his ignorance—and content for having participated in such an exotic ritual—while the court solemnly mocked the esteemed visitor for his naive participation in a sham ceremony—one that in no way obligated "the king" or the court to the requirements normally expected of blood brotherhood, whether enforced by social protocol or ritual power.

But it is not Rwandan poetics alone that is tied to the power of words in this study. Des Forges's entire work is lucidly presented in a narrative style that focuses on individuals and events—and which reaches out from there to embody principles and processes. In addition, the work is interspersed with proverbs; indeed in the original thesis the chapter headings were formed not of topic titles but exclusively of allusive proverbs, which could be read in several ways and would surely resonate with Rwandan readers. In choosing such a style Des Forges underscores her awareness that language was at the heart of the political game in Rwanda. Understanding the subtle sense of the relation of words and power in Rwandan political culture was undoubtedly a valuable lesson for her later work in post-genocide Rwanda.

Conclusion

All these elements are part of the political process in Rwanda: the intense and continuing internal factions, the enduring power of regional identities, the search for local control of multiple layers of outside interference, the objective of channeling of resources from the outside through elite networks, and the "creative" (but apparently sincere) use of language. And all these are also clearly part of the cultural field today. While they have been noted by others, an understanding of their current use can be enriched by an understanding of their use in earlier periods. Working on such themes for earlier periods provided Des Forges with unparalleled insights on the exercise of power in Rwanda in later periods as well.

Completing her fieldwork in 1969, Des Forges focused her dissertation on "the most clearly dramatic confrontations in modern times, those between Africans and the Europeans who came to rule them" (1972, i). But in a prescient comment, she noted that at the time she wrote, historians "[had] given [little] attention to penetrating the complexities of relations among Africans, and how the understanding of the divisions among them influence[s] their attitudes towards . . . foreign challenge[s]" (ibid.). Furthermore, the reign of Musinga, she noted, "provides excellent examples of the centuries-old struggle between the Court and its agents, who were trying to extend their control outward and downward, and the ordinary people, who opposed such expansion of central power" (ibid.). But such struggles were not confined to the early twentieth century. For this African polity at least, where colonial conquest occurred without massive casualties among the elite, the most dramatic confrontations were to come a quarter century after her fieldwork, and they were to include two elements she had placed at the center of her focus: the complexities of relations among Africans in the centers of power, and an understanding of "how divisions among them influenced their attitudes towards foreign challenges." These were indeed among the issues that Des Forges devoted her life to pursuing. By helping to clarify these elements, her historical training was an integral component of her extraordinary effectiveness in working on human rights issues as a "contemporary historian."

Notes

This paper was originally presented at a conference in Madison, Wisconsin, to honor the memory of Alison Des Forges. I am grateful to Scott Straus and Lars Waldorf for organizing the conference and for their comments on an early version of this chapter. Portions of this chapter have previously appeared in "Alison Des Forges and

Rwanda: From Engaged Scholarship to Informed Activism," *Canadian Journal of African Studies* 44, no. 1 (2010): 35–74.

1. By the 1950s only very few Hutu remained as subchiefs; in 1959 one of them became the target of an attack by Tutsi youth, an attack that was to set off a chain of events that eventually led to the overthrow of the monarchy. (On these events, see Murego 1975 and Reyntjens 1985.)

2. For the internal violence associated with Rwabugiri's reign, see Vansina 2004, chap. 7, "Nightmares."

3. It is noteworthy that this was written before the term came to be applied to the destruction of the Jews in Germany.

4. Heremans and Ntezimana 1987, 15: "Both oral traditions and written sources conjecture that the Abanyiginya dynastic lineage might have been completely exterminated if the Europeans had not arrived [when they did]." De Lacger 1961, 367, refers to the three principal Bega actors at the court as "le triumvirat sanglant," and notes that "a general slaughter preceded the holocaust." Pagès 1933, 206, states outright that "it is because of the arrival of the Europeans that the Banyiginya were not exterminated."

5. In fact she later published a long article detailing the difficulties of the court in their conquest in the northern areas (Des Forges 1986).

6. The effects of such "dual administration" on the peasants in the southwestern region of the country are illustrated in Newbury 1988.

References

de Lacger, Louis. 1961. *Le Ruanda*. Kabgayi, Rwanda: Imprimerie de Kabgayi. [First edition, Namur: Grands Lacs, 1939.]

Des Forges, Alison. 1972. "Defeat Is the Only Bad News: Rwanda under Musiinga, 1896–1931." PhD diss., Yale University.

———. 1986. "'The Drum Is Greater Than the Shout': The 1912 Rebellion in Northern Rwanda." In *Banditry, Rebellion and Social Protest in Africa*, edited by Donald Crummey, 311–31. London: James Currey.

———. 1999. *Leave None to Tell the Story: Genocide in Rwanda*. New York: Human Rights Watch.

Heremans, Roger, and Emmanuel Ntezimana. 1987. *Journal de la mission de Save, 1899–1905*. Ruhengeri: Editions Universitaires du Rwanda.

Kandt, Richard. 1921. *Caput Nili*. Berlin: Dietrich Reiner.

Murego, Donat. 1975. *La Révolution Rwandaise, 1959–1962*. Louvain: Institute des Sciences Politiques et Sociales.

Newbury, Catharine. 1988. *The Cohesion of Oppression: Clientship and Ethnicity in Rwanda, 1860–1960*. New York: Columbia University Press.

Newbury, David, and Filip Reyntjens. 2010. "Alison Des Forges and Rwanda: From Engaged Scholarship to Informed Activism." *Canadian Journal of African Studies* 44, no. 1: 35–74.

Pagès, A. 1933. *Au Ruanda sur les bords du Lac Kivu (Congo Belge): Un royaume hamite au centre de l'Afrique.* Brussels: Institut royal colonial belge.

Reyntjens, Filip. 1985. *Pouvoir et Droit au Rwanda.* Tervuren: Musée royal de l'Afrique centrale.

Vansina, Jan. 2004. *Antecedents to Modern Rwanda: The Nyiginya Kingdom.* Madison: University of Wisconsin Press.

Remaking Rwanda

Introduction

Seeing Like a Post-Conflict State

SCOTT STRAUS and LARS WALDORF

Where the utopian vision goes wrong is when it is held by ruling elites with no commitment to democracy or civil rights and who are therefore likely to use unbridled state power for its achievement. Where it goes brutally wrong is when the society subjected to such utopian experiments lacks the capacity to mount a *determined* resistance.

Scott 1998, 89

Official declarations are one thing; reality is another. . . . [N]ational reconciliation does not mean forcing people to subscribe to an ideology or to obey a new form of authority unquestioningly. . . . That is extremely dangerous. The country ha[s] already seen the results of a cult of authority.

Sibomana 1999, 139

Overview: Remaking Rwanda

In the early 1990s, Rwanda was devastated by civil war and genocide. During one hundred days in 1994, an interim regime orchestrated the systematic massacre of three-quarters of Rwanda's Tutsi minority and the murder of Hutu who opposed the regime and the genocide.[1] This genocide was undoubtedly one of the worst atrocities of the last century. It was committed during an armed conflict that had begun in October 1990 with the invasion of Rwanda by mostly Tutsi exiles fighting under the banner of the Rwandan Patriotic Front (RPF). The genocide ended in mid-July with the RPF's complete victory over the genocidal forces. Along the way, the RPF committed widespread and systematic massacres of Hutu civilians.[2]

Since 1994, the RPF-led government has practiced a deft authoritarianism that justifies its restrictions on political parties, civil society, and the media as necessary measures to guard against a recrudescence of ethnic violence.[3] The RPF has also pursued a highly ambitious policy of reconstruction and development that it adroitly frames in the preferred language of international donors: good governance, decentralization, gender mainstreaming, poverty reduction, rule of law, and transparency. Yet the RPF not only aims to alter Rwanda's governance and economic structures; it also seeks to alter social identities, cultural norms, and individual behavior. The RPF has undertaken a series of dramatic political, economic, and social projects, including the world's boldest experiment in transitional justice, comprehensive land tenure and agricultural reform, forced villagization, a de facto ban on ethnic identity, reeducation of the population, and the systematic redrawing and renaming of Rwanda's territory, among other things. In other words, the RPF has engaged in political, economic, and social engineering whose high-modernist ambitions and tactics resemble what James Scott (1998) described in *Seeing Like a State*. It is not an overstatement to compare the RPF's top-down reconstruction to those brought about by the French revolutionaries or by Kemal Ataturk.[4]

The RPF's boldness is not only evident in social engineering at home. It has also forced regime change and economic exploitation on neighboring Democratic Republic of Congo (DRC)—a country about ninety times larger than Rwanda. The RPF initiated two wars with the DRC. The first (1996–97) entailed a march across Congo's vast expanse that culminated some 1,500 miles west of Rwanda in the overthrow of Mobutu Sese Seko's thirty-two-year-long rule. The second (1998–2003) involved the capture of nearly one third of Congolese territory. Since then, Rwandan forces and Rwandan proxies have fought in the eastern Congo on various occasions. Rwanda entered the DRC partly for security reasons. In 1994 the rump genocidal regime relocated to the DRC with more than a million Hutu refugees and from there prepared to reinvade Rwanda. In later years, Rwanda faced a Congo-based Hutu rebel threat drawn in part from the former *génocidaires*. But in both cases, the RPF's ambitions exceeded its legitimate, short-term security needs. In the first invasion, its objective became to unseat a neighboring regime. In the second, the RPF funneled Congo's remarkable mineral wealth to Kigali. Rwanda was not alone: as many as seven states intervened in—and profited from—the DRC. But

Rwanda was the central, initiating external actor. And both times, Rwanda's actions in the various wars caused extensive suffering and death: as the chapters by Filip Reyntjens and Jason Stearns and Federico Borello show, Rwandan forces massacred tens of thousands of civilians, displaced many more, and contributed to the more than four million dead from conflict-related causes (see also Prunier 2009; Reyntjens 2009; Umutesi 2004). A leaked UN report (UNHCHR 2010) details the 1996–97 massacres and concludes that the Rwandan military committed crimes against humanity (and possibly genocide) against Hutu refugees.

By and large, many observers of Rwanda do not contest this empirical description, even if they emphasize different aspects. The principal source of disagreement is how to understand and evaluate Rwanda's post-genocide recovery in both normative and theoretical terms. On the normative side, the key question is: Will Rwanda's post-conflict reconstruction be successful and durable? The question has clear and vital implications for Rwanda, but it also has larger implications because the country is a high-profile case of post-conflict and post-atrocity reconstruction whose experience reverberates well beyond Central Africa. On the theoretical side, there are two central questions. First, what does Rwanda's experience of top-down, donor-supported, transformative authoritarianism teach us about existing models of post-conflict reconstruction? Second, what explains Rwanda's path of post-atrocity recovery? Rather than just examine the costs and benefits of particular policy choices, we ask what pushed (or permitted) Rwanda's post-genocide government to pursue the policies it did. We also examine the tensions and trade-offs between post-conflict reconstruction and human rights.

Objectives

Linked to those questions, this volume has three main objectives. First, it fills a crucial gap in the existing literature on Rwanda. Most of the books published on Rwanda over the past fifteen years are scholarly, journalistic, or personal treatments of the 1994 genocide as well as the international community's failure to intervene (e.g., Dallaire 2003; Kuperman 2001; Melvern 2000).[5] There is also a growing literature on international, national, and local efforts at genocide justice (e.g., Clark 2010; Cruvellier 2010; de Vulpian 2004; Jones 2009; Moghalu 2005; Neuffer 2001; Peskin 2008; Temple-Raston 2005; Tertsakian 2008). However, few scholarly books have been written on post-genocide Rwanda.[6] Johan Pottier (2002) published an important book some years back that mostly emphasized the RPF's successful manipulation of information and journalists about the war and refugees in the DRC. Nigel Eltringham (2004) examined post-genocide debates over ethnicity, history, memory, and guilt inside Rwanda and among the Rwandan exile community. Phil Clark and Zachary Kaufman (2009) brought together a group of authors who largely focus on transitional justice and reconciliation. Overall, then, *Remaking Rwanda* fills an important niche by presenting a comprehensive account of post-genocide reconstruction in Rwanda. Drawing on a range of scholars and practitioners from various backgrounds, the volume describes multiple dimensions of the country's recovery, including national and local governance, regional and international relations, economic development, international and local justice, education reform, and memory politics.

Second, the book's findings challenge what had been the prevailing positive assessments of Rwanda's post-genocide recovery up until mid-2010.[7] Rwanda was widely hailed as a remarkable success story, a showcase for post-conflict reconstruction, and the latest symbol of hope for the African continent. Well-known journalists, such as Stephen Kinzer (2008) and Philip Gourevitch (2009), were instrumental in shaping this glowing image of contemporary Rwanda. Similarly, the journalist and public intellectual Fareed Zakaria (2009) claimed that "Rwanda has become a model for the African renaissance. It is now stable, well ordered, and being rebuilt every month." Much of the praise was focused on President Paul Kagame, who the *Financial Times* and *Time* magazine named as one of the fifty most influential people of the new millennium (*Financial Times* 2009, Warren 2009). In late 2009 the Clinton Foundation awarded him a Global Citizen Award, stating: "From crisis, President Kagame has forged a strong, unified and growing nation with the potential to become a model for the rest of Africa and the world" (Clinton Foundation 2009). Aid agencies and private investors made similarly positive assessments. A Chicago businessman (now an adviser to President Kagame) nicely captured this sense of admiration in a British Broadcasting Corporation (BBC) interview: "Rwanda has gone from literally the bottom of the heap to become the beacon for Africa in fifteen years" (BBC 2010). Several scholars also praised Rwanda's achievements (see, e.g., Clark 2010; Clark and Kaufman 2009; Ensign and Bertrand 2009; Stansell 2009).

The contributors in *Remaking Rwanda* come to different conclusions based on observations, findings, and insights derived from extensive field research and historical reflection. Most contributors (including the editors) are relatively new to Rwanda and first came to the country to help document and understand the 1994 genocide and post-genocide challenges. Some contributors—such as Catharine Newbury, David Newbury, and Filip Reyntjens—are veteran scholars of Rwanda and the Great Lakes region. Many contributors have spent considerable time in rural areas outside the capital Kigali—where the RPF elite viewpoint prevails. This volume thus brings grounded, "from-below," and historically informed perspectives that are often missing from accounts of post-genocide Rwanda (see Newbury and Newbury 2000). Based on their research and experiences, most contributors to this volume have developed deep concern about the depth and durability of Rwanda's recovery, even while recognizing the country's achievements. One cannot yet know for certain what the medium- and long-term effects of Rwanda's model will be. Still, the volume calls attention to the social and political costs of repression, exclusion, growing inequality, a general climate of fear and intimidation, and impunity for crimes against humanity and war crimes committed in Rwanda and in the DRC. Several contributors also point out that the stability, order, and growth in contemporary Rwanda are not new when viewed in historical perspective. After all, pre-genocide Rwanda was a donor darling praised for many of the same qualities as the current regime (Uvin 1998). In short, the volume registers considerable concern.

We realize that debates on contemporary Rwanda are often polarized and polarizing.[8] Through this volume, we have tried to offer a more nuanced appraisal, though one that is ultimately critical. We acknowledge the enormity and impact of the Rwandan genocide of 1994. We recognize the enormous challenges of governing a state after genocide and the intense fear and insecurity that some Tutsi citizens feel. We appreciate Rwanda's undeniable accomplishments: visionary leadership, political stability, economic growth, pro-business environment, relative transparency, high proportion of women in parliament, and improved education and health care. Still, we have real concerns about the medium- and long-term social and political consequences of Rwanda's post-genocide model. For Rwanda's historical experience sadly teaches us that stability, order, and growth do not preclude severe breakdowns and violent conflict.

Third, the book aims to highlight Rwanda's importance for analyzing post-conflict recovery. Rwanda is, in our view, a critical case because of the international prominence of the genocide, the amount of international assistance the country has received since the 1994 genocide, and the way Rwanda is touted as a model post-conflict state. Rwanda has also emerged as a key player in the Great Lakes region and at the African Union. To be sure, Rwanda has specific characteristics, particularly the legacy of genocide. And as a small, landlocked, agrarian, and overpopulated state in a bad neighborhood (Central Africa), it has distinct physical and economic disadvantages.[9] Nonetheless, Rwanda is not a sui generis case. It has important similarities with other post-atrocity and post-conflict states, including East Timor, Cambodia, Guatemala, Burundi,

Liberia, Sierra Leone, and Uganda, on such salient features as physical, social, and psychological devastation, international assistance, and state building. Thus, this volume's analysis of post-conflict Rwanda has bearing on understanding post-conflict reconstruction more generally.

This book contributes to debates about post-conflict reconstruction in several ways. First, it provides a descriptive account of the nature and extent of Rwanda's reconstruction efforts for those interested in Rwanda as a case of post-conflict recovery. Second, by covering a wide range of topics and by bringing together multiple scholars and practitioners, we broaden the available discussion about post-genocide Rwanda. Finally, we seek to situate Rwanda's experience in the existing theoretical literature by asking what shaped Rwanda's trajectory and by asking what the case tells us about existing theories.

Rwanda's Social Engineering

In the aftermath of genocide, Rwanda's new leaders saw an opportunity to engage in ambitious social engineering.[10] Their central justification is that the prior social order produced genocide, so radical change is needed to prevent a future recurrence. This view is predicated on a specific, intentionalist interpretation of the genocide that sees it rooted in a racist Rwandan culture that consistently tolerated violence against Tutsi. That is, Rwanda's new leaders have a fairly one-dimensional and sharply negative view of past Rwandan society and culture. This is understandable as most of these leaders grew up in exile because their parents had fled identity-based violence and discrimination. Yet it is also self-serving in that it significantly downplayed the effect of the RPF-initiated civil war (Lemarchand 2008; McDoom 2009; Straus 2006). Furthermore, recent scholarship challenges the RPF's view that ethnic hatred, genocide ideology, and hate media motivated the *génocidaires* (Fujii 2009; McDoom 2009; Straus 2006).

The RPF's social engineering occurs in four main arenas. The first is behavioral and cultural. A central goal of Rwanda's current leadership is to change how Rwandans understand themselves and the social categories around them. This is done by inculcating a new ideology of "national unity and reconciliation" in all Rwandans (particularly youth). As part of that program, Rwandan citizens are commanded to drop their ethnic identity labels and to identify only as Rwandans. The government has also launched a national reeducation program as part of which various Rwandan groups are taught how to think about the past in solidarity camps (*ingando*) and civic education trainings (*itorero*). In a remarkable chapter, Susan Thomson describes how she was forced to undergo reeducation when her research project fell afoul of government officials. The community courts (*gacaca*) dealing with genocide cases, which are described by Max Rettig, were part of the larger effort to inculcate new social values. Rwandans were compelled to attend the proceedings, partly to learn about how the prior regime's bad governance had resulted in genocide. As An Ansoms and Bert Ingelaere show, peasants are being forced to comply with new regulations on personal hygiene and appearance. This has even included banning the cultural tradition of drinking *urwagwa* (banana beer) and other beverages through a shared straw—even though that symbolizes reconciliation and social trust. Interestingly, the RPF partly blames a Rwandan culture of obedience for the genocide, but its social engineering has sought only to reinforce habits of obedience in the population.

A second aspect of social engineering is the spatial reconfiguration of Rwanda. Catharine Newbury's chapter describes how the government has promoted—and often imposed—villagization (*imidugudu*) on a rural landscape of traditionally scattered homesteads in order to modernize, rationalize, and control the countryside. At a public meeting in Kigali in 2003, a Tanzanian reminded the audience that his country had tried that and failed in the 1970s (see Scott 1998, 223–61). The director of Lands responded curtly, "Tanzania did it wrong; we'll do it right." In addition, the government has transformed the state's administrative units and redistributed their powers and responsibilities as part of its decentralization policy. More dramatically, the government redrew and renamed Rwanda's map in 2005. This spatial reengineering can also be seen as an attempt to eradicate the regionalist loyalties and divisions that have played a significant role in Rwanda's ethnic violence. The country's ten provinces (with their historically evocative names) were reduced to four (with the rationalistic, legible names of Northern, Southern, Eastern, and Western). Practically overnight most cities, towns, and other places changed names and shapes. These changes, alongside the new flag, new national anthem, and new national language (English), have seemingly turned Rwanda into a new state. Indeed, as Carina Tertsakian writes, many long-term genocide detainees no longer recognize their country upon release.

A third arena for social engineering is the economy. Prior to 1994, Rwanda was an overwhelmingly rural society dominated by smallholder farming of subsistence crops and coffee. Rwanda's post-genocide leaders have a very different vision for economic growth. As An Ansoms and Chris Huggins detail, the government is replacing small-scale and subsistence agriculture with larger agribusiness and ranching ventures through land consolidation, land tenure reform, and mono-cropping. In addition, the RPF wants to make Rwanda a hub for information technology in Africa. And, as a UN panel of experts found, Rwanda's leaders have raised considerable revenue through the (mostly illegal) exploitation of mineral and other natural resources in the DRC. To be sure, post-genocide Rwanda needed alternative avenues for economic development; smallholder agriculture was simply not sustainable over the long term, particularly given the country's growing population, decreasing size of land holdings, and declining soil fertility. Some of these policies have created wealth and economic growth, at least in the short term. This, in turn, has encouraged a developmental state agenda that envisions Rwanda becoming the Singapore of Central Africa. There are three problems with this vision. Rwanda's growth owes a great deal to foreign aid and illegal resource exploitation. In addition, that growth is clearly not sustainable given the increasing overpopulation. Furthermore, the United Nations Development Programme (UNDP) raised concerns that "Rwanda's high growth rates are deceptive in that they hide large and growing inequalities between social classes, geographic regions and gender" (UNDP 2007).[11] Our point here is that these efforts to overhaul Rwanda's economy should be seen in the larger context of the leadership's top-down project to transform the society.

The final focus for the government's social engineering is politics. The new leadership does not allow any serious political opposition, independent media, or independent civil society to exist. The ruling RPF also seeks to incorporate most citizens into this vanguard party—known as the *umuryango* (family lineage)—through recruitment drives, "animation" sessions, and the harassment, cooption, and disbanding of other political parties (HRW 2003, 2010; ICG 2002). This resembles both Uganda's "Movement" system and former president Juvénal Habyarimana's one-party state in which all Rwandans were born members of his Mouvement républicain national pour la démocratie et le développement (National Republican Movement for Democracy and Development, MRND) party. Furthermore, as Ingelaere reveals, the RPF has increased its political control over the countryside by replacing elected local officials (even RPF party members) with appointed, nonlocal loyalists.

Findings and Themes

We identify five interrelated themes in this volume. First, researchers looking at various sectors find a pattern of authoritarian control, whose mechanisms vary from heavy-handed repression to subtle cooption. Mostly, though, the exercise of power is deft.[12] While the political system has multiple parties, regular elections, and a formal separation of powers, criticism of the RPF, let alone opposition, is rarely tolerated. As Timothy Longman shows, the RPF has consistently sidelined Hutu and Tutsi democrats who could pose any threat to its hegemony. In his recent autobiography, the former parliamentary speaker Joseph Sebarenzi (2009), who is Tutsi and was closely associated with the genocide survivor community, reveals how President Kagame had him removed from office because of his efforts to strengthen parliament. Furthermore, the RPF's inner circle has shrunk considerably since 2003 with the arrest, exiling, and departure of some of President Kagame's oldest allies including former prosecutor general Gerald Gahima, former presidential adviser Theogene Rudasingwa, former head of external intelligence Patrick Karegeya, and former army chief of staff General Nyamwasa Kayumba. There are also regular cabinet shake-ups with government ministers suddenly finding themselves demoted or charged with corruption. At a local level, Ingelaere's work reveals how the RPF has employed decentralization to expand the state's coercive reach in the countryside. He evocatively quotes an elder Rwandan who states the "drum" is louder than the "shout," a phrase harking back to pre-colonial times that signifies the state's power over the people.[13]

Meanwhile, as Paul Gready and Longman demonstrate, civil society organizations have mostly had to adopt a compliant and conciliatory tone to survive. Human rights organizations have been largely coopted, even if as Gready shows there still exists some narrow but important room for maneuver. The same pattern holds true for the media: multiple news outlets exist, but independent voices are subjected to violence, heavy fines, and imprisonment, leading Rwanda to earn Africa's worst ranking from international watchdog Reporters sans frontières (Reporters without Borders, RSF) in 2009.

A second clear finding from the chapters is that of exclusion. Viewpoints that diverge from the RPF line are excluded from political debate and often demonized as "genocide ideology." Contributors who spent time talking to Rwandans beyond the narrow, elite circle of mostly Anglophone Tutsi returnees in Kigali—whether peasants (see Ansoms, Ingelaere, Huggins, and Thomson), Hutu prisoners (see Tertsakian), Tutsi survivors (see Rettig), or youth (see Kirrily Pells and Lyndsay McLean Hilker)—consistently report hearing expressions of exclusion and marginalization. This is often accompanied by a palpable sense of fear and alienation. As Rettig, Tertsakian, Don Webster, and Lars Waldorf report, many Hutu fear being denounced for genocide or "genocide ideology" and then imprisoned. In his chapter on *gacaca* in Sovu, Rettig shows that the community courts have stoked social mistrust and conflict. In the economic context, there is increasing inequality. These findings undermine claims that post-genocide Rwanda is achieving reconciliation or rebuilding social trust.

A third clear finding in the book is the RPF's instrumentalization of genocide, identity, history, and memory. Whenever the RPF feels a need to reassert its legitimacy, justify a particular policy, or defend itself against criticism, it raises the specter of genocide. As Waldorf demonstrates, accusations of "genocide ideology" have been leveled against a range of international actors (including CARE International, the BBC, and Human Rights Watch), local civil society organizations, and ordinary Rwandans. In addition, *gacaca* was used to impose collective guilt on the Hutu majority—something that reinforces the RPF's social control over the population. Jens Meierhenreich's fascinating research on sites of memory attests to the ways in which the RPF controls how the genocide is remembered. Nigel Eltringham, McLean Hilker, and Pells show how the RPF's control over public discourse about identity and history runs contrary to Rwandans' lived experiences.

A fourth pattern is that strong donor support has facilitated Rwanda's post-conflict recovery. Donor assistance constitutes more than 50 percent of the national budget. In her chapter, Eugenia Zorbas persuasively argues that donors are eager for success stories in Africa and that the Rwandan government continues to wield the "genocide credit." The regime balances defiance and persuasion, shifting between strident rhetoric about Rwandan self-reliance and positive endorsement of donor priorities. As the chapters by Zorbas, Rachel Hayman, and Stearns and Borello show, Rwanda's donors have largely avoided confrontation with the regime over domestic repression, exclusion, and inequality. The only (limited) exception to this pattern is when Rwanda has overreached in the DRC, either by threatening to reinvade or by too blatantly supporting rebel warlords. Overall, donor assistance, particularly in the form of (general and sectoral) budgetary support and diplomatic support, has been critical for Rwanda's post-conflict recovery.

The final theme of the book, addressed in the chapters from Victor Peskin, Reyntjens, and Stearns and Borello, is impunity for crimes against humanity and war crimes committed by the RPF during the 1990–94 civil war, the 1997–2001 insurgency in Rwanda's northwest, and the two Congo wars. These crimes cannot be equated with the 1994 genocide in Rwanda. Nonetheless, victor's justice inside Rwanda and at the International Criminal Tribunal for Rwanda (ICTR) undermines the rule of law and international criminal justice, while also discrediting justice efforts for the genocide. Furthermore, as Alison Des Forges wrote in her last HRW report, "all victims . . . must have equal opportunity to seek redress for the wrongs done them" (HRW 2008, 90).

Taken together, the contributors reveal an underside to Rwanda's post-genocide recovery that belies the dominant public narrative and that raises serious concern about the extent of social repair in the country. Worryingly, they also show the presence of all four factors identified by James Scott as necessary for "the most tragic episodes of state-initiated social engineering": an administrative ordering of nature and society, a high-modernist ideology that believes in the rational re-design of human nature and social relations, an authoritarian state "willing and able to use the full weight of its coercive power to bring these high-modernist designs into being," and "a prostrate civil society that lacks the capacity to resist these plans" (Scott 1998, 4–5). This is not to suggest a crude determinism: Rwanda's leaders and populace still have the final say over what Rwanda's future will hold. But taken together the chapters underscore concerns about Rwanda's current trajectory and the top-down, state-led, post-conflict model of reconstruction that de-emphasizes human rights.

Theoretical Implications

In this final section, we place Rwanda's reconstruction in comparative perspective. We ask two main analytical questions. First, what led the post-genocide regime to choose the path it did, namely social engineering coupled with sophisticated authoritarianism? Second, what does the Rwandan case study tell us about the emerging theoretical literature on post-conflict reconstruction?

We identify six critical factors that help explain Rwanda's reconstruction that, in turn, have comparative implications. The first is the nature and scale of the violence that occurred. The genocidal violence destroyed infrastructure, discredited institutions (particularly political parties and churches), and devastated bonds of social trust. It also left many Rwandans deeply traumatized and some genuinely fearful that genocide would recur. This legacy of genocidal violence provided both an opportunity and a justification for the RPF to re-invent Rwanda and Rwandans—to respond to the past and build a bulwark for the future. This same legacy also created a powerful rhetorical weapon against domestic and international critics. When challenged, the RPF has routinely raised the issue of genocide to say that because the past produced the worst of all human evils, the RPF has a right to remake Rwanda. Many international donors also accepted Rwanda's authoritarianism precisely because of the history of genocide.

A second critical issue is the terms of settlement of the conflict. The RPF handily won a military victory with some regional help from Uganda, but with no major international assistance. To the contrary, many inside Rwanda and outside view the United Nations peacekeeping mission and influential Western states as direct and indirect contributors to the genocidal violence, either because they withdrew their forces (United Nations and Belgium) or because they supported the Habyarimana regime (France). As a result, the RPF came to power with a relatively free hand: they did not have to make any significant political concessions to their military adversaries (the defeated *génocidaires*), their political allies (the Hutu and Tutsi democrats), or the discredited international community. This helps to explain why the "government of national unity," set up by the RPF immediately after the genocide, lasted only about a year.

A third critical issue is the post-conflict regime's pathway to power. On the one hand, the most influential actors in the current government, starting with President Kagame, trained as soldiers. They are hierarchical and disciplined, and they place great value on security and military power. It is thus not surprising that a strong coercive, security state has been central to Rwanda's post-genocide recovery. On the other hand, the main ideological influences on the RPF leadership in exile were those of revolutionary vanguard movements, particularly Uganda's National Resistance Movement (NRM), Mozambique's Frente de Libertação de Moçambique (Liberation Front of Mozambique, FRELIMO) party, and South Africa's African National Congress (ANC). Little is known about the debates and influences within the RPF as the party has been quite successful at closing ranks and remaining opaque to outsiders. Nonetheless, it seems that the NRM/FRELIMO/ANC models of revolutionary transformation were instrumental in shaping the RPF's social engineering ambitions. Indeed, some of the RPF's mechanisms are borrowed from the NRM: the notion of the RPF as an all-embracing family resembles the "no-party" Movement system, and *ingando* solidarity camps are lifted from Uganda's *chaka-mchaka* camps (right down to the weapons training for students).

The fourth factor is institutional legacy. Many observers who compare Rwanda today with the destruction after the genocide and civil war come away understandably impressed. But contemporary Rwanda also should be compared with the pre-colonial, colonial, and post-independence regimes that preceded it. This historical perspective reveals that a strong, centralized state presence—one associated with social control—has been a constant feature of Rwandan regimes across time. Several scholars have traced Rwanda's centralizing, statist tradition to the pre-colonial period (Lemarchand 1970; Vansina 2004). Indeed, strong state institutions of control and labor mobilization were critical to the rapid, participatory nature of the Rwandan genocide (Straus 2006; Verwimp 2006). Even today's practices in rural areas echo the findings of Danielle de Lame's powerful ethnographic study of pre-genocide Rwanda (de Lame 2005). In short, current practices of state-centered social control are strongly rooted in Rwandan political culture and institutions, and thus post-genocide Rwanda exhibits strong patterns of continuity with pre-genocide Rwanda.

A fifth major issue is the regime's base of political support. The RPF has a very narrow base of core support: mostly Anglophone Tutsi who grew up in exile in Uganda—that is, a minority of the Tutsi minority (which comprises an estimated 10–14 percent of the population). The RPF has lost support among its base (due to internal purges), as well as among its natural allies of Tutsi survivors and Hutu democrats (due to repressive policies). The RPF also alienated many would-be Hutu supporters through the 1990–94 civil war, the massacre of some 2,000–4,000 Hutu displaced persons at Kibeho in 1995, the brutal counterinsurgency in the northwest in the late 1990s, the massacres of Rwandan Hutu in the DRC, and the mass arrests and accusations against Hutu in Rwanda (as well as public executions in 1998). With such a narrow—and narrowing—base of support, the RPF's paramount concern is to retain tight control of the political arena and population in the short term. In the long term, the objective is to change preferences—to mold the culture, norms, identities, and behavior of Rwandans through social engineering. In short, the RPF's choice of repression and transformation conforms to a political logic of survival given its narrow base of support.

A final factor is the international environment. A permissive international community has been central to the RPF's ability to reshape the political and social landscape. The RPF skillfully plays international donors: it exploits donor guilt over the genocide, invokes the Paris Principles on aid effectiveness, makes defiant assertions about Western neo-colonialism and Rwandan self-reliance, and adopts donor preferences and rhetoric on issues it considers peripheral and unthreatening (like gender mainstreaming). Given the RPF's successful control and co-option of political opposition and civil society, the only alternative source of counterpower to the state would have been international donors (Uvin 2003). Yet donors have been passive and pliant, thereby enabling the RPF's repression, exclusion, and social engineering. Once again, the development enterprise is underwriting and legitimizing inequality and exclusion—as it did in the 1980s (Uvin 1998).

What does the above analysis contribute to our thinking about post-conflict reconstruction more generally? Here, we can only sketch three sets of arguments. First, our analysis suggests that we need a more complex model to explain the trajectory—not merely the outcome—of post-conflict recovery. Existing theory sees such recovery largely as a function of three variables: the degree of preexisting conflict, the institutional capacity of the state, and the amount of international assistance (Doyle and Sambanis 2006). Our analysis indicates that while these factors are indeed important, so too are the regime's pathways to power, the degree of power-sharing flowing from the conflict settlement, the regime's political base of support, and the nature of the relationship between the regime and its principal donors.

Second, the Rwandan case casts some doubt on teleological models of political transitions and human rights norm diffusion (see Risse, Ropp, and Sikkink 1999). Rwanda is not transitioning toward democracy despite considerable efforts at democracy promotion by donors, consultants, and nongovernmental organizations (NGOs) (see Carothers 2002). Indeed, as Sarah Freedman and her colleagues discovered, the RPF was not willing to allow democratic teaching of history in secondary schools. Given the amount of financial and technical assistance to transitional justice and rule of law efforts, as well as the work of the ICTR, one would expect something of a "justice cascade" in Rwanda (Sikkink and Lutz 2001). Instead, as Peskin and Stearns and Borello show, victor's justice prevails. Rwanda thus attests to some of the limitations of current theorizing about norm diffusion and norm transmission through international engagement.

Finally, Roland Paris has made an influential argument that institutionalization before political and economic liberalization is critically important for post-conflict reconstruction (Paris 2004). The need for institution-building before political pluralism is emphasized in other work on post-conflict states (see, e.g., Barnett 2006). Yet Rwanda attests to some of that strategy's costs. First, a newly strengthened state has less incentive to introduce liberal democratic features down the road (see Peou, 2009; Sisk 2009). Second, the absence of effective feedback mechanisms from citizens, whether through independent political parties, independent civil society, or independent media, means that government policy will be less responsive to citizens' needs. At the same time, citizens are denied nonviolent channels for expressing political, economic, and social grievances. This may merely postpone a future reckoning.

In challenging what has been the prevailing view of post-genocide Rwanda and complicating existing theories of post-conflict reconstruction, this volume aims to contribute—in whatever way outsiders can—to a robust social and political system that will avoid the terrible violence of Rwanda's past. For many readers of this volume, this may seem anodyne or obvious, but in the highly fractious and politicized environment of post-genocide Rwanda, it is vital to emphasize that the objective of durable social and political repair is a shared one. We hope this collection will stimulate a productive debate about how this shared goal—to which Alison Des Forges devoted much of her life—can best be accomplished both within and beyond Rwanda. At bottom, this book underscores the central importance of human rights for any model of post-conflict and post-atrocity recovery.

Notes

We are very grateful to David Newbury, Victor Peskin, Filip Reyntjens, and three anonymous reviewers for their helpful comments on earlier drafts of the introduction.

1. Acknowledging the difficulties with calculating the number killed in the genocide, Alison Des Forges estimated there were at least half a million victims (Des Forges 1999, 15–16; see also Reyntjens 2004, 178n1).

2. In her landmark account of the 1994 period, Des Forges estimated that the RPF killed approximately 25,000–30,000 civilians (Des Forges 1999).

3. Given the RPF's dominance, we use the terms "RPF" and "government" interchangeably.

4. We thank an anonymous reviewer for this insight.

5. For scholarly works on the genocide, see, e.g., Des Forges 1999; Fujii 2009; Guichaoua 2005; Longman 2010; McDoom 2009; Prunier 1995; Straus 2006.

6. To be sure, a number of important articles and book chapters on post-genocide Rwanda exist by many of our contributors and others not represented in this volume (e.g., Burnet 2008; Doom and Gorus 2000; Lemarchand 2008; Reyntjens 2004; Stover and Weinstein 2004; Uvin 2001).

7. Media coverage of Rwanda and President Kagame turned sharply critical in mid-2010 in response to increased repression, shadowy assassinations (and a near-assassination), President Kagame's reelection with 93 percent of the vote, and the leak of a UN report documenting Rwandan troops' massacres of civilians in the DRC (see, e.g., Clarke 2010; French 2010; Gettleman 2010; Traub 2010; Wadhams 2010). These events are described in the chapters by Longman, Sebarenzi, and Stearns and Borello. Still, it remains to be seen whether these events will have any lasting impact on the tone of media coverage, and more importantly, whether it will affect donor policy toward Rwanda.

8. See for example the exchange between President Kagame and René Lemarchand in Clark and Kaufman 2009.

9. Rwanda falls into three of the four traps identified by Paul Collier (2007) in *The Bottom Billion*: the conflict trap, landlocked with bad neighbors, and a legacy of bad governance in a small country.

10. Scott (1998, 94) notes that "at its most radical, high modernism imagined wiping the slate utterly clean and beginning from zero." This explains why high modernist projects are usually launched after war, decolonization, and other decisive events that seem to sweep away the past (ibid., 5).

11. Notably, but not surprisingly, the UNDP made no reference to ethnic inequalities despite conspicuous consumption by a growing Tutsi elite connected to the RPF and resource exploitation in the Congo. Still, it is important to underline

that inequality is not reducible to ethnicity: there are important inequalities within each of the ethnic groups (e.g., urban/rural, returnee/nonreturnee, Anglophone/Francophone).

12. A notable exception was the run-up to the 2010 presidential elections, which is described by Sebarenzi in this volume.

13. As Ingelaere notes, Des Forges used this phrase as the title for a historical article on the Rwandan state's expansion in the colonial era.

References

Barnett, Michael. 2006. "Building a Republican Peace: Stabilizing States after War." *International Security* 30, no. 4: 87–112.

BBC. 2010. "What Is the True Price of Rwanda's Recovery?" BBC Newsnight, March 31. http://news.bbc.co.uk/2/hi/programmes/newsnight/8593734.stm.

Burnet, Jennie E. 2008. "Gender Balance and the Meanings of Women in Governance in Post-Genocide Rwanda." *African Affairs* 107:361–86.

Carothers, Thomas. 2002. "The End of the Transition Paradigm." *Journal of Democracy* 13, no. 1: 5–21.

Clark, Phil. 2010. *The Gacaca Courts, Post-Genocide Justice and Reconciliation in Rwanda: Justice without Lawyers.* Cambridge: Cambridge University Press.

Clark, Phil, and Zachary Kaufman, eds. 2009. *After Genocide: Transitional Justice, Post-Conflict Reconstruction and Reconciliation in Rwanda and Beyond.* London: Hurst.

Clarke, Jody. 2010. "Rwandan Leader Fails to Quell Despot Fears." *Financial Times,* August 7.

Clinton Foundation. 2009. "Former President Clinton Announces Winners of the Third Annual Clinton Global Citizen Awards." September 23. http://www.clintonglobalinitiative.org/Newsmedia/newsmedia_pressreleases_92309c.asp?Section=NewsMedia.

Collier, Paul. 2007. *The Bottom Billion: Why the Poorest Countries are Failing and What Can Be Done About It.* Oxford: Oxford University Press.

Cruvellier, Thierry. 2010. *Court of Remorse: Inside the International Criminal Tribunal for Rwanda.* Translated by Chari Voss. Madison: University of Wisconsin Press.

Dallaire, Roméo (with Brent Beardsley). 2003. *Shake Hands with the Devil: The Failure of Humanity in Rwanda.* Toronto: Random House.

de Lame, Danielle. 2005. *A Hill among a Thousand: Transformations and Ruptures in Rural Rwanda.* Translated by Helen Arnold. Madison: University of Wisconsin Press; Tervuren: Royal Museum for Central Africa.

Des Forges, Alison. 1999. *Leave None to Tell the Story: Genocide in Rwanda.* New York: Human Rights Watch.

de Vulpian, Laure. 2004. *Rwanda, un genocide oublié? Un procès pour mémoire.* Brussels: Éditions Complexe.

Doom, Ruddy, and Jan Gorus, eds. 2000. *Politics of Identity and Economics of Conflict in the Great Lakes Region.* Brussels: VUB University Press.

Doyle, Mark, and Nicolas Sambanis. 2006. *Making War and Building Peace*. Princeton, NJ: Princeton University Press.

Eltringham, Nigel. 2004. *Accounting for Horror: Post-Genocide Debates in Rwanda*. London: Pluto Press.

Ensign, Margee, and William Bertrand. 2009. *Rwanda: History and Hope*. Lanham, MD: University Press of America.

Financial Times. 2009. "Fifty Faces That Shaped the Decade." December 28.

French, Howard. 2010. "U.N. Congo Report Offers New View on Genocide." *New York Times*, August 27.

Fujii, Lee Ann. 2009. *Killing Neighbors: Webs of Violence in Rwanda*. Ithaca, NY: Cornell University Press.

Gettleman, Jeffrey. 2010. "Rwanda Pursues Dissenters and the Homeless." *New York Times*, April 30.

Gourevitch, Philip. 2009. "The Life After." *New Yorker*, May 4.

Guichaoua, André. 2005. *Rwanda 1994: Les politiques du génocide à Butare*. Paris: Karthala.

Human Rights Watch (HRW). 2003. "Preparing for Elections: Tightening Control in the Name of Unity." May 8. http://www.hrw.org/en/node/77843.

———. 2008. "Law and Reality: Progress in Judicial Reform in Rwanda." July 25. http://www.hrw.org/node/62098.

———. 2010. "Rwanda: End Attacks on Opposition Parties." February 10. http://www.hrw.org/en/news/2010/02/10/rwanda-end-attacks-opposition-parties.

International Crisis Group (ICG). 2002. "Rwanda at the End of the Transition: A Necessary Political Liberalisation." November 13. http://www.grandslacs.net/doc/2555.pdf.

Jones, Nicholas. 2009. *The Courts of Genocide: Politics and the Rule of Law in Rwanda and Arusha*. London: Routledge-Cavendish.

Kinzer, Stephen. 2008. *A Thousand Hills: Rwanda's Rebirth and the Man Who Dreamed It*. Hoboken, NJ: John Wiley and Sons.

Kuperman, Alan. 2001. *The Limits of Humanitarian Intervention: Genocide in Rwanda*. Washington, DC: Brookings.

Lemarchand, René. 1970. *Rwanda and Burundi*. New York: Pall Mall.

———. 2008. *The Dynamics of Violence in Central Africa*. Philadelphia: University of Pennsylvania Press.

Longman, Timothy. 2010. *Christianity and Genocide in Rwanda*. Cambridge: Cambridge University Press.

Lopez, Humberto, and Quentin Woden. 2005. "Economic Impact of Armed Conflict in Rwanda." *Journal of African Economies* 14:586–602.

McDoom, Omar. 2009. "The Micro-Politics of Mass Violence: Authority, Security, and Opportunity in Rwanda's Genocide." PhD diss., London School of Economics.

Melvern, Linda. 2000. *A People Betrayed: The Role of the West in Rwanda's Genocide*. London: Zed Books.

Moghalu, Kingsley Chiedu. 2005. *Rwanda's Genocide: The Politics of Global Justice*. New York: Macmillan.

Neuffer, Elizabeth. 2001. *The Key to My Neighbor's House: Seeking Justice in Bosnia and Rwanda*. New York: Picador.

Newbury, David, and Catharine Newbury. 2000. "Bringing the Peasants Back In: Agrarian Themes in the Construction and Corrosion of Statist Historiography in Rwanda." *American Historical Review* 105:832–77.

Paris, Roland. 2004. *At War's End: Building Peace after Civil Conflict*. New York: Cambridge University Press.

Peou, Sorpong. 2009. "Re-examining Liberal Peacebuilding in Light of Realism and Pragmatism: The Cambodian Experience." In *New Perspectives on Liberal Peacebuilding*, edited by Edward Newman, Roland Paris, and Oliver P. Richmond, 316–35. New York: United Nations University Press.

Peskin, Victor. 2008. *International Justice in Rwanda and the Balkans: Virtual Trials and the Struggle for State Cooperation*. New York: Cambridge University Press.

Pottier, Johan. 2002. *Re-Imagining Rwanda: Conflict, Survival and Disinformation in the Late Twentieth Century*. Cambridge: Cambridge University Press.

Prunier, Gérard. 1995. *The Rwandan Crisis: History of a Genocide*. New York: Columbia University Press.

———. 2009. *From Genocide to Continental War: The "Congolese" Conflict and the Crisis of Contemporary Africa*. London: Hurst.

Reyntjens, Filip. 2004. "Rwanda, Ten Years On: From Genocide to Dictatorship." *African Affairs* 103:177–210.

———. 2009. *The Great African War: Congo and Regional Geopolitics, 1996–2006*. Cambridge: Cambridge University Press.

Risse, Thomas, Stephen Ropp, and Kathryn Sikkink. 1999. *The Power of Human Rights: International Norms and Domestic Change*. Cambridge: Cambridge University Press.

Scott, James. 1998. *Seeing Like a State: How Certain Schemes to Improve the Human Condition Have Failed*. New Haven, CT: Yale University Press.

Sebarenzi, Joseph. 2009. *God Sleeps in Rwanda*. New York: Simon and Schuster.

Sibomana, André. 1999. *Hope for Rwanda: Conversations with Laure Guilbert and Hervé Deguine*. Translated by Carina Tertsakian. London: Pluto Press.

Sikkink, Kathryn, and Ellen Lutz. 2001. "The Justice Cascade: The Evolution and Impact of Foreign Human Rights Trials in Latin America." *Chicago Journal of International Law* 2, no. 1: 1–33.

Sisk, Timothy D. 2009. "Pathways of the Political: Electoral Processes after Civil War." In *The Dilemmas of Statebuilding: Confronting the Contradictions of Postwar Peace Operations*, edited by Roland Paris and Timothy D. Sisk, 196–223. London: Routledge.

Stansell, Christine. 2009. "The Aftermath and After." *New Republic*, September 5.

Stover, Eric, and Harvey M. Weinstein, eds. 2004. *My Neighbor, My Enemy: Justice and*

Community in the Aftermath of Mass Atrocity. Cambridge: Cambridge University Press.

Straus, Scott. 2006. *The Order of Genocide: Race, Power, and War in Rwanda.* Ithaca, NY: Cornell University Press.

Temple-Raston, Dina. 2005. *Justice on the Grass: Three Rwandan Journalists, Their Trial for War Crimes, and a Nation's Quest for Redemption.* New York: Free Press.

Tertsakian, Carina. 2008. *Le Château: The Lives of Prisoners in Rwanda.* London: Arves Books.

Traub, James. 2010. "Foreign Policy: Holding Rwanda Accountable." National Public Radio, September 7. http://www.npr.org/templates/story/story.php?storyId =129696478.

Umutesi, Marie-Béatrice. 2004. *Surviving the Slaughter: The Ordeal of a Rwandan Refugee in Zaire.* Madison: University of Wisconsin Press.

United Nations Development Programme (UNDP). 2007. "Turning Vision 2020 into Reality: From Recovery to Sustainable Human Development." http://hdr.undp .org/en/reports/nationalreports/africa/rwanda/RWANDA_2007_en.pdf.

United Nations High Commissioner for Human Rights (UNHCHR). 2010. "Democratic Republic of the Congo, 1993–2003: Report of the Mapping Exercise Documenting the Most Serious Violations of Human Rights and International Humanitarian Law Committed within the Territory of the Democratic Republic of the Congo between March 1993 and June 2003." August draft.

Uvin, Peter. 1998. *Aiding Violence: The Development Enterprise in Rwanda.* West Hartford, CT: Kumarian Press.

———. 2001. "Difficult Choices in the New Post-Conflict Agenda: The International Community in Rwanda after the Genocide." *Third World Quarterly* 22, no. 2: 177–89.

———. 2003. "Wake Up! Some Personal Reflections and Policy Proposals." Unpublished report. June. http://fletcher.tufts.edu/faculty/uvin/pdfs/reports/wakeup.pdf.

Vansina, Jan. 2004. *Antecedents to Modern Rwanda: The Nyiginya Kigdom.* Madison: University of Wisconsin Press.

Verwimp, Philip. 2006. "Peasant Ideology and Genocide in Rwanda under Habyarimana." In *Genocide in Cambodia and Rwanda: New Perspectives*, edited by Susan Cook, 1–40. New Brunswick, NJ: Transaction Publishers.

Wadhams, Nick. 2010. "Is Rwanda's Hero Becoming Its Oppressor?" *Time*, April 24. http://www.time.com/time/world/article/0,8599,1984315,00.html.

Warren, Rick. 2009. "The 2009 Time 100: Paul Kagame." *Time*, April 30. http://www .time.com/time/specials/packages/article/0,28804,1894410_1893847_1893843,00 .html.

Zakaria, Fareed. 2009. "Africa's New Path: Paul Kagame Charts a Way Forward." *Newsweek*, July 18. http://www.newsweek.com/id/207403.

Part I

Governance and
State Building

1

Limitations to Political Reform

The Undemocratic Nature of Transition in Rwanda

TIMOTHY LONGMAN

For much of the international community, post-genocide Rwanda stands as a glowing story of successful postwar reconstruction. The journalist Stephen Kinzer (2008) argues that Rwanda has "rebelled against its destiny. It has recovered from civil war and genocide more fully than anyone imagined possible and is united, stable, and at peace. Its leaders are boundlessly ambitious. Rwandans are bubbling over with a sense of unlimited possibility" (1–2). Diplomats and businesspeople praise the high level of competence displayed by civil servants and the government's strong commitment to economic development (Chu 2009). International church and school groups now regularly visit Rwanda to learn about reconciliation and contribute to the country's reconstruction (Smith 2009; Van Eyck 2009; Lerner 2009).

Rwanda's supposed remarkable recovery is generally credited to the post-genocide government led by the Rwandan Patriotic Front (RPF). Many observers heap particular praise on Paul Kagame, president of Rwanda since 2000. Shortly after the genocide, *New Yorker* writer Philip Gourevitch praised Kagame (then vice president) as a new type of African leader, both competent and democratic, and such praise has only increased over time (Gourevitch 1997). Kinzer (2008, 337) writes:

Two things about President Kagame are evident to all who consider his situation honestly. First, he has accomplished something truly remarkable. The contrast between where Rwanda is today and where most people would have guessed it would be today in the wake of the 1994 genocide is astonishing. Second, Kagame is the man of the hour in modern Africa. The eyes of all who hope for a better Africa are upon him.

As this volume suggests, the image drawn by numerous scholars and human rights activists is at sharp variance with this generally positive view of Rwanda. Johan Pottier (2002) has effectively studied the RPF's savvy manipulation of the international media to promote a restricted narrative about Rwanda's recent history that paints the RPF in a heroic light. According to Pottier (2002, 51):

Rwanda's RPF-led regime has views about the past, present and future which are being propagated via a wide range of intersecting channels: academic outlets, diplomatic activity, media broadcasting, policymaking for refugees and the writing of rural development policy. Outsiders unfamiliar with the intricate interplay of local, national, regional and international dynamics have ended up "feeling inspired" by the remarkable consistency with which Rwanda's post-genocide leaders have spoken about society, history and economy.

In this essay, I explore one aspect of Rwanda's supposed miracle of recovery, the ostensible transition to democratic rule. Beginning in 1999, Rwanda's post-genocide government began to organize elections, starting at the local level and culminating in 2003 with presidential and parliamentary elections. Many observers praised the RPF and its leader for courageously implementing a transition to democracy less than a decade after the genocide. In a recent *Time* magazine profile of one hundred of "the world's most influential individuals," Reverend Rick Warren, one of America's best-known evangelical preachers, applauded Kagame for having "successfully modeled the transition from soldier to statesman," and praised "his willingness to listen to and learn from those who oppose him" (Warren 2009).

Based on an analysis of the elements that are widely recognized to constitute democratic governance, Rwanda continues to fall far short of the standards of liberal democracy.[1] In the post-genocide era, Rwanda has made a transition from one type of authoritarian regime to another. The RPF regime has systematically intimidated, co-opted, and suppressed civil society, so that Rwanda today lacks independent social organizations capable of articulating most public interests. The regime tolerates very little public criticism, strictly limiting freedoms of speech, press, and association. Political parties are restricted and intimidated, while constraints and manipulation of the electoral process have prevented elections from being truly free and fair.[2] Defenders of the RPF regime simultaneously deny these criticisms and claim that restrictions on freedoms are necessary for national unity, given the history of genocide, and that benign authoritarian rule is necessary for economic development, their top priority.[3] Rwanda's persistent authoritarian rule may ultimately prove disastrous for the country's long-term stability, as it prevents the public from expressing its interests through productive, peaceful political means and also prevents the regime from benefiting from the contributions of much of the population.

Stifling Civil Society

The protection of civil liberties is an essential aspect of liberal democracy. According to Diamond, Linz, and Lipset (1990), freedom of expression, the press, and association are key "to ensure the integrity of political competition and participation" (7). Civil society is a crucial aspect of freedom of association. Democratic theorists generally regard a vibrant civil society as essential to democratic governance, because free associations allow the open competition of ideas and provide means for the public to express their interests vis-à-vis the government. Civil society presents an important check on the concentration of political power in the hands of a limited group (Rosenblum and Post 2002; Gellner 1994).

In the years preceding the 1994 genocide, Rwandan civil society experienced impressive expansion. A proliferation of human rights organizations, women's groups, farmers' cooperatives, and other independent associations, most of them intentionally multi-ethnic, played a major role in pushing for democratic reform. As a result, the genocide targeted civil society groups, and many of their leaders—both Tutsi and Hutu—were killed. In the immediate aftermath of the genocide, however, Rwanda's civil society remained vibrant. Many existing organizations quickly regrouped, while new associations were founded—such as those for widows and genocide survivors. Even today, many visitors to Rwanda are impressed by the number of active civil society groups and the dynamic, articulate individuals who lead them.

Unfortunately, civil society in Rwanda today, despite the continuing appearance of vitality, fails to stand as an independent social voice, having been effectively suppressed and co-opted by the RPF.[4] The RPF regards former Tutsi refugees returned from Uganda, Burundi, and the Democratic Republic of

Congo (DRC) as its core constituency and has strongly favored civic groups run by the returnees, allowing them to function relatively freely. A group like the women's network Profemmes Twese Hamwe, founded in 1991 but relaunched in 1995 under the leadership of several dynamic women returnees from Congo, could freely demand reform on issues such as inheritance rights, because the government trusted that in the end, the group shared its vision for Rwandan society and supported its leadership. However, groups led by Hutu, while initially tolerated under the RPF's strategy of appearing to promote national unity and embrace diversity, gradually faced increased limitations on their actions and pressure to change their leadership.

The strategy of co-opting civil society by forcing groups to accept pro-RPF leaders was first seen in RPF policy toward the country's religious groups. Christian churches have historically been a very powerful force within Rwanda, closely allied with the state in a mutually beneficial cooperative relationship (Longman 2010). The new RPF leadership, however, regarded the churches skeptically, both because of the challenge that the churches posed to RPF hegemony and because they blamed the churches for supporting the 1959 uprising that drove Tutsi out of power and into exile, helping to make possible the 1994 genocide. The RPF thus moved aggressively to bring the churches under its control. Several churches sought to appease the regime by appointing leaders allied with the RPF. The Presbyterian Church, for example, appointed as president a Tutsi who had been living in Nairobi. The Vatican likewise appointed leaders acceptable to the regime, opting, for example, not to give a permanent appointment to André Sibomana, a prominent moderate Hutu who had been acting bishop of Kabgayi, after the regime objected to his speaking out on prison conditions. In other cases, the regime intervened to force changes to church leadership. Most notoriously, RPF soldiers massacred the archbishop of Kigali and twelve other Catholic clergy under their protection in June 1994.[5] In 1995, RPF troops surrounded a meeting of the Free Methodist Church to force the delegates to select a favored candidate as church leader. The government froze the bank accounts of the Episcopal and Pentecostal churches to compel the churches to remove Hutu from leadership. In addition to promoting preferred leaders, the RPF has made clear its dominance over churches in a variety of ways, including executing two Catholic priests (among the twenty-two convicted *génocidaires* publically executed in 1997) and putting a Catholic bishop on trial on genocide charges. Although Bishop Augustin Misago was eventually acquitted, his very public trial allowed the government to demonstrate its preeminence.

The regime has similarly used a combination of coercion and co-optation to neutralize challenges from human rights organizations. An active human rights community emerged in Rwanda in the early 1990s, with four groups represented in the Collectif des ligues et associations de défense des droits de l'homme au Rwanda (Collective of Alliances and Leagues for the Defense of Human Rights in Rwanda, CLADHO) at the time of the genocide. Following the genocide, the Association des volontaires de la paix (Association of Volunteers for Peace, AVP) was led by Tutsi genocide survivors, who allied themselves closely with the regime. The president of CLADHO's board was Dr. Josué Kayijaho, a Tutsi genocide survivor, who discouraged CLADHO from focusing on RPF human rights abuses. The Association rwandaise pour la défense des droits de la personne et des libertés publiques (Rwandan Association for the Defense of Human Rights and Civic Liberties, ADL) was very active prior to, and immediately following, the genocide, but the RPF's intimidation and subsequent complicity in the death of ADL's president, Bishop Sibomana, largely silenced the group (Tertsakian 1999; Deguine 1998). The Association rwandaise pour la défense des droits de l'homme (Rwandan Association for the Defense of Human Rights, ARDHO), led by Alphonse-Marie Nkubito, the first post-genocide minister of justice, was the most outspoken group immediately after the genocide. After Nkubito died in mysterious circumstances in 1997, ARDHO was effectively neutralized when RPF supporters joined the membership in large numbers and used democratic procedures to replace the group's elected leadership; the new leadership then redirected the paid staff away from investigating government abuses. ARDHO's executive secretary, Richard Nsanzabaganwa, himself a Tutsi genocide survivor, eventually fled Rwanda, finding it impossible to continue to engage in human rights work.

As CLADHO, ADL, and ARDHO became increasingly unwilling or unable to investigate RPF abuses, the Ligue rwandaise pour la promotion et la défense des droits de l'homme (Rwandan League for the Promotion and Defense of Human Rights, LIPRODHOR) emerged as the country's leading voice for human rights. In the absence of defense attorneys for most defendants, a group of young LIPRODHOR activists organized a program in 1997 to monitor genocide trials, and for several years LIPRODHOR provided excellent monitoring and reporting on Rwanda's legal system. The group also carried out research on a number of ongoing human rights issues, though they intentionally balanced their reporting of RPF abuses with reports on topics the RPF would approve, such as threats against genocide survivors. Government repression, however, ultimately crippled LIPRODHOR. The group was named in a 2003 parliamentary report condemning the country's last remaining effective opposition political party. Then, in 2004, the Rwandan parliament established a commission to investigate the presence of "genocidal ideology" in the country. The report, released in June that year, mixed information about actual cases of threats against genocide survivors with accusations that a variety of civil society groups and individuals harbored "genocide ideology," implying that they were linked to attacks on Tutsi survivors (Parliament of Rwanda 2004). The report recommended that five groups be banned, including LIPRODHOR. An ostensibly secret list of LIPRODHOR members to be arrested was leaked to the public, encouraging a dozen individuals to flee the country, which the RPF claimed was evidence of their guilt. A few remaining LIPRODHOR members, seeking to save themselves, issued a public apology, which inaccurately confirmed the commission's accusations (Amnesty International 2003a, 2004; Front Line 2005). Nevertheless, the LIPRODHOR leader who issued the apology, François-Xavier Byuma, was subsequently tried in a *gacaca* court in 2007 and sentenced to nineteen years in prison (Amnesty International 2007; Mukantaganzwa 2007).

In some cases, intimidation of civil society activists has gone beyond threats of arrest to include disappearances and assassinations. Father Vjeko Curic, a Franciscan father from Croatia and close associate of Sibomana, was gunned down in Kigali in 1998 (Green 1998). Sibomana himself was denied the right to leave the country in 1998 to seek medical treatment and subsequently died. In March 2003, Augustin Cyiza, a Hutu democrat who had opposed the genocide and served as vice president of the Supreme Court after the genocide, disappeared. He was a founding member of ARDHO and also served on the boards of Hagaruka, a women's rights group, and the Conseil de concertation des organisations d'appui aux initiatives de base (Consultative Council of Organizations to Support Grassroots Initiatives, CCOAIB), the umbrella group for development cooperatives (Front Line 2005, 14–15).

While Hutu civil society activists have been killed, arrested, or forced out of leadership positions through accusations of involvement in the genocide or of supporting "divisionism" or "genocide ideology," Tutsi civil society leaders have not been immune from government intimidation and harassment. Genocide survivors in particular are sometimes harassed. Significantly, leaders of IBUKA ("Remember"), the umbrella group for genocide survivor organizations, faced harassment that ultimately led several to flee the country. In the late 1990s, IBUKA had become increasingly critical of the government's neglect of genocide survivors, in particular their failure to deliver substantial economic opportunities. In 2000, Assiel Kabera, the former prefect of Kibuye Prefecture, was assassinated, and when his brother, the IBUKA vice president Josué Kayijaho (also of CLADHO), tried to leave the country, he was detained and his passport confiscated. Kayijaho was eventually able to leave the country and was joined in exile by another brother, who was the executive secretary of the Fonds d'assistance aux rescapés du génocide (National Fund for the

Assistance of Genocide Survivors, FARG), and by the IBUKA founder Bosco Rutagengwa and Secretary-General Anastase Muramba. Antoine Mugesera, a member of the central committee of the RPF who had previously helped neutralize the Centre de formation et de recherché cooperatives (Center for Training and Research on Cooperatives, Centre Iwacu), stepped in as president of IBUKA, and the organization has since largely followed the RPF line (ICG 2002, 12–13; Front Line 2005). In 2010 the government arrested five of IBUKA's senior officials on accusations of corruption and mismanagement of funds for genocide survivors (Ssuuna 2010).

As a result of concerted RPF policy, Rwanda today has a civil society that includes many organizations but has little independence. Groups have been intimidated into docility or taken over by RPF sympathizers who reorient them toward supporting government programs. Even the Association des veuves du génocide (Association of Genocide Widows, AVEGA-AGAHOZA) is now led by a Tutsi returnee rather than a genocide survivor. The government has sought to make its relationship with civil society increasingly corporatist in nature, using civil society groups to carry out official policy rather than allowing civil society to represent public interests.[6] A nongovernmental organization (NGO) law adopted in 2002 gave the government wide latitude in authorizing civil society groups and regulating their internal affairs. In practice, the government has required civil society groups to register since at least 1995 and used this power to restrict certain groups and even to expel several international NGOs; the 2002 law simply formalized and strengthened government control. In 2004, four leading umbrella groups for different areas of civil society—CCOAIB, for development organizations; CLADHO, for human rights; IBUKA, for survivors' groups; and Pro-Femmes Twese Hamwe, for women—came together at government urging to form a Civil Society Platform to regulate relations between most NGOs and government, moving Rwanda even closer to a corporatist structure for its civil society (Front Line 2005, 28–30). While numerous additional cases of civil society groups that have faced government harassment could be included, Filip Reyntjens's review of Rwandan civil society in 2004 remains true today: "In sum, 'civil society' is controlled by the regime" (Reyntjens 2004, 185; but see Gready, chap. 5, this volume).

Constraining Political Parties

Political parties are another key element of freedom of association, allowing the public to organize to elect candidates of their choosing and to influence public policy directly. As with civil society, political parties flourished in Rwanda for a brief period in the 1990s, but Hutu extremists in the Habyarimana regime effectively divided and co-opted the various political parties, and as a result, many became deeply implicated in the 1994 genocide. After taking power in July 1994, the RPF installed a "Government of National Unity," loosely based on the power-sharing agreement articulated in the August 1993 Arusha Peace Accords, which distributed ministries among the RPF, parties supporting the Habyarimana regime, and opposition parties. While excluding the Hutu extremist parties in its first government, the RPF included ministers from the former opposition parties—the Mouvement démocratique républicain (Democratic Republican Movement, MDR), Parti social démocrate (Social Democratic Party, PSD), and Parti libéral (Liberal Party, PL)—and appointed a Hutu MDR leader, Faustin Twagiramungu, as prime minister.

In reality though, the RPF retained control over all government ministries. Where a Hutu led a ministry, a Tutsi RPF officer (usually a former refugee from Uganda) serving in the second- or third-ranking post actually called the shots. This was true even at the highest level of power: Pasteur Bizimungu, a Hutu RPF member, served as president, but Paul Kagame, then vice president and minister of defense, maintained real control. In August 1995, just a year after the Government of National Unity was named, Faustin Twagiramungu and four other Hutu ministers resigned from the government, protesting their lack of actual power. Twagiramungu and the interior minister, Seth Sendashonga, a Hutu RPF member, fled Rwanda, while the justice minister, Nkubito, remained in Rwanda. Sendashonga was attacked in Nairobi in 1996 and then assassinated in 1998. Nkubito died in 1997.

Although the five Hutu ministers were replaced by other Hutu and parties other than the RPF continued to occupy ministerial posts, none of the new officials had the stature of Twagiramungu, Sendashonga, and Nkubito, whose departure from government marked the beginning of a steady and more obvious concentration of power in RPF hands. Although the MDR, PSD, and PL continued to have representation in the government and the Transitional National Assembly (TNA), the RPF used strategies much like those used against civil society to suppress and co-opt the political parties. Members of the MDR, PSD, and PL who spoke against the prescribed government line risked harassment, arrest, or even assassination. By the late 1990s, even politicians in the RPF found their room for political independence constrained, as Kagame sought further to consolidate his power. In 2000 the highly respected Speaker of the TNA, Joseph Sebarenzi, a Tutsi PL member identified with the survivor community, was forced to resign and flee the country, amid accusations from Kagame and others of engaging in financial misconduct and supporting the return of the Rwandan king (Sebarenzi 2009; see also Sebarenzi, chap. 22, this volume). Within three months, Prime Minister Pierre-Celestin Rwigema, a Hutu from the MDR, and President Bizimungu of the RPF were also forced from office. Kagame then assumed the post of president and hand-picked the new prime minister and speaker (Reyntjens 2004, 180–81; see also HRW 2000).

The RPF has aggressively and consistently suppressed independent politi-cal activity. In May 2001, Bizimungu announced the formation of a new po-litical party, the Parti pour la democratie et le renouveau-Ubuyanja (Party for Democratic Renewal-Ubuyanja, PDR-Ubuyanja). The party was immediately banned, and Bizimungu was placed under house arrest. Others associated with the party were arrested or harassed. Bizimungu and Charles Ntakirutinka, a former minister in Bizimungu's government, were beaten in August, then arrested and put in jail. One party member, Gratien Munyarubuga, was assas-sinated in December; Frank Bizimungu disappeared; Pasteur Bizimungu and Ntakirutinka were ultimately tried and convicted of spreading rumors to incite rebellion and creating a criminal association. President Kagame pardoned Bi-zimungu in 2007, but as of this writing, Ntakirutinka was still in jail. Despite the lack of any apparent party organization outside Kigali, the crackdown on the PDR-Ubuyanja was used to justify the arrest of a number of individu-als throughout the country in 2001–3 (Reyntjens 2004, 193).

During the run-up to the 2003 elections, the government sought to crush the MDR, the party that posed the greatest credible threat to RPF dominance because of its wide base of popular support, particularly among the Hutu majority. In January 2002 the MDR secretary general Pierre Gakwandi was arrested and charged with promoting ethnic divisions after criticizing the RPF in a press interview. In March 2003 a parliamentary commission issued a re-port accusing the MDR of promoting "divisionism" and "genocide ideology," and urged that the party be banned. In April, Leonard Hitimana, an MDR parliamentarian and one of forty-seven individuals named in the parliamen-tary report, disappeared. Two high-ranking Hutu military officers named in the report fled the country, and several of their associates disappeared or were arrested. That month the parliament voted unanimously to ban the MDR (HRW 2003, 4–9; Amnesty International, 2003a).

Although the RPF has allowed the PSD and PL as well as several smaller political parties to continue to function, the actions taken against PDR-Ubuyanja and MDR made clear that the RPF would tolerate no challenges to its authority or criticisms of its policies. The RPF organized all political parties represented in the TNA into a "Forum of Political Parties," a body that assumed the right to approve all members of parliament put forward by their parties and to censure and remove members that they accuse of promoting "divisionism" or "genocide ideology," which in practice is equated with any criticism of the RPF (ICG 2001). Despite criticisms that the forum was dominated by the RPF and stifled the independence of other political parties, the 2003 Constitution made the forum a permanent, codified institution (RoR 2003). Now, the Forum of Political Parties has made Rwanda a de facto one-party state. Meanwhile, harassment of other parties continues. Alfred Mukezamfura of the Centrist Democratic Party served as speaker of the National Assembly from 2003 to 2008 but was consistently dogged by accusations of complicity in the genocide. He fled Rwanda in late 2008 and was tried in absentia by a *gacaca* court and sentenced to life imprisonment in September 2009 (Musoni 2009). Even the PL, a party closely identified with genocide survivors, has faced accusations of promoting "divisionism," which have constrained its ability to challenge the RPF (Waldorf 2007).

The harassment of opposition political parties was even more severe in the run-up to the 2010 presidential elections. A group of dissident, mostly Anglophone RPF members who sought to form a Rwandan branch of the Green Party was prevented for several months in 2009 from holding a founding political convention and afterward faced harassment and intimidation (Howden 2010). Victoire Ingabire, the presidential candidate of the Forces démocratiques unifiées-Inkingi (United Democratic Forces, FDU-Inkingi), faced death threats after returning to Rwanda in January 2010 and calling for perpetrators of both the genocide of Tutsi and crimes against humanity against Hutu to be held accountable. In February she and an aide were physically attacked at a local government office, and she was later arrested (though subsequently released on bail). On July 13 the vice president of the Democratic Green Party of Rwanda (DGPR), André Kagwa Rwisereka, was assassinated (Brown 2010; Rice 2010).

Limiting Freedom of the Press

The last years of the Habyarimana regime marked a "golden era" for freedom of the press in Rwanda. A wide variety of newspapers and journals began publishing, representing a broad range of political positions, and the printed press played an important part in challenging the authoritarian nature of the regime (LDGL 2001, 9–15). The genocide devastated the press, both because reformist journalists were targeted and also because extremist anti-Tutsi journalism contributed directly to the genocide, thereby discrediting the free press (Chrétien et al. 1995). The press in Rwanda has never fully recovered.

Since taking power, the RPF has maintained tight control on the press, allowing only newspapers favorable to the regime to publish without harassment or closure. As one regional human rights group noted after the genocide, "The written press saw a new proliferation of titles, but some of them quickly faced diverse threats. . . . Some journalists were arrested, others intimidated, others are the object of aggression, even attempts at murder" (LDGL 2001, 20). The situation for the press has evolved little since 1994, as the regime has regularly arrested journalists, seized issues of journals, and closed publications. Papers run by Hutu are at greatest risk, but even those published by Tutsi returnees face threats and closure when they openly challenge regime policy (LDGL 2002, 135–38; HRW 2000; LDGL 2001, 21–28).

A few recent examples of intimidation of the press suggest the general pattern of restrictions of press freedom that has persisted since 1994.[7] In February 2007 the editor of *Umuvugizi* was beaten unconscious after he published allegations of corruption and mismanagement by several top government and military officials. In April 2007 the editor of *Umurabyo* was sentenced to a year in prison after pleading guilty to "creating divisions," "sectarianism," and "defamation" after publishing a column headlined "You have problems if you kill a Tutsi, but you go free if you kill a Hutu" (RSF 2007a). Bonaventure Bizumuremyi, the editor of *Umuco*, went into hiding (Committee to Protect Journalists 2008). The editor of *Umuseso*, Gérard M. Manzi, was detained for more than a week on trumped-up rape charges in August 2007, while the deputy managing editor, Furaha Mugisha, was deported in July 2008 (RSF 2007b, 2008). In August 2009 the Ministry of Information banned *Umuseso* for three months (RSF 2009a). In April 2010, *Umuseso* and *Umuvugizi* were suspended for six months (Committee to Protect Journalists 2010a). On June 24 the deputy editor of *Umuvugizi*, Jean-Léonard Rugambage, was murdered outside his home after he reported on the newspaper's online edition about the attempted assassination in South Africa of former Kagame ally General Kayumba Nyamwasa. Although the government soon secured confessions from two men who claimed that it was a nonpolitical revenge killing, few outside observers believed this version of events (Committee to Protect Journalists 2010b).

The situation for radio has seen greater evolution since 1994. The radio's role in the genocide was particularly pernicious, especially the notorious Radio télévision libre des Mille Collines (RTLM). In the immediate aftermath of the genocide, the only domestic network allowed to broadcast was the official Radio Rwanda, although the British Broadcasting Corporation (BBC) and Voice of America (VOA) also opened branches in Rwanda. In 2005 the government authorized private radio stations for the first time. Several new stations have since begun to broadcast, but they are heavily regulated and focus mostly on music or other noncontroversial content. In April 2009 the regime suspended the Kinyarwanda service of the BBC, one of the only sources of unbiased news in Rwanda, accusing the BBC of "blatant denial of the 1994 genocide against the Tutsi of Rwanda" (quoted in HRW 2009).

In August 2009, President Kagame signed a controversial new press law that allows the government to regulate journalists by setting educational and other standards, and allowing the government to review the content of publications (Kagire 2009). Another proposed law will further hamper the press by requiring those seeking a license to publish or broadcast to demonstrate substantial capital reserves, ranging from $41,000 for newspapers to $187,500 for television stations. Officially these cash reserves are meant to prevent media outlets from being susceptible to manipulation, but their effect will be to prevent most individuals from publishing or broadcasting (RSF 2009b). As in other areas of civil and political society, the RPF has set up a corporatist institution, the Media High Council, that regulates the content of the press. As a regional human rights group has stated, "The quasi-monopoly of the RPF over the different institutions, the means of mass communication, the most profitable sectors of the economy recalls the practices of the preceding regime and leads one to doubt the will of authorities to promote any open debate" (LDGL 2001, 27).

Suppressing Freedom of Speech

As with restraints on political party organization, restraints on speech became increasingly pronounced as Rwanda moved toward the end of its supposed democratic transition. The RPF was never particularly tolerant of criticism, and as power consolidated progressively in the hands of a few individuals, the parameters for allowable speech became increasingly limited. Regulations on free speech that began informally became increasingly codified. For example, when I lived in Rwanda in 1995–96, discussion of ethnic identities was fairly open, as people freely discussed how ethnicity had tragically divided their communities. Within a few years, however, the government's program encouraging all people to identify only as Rwandan and discouraging ethnic identification had made such discussion taboo. In research I conducted in 2001–3, many people were uncomfortable naming their ethnic identity, fearing possible consequences: even talking about ethnicity had become equated with supporting genocide. In 2002 the government began to enforce a law against "divisionism," a crime that was only vaguely defined but in practice was used to punish any discussion of ethnicity. The 2003 Constitution made supporting "genocide ideology" illegal (RoR 2003), and a 2008 law against "genocide ideology" went even farther in limiting people's ability to discuss identity issues (HRW 2008, 38–39; see also Waldorf, chap. 2, this volume).

Concern over how ethnicity is invoked is understandable given Rwanda's history of ethnic violence, yet the government's crackdown on discussing ethnicity masks the reality that political, social, and economic power have become more and more concentrated in the hands of a small group of Tutsi returnees, particularly from Uganda. Banning discussion of ethnicity prohibits people from complaining not only about unequal economic development but also about active discrimination, which my research has indicated remains prevalent. The restrictions against "divisionism" and "genocide ideology" have been applied broadly, so that in practice, criticism of the regime is treated as support for genocide. As the two preceding sections indicate, the laws are also used to suppress the press and political party organization. The history of the genocide and the threat of renewed ethnic violence are thus used to justify political repression whose real purpose is to consolidate the power of the RPF regime.

In the aftermath of the 2003 elections, many observers hoped that the government would relax the tight controls on public life. However, suppression of civil society, political parties, and free speech have all continued. The parliamentary report on genocide ideology was released in June 2004, less than a year after the parliamentary elections. That report accused not only the human rights group LIPRODHOR of harboring genocide ideology, but also a variety of other domestic and international NGOs, including Care, Pax Christi, many of the country's churches, and a number of schools (Parliament of Rwanda 2004; Amnesty International 2004). The accusations of genocide ideology have been particularly stifling for free discussion within schools. In October 2004 the Ministry of Education followed up on the parliamentary report with a communiqué that accused a number of secondary school administrators, teachers, and students of "divisionism" and suspended them (Front Line 2005, 24–25). In a project I was involved in working with the Ministry of Education to develop a new history curriculum for Rwandan secondary schools, we found that despite official support for the idea of free debate and discussion within schools, teachers and students alike felt highly constrained in what they were able to say (see Freedman et al., chap. 19, this volume). The practice of accusing people who question the government of supporting genocide ideology or divisionism has continued, and many people have been arrested, suspended from their jobs, or forced to flee the country (Amnesty International 2010;

cf. the Rwanda articles in Human Rights Watch, *World Report*, 2005–8). In the 2010 presidential election, accusations of supporting genocide ideology were widely used to discredit and disqualify opposition candidates.

Tightly Controlling Elections

I have intentionally waited until the end of my discussion to turn to elections, which many observers consider the ultimate measure of democracy, because of the importance of understanding the context of severe political constraint within which elections have occurred in Rwanda. According to the RPF, the adoption of the new constitution and national elections in 2003 marked the culmination of a decade-long transition to democracy. Many observers have concluded that Rwanda's elections have been free and fair due to the lack of violence and little obvious intimidation or irregularities. In reality, the RPF has used elections to guarantee its hegemony by actively manipulating the process leading up to the actual casting of votes, by limiting who could and could not run for office and heavily regulating campaigning (HRW 2001, 2003). Hence, far from allowing true input from the public, elections have served to consolidate and legitimize RPF control over Rwanda's political system.

The post-genocide government began the process of democratic transition with elections for local cell and sector councils in March 1999. Candidates for these positions campaigned on an individual basis, since the government did not allow candidates to identify themselves with a political party and did not allow the parties to organize below the national level. Most of the criticism of the election focused on the use of a queuing system for voting, in which community members publicly lined up behind the candidate of their choice. As Kimonyo, Twagiramungu, and Kayumba (2004, 15) wrote, "This method of voting is cheaper and logistically simpler, but it also permits strong political control." District-level elections in March 2001 were run similarly on a nonparty basis, but with a secret ballot. Human Rights Watch pointed out that in a large number of constituencies, voters had no choices at all because only one candidate per position ran for office (HRW 2001). In addition, despite regulations on political party activity, the RPF informally campaigned in many communities. Mayors were chosen indirectly by cell and sector electors (ICG 2001, 10).

My research in local communities in Kibuye, Butare, and Byumba Provinces in 2001–3 revealed more serious problems with the two local elections. According to people I interviewed, RPF officials actively manipulated the candidate roles, pushing some people to run for office and telling others to withdraw their candidacy. As one farmer in Kibuye told us, "[The elections] weren't at all democratic. They secretly prevented some people from posing as candidates at the same time that they forced others to run against their will" (interview, December 8, 2001). Even more troubling was the degree to which the RPF failed to respect the choices of the public, as they freely removed elected office-holders from their positions if they found them to be insufficiently compliant. In many cases, local government officials were arrested as a pretense for removing them, with Hutu accused of participation in the genocide or genocide ideology and Tutsi accused of corruption. Four of the five elected mayors in the districts I studied were arrested during the two-year period of my research (Longman, forthcoming).

The process of controlling elections through manipulation of candidate lists continued in the national elections in 2003. The formal attack on the MDR prevented the most credible alternative to the RPF from fielding candidates. Faustin Twagiramungu, prime minister from 1994 to 1995, returned to Rwanda to run for president, but the de facto banning of the MDR forced him to run as an independent. He faced serious constraints on his ability to campaign, including death threats, confiscation of his campaign literature, and prohibitions on holding rallies (Amnesty International 2003b; HRW 2003). Bizimungu was banned from running and remained in detention throughout the campaign. In the end, much of the population apparently believed that they lacked a real choice. Kagame officially won the election with 95.1 percent of the vote. According to some well-informed observers, Kagame won the election, but Twagiramungu earned a much higher percentage than the 3.6 percent officially reported; the results were tampered with to demonstrate a more ringing endorsement of Kagame.[8] An electoral observation mission from the European Union concluded that voters had been intimidated during the campaign period and that the election itself had "irregularities and instances of fraud" (Economist Intelligence Unit 2004). An observer team from the Norwegian Center for Human Rights concluded that

even though the presidential elections were conducted in a technically good manner, the degree of pressure to vote for the incumbent candidate cannot be underestimated. . . . The RPF used its hold of the state's administrative and military power to exert various forms of influence on potential voters. This process started long before the electoral campaign. . . . The lack of transparency in the consolidation process served to nurture the team's impression that single cases of irregularities and fraud did constitute a part of a pattern, or a system, geared to make sure that the ruling party emerge victorious of the electoral battle. (Samset and Dalby 2003, 40)

The 2003 parliamentary elections were only slightly more competitive. The National Electoral Commission vetted candidates, allowing those from the PSD, PL, and the newer Party for Progress and Concord as well as a few independent candidates, but the overwhelming majority of approved candidates were from the RPF and five satellite parties that ran under its umbrella. Furthermore, the method for electing legislators limited the impact of the popular vote. In the lower house, the National Assembly, only fifty-three of eighty seats were chosen through direct popular ballot. The RPF and its allies won 73.8 percent of the vote, garnering forty seats. The PSD won seven seats, and the PL won six. The remaining twenty-seven seats were reserved seats for women, youth, and the disabled, chosen through a system of indirect voting (EU EOM 2003). The combination of reserved seats and party-list quotas allowed Rwanda to achieve the highest percentage of women (48.8 percent) in any parliament in the world in the 2003 elections (Longman 2006).[9] None of the twenty-six-seat Senate is elected through direct suffrage. Twelve members are chosen through electoral colleges in each of the provinces, two are chosen by university professors, while the rest are named by the president and the Forum of Political Parties. Senators are not elected as part of a political party, which has had the effect of allowing the Senate to be populated entirely with strong supporters of the RPF (Samset and Dalby 2003).

Rwanda held local-level elections in 2006 and parliamentary elections again in 2008. The official results of the 2008 elections were similar to those in 2003, with the RPF coalition winning 78.8 percent and forty-two seats, the PSD winning 13.1 percent and seven seats, and the PL winning 7.5 percent and four seats. The European Union Election Observation Mission (EU EOM), however, carried out sampling in a large number of districts that found the actual results were 98.4 percent for the RPF (EU EOM 2008). Whereas in 2003, results were apparently altered to favor the RPF presidential candidate in order to demonstrate his wide popular support, the 2008 parliamentary results were altered to give Rwanda the appearance of being a more vigorous democracy than is in fact the case. The Rwandan population treated the election as a plebiscite, fearing the type of negative consequences that allegedly befell communities that did not give Kagame a sufficiently lopsided vote in 2003. Rwandan voters realized that all real power currently rests in the hands of the RPF. From that perspective, voting for another party offered no benefits, while voting against the RPF could potentially have negative consequences.

In many ways, the 2010 presidential elections resembled those in 2003, with the major potential opposition parties prevented from registering and major opposition candidates discredited and prevented from campaigning. Neither the DGPR nor FDU-Inkingi were allowed to register, and not only

Table 1.1 Election results, EU EOM research compared with
official tallies, 2008

	RPF	PL	PSD
EU EOM research	98.38%	0.61%	0.53%
Official tallies	78.76%	7.50%	13.13%

Source: European Union Election Observation Mission (EU EOM) 2008.

was FDU-Inkingi leader Victoire Ingabire arrested, but the American lawyer
who came to Rwanda to defend her was imprisoned as well (Kron and Gettleman 2010). In the end, Kagame won re-election handily, with 93 percent of
the vote (Baldauf 2010).

Conclusion: Restricting Democracy in the Name of the Developmental State

Paul Kagame was once lauded as a "new African leader," one
of a new generation of progressive leaders that also included the presidents
of Uganda, Ethiopia, Eritrea, and the Democratic Republic of Congo, who
would drive development on the continent and establish democracy on their
own terms (Ottaway 2000; Gourevitch 1997, 42–55). As my account here suggests, Kagame actually resembles an older generation of African leaders who
protected their political power by restricting civil society and civil liberties, and
staging noncompetitive elections in the name of national unity.

Like the first generation of African leaders, Kagame and the RPF have
justified restrictions on democracy not only to prevent ethnic violence but
also in the name of economic development. In the aftermath of the genocide,
the international community poured money into rebuilding Rwanda in part
because of guilt over failure to stop the genocide. The RPF generally managed
this development quite well, building an image of technocratic competence.
Kagame has portrayed Rwanda as a developmental state, along the lines of the
"Asian Tigers," whose governments actively intervened in driving economic
development while tightly limiting political freedoms (Woo-Cumings 1999).
Kagame seems to be relying on a strategy of "performance legitimation," in
which the public will not care about political liberties if the government brings
them prosperity.

Many of Kagame's admirers are quick to admit that he has authoritarian tendencies, but they also tend to dismiss the possibility of democracy in

Rwanda given the history of the genocide. They also appreciate Kagame's apparent probity and his seriousness about economic development.[10] In a recent portrait of Kagame, Philip Gourevitch wrote approvingly: "Today, Kagame will tell you that the No. 1 threat to the country is not ethnic extremism or violence but the underlying scourge of poverty" (Gourevitch 2009, 36–48, quotation on 46). Some observers suggest that Rwanda could follow the model of South Korea or Taiwan, in which democracy comes only after solid economic growth. In fact, Kagame seems to be taking Singapore as a prime model. The state in Rwanda governs with an extremely heavy hand. With little public consultation, the government has implemented a series of quality-of-life laws such as mandating seat-belt usage, banning the use of plastic bags, forbidding public urination and spitting, and requiring people to wear shoes when in public, even in rural areas. While each of these proposals makes sense in terms of public safety or environmental protection, the Rwandan public experiences them as additional government efforts to exercise authority, as in the massive mobilizations for *gacaca* and elections, the implementation of mandatory participation in *umuganda* public labor programs, the decision to shift education from French to English, the repeated redrawing and renaming of geographic political boundaries, and the replacement of all the country's national symbols. To the general public, most of these decisions and programs seem arbitrary, and they contribute to a political climate of submission and fear.

For the time being, Rwanda is relatively peaceful, but how long the suppression of democracy can remain sustainable is unclear. Much like African states from the first decades after independence, Rwanda is effectively a one-party state with a corporatist civil society and a leader elected by plebiscite. The strategy of performance legitimation assumes that prosperity will earn public support, but in Rwanda the lack of democracy is contributing to unequal development, in which wealth is concentrated disproportionately in the hands of a small group, primarily Anglophone returnees from Uganda. Rwanda's Gini coefficient rose from 0.47 in 2001 to 0.51 in 2006, and that trend appears only to be getting worse (Ansoms 2009). Since the public is neither free to complain nor to organize to address this inequality, frustration is likely to mount.

For those of us who lived in Rwanda under the Habyarimana regime, the attitude of those who are willing to postpone democratic reform in the name of economic development is disturbingly familiar. As Catharine Newbury noted in 1992, "a 1989 World Bank report singled out Rwanda as a 'successful case of adaptation,' where government policies had successfully encouraged growth in agricultural production. . . . The report praises the Rwandan government for providing an 'enabling environment' that encouraged growth in agricultural production" (Newbury 1992, 193; see also Uvin 1998). The willingness to forgive authoritarianism during the Habyarimana regime in the name of unity and development made genocide possible. Will the world allow the same mistake to be repeated under Kagame?

Notes

1. For a definition of democracy, see Dahl 1989, which defines democratic governance (what Dahl calls polyarchy) as involving constitutionally empowered leaders elected in free and fair competitive elections, protection of basic civil liberties including freedom of speech and a free and diverse media, and vibrant interest groups.

2. I intentionally discuss elections last because it is important to understand the context of severe political constraint within which they have occurred.

3. When I presented a version of this paper at Harvard University in November 2009, the Rwandan ambassador to the United States, along with several RPF members in attendance, challenged my qualifications and my facts, claimed that I was imposing a Western idea of democracy on Rwanda, argued that the attempt to promote human rights in Rwanda was an example of Western imperialism, but ultimately conceded that given the genocide, Rwanda could not tolerate democracy and really needed economic development instead.

4. To reflect political reality, I refer to the RPF as being in power, though officially they shared power with other political parties until the 2003 elections. I do not distinguish between the Rwandan Patriotic Army and its political wing, the RPF, because of their functional unity.

5. The RPF finally prosecuted this crime in 2008 under pressure from the international community (see Peskin, chap. 10, this volume).

6. For a useful discussion of corporatism, see Wiarda 1981.

7. For an overview of attacks on press freedom prior to 2007, see Waldorf 2007, as well as regular reports from Reporters sans frontières (Reporters without Borders, RSF) and the Committee to Protect Journalists.

8. Alison Des Forges reported that several electoral observers and diplomatic sources told her that, based on their observations, Kagame had won more than 50 percent of the vote but that Twagiramungu may have won as much as 30 percent. Personal communication, November 2003.

9. As I have argued elsewhere, however, diversity in terms of ascriptive characteristics served in some ways to mask uniformity in political position.

10. Rwanda's position on Transparency International's annual Corruption Index has been consistently lower than most of its neighbors.

References

Amnesty International. 2003a. "Rwanda: Escalating Repression Against Political Opposition." AFR 47/004/2003. April 22. http://www.amnesty.org/en/library/info/AFR47/004/2003.

———. 2003b. "Rwanda: Run-up to Presidential Elections Marred by Threats and Harassment." August 22. http://www.amnesty.org/en/library/info/AFR47/010/2003.

———. 2004. "Rwanda: Deeper into the Abyss—Waging War on Civil Society." AFR 47/013/2004. July 6. http://www.amnesty.org/en/library/info/AFR47/013/2004.

———. 2007. "Rwanda: Further Information on Fear for Safety/Legal Concern; François-Xavier Byuma." AFR 47/009/2007. July 9. http://www.amnesty.org/en/library/info/AFR47/009/2007.

———. 2010. "Safer to Stay Silent: The Chilling Effect of Rwanda's Laws on 'Genocide Ideology' and 'Sectarianism.'" AFR 47/005/2010. March 19. http://www.amnesty.org/en/library/info/AFR47/005/2010/en.

Ansoms, An. 2009. "Reengineering Rural Society: The Visions and Ambitions of the Rwandan Elite." *African Affairs* 108, no. 431: 1–21.

Baldauf, Scott. 2010. "Kigali Grenade Attack Follows Kagame's Rwanda Election Win." *Christian Science Monitor.* August 11.

Brown, Eric. 2010. "Rwandan Genocide: Is Rwanda Gearing up for Another Genocide?" *Human Rights First*, February 23.

Chrétien, Jean-Pierre, et al. 1995. *Rwanda: Les médias du génocide.* Paris: Karthala.

Chu, Jeff. 2009. "Rwanda Rising: A New Model of Economic Development." *Fast Company*, April 1.

Committee to Protect Journalists. 2008. "Rwanda Newspaper Editor Flees, Publication Suspended." March 21. http://cpj.org/2008/03/rwandan-newspaper-editor-flees-publication-suspend.php.

———. 2010a. "Rwanda Shuts Critical Papers in Run-up to Presidential Vote." April 13. http://cpj.org/2010/04/rwanda-shuts-critical-papers-in-run-up-to-presiden.php.

———. 2010b. "Skepticisms Greets Arrests in Rwandan Journalist's Murder." June 29. http://cpj.org/2010/06/skepticism-greets-arrests-in-rwandan-journalists-m.php.

Dahl, Robert. 1989. *Democracy and Its Critics.* New Haven, CT: Yale University Press.

Deguine, Hervé. 1998. *Enquête sur la mort d'André Sibomana.* Paris: Reporters sans frontières.

Diamond, Larry, Juan J. Linz, and Seymour Martin Lipset. 1990. "Introduction." In *Politics in Developing Countries: Comparing Experiences with Democracy*, edited by Diamond, Linz, and Lipset, 1–66. Boulder, CO: Lynne Rienner.

Economist Intelligence Unit. 2004. "Rwanda." *Country Report.* April 12.

European Union Election Observation Mission (EU EOM). 2003. *Rwanda: Election presidentielle 25 Août 2003; Élections législatives 29 et 30 Septembre, 2 Octobre 2003* (final report). Brussels: European Union.

———. 2008. "Final Report: Legislative Elections to the Chamber of Deputies, 15–18 September 2008." http://www.eueomrwanda.org/EN/Final_Report.html.

Front Line. 2005. "Front Line Rwanda: Disappearances, Arrests, Threats, Intimidation and Co-option of Human Rights Defenders 2001–2004." March. http://www.frontlinedefenders.org/files/en/FrontLineRwandaReport.pdf.

Gellner, Ernest. 1994. *Conditions of Liberty: Civil Society and Its Rivals*. New York: Penguin, 1994.

Gourevitch, Philip. 1997. "Letter from the Congo: Continental Shift." *New Yorker*, August 4.

———. 2009. "The Life After: Fifteen Years after the Genocide in Rwanda, the Reconciliation Defies Expectations." *New Yorker*, May 4.

Green, Sonya Laurence. 1998. "Foreign Priest Killed in Kigali." *Voice of America*, February 1.

Howden, Daniel. 2010. "Rwanda's Democratic Credentials Under Fire: Host of UN Environmental Event Accused of Clamping Down on its Green Party." *Independent*, March 15.

Human Rights Watch (HRW). 2000. "Rwanda: The Search for Security and Human Rights Abuses." April 1. http://www.hrw.org/reports/2000/rwanda/.

———. 2001. "No Contest in Rwandan Elections." March 8. http://www.hrw.org/en/news/2001/03/09/no-contest-rwandan-elections.

———. 2003. "Preparing for Elections: Tightening Control in the Name of Unity." May 8. http://www.hrw.org/en/node/77843.

———. 2008. "Law and Reality: Progress in Judicial Reform in Rwanda." July 25. http://www.hrw.org/node/62098.

———. 2009. "Rwanda: Restore BBC to the Air." April 27. http://www.hrw.org/en/news/2009/04/27/rwanda-restore-bbc-air.

International Crisis Group (ICG). 2001. "'Consensual Democracy' in Post-Genocide Rwanda: Evaluating the March 2001 District Elections." October 9.

———. 2002. "Rwanda at the End of the Transition: A Necessary Political Liberalisation." November 13.

Kagire, Edmund. 2009. "President Kagame Signs Media Law." *New Times*, August 14.

Kimonyo, Jean-Paul, Noel Twagiramungu, and Christophe Kayumba. 2004. "Supporting the Post-Genocide Transition in Rwanda: The Role of the International Community." Democratic Transition in Post-Conflict Societies Project, Working Paper 32. http://www.clingendael.nl/publications/2004/20041200_cru_working_paper_32.pdf.

Kinzer, Stephen. 2008. *A Thousand Hills: Rwanda's Rebirth and the Man Who Dreamed It*. Hoboken, NJ: John Wiley and Sons.

Kron, Josh, and Jeffrey Gettleman. 2010. "American Lawyer for Opposition Figure Is Arrested in Rwanda." *New York Times*, May 29.

Lerner, Nadia. 2009. "Rwanda Rises from the Ashes of Civil War: Canadian Mission Group Helps to Rebuild Rwanda." July. http://www.suite101.com/content/rwanda-rising-from-the-ashes-of-civil-war-a131651.

Ligue des droits de la personne dans la région des Grands Lacs (LDGL). 2001. "La problématique de la liberté d'expression au Rwanda: Cas de la presse." November. http://www.grandslacs.net/doc/2511.pdf.

———. 2002. "Entre la violence impunie et la misère: Rapport sur la situation des droits de l'homme; Burundi, RDC et Rwanda, Années 2000–2001." May. http://www.grandslacs.net/doc/2384.pdf.

Longman, Timothy. 2006. "Rwanda: Achieving Equality or Serving an Authoritarian State?" In *Women in African Parliaments*, edited by Gretchen Bauer and Hannah Britton, 133–50. Boulder, CO: Lynne Reinner.

———. 2010. *Christianity and Genocide in Rwanda*. New York: Cambridge University Press.

———. Forthcoming. "Memory, Justice, and Power in Post-Genocide Rwanda."

Mukantaganzwa, Domatilla. 2007. "Byuma Francois Xavier's Case." Service national des juridictions gacaca (National Service of Gacaca Jurisdictions, NSGJ). Kigali, June 12. http://www.inkiko-gacaca.gov.rw/pdf/June%20Byuma%20Final%20copy.pdf.

Musoni, Edwin. 2009. "Former Speaker Gets Life Sentence." *New Times*, September 4.

Newbury, Catharine. 1992. "Rwanda: Recent Debates over Governance and Rural Development." In *Governance and Politics in Africa*, edited by Goran Hyden and Michael Bratton, 193–219. Boulder, CO: Lynne Rienner.

Ottaway, Marina. 2000. *Africa's New Leaders: Democracy or State Reconstruction?* Washington, DC: Carnegie Endowment for International Peace.

Parliament of Rwanda. 2004. "Là où l'idéologie génocidaire se fait observer au Rwanda." Kigali, June. http://www.grandslacs.net/doc/3301.pdf.

Pottier, Johan. 2002. *Re-Imagining Rwanda: Conflict, Survival and Disinformation in the Late Twentieth Century*. Cambridge: Cambridge University Press.

Reporters sans frontières (RSF). 2007a. "Woman Editor Gets a Year in Prison for Article about Ethnic Discrimination." April 20. http://en.rsf.org/rwanda-woman-editor-gets-a-year-in-prison-20-04-2007,20399.html.

———. 2007b. "Editor Released after Being Held for Eight Days on Rape Charge." August 30. http://en.rsf.org/rwanda-editor-released-after-being-held-30-08-2007,23422.html.

———. 2008. "Government Deports Independent Weekly's Deputy Managing Editor." July 17. http://en.rsf.org/rwanda-government-deports-independent-17-07-2008,27867.html.

———. 2009a. "Independent Weekly Suspended for Three Months for Article Comparing Kagame's Government to Habyarimana's." August 7. http://en.rsf.org/rwanda-independent-weekly-suspended-for-07-08-2009,34113.html.

———. 2009b. "Government to Demand Exorbitant Sums to Launch New News Media." September 24. http://en.rsf.org/rwanda-government-to-demand-exorbitant-24-09-2009,34580.html.

Republic of Rwanda (RoR). 2003. Constitution. May 26. http://www.mod.gov.rw/IMG/doc/Constitution_of_the_Republic_of_Rda.doc.

Reyntjens, Filip. 2004. "Rwanda, Ten Years On: From Genocide to Dictatorship." *African Affairs* 103:177–210.

Rice, Xan. 2010. "Democracy and Ethnicity a Murderous Mix in Rwanda Still Haunted by 1994 Genocide: Kagame's Bid for Re-Election Overshadowed by Killings and Banning of Opposition Parties." *The Guardian*, August 7.

Rosenblum, Nancy L., and Robert C. Post, eds. 2002. *Civil Society and Government.* Princeton, NJ: Princeton University Press.

Samset, Ingrid, and Orrvar Dalby. 2003. "Rwanda: Presidential and Parliamentary Elections 2003." Norwegian Centre for Human Rights, Oslo. http://www.cmi.no/publications/file/1770-rwanda-presidential-and-parliamentary-elections.pdf.

Sebarenzi, Joseph. 2009. *God Sleeps in Rwanda.* New York: Simon and Schuster.

Sibomana, André. 1999. *Hope for Rwanda: Conversations with Laure Guilbert and Hervé Deguine.* Translated by Carina Tertsakian. London: Pluto Press.

Smith, James F. 2009. "In Rwanda, a Lesson in Understanding: Area Students Travel to Learn About Genocide." *Boston Globe*, September 9.

Ssuuna, Ignatius. 2010. "Two More IBUKA Officials Arrested." *New Times*, April 29.

Tertsakian, Carina. 1999. "Postscript: What Future for the Defence of Human Rights in Rwanda?" In André Sibomana, *Hope for Rwanda: Conversations with Laure Guilbert and Hervé Deguine*, translated by Carina Tertsakian, 158–71. London: Pluto Press.

Uvin, Peter. 1998. *Aiding Violence: The Development Enterprise in Rwanda.* West Hartford, CT: Kumarian Press.

Van Eyck, Masarah. 2009. "High School Teachers Leave for Rwanda on UW–Madison Fulbright Grant." June 30. http://www.news.wisc.edu/16870.

Waldorf, Lars. 2007. "Censorship and Propaganda in Post-Genocide Rwanda." In *The Media and the Rwandan Genocide*, edited by Allan Thompson, 404–16. London: Pluto Press.

Warren, Rick. 2009. "Paul Kagame." *Time*, May 4.

Wiarda, Howard J. 1981. *Corporatism and National Development in Latin America.* Boulder, CO: Westview Press.

Woo-Cumings, Meredith, ed. 1999. *The Developmental State.* Ithaca, NY: Cornell University Press.

2

Instrumentalizing Genocide

The RPF's Campaign against "Genocide Ideology"

LARS WALDORF

Introduction

I was at a June 2008 conference in Kigali when Rwanda's minister of justice publicly accused Alison Des Forges of becoming "a spokesperson for genocide ideology." She took that in stride. After all, Des Forges was in good company: the government had already accused CARE International, Trócaire, Norwegian People's Aid (NPA), the British Broadcasting Corporation (BBC), and the Voice of America (VOA) of propagating genocide ideology. Subsequently, the government prevented her from entering the country—without giving any reason. She took that in stride as well. Perhaps Des Forges saw her exclusion as conclusive proof that Rwanda's new law on genocide ideology was, as she had written, an "abusive restriction on free speech" intended to punish any criticism of the ruling Rwandan Patriotic Front (RPF) (HRW 2008b, 42).

Des Forges never disputed Rwanda's need for laws to prevent hate speech and incitement to genocide.[1] She knew only too well what a real genocide ideology had wrought in 1994. In her tireless efforts to document the genocide and bring *génocidaires* to justice, she repeatedly emphasized the key role that ideology and "hate media" had played in inciting Rwanda's genocide (Des Forges 2007; Des Forges 1999, 65–95). Yet she was also able to see, more clearly than most, how the RPF was instrumentalizing the genocide—through *gacaca* and its genocide ideology campaigns—to maintain its hold on power. She worried that in the long run, this could trivialize the genocide and fuel further negationism.[2]

This chapter begins by examining the tensions between the government's discourse on reconciliation and its fight against negationism. It then shows how the government's campaign against genocide ideology has taken shape. Next, the chapter looks briefly at the accusations against Des Forges, the BBC, and political opponents. The chapter concludes that the government's misuse of the genocide ideology law to repress political dissent and civil society voices does not augur well for Rwanda's future.

Background

There has always been an inherent tension between the government's forward-looking reconciliation narrative, which seeks to erase ethnicity, and its backward-looking genocide narrative, which inevitably emphasizes ethnicity (see Eltringham, chap. 17, this volume). As Nigel Eltringham (2004, 72–99) has observed, the government risks replacing the old ethnic labels (Hutu, Tutsi) with new, but equally divisive, labels (*génocidaire*, victim). During a brief period, the government made serious efforts to avoid ethnic labeling—even in its discourse on genocide. For example, President Paul Kagame elided ethnicity in his speech at the 2006 genocide commemoration ceremony: "the citizens of the country" were mobilized "into killing their fellow Rwandans" (Kagame 2006). Since 2007, however, the government has reemphasized ethnicity in describing the 1994 genocide. The 2003 Constitution was amended by replacing "genocide" with "the 1994 Tutsi genocide" (RoR 2003a, arts. 51 and 179). At a 2008 conference in Kigali, a government official gently chided an audience member for using the term "Rwandan genocide" and reminded him that the new term was "Tutsi genocide."[3] One longtime Rwanda observer worried that the term "Tutsi genocide" winds up "making ethnicity paramount" again (interview, Kigali, July 2008). Furthermore, this emphasis on collective Tutsi victimization implicitly imposes collective guilt on Hutu and consequently makes it more difficult to achieve sustainable coexistence in Rwanda.

Genocide denial and "genocide ideology" are separate and distinct phenomena that the RPF has conflated. To understand why, it is first necessary to set out the basic outlines of the RPF's genocide narrative. The RPF views the 1994 genocide as the culmination of a series of (smaller) genocides that began with the so-called social revolution of 1959, when Belgian colonialists and missionaries switched allegiance from the Tutsi minority to the Hutu majority and condoned anti-Tutsi violence. According to the RPF, the 1994 genocide resulted from a combination of "colonial divide and rule," "bad leadership," extremist political parties, a virulently anti-Tutsi ideology, the "hate media" that disseminated this ideology, and an uneducated peasantry steeped in habits of obedience.[4] This is then used to justify the need for tight restrictions on multiparty democracy, freedom of speech, and freedom of the press (see Longman, chap. 1, this volume), as well as the reeducation of the population through *ingando* and *itorero* (see Thomson, chap. 21, this volume). The RPF views alternative historical interpretations as challenges to its legitimacy and its policies. As President Kagame (2009, xxii) made clear:

Those who have divergent interpretations of how and why the genocide occurred are revisionists and/or proponents of the theory of double genocide. This, as we know, is another phase of genocide.

In a similar vein, Foreign Minister Louise Mushikiwabo stated, "From Day 1, there has been acknowledgment of Hutu that were killed. They try to ignore that R.P.A. [Rwandan Patriotic Army] soldiers have been tried. Anything in addition to that is diminishing the genocide" (Kron 2010).

Genocide Denial

Government concerns about negationism are not unfounded: genocide denial thrives within certain Rwandan exile circles in Europe and Congo, and is then channeled to wider audiences using the Internet (see Ndahiro 2009). This denial takes several familiar forms: (1) asserting that war alone was responsible for the civilian casualties, (2) blaming the victim group, and (3) promoting moral equivalency.[5] Negationists insist that what occurred in 1994 was simply war and self-defense, not genocide. This argument is made easier by the fact that the Rwandan genocide, like other twentieth-century genocides, happened in the context of war. Negationists usually blame the Tutsi-led RPF for restarting the war, and by extension the death of Tutsi civilians, with the shooting down of President Juvénal Habyarimana's plane in 1994. In late 2006 a French anti-terrorist judge charged President Kagame and his top military advisors with bringing down the plane (Bruguière 2006). In response, the Rwandan government set up its own commission to investigate the plane crash, which, not surprisingly, found it was the work of Hutu extremists (RoR 2010). The truth may never be known, but regardless of who shot down the plane, Habyarimana's assassination served as a pretext for launching an extermination campaign against the Tutsi.

Genocide denial often comes disguised as moral equivalency. Some claim that there are as many (or even more) Hutu victims of the RPF than Tutsi victims of the genocidal government (Davenport and Stam 2009).[6] André Sibomana, a Rwandan human rights activist, once described this as "a more furtive but equally dangerous" form of denial. As he observed: "Deaths don't compensate for each other; they don't cancel each other out; they simply add up" (Sibomana 1999, 117).

Several factors in contemporary Rwanda may make the population more susceptible to negationist propaganda. First, Rwandan history has not been taught in primary and secondary schools since the genocide (see Freedman et al., chap. 19, and McLean Hilker, chap. 20, this volume). As a consequence, children learn history partly from their parents, who were schooled under the Habyarimana regime, which taught a very different version of Rwandan history. Second, the imposition of collective guilt on Hutu and the lack of official accountability for RPF war crimes encourage talk of double genocide and victor's justice.[7] Third, the government's campaign against what it terms "genocide ideology" has made it much harder to distinguish true negationism from unwanted political criticism. Finally, the RPF's politicization of the genocide to justify and legitimate its repressive rule prompts a counternarrative of genocide denial that challenges the RPF's right to rule.

To combat genocide denial, the government adopted several legal instruments. The 2003 Constitution criminalizes "[r]evisionism, negationism, and trivialization of genocide" although it does not define those terms (RoR 2003a, art. 13).[8] It also commits the state to "fighting the ideology of genocide and all its manifestations" (art. 9), though it provides no definition of that term either. The 2003 Law Punishing Genocide is more precise, referring to "any person who will have publicly shown, by his or her words, writings, images, or by any other means, that he or she has negated the genocide committed, rudely minimized it or attempted to justify or approve its grounds" (RoR 2003b, art. 4). Under that law, which provides for prison terms ranging from ten to twenty years, Rwandan prosecutors charged 243 people with revisionism and negationism between mid-2007 and mid-2008 (HRW 2008b, 40). Roughly half were acquitted, with the remainder receiving prison sentences (including eight who were given life terms) (ibid.). There have been abuses of this law: in one case, a person was sentenced to twenty years for "gross minimization of the genocide" after having publicly testified about RPF war crimes in *gacaca* (ibid.). Given that the 2003 law punishes both negationism (art. 4) and incitement to genocide (art. 17[3]), why did the government feel the need to pass a new law criminalizing the separate and vague offense of "genocide ideology"?

The Government's Campaign against "Genocide Ideology"

Over the past few years, "genocide ideology" has become the dominant accusation to stifle political dissent and independent civil society voices. The RPF has long used "accusatory practices" (Fitzpatrick and Gellately 1997) to silence its critics. Between 1995 and 2000 it branded Hutu critics "génocidaires" and Tutsi critics "monarchists" (Reyntjens 2004; Sebarenzi 2009). Starting in 2001 the government's accusatory language changed and evolved: prominent Hutu critics have been successively charged with "divisionism," "negationism," and, most recently, "genocide ideology," while Tutsi critics are usually accused of corruption.[9] Genocide ideology has several advantages over those previous accusations: (1) it can be applied to any Hutu, not just those implicated in the genocide; (2) it is less embarrassing to charge long-serving, reintegrated Hutu members of government with genocide ideology than with genocide; and (3) it evokes a more immediate threat of a return to genocidal killings.[10]

The 2003 Law Punishing Genocide made no mention of genocide ideology. The government first deployed accusations of genocide ideology against political opponents in 2003 in the lead-up to presidential and parliamentary elections that year. A parliamentary commission accused the leading opposition party, the Mouvement démocratique républicain (Democratic Republican Movement, MDR), of divisionism and genocide ideology, and called for its banning.[11] In a 2003 radio broadcast, Tito Rutaramera, a prominent RPF ideologue and then president of the constitutional commission, accused former prime minister (and then presidential contender) Faustin Twagiramungu of genocide ideology (BBC 2003)—even though Twagiramungu was targeted during the genocide and had to be spirited out of the country by UN peace-keeping forces. During the same period, Tom Ndahiro, then a member of the government's human rights commission, accused the country's most independent human rights nongovernmental organization (NGO), Ligue rwandaise pour la promotion et la défense des droits de l'homme (Rwandan League for the Promotion and Defense of Human Rights, LIPRODHOR) and most independent newspaper, *Umuseso*, of promoting genocide ideology.[12]

In January 2004 the Rwandan Parliament established a commission to investigate the murder of three genocide survivors.[13] Its official title was the "Ad Hoc Parliamentary Commission to Profoundly Analyse the Killings Perpetrated in Gikongoro Province, Genocide Ideology, and Those Who Propagate it Everywhere in Rwanda" (Commission Parlementaire 2004). The commission issued its report shortly after the tenth commemoration of the genocide in April 2004. That report not only accused the usual suspects (LIPRODHOR and *Umuseso*), but it also charged the international community with "sowing division within the Rwandan population" through international nongovernmental organizations (INGOs) "like . . . Trócaire, CARE International, NPA, etc." (ibid.). The report also denounced the BBC, Voice of America, and a multitude of Christian churches as conduits of genocide ideology (ibid.).

The Rwandan government endorsed the commission's report and issued a communiqué exhorting national and international NGOs harboring genocide ideology to engage in self-criticism and "house-cleaning" (Ministry of Information 2004, para. 5). The communiqué also criticized international donors for supporting organizations implicated in genocide ideology (ibid.). That prompted a response from the European Union, which expressed concern over "the liberal use of the terms 'ideology of genocide' and 'divisionism'" and called on the government to "clarify the definition of these terms and how they relate to the laws on discrimination and sectarianism and to the freedom of speech in general" (European Union 2004). President Kagame reacted strongly:

I wish to say that genocide and divisionism are not Kinyarwanda words and I don't know what it means in their [the EU] context. I suggest that they explain it themselves. What we should be asked is whether what we are doing for the country is good or not, and we will be ready to explain this. (*New Times* 2004)

The Ministry of Foreign Affairs (2004, para. 4) also responded to the EU with a "Note Verbale," stating, in part, "If [the] European Union has no problem understanding 'discrimination' and 'sectarianism' as described in the law on discrimination and sectarianism it should not have any problem understanding the terms 'ideology of genocide' and 'divisionism' since they describe the same phenomenon." The Note Verbale continued:

The government of Rwanda wishes to remind that in 1994 some governments in the western world were begged to use their technological advances to silence the infamous Radio Television of Mille Collines (RTLM) which was calling for the extermination of Tutsis. The unequivocal answer was that silencing this terrible radio would be an infringement to the freedom of expression and/or press of those who were using RTLM. Rwanda cannot subscribe to this liberal interpretation of the freedom of expression and freedom of press. (ibid., para. 5)

In that paragraph, the Rwandan government not only played on Western guilt, but it also implicitly equated the BBC and VOA with the notorious Radio télévision libre des Mille Collines (RTLM).

Following the 2004 report, the Senate created a commission to look into genocide ideology's causes and cures. This commission released a two-hundred-page report in 2006 that concluded that genocide ideology was "persisten[t]" but "not pervasive" (Rwandan Senate 2006). The report recognized the difficulty of providing "a systematic definition" of genocide ideology (16), but then proceeded to define it in very broad terms:

The ethnicist, anti-Tutsi, genocidal or pan-Hutu ideology takes the form of revisionism by denying genocide and its consequences, or by minimizing it. It takes a revisionist form by vaguely acknowledging genocide but, in the same breath, trying to justify it through counter accusations in order to cleanse the real culprits of any responsibility. In particular, the genocide ideology takes on the subtle form of a merciless war against any effort to rebuild consciousness of national citizenship and strives to encapsulate the Rwandan society for ever in the ethnicist deadlock. Finally, the genocide ideology takes the form of a political broadside, more often than not biased and unjust. (17)

The Senate Commission provided numerous examples of "revisionism," which include saying that "Hutus [are] detained on the basis of some simple accusation" or that "[there are] unpunished RPF crimes" (17nn5–6). It also listed examples of "political broadside[s]" that constitute genocide ideology: "totalitarian regime muzzling the opposition, the press, freedom of association and of speech; accusation of divisionism against political opponents and civil society associations; guilty conscience of the international community that does not condemn sufficiently the post-genocide regime; appeals to suspend international assistance, ..." (17n8). The Senate Report thus conflates genocide ideology with any ethnic discourse, political criticism, revisionism, and negationism. According to its definition, any mention of alleged RPF war crimes or human rights abuses constitutes genocide ideology.

In 2007 a fourth parliamentary commission issued a report uncovering alleged genocide ideology in twenty-six schools. This was a follow-up to the 2004 Commission, which had accused several principals, teachers, and students of manifesting genocide ideology (Commission Parlementaire 2004). A Ministry of Education communiqué in October 2004 had suspended thirty-seven secondary school educators from their posts and twenty-seven students from school without due process (RoR 2004).[14] Similarly, in the wake of the 2007 report, educators were again fired from their posts and efforts taken to root out genocide ideology (HRW 2008b, 39).

The Genocide Ideology Law

In 2008 the government finally passed a law punishing acts and expressions of genocide ideology (RoR 2008b).[15] Even before that law was put in place, government officials had been reporting and prosecuting genocide ideology as a crime (apparently using the 2001 law against "sectarianism"). In 2005, Eugenia Zorbas (2007, 104) found that local officials in two communities "almost arbitrarily branded" common crimes as genocide ideology if the victims were Tutsi genocide survivors. Interestingly, genocide ideology cases appear to have dropped after the law came into effect: there were 792 in 2007, 618 in 2008, and 435 in 2009 (Amnesty International 2010, 17). In addition, there were 749 cases of "genocide revisionism and other related crimes" in 2009—some of which may have been prosecuted under the 2008 genocide law (ibid.).[16]

The 2008 law defines genocide ideology in sweeping terms. The article titled "Characteristics of the Crime of Genocide Ideology" reads:

The crime of genocide ideology is characterized in any behavior manifested by facts aimed at dehumanizing a person or a group of persons with the same characteristics in the following manner:

1. Threatening, intimidating, degrading through defamatory speeches, documents, or actions which aim at propounding wickedness or inciting hatred.
2. Marginalizing, laughing at one's misfortune, defaming, mocking, boasting, despising, degrading, creating confusion aiming at negating the genocide which occurred, stirring up ill feelings, taking revenge, altering testimony or evidence for the genocide which occurred.
3. Killing, planning to kill, or attempting to kill someone for purposes of furthering genocide ideology. (RoR 2008b, art. 3)[17]

The law is deliberately vague: it was passed despite serious concerns raised by a donor-driven Joint Governance Assessment about the draft law's conformity with "the principles of legality, intentionality and supporting freedom of expression" (RoR 2008a, 79; see also ibid., 34). The law also purposefully conflates criminal defamation (and a host of lesser offences) with genocide.[18] As Human Rights Watch (2008b, 42) pointed out:

The Rwandan law on genocide ideology is largely disconnected from the crime of genocide itself. It does not require that the perpetrator intend to assist or facilitate genocide, or be aware of any planned or actual acts of genocide.

Under this law, genocide ideology will be punished harshly with prison sentences ranging from ten to fifty years (RoR 2008b, arts. 4 and 8). Even children under the age of twelve could be held criminally responsible, although they would receive only a maximum sentence of one year in a rehabilitation center (arts. 9 and 10). A child's parent or teacher could also face prosecution (and a possible prison term of fifteen to twenty-five years) (art. 11). Furthermore, the state is able to prosecute political organizations and NGOs for genocide ideology, with convictions leading to dissolution, heavy fines, and possibly individual prosecutions (art. 7). It remains to be seen whether this law will encourage more false accusations of genocide ideology.[19]

Accusations against the BBC and Human Rights Watch

Since the passage of the genocide ideology law, the government has continued to make sweeping accusations of genocide denial and genocide ideology against its critics. In April 2009, just days before Rwanda was to host a regional conference for World Press Day, Mushikiwabo, then minister of information, suspended the BBC's Kinyarwanda radio service, claiming that it was propagating genocide denial. She objected to its preview for a debate on reconciliation in post-genocide Rwanda, which featured former prime minister Faustin Twagiramungu opposing government efforts to have the Hutu population apologize for the genocide, and a man of mixed Hutu-Tutsi ethnicity questioning the government's refusal to allow people to mourn those killed by the RPF (HRW 2009). The minister claimed the program "undermines efforts at national unity and reconciliation and amounted to blatant denial of genocide" (ibid.). She also told one foreign journalist that the program's speakers "won't deny the genocide outright. But we know the hidden messages, and they know exactly what they are doing" (Kron 2009). The ban on the BBC's local service was lifted two months later.[20]

In March 2008, Human Rights Watch (HRW) filed amicus briefs opposing the transfer of genocide suspects from the International Criminal Tribunal for Rwanda (ICTR) to Rwanda on the grounds that they would not receive a fair trial in Rwanda. As part of its argument, HRW contended that potential defense witnesses might refuse to testify for fear of being accused of genocide ideology (HRW 2008a, paras. 30–40). The president of IBUKA (an organization for genocide survivors) reacted to HRW's amicus brief with a letter to the ICTR president, in which the association "strongly condemn[ed]" Des Forges for having "taken the side of our executioners" and accused her of trivializing the genocide.[21] A few months later, at the June 2008 conference in Kigali, the minister of justice publicly accused her of becoming "a spokesperson for genocide ideology" after she had critiqued the justice sector.[22] That outburst substantiated HRW's argument that the government uses sweeping accusations of genocide ideology to intimidate or silence its critics. If Des Forges could be labeled a proponent of genocide ideology, how much easier would it be to level the same accusation against any Rwandan who testifies in defense of genocide suspects?

As it turned out, ICTR judges repeatedly ruled against the proposed transfers of ICTR suspects, relying, in part, on the possibility that accusations of genocide ideology would impede a fair trial. In one case, for example, the ICTR (2008) held:

[T]he 2003 Genocide Law prohibits the negation of genocide. This in itself is legitimate and understandable in the Rwandan context. The Chamber recalls that many countries criminalise the denial of the Holocaust, while others prohibit hate speech in general . . . in several instances, the concept [of genocide ideology] has been given a wide interpretation . . . the Trial Chamber cannot exclude that some potential Defense witnesses in Rwanda may refrain from testifying because of fear of being accused of harboring "genocidal ideology."[23]

Ironically, then, the government's campaign against genocide ideology has made it more difficult for Rwanda to gain custody over prominent genocide suspects.[24]

Accusations against Political Opponents

The government's campaign against genocide ideology took on new momentum in the lead-up to the August 2010 presidential elections. In January 2010 the chairman of the Parliamentary Standing Committee on Unity, Human Rights, and the Fight Against Genocide stated the intention to use local leaders to uproot genocide ideology (*New Times* 2010). Three prominent political opponents were subsequently arrested on genocide ideology charges: the Hutu presidential contenders Victoire Ingabire and Bernard Ntaganda, and the Tutsi leader of a political movement in exile, Deogratias Mushayidi.[25] The case that attracted the most attention was that of Ingabire, partly because the government arrested her American defense lawyer for genocide denial.

Ingabire was charged with genocide ideology, minimizing the genocide, and divisionism partly based on a speech she had delivered at the main genocide memorial in Kigali in January. In that speech, she stated in part:

[W]e are here honouring at this Memorial the Tutsi victims of the Genocide; there are also Hutu who were victims of crimes against humanity and war crimes, not remembered or honoured here. Hutus are also suffering. They are wondering when their time will come to remember their people.

In order for us to get to that desirable reconciliation, we must be fair and compassionate towards every Rwandan's suffering. It is imperative that for Tutsi survivors, Hutu who killed their relatives understand the crimes they committed and accept the legal consequences.

It is also crucial that those who may have killed Hutus understand that they must be equally punished by the laws. (Ingabire 2010)

After Ingabire's arrest, Rwanda's prosecutor general Martin Ngoga gave an interview to *Time* magazine justifying her prosecution:

The statement that, "Yes, there was a genocide, but there were some other people also killed," made on top of the graves of victims of the genocide, a few minutes, 10 minutes from the time of her arrival in the country—is it the same as the visit by many other people who come to Rwanda and go straight to the memorial with flowers to pay homage to the victims of the genocide? Are you saying she had gone there really, contextually, to do that?

The issue is the philosophy behind it. It's not one of criminality, it's one of philosophy. The insistence is not based on the concern that this is a group that will be forgotten. No, it is based on an attempt to play down the bigger project of the genocide. (quoted in Wadhams 2010)[26]

Ngoga also explained the rationale behind the genocide ideology law in the following terms:

There are people who, given the opportunity, would do it again. There are politicians who would like it to happen. There are armed groups that want it to happen. There is a population that we continue to educate but is not educated enough to the extent that they will not be manipulated again. (ibid.)

Here, Ngoga made clear that freedom of speech about RPF crimes will not be permitted—at least until the population is sufficiently reeducated.

After her arrest, Ingabire hired American law professor and ICTR defense attorney Peter Erlinder, who was well known for minimizing the 1994 genocide and for filing a wrongful death lawsuit against President Kagame over the shooting down of Habyarimana's plane. Ingabire's choice showed spectacularly poor judgment or perhaps something more sinister. Either way, it played straight into the government's hands, seeming to confirm some of the charges against her. After Erlinder arrived in Kigali in May to defend his new client, the government arrested him on charges of denying and minimizing the genocide in contravention of the 2003 law (NPPA 2010, 2).[27] At a bail hearing, the Rwandan prosecutor stated in part: "While he was Defence Counsel at the International Criminal Tribunal for Rwanda, Carl Peter Erlinder submitted that what had happened was a massacre of members of the population [i.e., not a genocide]" (ICTR 2010, 1). That statement and other similar ones prompted the UN's Office of Legal Affairs and the ICTR to assert immunity for Erlinder for statements made at the ICTR in his capacity as defense counsel, and to request his immediate release (ibid.). In addition, the United States called for Erlinder's release after he was hospitalized (partly due to poor treatment in detention). Rwanda finally released Erlinder on bail for medical reasons and permitted him to leave Rwanda—nineteen days after his arrest. Although the case against Erlinder involved genocide denial—not genocide ideology—that legal distinction was lost on Foreign Minister Mushikiwabo, who justified Erlinder's prosecution on the grounds that "flagrant and orchestrated breaches of our genocide ideology laws will be met with the full force of the law" (Kron 2010). Indeed, Erlinder's arrest brought heightened international scrutiny to Rwanda's genocide denial and genocide ideology laws.

Conclusion

No one would dispute the urgent need for strict laws to counter hate speech and incitement to genocide in a country still recovering from genocide. Yet Rwanda's law on genocide ideology is so broadly drafted that it is easily manipulated for personal and political reasons. It also conflates any challenges to the government's master narratives on the genocide and reconciliation with genocide ideology. While the government has indicated some willingness to amend the law (Amnesty International 2010, 34), that did not prevent it from using the law to prosecute three high-profile political opponents in 2010.

Already the campaign against genocide ideology has had several negative consequences. First, it has inadvertently trivialized the genocide. Calling the BBC and Des Forges exponents of genocide ideology makes it that much more difficult to distinguish and combat the true negationist propaganda being spewed by extremist groups in the Congo and Europe. Second, the campaign has reinforced Rwanda's current culture of accusatory practices. Denunciation of genocide ideology at both the national and local levels engenders fear and mistrust among the population. As Rwanda's Roman Catholic bishops warned in 2004, government allegations of genocide ideology "could serve as a pretext to spread rumors, pre-judge people, and to generate interminable hatred" (Rwandan Bishops 2004).[28] Third, genocide ideology accusations and prosecutions have further chilled freedom of speech and promoted self-censorship in an already repressive atmosphere (see Amnesty International 2010, 26–29). Fourth, they reinscribe ethnic divisions and impose collective guilt because they are mostly leveled against Hutu.[29] Fifth, genocide ideology accusations and genocide denial claims feed off each other, crowding out the possibility for a middle ground in which there is room both for acknowledging the genocide and for critiquing the RPF—a middle ground that Des Forges strove to preserve through her work with the ICTR and HRW. Finally, the campaign against genocide ideology has made it more difficult for Rwanda to gain custody over prominent genocide suspects currently at the ICTR. It is certainly a sad irony that Rwanda's genocide ideology law is making it less likely that some accused *génocidaires* will be tried in the very country where they committed their crimes—especially because such trials could provide an instructive lesson on the punishment of what is truly genocide ideology.

Notes

This is a condensed, updated, and revised version of "Revisiting *Hotel Rwanda*: Genocide Ideology, Reconciliation, and Rescuers," *Journal of Genocide Research* 11, no. 1 (March 2009): 101–25.

1. In her last report, she contended that genocide denial should be criminalized where it amounts to hate speech (HRW 2008b, 43).

2. Indeed, there is some evidence that the government's accusations of genocide ideology against Hutu political opponents have prompted the latter to adopt more extreme positions of minimizing the 1994 genocide or accusing the RPF of committing genocide against Hutu. So, for example, President Paul Kagame's denunciations of Paul Rusesabagina, whose heroism during the genocide inspired the film *Hotel Rwanda*, has encouraged Rusesabagina to accuse the RPF of attempting to "exterminate an entire people [i.e., the Hutu]" (Rusesabagina 2006; see also Ndahiro and Rutazibwa 2008; Waldorf 2009).

3. International Conference on the Tutsi Genocide and Reconstruction of Knowledge, Kigali, July 23, 2008 (author's notes).

4. A thorough presentation of the RPF's historical narrative can be found in Rwan-

dan Senate (2006, 13–58). For a critical reading of earlier versions of the RPF's narratives, see Eltringham 2004.

5. For a comprehensive analysis of different manifestations of denial, see Cohen 2001.

6. While the RPF committed crimes against humanity and war crimes against Hutu civilians in Rwanda (see Peskin, chap. 10, this volume), there is no moral equivalency because the intent was very different from that of the genocide against Tutsi civilians in 1994 (see Des Forges 1999, 701–35; Verwimp 2003). The more difficult question is whether the RPF committed genocide against Hutu civilians in the DRC. A leaked UN report (UNHCHR 2010, para. 518) stated that "it seems possible to infer a specific intention on the part of certain [RPF military] commanders to partially destroy the Hutus in the DRC, and therefore to commit a crime of genocide. . . . It will be for a court with proper jurisdiction to rule on this question." Still, the evidence of genocide in DRC is equivocal (at best), while that for Rwanda is unequivocal.

7. This is not to suggest the government should treat genocide and war crimes in like fashion. Yet the government has made little effort to prosecute RPF war crimes (see HRW 2008b; Waldorf 2010) while, at the same time, rejecting nonprosecutorial mechanisms (such as a truth commission).

8. The Constitution also created a National Commission for the Fight against Genocide, which focuses on education, research, and advocacy.

9. "Divisionism" appears to be a variant on "sectarianism," which is criminalized (see RoR 2001, art. 1). At one point, though, Prosecutor General Martin Ngoga defined "divisionism" as "the deliberate propagation of genocide ideology" (Ngoga 2009, 327). More recently, the Ministry of Justice acknowledged that "Rwanda does not have a particular law defining divisionism," but claimed it can be "considered illegal" because it is "generally understood" (Ministry of Justice 2009, 22). For a legal critique of "divisionism," see Amnesty International 2010, 15–17.

10. For example, Celestin Rwigema, who served as prime minister from 1995 to 2000, fled to the United States in 2000, whereupon the Rwandan government accused him of genocide and unsuccessfully sought his extradition.

11. Following the disappearance of Dr. Leonard Hitimana, an MDR parliamentarian who was well known for saving Tutsi during the genocide, the party simply ceased to exist.

12. Author's notes from Coexistence Network meeting, Kigali, May 30, 2003.

13. For more details on those killings, see PRI 2004, 50.

14. Following the communiqué, the police arrested several teachers and students (Front Line 2005, 24–25).

15. The law took effect in October 2008.

16. Amnesty International pointed out that the "absence of transparent, comprehensive and reliable statistics on the number of 'genocide ideology' and 'sectarianism' cases reported and prosecuted and on sentences . . . adds to the difficulty in assessing how these vague laws are being used and potentially misused" (2010, 20).

17. Some misspellings and punctuation are corrected here.

18. For legal critiques of the genocide ideology law, see Amnesty International 2010, 13–15; Article 19 2009, 6–12; HRW 2008b, 41–43. Taking an absolutist stance, the human rights NGO Article 19 (2009, 12) called on the "Rwandan Legislature [to] immediately repeal the Genocide Ideology Law in its entirety." Amnesty International (2010, 8) adopted a more pragmatic position, encouraging Rwanda to revise the law so it meets Rwanda's legitimate concerns *and* complies with international human rights law.

19. An earlier draft of the law included a provision for punishing false accusations, but that was struck from the final version (*New Times* 2008).

20. In a 2010 interview, Mushikiwabo, now foreign minister, stated, "BBC has toned it down. . . . When they agreed to change, we brought them back" (Kron 2010).

21. IBUKA (2008, 1) dismissed Des Forges's role as a prosecution expert in ICTR trials, claiming that "[t]o give herself credibility, [she] accuses certain criminals in order to be able to defend others." It also falsely claimed that she had served as an expert witness for the defense (2).

22. Author's notes from Judicial Sector conference. The 2006 Senate Commission made the accusation more obliquely: "The ideology of genocide and the sets of ideas that generated it are not only maintained by some Rwandans but that they are also propagated by foreigners, political organizations and international NGOs, particularly through the media and those claiming to be specialists on Rwanda and the Great Lakes Region" (Rwandan Senate 2006).

23. Similarly, the United Kingdom's High Court refused to extradite four Rwandan genocide suspects to Rwanda on fair trial grounds, noting that "the possibility of accusations of 'genocide minimization' is especially troubling" (High Court 2009, para. 62).

24. In an effort to rectify this difficulty, the Rwandan government passed a law exempting witnesses in transfer or extradition cases from prosecution "for anything said or done in the course of trials" (RoR 2009, art. 2). It remains to be seen whether the ICTR or national judges will find this sufficient without a change in the genocide ideology law.

25. Ingabire and Mushayidi were also accused of collaboration with a terrorist organization, the Forces démocratiques de libération du Rwanda (Democratic Forces for the Liberation of Rwanda, FDLR) based in the Democratic Republic of Congo. As of September 2010, Ingabire was on bail, Ntaganda was in pretrial detention, and Mushayidi was on trial. For more details about their cases, see Amnesty International 2010, 21–23; Sebarenzi, chap. 22, this volume.

26. Foreign Minister Mushikiwabo took a similar position: "For the foreseeable future, Rwanda will not allow any politician, political party, any individual, to tamper with the reconciliation and unity in Rwanda. . . . Neither [Ingabire], nor anyone else will start dividing people and rewriting history" (Kron 2010).

27. Prosecutors also charged Erlinder with the "malicious spread of rumours" that threaten or could threaten national security. That charge was based on his assertions

that President Kagame had caused the 1994 massacres by shooting down Habyarimana's plane (NPPA 2010, 2).

28. The denunciations in the four parliamentary reports between 2003 and 2008 "were rarely followed by judicial proceedings, leaving many accused without any opportunity to clear their names" (Amnesty International 2010, 11).

29. In an exceptional case, the government has put Deogratias Mushayidi, a Tutsi opposition politician who lost family members during the genocide, on trial for genocide ideology, among other charges (Amnesty International 2010, 22–23).

References

Amnesty International. 2010. "Safer to Stay Silent: The Chilling Effect of Rwanda's Laws on 'Genocide Ideology' and 'Sectarianism.'" AFR 47/005/2010. March 19. http://www.amnesty.org/en/library/info/AFR47/005/2010/en.

Article 19. 2009. "Comment on the Law Relating to the Punishment of the Crime of Genocide Ideology of Rwanda." London, September. http://www.article19 .org/pdfs/analysis/rwanda-comment-on-the-law-relating-to-the punishment-of-the -crime-of-genocid.pdf.

BBC. 2003. Morning broadcast. April 19.

Bruguière, Jean-Louis. 2006. "Délivrance de mandats d'arrêt internationaux." November 17. http://rwandahope.com/bruguiere.pdf

Cohen, Stanley. 2001. *States of Denial: Knowing about Atrocities and Suffering*. Cambridge: Polity Press.

Commission Parlementaire. 2004. "Rapport de la Commission Parlementaire ad hoc, crée en date du 20 janvier 2004 par le Parlement, Chambre des Députes pour analyser en profondeur les tueries perpétrées dans la province de Gikongoro, idéologie génocidaire et ceux qui la propagent partout au Rwanda." June 28. (Unofficial French translation from the official Kinyarwanda report on file with the author.)

Davenport, Christian, and Allan C. Stam. 2009. "What Really Happened in Rwanda?" October 6. http://www.thirdworldtraveler.com/East_Africa/Rwanda _WhatReallyHappened.html.

Des Forges, Alison. 1999. *Leave None to Tell the Story: Genocide in Rwanda*. New York: Human Rights Watch.

———. 2007. "Call to Genocide: Radio in Rwanda, 1994." In *The Media and the Rwanda Genocide*, edited by Allan Thompson, 41–54. London: Pluto Press.

Eltringham, Nigel. 2004. *Accounting for Horror: Post-Genocide Debates in Rwanda*. London: Pluto Press.

European Union. 2004. "Declaration by the Presidency on behalf of the European Union on the Statement of the Rwandan Government to the Parliamentary Report on Genocidal Ideology." Brussels, October 6.

Fitzpatrick, Sheila, and Robert Gellately. eds. 1997. *Accusatory Practices: Denunciation in Modern European History, 1789–1989*. Chicago: University of Chicago Press.

Front Line. 2005. "Front Line Rwanda: Disappearances, Arrests, Threats, Intimidation and Co-option of Human Rights Defenders 2001–2004." March. http://www.frontlinedefenders.org/files/en/FrontLineRwandaReport.pdf.

High Court, United Kingdom. 2009. *Vincent Brown et al. v. Government of Rwanda and the Secretary of State for the Home Department.* EWHC 770, April 8. http://www.unhcr.org/refworld/docid/49f848212.html.

Human Rights Watch (HRW). 2008a. "Brief of Human Rights Watch as *Amicus Curiae* in Opposition to Rule 11 *bis* Transfer, *Prosecutor v. Yussuf Munyakazi*, Case No. ICTR-1997-36-I." February 27.

———. 2008b. "Law and Reality: Progress in Judicial Reform in Rwanda." July 25. http://www.hrw.org/node/62098.

———. 2009. "Rwanda: Restore BBC to the Air." April 27. http://www.hrw.org/en/news/2009/04/27/rwanda-restore-bbc-air.

IBUKA. 2008. "Letter to The Honorable Justice Dennis Byron, President, International Criminal Tribunal for Rwanda re: The Reaction of Genocide Survivors to the Defense of Genocide Suspects by Mrs. Alison Des Forges and Human Rights Watch." April 23.

International Criminal Tribunal for Rwanda (ICTR). 2008. "Decision on Prosecutor's Request for Referral to the Republic of Rwanda, *Prosecutor v. Gaspard Kanyarukiga*, Case No. ICTR-2002-78-R11 *bis*." June 6. http://www.haguejusticeportal.net/Docs/Court%20Documents/ICTR/Kanyarukiga_Decision_Referral_EN.pdf.

———. 2010. "Note Verbale." ICTR/RO/0610/175. June 15.

Ingabire, Victoire. 2010. "Letter to *New Times*." http://rwandinfo.com/eng/mrs-victoire-ingabire-about-false-allegations-in-the-new-times/.

Kagame, Paul. 2006. "Address by His Excellency Paul Kagame, President of the Republic of Rwanda, at the Twelfth Commemoration of the Rwandan Genocide." April 7.

———. 2009. "Preface." In *After Genocide: Transitional Justice, Post-Conflict Reconstruction and Reconciliation in Rwanda and Beyond*, edited by Phil Clark and Zachary D. Kaufman, xxi–xxvi. London: Hurst.

Kron, Josh. 2009. "BBC Genocide Talk Show Pulled off Air in Restive Rwanda." *East African*, May 11.

———. 2010. "American Lawyer Denied Bail in Rwanda." *New York Times*, June 7.

Ministry of Foreign Affairs. 2004. "Note Verbale." October 13.

Ministry of Information. 2004. "Statement by Cabinet, Meeting in Its Session of September 17, 2004, on the Report of the Chamber of Deputies about the Gikongoro Killings and Genocide Ideology in Rwanda." September 18.

Ministry of Justice. 2009. "The 9th and 10th Periodic Report of the Republic of Rwanda Under the African Charter on Human and Peoples' Rights." Period covered by the report 2005–July 2009. Kigali.

National Public Prosecution Authority (NPPA). 2010. "Prosecution's Submissions to Court in the Pretrial Case, *Prosecution v. Prof. Carl Peter Erlinder*, Case No. 0678/10/kig/nm." June 4.

Ndahiro, Alfred, and Privat Rutazibwa. 2008. *Hotel Rwanda, or, The Tutsi Genocide as Seen by Hollywood*. Paris: L'Harmattan.

Ndahiro, Tom. 2009. "Genocide Laundering: Historical Revisionism, Genocide Denial and the *Rassemblement Républicain pour la Démocratie au Rwanda*." In *After Genocide: Transitional Justice, Post-Conflict Reconstruction and Reconciliation in Rwanda and Beyond*, edited by Phil Clark and Zachary D. Kaufman, 101–24. London: Hurst.

New Times. 2004. "'Genocide Ideology' not Kinyarwanda—Kagame." October 25–26.

———. 2008. "Senate Strikes Clause out of Genocide Ideology Bill." June 13.

———. 2010. "Rwandan MP Says Genocide Ideology Still Rife in Country." January 12.

Ngoga, Martin. 2009. "The Institutionalisation of Impunity: A Judicial Perspective of the Rwandan Genocide." In *After Genocide: Transitional Justice, Post-Conflict Reconstruction and Reconciliation in Rwanda and Beyond*, edited by Phil Clark and Zachary D. Kaufman, 321–32. London: Hurst.

Penal Reform International (PRI). 2004. "From Camp to Hill: The Reintegration of Released Prisoners." Research Report on the Gacaca VI. London, May. http://www.penalreform.org/files/rep-ga6-2004-released-prisoners-en_0.pdf.

Republic of Rwanda (RoR). 2001. "Law No. 47/2001 of 18/12/2001 Instituting Punishment for Offences of Discrimination and Sectarianism." *Journal Officiel* No. 4, February 15, 2002. http://www.grandslacs.net/doc/4040.pdf.

———. 2003a. Republic of Rwanda. 2003. Constitution. May 26. http://www.mod.gov.rw/IMG/doc/Constitution_of_the_Republic_of_Rda.doc.

———. 2003b. "Law No. 33 bis/2003 of 6/9/2003 Repressing the Crime of Genocide, Crimes Against Humanity and War Crimes." November 1. http://www.cnlg.gov.rw/Laws/Law%20repressing%20the%20crime%20of%20genocide.doc.

———. 2004. "Communiqué de l'Etat No. 045/12.00/2004." *Imvaho* no. 1569, October 4–10.

———. 2008a. "Rwanda: Joint Governance Assessment." August 3. http://www.minaloc.gov.rw/IMG/pdf_JGA_PGF_23-09-08.pdf.

———. 2008b. "Law No. 18/2008 of 23/07/2008 Relating to the Punishment of the Crime of Genocide Ideology." http://www.unhcr.org/refworld/docid/4acc9a4e2.html.

———. 2009. "Organic Law Modifying and Complementing the Organic Law No. 11/2007 of 16/03/2007 Concerning the Transfer of Cases to the Republic of Rwanda from the International Criminal Tribunal of Rwanda and from Other States." *Official Gazette*, May 26.

———. 2010. "Report of the Investigation into the Causes and Circumstances of and Responsibility for the Attack of 06/04/1994 against the Falcon 50 Rwandan Presidential Airplane, Registration Number 9XR-NN." http://mutsinzireport.com/wp-content/uploads/2010/01/Falcon-Report-english.pdf.

Reyntjens, Filip. 2004. "Rwanda, Ten Years On: From Genocide to Dictatorship." *African Affairs* 103:177–210.

Rusesabagina, Paul. 2006. "Compendium of RPF Crimes—October 1990 to Present: The Case for Overdue Prosecution." Brussels, November. http://www.iwacu1.com/pdf/2006/11/Compendium_of_RPF_Crimes.pdf.

Rwandan Bishops. 2004. "Réaction au rapport parlementaire de juin 2004." *Dialogue* 235, July–August.

Rwandan Senate. 2006. "Rwanda: Genocide Ideology and Strategies for its Eradication." Kigali.

Sebarenzi, Joseph. 2009. *God Sleeps in Rwanda*. New York: Simon and Schuster.

Sibomana, André. 1999. *Hope for Rwanda: Conversations with Laure Guilbert and Hervé Deguine*. Translated by Carina Tertsakian. London: Pluto Press.

United Nations High Commissioner for Human Rights (UNHCHR). 2010. "Democratic Republic of the Congo, 1993–2003: Report of the Mapping Exercise documenting the most serious violations of human rights and international humanitarian law committed within the territory of the Democratic Republic of the Congo between March 1993 and June 2003." August draft.

Verwimp, Philip. 2003. "Testing the Double-Genocide Thesis for Central and Southern Rwanda." *Journal of Conflict Resolution* 47, no. 4: 423–42.

Wadhams, Nick. 2010. "Rwanda: Anti-Genocide Law Clashes with Free Speech." *Time*, May 5. http://www.time.com/time/world/article/0,8599,1986699,00.html.

Waldorf, Lars. 2009. "Revisiting *Hotel Rwanda*: Genocide Ideology, Reconciliation, and Rescuers." *Journal of Genocide Research* 11, no. 1: 101–25.

———. 2010. "'A Mere Pretense of Justice': Complementarity, Sham Trials and Victor's Justice at the Rwanda Tribunal." *Fordham International Law Journal* 33:101–55.

Zorbas, Eugenia. 2007. "Reconciliation in Post-genocide Rwanda: Discourse and Practice." PhD diss., London School of Economics and Political Science.

3

The Ruler's Drum and the People's Shout

Accountability and Representation on Rwanda's Hills

BERT INGELAERE

Introduction

I was interviewing peasants in southeast Rwanda in 2006 about their experience of political representation when an old man made a cryptic remark: "The cry [shout] is not winning from the drum [*Induru ntirwana n'ingoma*]." I wasn't surprised by this response, as Rwandans tend to speak in proverbs. But it wasn't until I came across an article by Alison Des Forges that I began to understand what he had meant. As Des Forges explained: "During the nineteenth century the Rwandan state grew stronger and the rulers more ambitious. 'The drum is greater than the shout' became an accepted proverb, meaning the power of the state exceeds that of the people" (Des Forges 1986, 312).[1] As part of that state expansion, nobles from the largely Tutsi court had been sent north to govern what had previously been an autonomous and predominantly Hutu region. By invoking this proverb, the elderly peasant sought to explain the post-genocide present in terms of the pre-colonial past—not the

Rwandan Patriotic Front's (RPF's) imagined past of nonethnic harmony, but rather a past marked by the central state's political (and ethnic) domination over the periphery.

In this chapter, I examine the interplay between state power and peasants at the local level. Despite the recent proliferation of writings on the post-genocide regime, political representation and governance at the local level remain largely unexplored. Such a bottom-up perspective helps "bring peasants back into an understanding of the political and social processes of the state" (Newbury and Newbury 2000, 874). I argue that, under the guise of "decentralization," the RPF has actually expanded the central state's political reach down to the local level. Crucial to understanding this process is the fact that locally elected representatives have been displaced by centrally appointed authorities. Not surprisingly, then, accountability in local governance structures flows upward to central authorities, not downward to the population. This chapter shows how the RPF has created parallel channels of command and control in the countryside to maintain centralized control over the population. These developments are worrying because top-down and authoritarian power structures are precisely what made the administration of violence so viciously efficient in 1994.

The chapter begins with a brief overview of how the RPF has restructured the state at the local level as part of its larger social engineering campaign. It then describes local elections on a rural hill in 2006 and the subsequent marginalization of those elected representatives. Finally, it describes governance practice in the periphery.

Restructuring Governance in the Countryside

During the First (1962–73) and Second (1973–94) "Hutu Republics," Rwandan society was hierarchically organized into prefectures (provinces), communes (municipalities), sectors, cells, and, at the lowest level, *nyumbakumi* (groupings of ten households). Each commune was run by a *bourgmestre* (mayor) directly appointed by the president. Their position was similar to the chiefs who had existed prior to the so-called 1959 Hutu social revolution (Lemarchand 1970, 183–88; Reyntjens 1987). A consultant for the U.S. Agency for International Development (USAID) found that the appointment of *bourgmestres* "gives central authorities strong control and monitoring powers over the activities of the commune" (Goetz et al. 1994, 5). Ironically, the consultancy report was published in May 1994 when the state was mobilizing many *bourgmestres* to direct genocidal killings in their communes.

Several years after the genocide, the idea of restructuring the state in the countryside surfaced during the so-called *Urugwiro* meetings between May 1998 and March 1999 (RoR 1999). Every Saturday, then-president Pasteur Bizimungu met "representatives of Rwandan society" to discuss pressing issues and debate possible solutions. Some participants in these meetings identified centralized state structures as a major factor in the genocidal violence and so proposed decentralization for future conflict prevention. Decentralization also chimed with donor priorities for good governance (USAID 2002; Oxfam 2002; SIDA 2004; UNDP 2005).

The RPF-led government adopted a decentralization policy in 2000 (RoR 2001). Following that, it abolished the *sous-prefectures* and replaced *communes* with districts. The main changes to the administrative structures took effect after a sweeping "territorial reform" in January 2006 that reduced the number of provinces (from 11 to 4), districts (from 106 to 30), sectors (from 1,545 to 416), and cells (*cellules*) (down from 9,201) (RoR 2005). This was matched by redrawing their boundaries and renaming them. Practically overnight, most localities and major towns took on new names, some of which were inspired by pre-colonial Rwanda. The government also redefined the administrative roles of these territorial entities: provinces lost their autonomy (and are due to be abolished); districts have primarily coordinating and financial functions; sectors coordinate, manage, and execute development and service delivery; and cells mobilize and "sensitize" the local population. Although hardly mentioned in policy documents, the government also introduced a new administrative structure below the cell level: the *umudugudu* (plural: *imidugudu*) or agglomeration. Importantly, this is the same term that was used to refer to the (often forced) villagization policy that started in the second half of the 1990s (see C. Newbury, chap. 14, this volume).

The "territorial reform" and administrative restructuring fundamentally altered local-level posts and accomplished a personnel reform. Figure 3.1 gives an overview of the local governance structure since 2006. Sector and cell level authorities are the backbone of the local government. There is a clear hierarchy between appointed and elected postholders, with only those in appointed positions receiving a regular salary from the central/district administration.[2] The executive secretary is the most powerful person at the sector and cell levels. He or she is appointed by the central authorities in Kigali and mostly comes from outside the sector. The executive secretary is flanked by a consultation committee of elected sector residents (*njyanama*).

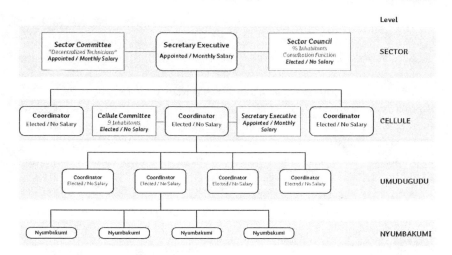

Figure 3.1 Local government structure beginning in 2006

The 2006 reforms also introduced a new norm into local governance: accountability, which is in vogue with contemporary thinking on development and good governance. The government insists that accountability is at the heart of decentralized service delivery: "Both policymakers and providers [should] be accountable to citizens, who should have strong influence over the availability and quality of services" (RoR 2006, 9). Local administrative structures, such as the cell committee and sector council, are supposed to provide "an important vehicle for the citizens' voice" (ibid., 2). Citizen report cards and community score cards also enable participatory governance, as well as tools facilitating participatory community development planning (ibid., 13).

In the wake of this territorial reform, the government has introduced a homegrown variant of accountability, which it named *imihigo* after the "traditional" public vow to honor the community with one's bravery (OSSREA 2007, 17–19).[3] *Imihigo*'s modern source of inspiration is "performance-based financing" in the public sector. This approach remunerates staff partly on the services they deliver and empowers them to search for creative solutions to improve service provision. Since 2002, Rwanda has been experimenting with several performance-based plans in the health sector, which has increased services while also introducing new norms (Meessen et al. 2006; Rusa et al. 2009). During a government retreat in March 2006, the idea of an *imihigo* ritual surfaced as a variant of the performance-based approach for local governance in general (RoR 2006, 49–50; OSSREA 2007, 12–16).

In its modern, adapted form, *imihigo* refers to the vow that local authorities make to higher-level authorities to execute their tasks with bravery and zeal. These tasks primarily consist of reaching specific (human) development targets in a given time period. Higher-level authorities, in return, commit themselves to give the necessary assistance to make the execution of the vow possible. Initially, district mayors signed such an *imihigo* with President Paul Kagame. Since then, *imihigo* has been introduced at all levels of government with authorities vowing to authorities at another level. Furthermore, individual households now sign an *imihigo* with their local authorities promising progress in their human development (*New Times* 2007a, 2008). Progress on meeting these promised development targets is periodically measured, and an annual, evaluative ceremony is held. Government officials who fail to live up to the vow are often replaced (*New Times* 2007b).

According to the government, the *imihigo* approach is a "genuine and meaningful way to give the population a chance to understand and to take an active part to the decentralization reform" (RoR 2006, vii). In practice, however, the selection of local officials and their implementation of central policies at the local level mostly coerce ordinary peasants.

Representation and Accountability at the Local Level

After administrative restructuring took effect on January 1, 2006, local elections were held around the country. I witnessed the elections and the behind-the-scenes manipulation in Ntabona, a rural hill where I was living in February and March 2006.[4] In Ntabona, as elsewhere, the elections were fairly complicated, as they combined direct and indirect elections for local officials and local committee representatives. For example, cell committee members were directly elected by the population, but they then selected the representatives for the sector committees among themselves.[5]

Despite restrictions on political party activity at the local level, local RPF representatives organized a meeting on February 3 for so-called opinion leaders in the community—that is, persons able to "sensitize" the population thanks to their social status, education level, or job. Most opinion leaders in Ntabona are teachers or small traders. Some of the teachers informally told me they could not refuse to participate in the sensitization campaign as that would bring "problems in other areas of life."[6] During that meeting, candidates were proposed to fill each post for each cell's executive committee. All the candidates were RPF members, and they were subtly screened by soldiers who had been sent to the region some weeks before the election.

On February 6 a direct election took place at the cell level to fill ten posts, ranging from the "cell coordinator" to the person in charge of the "sociology of the population." A member of the election committee, who had participated in the RPF's sensitization campaign, told me, "We presented more than one candidate to give the impression of free elections." Voters were required to line up behind the candidate of their choice. The opinion leaders were the first in line. Soldiers, who had been bivouacking in the nearby woods to "provide security," watched the elections from a nearby banana grove, while others circulated in civilian clothing. All the RPF's proposed candidates (with one exception) were elected.[7] One female resident told me: "Yes, I voted. But I only followed what the others did. If there are 40 persons queuing behind someone, you will also follow what the others do."[8] On March 3 the "elected" members of the cell committee were sworn in by the sector coordinator: they placed one hand on the Rwandan flag and swore they were "free of the spirit of sectarianism."

During the February 20 direct election for the sector representative to be sent to the district level, there was only a single candidate: the one proposed by the RPF. There were several residents who had wanted to contest the post, including the previous occupant, but their candidacies were rejected beforehand. The only candidate was a Hutu teacher whose husband had allegedly been killed by RPF soldiers after the genocide. Some rumors interpreted her selection as a way to "console" or "silence" her. This time, voters cast a ballot instead of lining up. The election committee decided that although the candidate had won, she had not received enough yes votes, so they added a significant number. When I asked a committee member afterward about that, he told me: "In Rwanda you want to win 'completely' by showing that a person is 'popular' and entirely selected for the post." The committee had learned its lesson after the 2003 presidential elections. Then, soldiers had forced the election committee "to destroy votes for presidential candidate Twagiramungu and add votes for president Kagame." This time around, the local teacher won the elections, in which she was the only candidate, with 94.3 percent of the votes.

Despite all the effort taken to make sure that RPF candidates won, these locally elected officials were mostly powerless. The real power lies with appointed "executive secretaries" who run the elected cell and sector committees. These authorities initially worked in conjunction with locally elected officials, probably because as outsiders they lacked local knowledge and local legitimacy. Yet over the years, the executive secretaries have totally usurped power at the local level. Appointed officials are accountable to the central government as a result of their salaries and *imihigo*—not to the local population they ostensibly serve. The sector and cell committees composed of elected community inhabitants mostly function to rubber-stamp decisions taken higher up that the executive secretary needs to implement.[9]

Although state restructuring was partly justified by the need to overcome ethnic divisions, it has perpetuated the very cleavages it was supposed to eradicate. Local officials in key positions, such as the executive secretaries, are often Tutsi. These positions were previously occupied almost exclusively by Hutu. Meanwhile, the much less powerful elected positions are often filled by Hutu originating from the area. This identity of power holders will inevitably give an ethnic dimension to the political and economic grievances experienced in rural Rwanda (Ingelaere 2010).

Coercive Policy Implementation at the Local Level

These local, appointed representatives of the central government are responsible for imposing the RPF's vision of progress on to the rural peasantry. Both the RPF's coercive means and its ambitious goals are reflected in the "system of fines used for the implementation of measures improving general well-being," which I came across when visiting a sector-level executive secretary's office in 2006 (see table 3.1). The underlying policy behind this document is certainly laudable: improving the standards of health and hygiene in rural areas. However, peasants cannot comply with these demands due to their financial straits so they sometimes end up in the local *cachot* (jail). These fines of 10,000 Rwandan francs are not adjusted to the reality of the countryside, where most people earn just 300 Rwandan francs a day.[10] Thus, while these measures are designed to make a significant portion of rural dwellers "look" less poor, they are likely to "be and feel" as poor, or even poorer, than before (Ingelaere 2006, 78–80; Ansoms 2009; Ansoms, chap. 15, this volume).

Survey results show that almost 60 percent of respondents indicate that activities linked to *imihigo* involve coercion (OSSREA 2007, 45). Force, as in the fines listed in the table, is used because local officials fear that they will lose honor and even their jobs at the annual *imihigo* ceremonial meetings if they have not reached their performance targets. Furthermore, there are few restrictions on the use of coercion because there are no channels through which local populations can voice their disagreement or discontent. The most important players in local government are appointed, so they cannot be voted out during elections. The community score cards and citizenship reports are survey instruments to capture progress toward service delivery targets (OSSREA 2006),

Table 3.1 System of fines used for the implementation of measures improving general well-being

	Forbidden or obligatory activity	Fine
1	Tending livestock on "public places"	10,000
2	Cultivating on riverbeds	10,000
3	Refusal to dig anti-erosion canals	10.000
4	Absence of roof gutter and receptacle near house	10,000
5	"Having" a second wife	10,000
6	Churches without chapel (building)	10,000
7	Religious groups praying at night	10,000
8	Refusal to participate in nocturnal security patrols	10,000
9	Parents who refuse to send children to school	10,000
10	Teacher or other person sending child from school for not paying tuition fee	10,000
11	Consulting traditional "healer" without authorization	10,000
12	Cutting trees without permission	10,000
13	Heating wood to fabricate charcoal	10,000
14	Selling wood products without authorization	10,000
15	Refusal to make/use a "modern cooking stove"	10,000
16	Selling homemade products like cheese, milk, etc., without authorization	10,000
17	House without compost bin	2,000
18	House without clothesline	2,000
19	House without closed toilet	2,000
20	House without table to put cooking utensils on	2,000
21	House without conservation place for drinking water	2,000
22	Someone without clean clothing & body hygiene	2,000
23	Teacher without clean clothing & body hygiene	10,000
24	Consumption of beers in cabarets or at home with straw	10,000
25	Commercial center without toilet	10,000
26	Restaurant without toilets or not clean	10,000
27	School compound not clean	10,000
28	Health center without hygiene	10,000
29	Market with no toilets and/or not clean	10,000

Source: Letter from a district mayor addressed to the executive secretaries at the sector level (fieldwork observation June 2006, Northern Province); fines given in Rwandan francs.

but they say nothing about how democratic or "good" governance is. While the *umuganda* communal labor activities are supposed to provide a forum for discussing development issues, the central government announces the topics of discussion beforehand. Similarly, the supposedly participatory community development process, known as *ubudehe*, is, as the government itself has acknowledged, "not meaningfully linked to national planning mechanisms or to the broader decentralization program" (RoR 2006, 14).

Classes Begin for 2nd 6 week classes ....

Official Day of Record 2nd 6 week classes.....

Friday closings end ....

Last Day to Drop 2nd 6 week Classes.........

Final Examinations for 2nd 6 week classes

Grades Due in Registrar's Office for 2nd 6 we

Fall,

Faculty Report for Fall Semester...................

NE Campus Academics Day ....

District Faculty and Staff Meeting (Breakfast & Dist)

Regular 16 Week Classes Begin...................

Labor Day Holiday ....

Weekend Classes Begin ....

NE/VP Student Development: 2016

Conclusion

Accountability is a central notion in Rwanda's decentralization policy. Under the *imihigo* system, all Rwandan households and communities are now accountable to appointed political leaders and ultimately to the president. This is the inverse of democratic governance where the leadership is accountable to the citizenry. *Imihigo* is meant to promote courage and voice; instead, it may be generating unspoken fear and resentment.

I started this chapter on local governance in post-genocide Rwanda by referring to Des Forges's discussion of how the power of the state exceeded the power of the people in nineteenth-century Rwanda. In her conclusion, she returned to the image of the drum as a symbol of power, writing that the 1912 rebellion "foreshadow[ed] the time when the shout would prove greater than the drum"—a reference to the 1959 social revolution that overthrew the monarchy and ushered in the post-colonial Hutu regimes (Des Forges 1986, 327).[11] One of my informants, an educated member of the predominantly Hutu peasantry, also invoked reversals of power in talking about the drum:

Why are you asking questions about power-sharing and democracy? In Rwandan tradition and custom, power is symbolized by the drum [*Ngoma*]. If you put your hands on the drum, it means you have power. . . . The only means for [others] to access the drum and thus power is to violently chop off the arm reaching for the drum and holding up those other arms. The drum comes in the hands of another and other arms are mustered to support and to be supported by the drum.[12]

Notes

1. Drums, and especially the royal drum (Karinga), were the symbols of power in pre-colonial Rwanda.

2. Several sources told me that the appointed authorities received a special "politico-military" training in the months before the administrative restructuring and the 2006 elections. While reeducation in *ingando* camps has become widespread in post-genocide Rwanda (see Thomson, chap. 21, this volume), these trainings apparently took place in military camps and not the more typical civilian camps.

3. It is not surprising that the RPF has given governance an "indigenous" twist. For one of the ideological vectors of this regime is the replacement of imported and divisive Western practices with homegrown traditions derived from Rwanda's socio-cultural fabric (*New Times* 2009). *Imihigo* thus joins *gacaca* (genocide community courts), *abunzi* (mediation committees), *ingando* (solidarity or reeducation camps), *ubudehe* (community development planning), and *umuganda* (community work), etc. For more discussion of *gacaca* and *ingando*, see Rettig (chap. 12) and Thomson (chap. 21) in this volume.

4. The place name has been changed to ensure confidentiality.

5. I do not discuss those indirect elections, which lacked transparency as they happened in private. The indirect elections are open to manipulation. Researchers of the Institut de recherche et de dialogue pour la paix (Institute of Research and Dialogue for Peace, IRDP) noted in their assessment of democracy in Rwanda that "the people we interviewed believe that this group [the group selected to cast an indirect vote] can be influenced easily in such a way that the elected person will defend the interests of unknown people at the central level" (IRDP 2005, 110).

6. Informal conversations, Ntabona, February–March 2006.

7. A group of residents, who allegedly sympathized with another political party, managed to get their favorite candidate elected. Another instance of "civil disobedience" occurred in a neighboring cell when people refused to accept the RPF candidate as the winner because he had received fewer votes than the non-RPF candidate. The soldiers intervened, but the population refused to continue voting for other posts in the cell committee as long as the election organizers refused to acknowledge the RPF candidate's loss.

8. Interview, *cellule* Ruhoke, Ntabona, June 2006 (peasant, Tutsi survivor, widow, four children, fifty-eight years old).

9. These observations were made during field trips in 2008 and 2009.

10. Research regarding the "performance initiative" in the rural health sector in Rwanda—one of the sources of inspiration for the *imihigo*—has in the meantime revealed some important negative side effects such as "irrational behavior in order to fulfill requirements" (Kalk et al. 2010, 186).

11. The relationship between the rulers and the ruled is also captured in two opposing proverbs: "One dances the way the drums are being beaten" (*uko zivuze ni ko zitambirwa*) and "One does not dance to the beat of the drum" (*uko zivuze si ko zitambirwa*).

12. Interview, Central Rwanda, February 2007 (Hutu, male, teacher, forty-five years old).

References

Ansoms, An. 2009. "Re-Engineering Rural Society: The Visions and Ambitions of the Rwandan Elite." *African Affairs* 108, no. 431: 289–309.

Des Forges, Alison. 1986. "'The Drum Is Greater than the Shout': The 1912 Rebellion in Northern Rwanda." In *Banditry, Rebellion and Social Protest in Africa*, edited by Donald Crummey, 311–31. London: James Currey.

Goetz, Daniel, Pascal Blacque-Belair, and Jacques Gagnon. 1994. "Assessment of Rwandan Local Authorities' Capacity and Formulation of Strategic Framework for Local Government Development." Consultancy Report, RTI-USAID. Kigali, May.

Ingelaere, Bert. 2006. "Political Transition(s) and Transitional Justice: Case Study on Rwanda. A View from Below." Unpublished manuscript.

———. 2010. "Peasants, Power and Ethnicity: A Bottom-Up Perspective on Rwanda's Political Transition." *African Affairs* 109, no. 435: 273–92.

Institut de recherche et de dialogue pour la paix (IRDP). 2005. "Democracy in Rwanda." December. http://www.irdp.rw/docs/democracy.pdf.

Kalk, Andreas, Friederike Paul, and Eva Grabosch. 2010. "Paying for Performance in Rwanda: Does it Pay Off?" *Tropical Medicine and International Health* 15, no. 2: 182–90.

Lemarchand, René. 1970. *Rwanda and Burundi.* London: Pall Mall Press.

Meessen, Bruno, Laurent Musango, Jean-Pierre I. Kashala, and Jackie Lemlin. 2006. "Reviewing Institutions of Rural Health Centres: The Performance Initiative in Butare, Rwanda." *Tropical Medicine and International Health* 11, no. 8: 1303–17.

Newbury, David, and Catharine Newbury. 2000. "Bringing Peasants Back In: Agrarian Themes in the Construction and Corrosion of Statist Historiography in Rwanda." *American Historical Review* 105, no. 3: 832–77.

New Times. 2007a. "Performance Contracts to Be Signed at Household Level." November 19.

———. 2007b. "Deliver or Resign, District Leaders Told." November 26.

———. 2008. "Upcountry Insight: Lessons from Imihigo." November 10.

———. 2009. "Rwanda: Home Grown Ideas Working for Country—Kagame." December 12.

Organisation for Social Science Research in Eastern and Southern Africa (OSSREA). 2006. "Rwanda Citizen Report and Community Score Cards." February. http://www.ansa-africa.net/uploads/documents/publications/Rwanda_Citizen_Report_Community_Score_Card2006.pdf.

———. 2007. "Rapid and Extensive Assessment of Performance Management Contracts—Imihigo." July.

Oxfam GB. 2002. "Survey of Decentralization Policy and Practice in Rwanda." October.

Republic of Rwanda (RoR). 1999. "Report on the Reflection Meetings Held in the Office of the President of the Republic from May 1998 to March 1999." August. http://www.grandslacs.net/doc/2378.pdf.

———. 2001. "National Decentralization Policy." May. http://www.minaloc.gov.rw/IMG/doc/decentr/dec_pol_uk2.pdf.

———. 2005. "Programme de Reforme de l'Administration du Territoire." August. http://www.minaloc.gov.rw/IMG/doc/terradmin/Reforme_Territoire.pdf.

———. 2006. "Making Decentralized Service Delivery Work in Rwanda: Putting the People at the Center of Service Provision." October. http://www.minaloc.gov.rw/IMG/pdf_Rwanda_Policy_Note_-_16_octobre.pdf.

Reyntjens, Filip. 1987. "Chiefs and Burgomasters in Rwanda: The Unfinished Quest for a Bureaucracy." *Journal of Legal Pluralism* 25/26:71–97.

Rusa, Louis, Miriam Schneidma, Gyuri Fritsche, and Laurent Musango. 2009. "Rwanda: Performance-Based Financing in the Public Sector." In *Performance*

Incentives for Global Health: Potential and Pitfalls, edited by Rena Eichler and Ruth Levine, 189–214. Washington DC: Center for Global Development.

Swedish International Development Cooperation Agency (SIDA). 2004. "Swedish Support to Decentralisation Reform in Rwanda." SIDA Evaluation 04/33. December.

United Nations Development Programme (UNDP). 2005. "Support to the Five Year Decentralisation Implementation Programme (DIP 5)." October. http://www.undp.org.rw/Pmu_Project43228.html.

U.S. Agency for International Development (USAID). 2002. "Rwanda Democracy and Governance Assessment." November. http://pdf.usaid.gov/pdf_docs/PNACR569.pdf.

4

Building a Rwanda "Fit for Children"

KIRRILY PELLS

You children must be worthy of Rwanda. Children are the Rwanda of tomorrow.

> Minister of gender and family rights, National Summit, July 2007

You say many goals that inspire us but you should come to the grassroots level and see the exact situation.

> Rwandan youth to the minister of youth, culture and sports at NGO-organized
> *Ingando*, April 2006

Globally, childhood is a political space where society's present anxieties and future aspirations play out. In times of uncertainty and transition, the symbolic positioning of children in nation-building narratives assumes greater importance.[1] As demonstrated by the first quotation above, post-genocide Rwanda is a paradigmatic case in which the language and symbolism around children are central to a new metanarrative of national rebirth. Nowhere is this more apparent than at the National Summit for Children and Young People, where discourses of children's rights are used by government actors to consolidate certain historical narratives and to project moral authority upward to the international community and downward to the Rwandan people. However, as illustrated by the second quotation above, Rwandan children are not passive consumers of these discourses. Instead, children and young people are actively engaged in reframing these narratives, thus highlighting a tension between national rhetoric and local, lived experience.[2]

This chapter begins by exploring the government's symbolic constructions of childhood in the new national metanarrative and how this is enacted through the National Summit for Children and Young People. It then draws on focus group research, conducted between 2006 and 2008 with children and young people, to argue that children's everyday experiences lead them to challenge the dominance of the nation-building narrative—not on ideological grounds but on its failure to address the practicalities of daily life.

"Umwana Ni Umutware": Children and Nation-Building

During the 1994 genocide, children were victims and (less often) perpetrators of murder, mutilation, rape, theft, and destruction (Des Forges 1999; HRW 2003).[3] An estimated 300,000 children were slaughtered and approximately 10 percent lost one or both parents. Many children still suffer the consequences of the genocide: 110,000 children live in child-headed households (due to the death or imprisonment of their parents), 7,000 live on the streets, and 19,000 under the age of fifteen are infected with HIV/AIDS.[4]

Since the genocide, the new government has made serious efforts to protect children's rights. It incorporated aspects of the Convention on the Rights of the Children (CRC) into domestic legislation in 2001, and it enshrined children's rights in the 2003 Constitution (RoR 2003). The government has included children's rights perspectives in various policies, including the National Policy on Orphans and Vulnerable Children (MINALOC 2004) and the five-year National Strategic Plan (MIGEPROF 2006).

In line with political transitions elsewhere, the Rwandan government symbolically links children and children's rights to a national rebirth and a reimagined future (see Cheney 2007). This is typified by President Paul Kagame, who grew up in exile and returned victorious in 1994 to become "the father of all orphans" (MIGEPROF 2007). Children also represent all their family members who died: "you live in place of your parents, you are the future generation" (MIJESPOC 2006).[5]

"Igiti Kigororwa Kikiri Gito": National Summit for Children and Young People

Since 2006 the Ministry of Gender, and Promotion of Child and Family Rights (MIGEPROF) has organized an annual National Summit for Children and Young People.[6] One child is peer-elected from every sector to attend a series of preparatory meetings, which is followed by a two-day event where delegates are given the opportunity to present their opinions, ideas, and concerns to various government and nongovernmental organization (NGO) representatives. The image of Rwanda as a country "fit for children" is projected up to the international level through the presence of large numbers of representatives from international nongovernmental organizations (INGOs), donors, and diplomats, and down to the local level through the mobilization of children for government programs such as Vision 2020 and the Economic Development and Poverty Reduction Strategy (EDPRS).[7]

The 2007 summit was presented as an opportunity for children to offer recommendations for developing the country that could be incorporated into the EDPRS. Opening the summit, the prime minister stated that "children are not beneficiaries but partners" in Rwanda's development. He then encouraged delegates to "speak up for yourselves, advocate for your rights. Don't expect others to come and do it for you as they might not do."[8] The summit was replete with ministers and officials stressing that "we adults want to learn from your wisdom" (MIGEPROF 2007). Despite this emphasis on children's voices, ideas, and opinions, government officials were quick to silence children who expressed anything contrary to government rhetoric. At one point, a child stated that "we children who have our parents in prison we do not like the Government of National Unity. We want the government to help us like the others." The child was severely rebuked for a long time by the representative of the Commission nationale des droits de l'homme (National Human Rights Commission, CNDH) for propagating genocidal ideology (discussion at National Summit, 2007). Likewise, when children reported that parents were selling their children as slaves to other households, they were criticized by ministers and told slavery did not exist in Rwanda (ibid.).

The summit was a way to demonstrate the "moral legitimacy" of the government as symbolized through its commitment to children and children's participation. For example, the minister of gender and family rights welcomed those participants from the Rwandan diaspora community "to see how Rwanda has developed and how children are given a forum and a voice under the excellent leadership of Kagame" (MIGEPROF 2007). At the same time, the government is controlling the space and form of children's rights discourses domestically by representing these rights as a form of beneficence or patronage. As the minister told summit participants: "Kagame because of good leadership has accepted the role of children to participate in all the programs of the country" (ibid.). Rather than being inherent to the child, rights are seen as a privilege, dependent on children performing as model citizens—proving they are "worthy of Rwanda" (ibid.).[9]

"Utazi Umukungu Yima Umwana": Children, Youth, and the Everyday

In their statements at the National Summit and my focus groups, children proffer two principal challenges to the nation-building metanarrative.[10] The first contests the rhetoric around national unity and reconciliation. While children and young people are well versed in this rhetoric, some question the practicality of reconciliation. As one asked, "How is it possible for us to unite with those who killed us during the genocide? Even today they are killing us" (focus group 2006). The decision to forgive is based on pragmatic considerations rather than political decrees or philosophical principles. One youth told me:

If people come and ask you for forgiveness you can say "no I don't forgive you" but you gain nothing. You can say "yes I forgive you" because they are your neighbors and then maybe you need something for cooking like salt or oil and you can go and ask them for some. But in your heart you can't forgive them because nothing can bring your family back. It is just what you say. (youth, interview, 2007)

Another acknowledged her difficulty with following the national policy of reconciliation:

There is the President's law but we cannot forgive. Maybe you have it in your heart to forgive one day but then the next day you have a problems and need something. You think "I have this problem because I don't have parents. They have everything they need because they have parents." And then you can't forgive. (youth, interview, 2007)

Children describe social relations as more complex than the official narrative of coexistence, but they see divisions beyond the narrow Hutu-Tutsi binary. Focus group participants talked about a bond among all children and young people who have been orphaned, whatever the cause: "We are all orphans together and face the same problems" (focus group 2006). They detailed how they visited one another and swapped clothes. By contrast, they portrayed a divide between orphans and those who have parents. Other children similarly mentioned not talking or playing with "the children who have parents" (focus group 2007). Some young people during the 2007 National Summit challenged ministers for not allowing them to gather views from children in prison. Thus, children and young people highlight both the practical difficulties of living together after genocide as well as other forms of division and segregation that are not predicated solely on ethnicity.

Children and youth also implicitly critique the government's metanarrative by asserting the hardships they face in everyday life. As one youth told the minister of youth, culture and sports, "You say many goals that inspire us but you should come to the grassroots level and see the exact situation" (NGO-organized *Ingando*, April 2006). Children and youth see the clear discrepancy between the nation-building narrative and local lived realities: "We can't enter Vision 2020 because of the life we are living today" (focus group 2007).[11] This highlights the government's problematic emphasis on "children as the Rwanda of tomorrow" rather than children as the Rwanda of today.

In contrast to the future-oriented nation-building narrative, children and young people repeatedly stressed the importance of the present. They raised concerns about social relationships and the community, economic livelihoods and education, a sense of belonging and meaning-making, and rights and participation. The loss or absence of parents seems to be the single biggest factor in making their daily life a struggle. The participants in my focus groups presented the legacies of the genocide—namely their parents' deaths—as more problematic than "traumatic memory" of the genocide. For example, one girl, who heads a household of eight siblings and other relatives, stated that "we've got used to the genocide, it's daily life that is the problem" (see Pells 2009b).

Looking to the future, youth see education as "the only way out" (focus group 2007). They associate education with being able to get a job and provide for themselves and their families. Consequently, inability to attend or to succeed in school creates a sense of despair for the future. Barriers to education largely stem from economic factors: the inability to pay for secondary school fees, materials, and transportation; the need to earn a living to support their family; or even the fear that their land and houses will be stolen while they are at school. Some children stated they did not want to go to school because of the stigmatization associated with their impoverished state: "'I have only one set of clothes and I get laughed at by the other kids so I would rather stay at home" (focus group 2006). Others reported that some headmasters turn away pupils who lack uniforms or shoes. Genocide survivors, whose fees are paid by the Fonds d'assistance aux rescapés du genocide (Fund for Assistance to Genocide Survivors, FARG), also complain that the money did not always reach the schools at the beginning of the term, which resulted in the students being turned away.

Conclusion

This chapter has traced two juxtaposing narratives about children in post-genocide Rwanda. At the national level, the symbolism of children and childhood is central in the coming together of selected historical narratives and human rights discourses to bestow moral authority on the government and chart a development trajectory in which children will move from being victims of the past to leaders of tomorrow. Despite the progress that has been made, children and young people stress the social and economic barriers faced in their daily lives that will prevent them from partaking in and benefiting from that vision.

Numerous consultations conducted by the government and NGOs engender disillusionment: "They come, talk with us, leave, then we never hear from them again" (focus group 2006). This results in "performed participation," which fails to take account of the current socioeconomic contexts of children and young people's daily lives (Pells 2009b). Instead, what is needed is "lived participation" (focus group 2007), such as regular meetings between local authorities and youth to discuss how children can assert their socioeconomic rights (Pells 2009b).[12] It is only by addressing everyday reality that the true potential of children and young people to contribute to building the nation—in a meaningful rather than a purely symbolic way—will be realized.

Notes

The quote "fit for children" in the chapter title is taken from a speech delivered by the minister of gender and family rights at the First National Summit for Children and Young People in April 2004 (UNICEF and NURC 2004, 49). Fieldwork for this study was conducted in three phases between 2006 and 2008. I wish to thank the School of Advanced Study for funding the doctoral research and the Central Research Fund, University of London, for partially funding fieldwork in Rwanda. In addition, I offer sincere appreciation to the children and young people of Rwanda for their generous input into this research and to the editors for their valuable comments.

1. For other cases, such as Uganda and Sierra Leone, see Burman 2008, 15–16; Cheney 2007, 10–11; Maria and Soep 2005, xv; Shepler 2005, 120.

2. This accords with the "new social studies of childhood," which call for a paradigm shift from viewing children as passive to active agents in the construction of their lifeworlds. See James and Prout 1997; James, Jenks, and Prout 1998; Mayall 2000; Jenks 2005; Qvortrup 2005.

3. *Umwana ni umutware* is a Rwandan proverb meaning "a child is king."

4. These figures are taken from HRW 2003 and UNICEF n.d.

5. Wardi observed a similar phenomenon among families of Holocaust survivors (1992).

6. *Igiti kigororwa kikiri gito* is a Rwandan proverb used with reference to children, meaning "a stick can be straightened while it is still young" (UNICEF and NURC 2004, 37). The first summit was initiated in 2004 by the National Unity and Reconciliation Commission (NURC).

7. Vision 2020 is a government strategy that sets out the key development priorities

and indicators to be achieved by 2020 (MINECOFIN 2000). The EDPRS replaced the Poverty Reduction Strategy Paper (PRSP) and is a medium-term framework (2008–12) for achieving the longer-term development goals of Vision 2020 and the Millennium Development Goals (MINECOFIN 2007).

8. Emphasizing the need for participation, the prime minister went so far as to say that "if there had been opportunities to come together, to talk together with the leadership and discuss problems then there would not have been a genocide" (prime minister, speech delivered at National Summit, July 30, 2007).

9. Cheney notes a similar phenomenon in Uganda, where "rather than freeing children, normative discourses of childhood based on international rights were often used to constrain children by suggesting to them how they should be, what they should have, and how they should behave" (2007, 66–67).

10. *Utazi umukungu yima umwana* is a Rwandan proverb meaning "'if you give a child opportunities you never know what they will achieve in the future" (UNICEF and NURC 2004, 39).

11. Among Ugandan children Cheney observed "deep personal commitments to national development but also the paradox of powerlessness that many children experience on a daily basis" (2007, 3).

12. For example, Save the Children UK has piloted Child Protection Networks in Rwanda that are comprised of adults, children, and sector and cell authorities working together to realize children's rights, protection, and participation in local development planning.

References

Burman, Erica. 2008. *Developments: Child, Image, Nation.* New York: Routledge.

Cheney, Kristen E. 2007. *Pillars of the Nation: Child Citizens and Ugandan National Development.* Chicago: University of Chicago Press.

Des Forges, Alison. 1999. *Leave None to Tell the Story: Genocide in Rwanda.* New York: Human Rights Watch.

Human Rights Watch (HRW). 2003. "Consequences of Genocide and War for Rwanda's Children." April 2. http://www.hrw.org/en/reports/2003/04/02/lasting-wounds.

James, Allison, and Alan Prout, eds. 1997. *Constructing and Reconstructing Childhood: Contemporary Issues in the Sociological Study of Childhood.* King's Lynn: Routledge-Falmer.

James, Allison, Chris Jenks, and Alan Prout. 1998. *Theorizing Childhood.* Cambridge: Polity Press.

Jenks, Chris. 2005. *Childhood.* 2nd ed. London: Routledge.

Maria, Sunaina, and Elisabeth Soep. 2005. *Youthscapes: The Popular, the National, the Global.* Philadelphia: University of Pennsylvania Press.

Mayall, Berry. 2000. "The Sociology of Childhood in Relation to Children's Rights." *International Journal of Children's Rights* 8:243–59.

Ministry of Gender, and Promotion of Child and Family Rights (MIGEPROF). 2006. "Government of Rwanda Strategic Plan of Action for Orphans and Other Vulnerable Children 2007–2011." http://www.ovcsupport.net/sw52167.asp.

———. 2007. Minister's speech delivered at National Summit for Children and Young People. July 30.

Ministry of Youth, Culture and Sports (MIJESPOC). 2006. Minister's speech delivered at NGO-organized *Ingando*, April.

Ministry of Local Government (MINALOC). 2004. "National Policy for Orphans and Vulnerable Children." http://www.youth-policy.com/Policies/Rwanda_National_Policy_for_OVCY.cfm.

Ministry of Finance and Economic Planning (MINECOFIN). 2000. "Rwanda Vision 2020." July. http://www.minecofin.gov.rw/docs/LatestNews/Vision-2020.pdf.

———. 2007. "Economic Development and Poverty Reduction Strategy, 2008–2012." July 9. http://www.rada.gov.rw/IMG/pdf/EDPRS_Version_July_9th.pdf.

Pells, Kirrily. 2009a. "'No One Ever Listens to Us': Challenging Obstacles to the Participation of Children and Young People in Rwanda." In *A Handbook of Children's Participation: Perspectives from Theory and Practice*, edited by Barry Percy-Smith and Nigel Thomas, 196–203. London: Routledge.

———. 2009b. "We've Got Used to the Genocide; It's Daily Life That's the Problem." *Peace Review* 21, no. 3: 339–46.

Qvortrup, Jens, ed. 2005. *Studies in Modern Childhood: Society, Agency, Culture*. Basingstoke: Palgrave Macmillian.

Republic of Rwanda (RoR). 2003. Constitution. May 26. http://www.mod.gov.rw/IMG/doc/Constitution_of_the_Republic_of_Rda.doc.

Shepler, Susan. 2005. "Globalizing Child Soldiers in Sierra Leone." In *Youthscapes: The Popular, the National, the Global*, edited by Sunaina Maria and Elisabeth Soep, 119–33. Philadelphia: University of Pennsylvania Press.

United Nations Children's Fund (UNICEF). n.d. "Rwanda: Statistics." http://www.unicef.org/infobycountry/rwanda_statistics.html.

United Nations Children's Fund (UNICEF) and National Unity and Reconciliation Commission (NURC). 2004. "Children's Summit Report." Intercontinental Hotel Kigali, April 29–30, 2004.

Wardi, Dina. 1992. *Memorial Candles: Children of the Holocaust*. London: Routledge.

5

 # Beyond "You're with Us or against Us"

Civil Society and Policymaking in Post-Genocide Rwanda

PAUL GREADY

Introduction

A major challenge of post-conflict and post-authoritarian transitions is the reconfiguration of relations between civil society and the state (Backer 2003; Bell and Keenan 2004; Crocker 2000). Negotiating roles, relationships, and spheres of influence represents a foundational lesson in democracy for both civil society and the state; and it is not always an easy set of lessons to learn. Tensions in this area are particularly pronounced in transitional states such as Rwanda that occupy the "political gray zone"—meaning they are neither straightforward dictatorships nor democracies (Carothers 2002, 9–14, 19).

Civil society itself can be weak: internally divided, mired in clientship relationships and service-delivery functions, dependent on the state or international donors, partisan, undemocratic, uncivil, or reflecting societal divisions rather than rising above them. Civil society actors can learn to balance and shift between collaboration on the one hand, and monitoring, lobbying, critique, and outright confrontation on the other. But, even for robust civil society actors, moving beyond an oppositional stance toward a previously repressive state requires not only macropolitical change but also more micropolitical processes and institutional arrangements through which new relationships can be negotiated.

On arrival in Rwanda in 2006, I focused on two seminal policy processes for post-conflict state building and human rights: land reform and the *gacaca* courts. More specifically, the research aimed to assess the impact of North-South civil society partnerships on policy processes, through an analysis of (1) LANDNET, a land reform network comprising mainly international and local nongovernmental organizations (NGOs), but also government representatives and donors; and (2) Penal Reform International (PRI), a northern-based international nongovernmental organization (INGO), utilizing a much more ad hoc set of partnerships in its monitoring of the *gacaca* process.

I was immediately struck by something of a paradox in the different attitude of human rights and development INGOs to partnership. Many human rights INGOs were reticent about partnership per se and were hesitant to enter into partnerships on the grounds that local human rights NGOs lacked independence.[1] Human rights INGOs had their own "justice forum" and tended to work in partnerships with one another, while also seeking individually and collectively to secure influence through donors.[2]

In contrast to the self-positioning of human rights INGOs, development INGOs, particularly those adopting a rights-based approach, forged partnerships with local human rights NGOs to build capacity, including in relation to the *gacaca* process (e.g., Trócaire and the Ligue rwandaise pour la promotion et la défense des droits de l'homme [Rwandan League for the Promotion and Defense of Human Rights, LIPRODHOR]). In part, this different approach was about a partnership ethos that privileged sustainability and local ownership. There was a greater emphasis on local context, caution about judging partners, and a belief that independence is not simply about confrontation with governments but also requires a relational, cooperative dimension. Yet some of these international agencies, which sought to build local capacity, particularly in the field of advocacy, had been targeted by the government, along with their partners, for alleged "divisionism" and the spreading of "genocidal ideology."

Rwandan Civil Society

What space is there for civil society to flourish in contemporary Rwanda? Prior to 1994, Rwanda had a dense associational sector, but—in a very strong rebuttal of the "if civil society then democracy" argument—the

Beyond "You're with Us or against Us"

sector was essentially clientist in nature, worked to an apolitical partnership or service-delivery model of development, reproduced ethnic divisions and other exclusions, depended on external drive and funding from the government and the international community, and operated within an authoritarian and hierarchical state (see Uvin 1998, 163–79). In short, it was part of the problem, not part of the solution. Civil society, therefore, had no track record of influencing policy.

The current regime's preferred modus operandi for civil society remains service delivery and gap filling. A "you're with us or against us" rationale prevails. As Johnston Busingye, the former secretary general of the Ministry of Justice, explained in an interview with me: "When civil society sees itself as something different to government, as almost opposed, then it is a problem." Linked to a stated policy of small government and decentralization, the government uses a discourse of both service delivery and consultation. Certain trends in the processes of consultation can be identified.

First, there are major consultative moments, such as the *Urugwiro* consultations (national level consultations) from May 1998 to March 1999, to guide national policymaking. These consultations are credited with informing policymaking vis-à-vis the Vision 2020 document, decentralization, controlled democratization, the establishment of the National Unity and Reconciliation Commission (NURC), and *gacaca* (Kimonyo et al. 2004, 7, 14–15; Musahara and Huggins 2005, 280). With regard to land reform and *gacaca*, there is no shortage of consultation in a quantitative sense. But the government has a very clear sense of its preferred policy vision or direction, and as a second feature of consultation, it often takes the form of information sharing and instruction, particularly at a more local level ("this is what we are going to do; any questions?" [INGO, human rights, interview]). Third, consultation often declines over time, and policies are periodically reclaimed by the government, sometimes for long periods. Civil society, lacking a clear sense of the internal politics of the Rwandan Patriotic Front (RPF) or the policymaking process—one interviewee referred to "developmental" and "ideological" factions within the government (INGO, development, interview)—simply loses sight of a given policy and understandably fears that the gains of the consultations will be lost.[3]

Otherwise, the government employs various strategies of management and control in relation to civil society. Legislation enacted in April 2001 gave the government powers to control the management, finances, and projects of national and international NGOs. From the government perspective, the legislation represents a requirement "to be organized, to report" (Sylvie Zainabu, president, Commission nationale des droits de l'homme [National Human

Rights Commission, CNDH], interview). In the pipeline is new legislation that seeks greater control over NGO activities. In this context, RPF cadre, or those with close ties to the government, have infiltrated the top jobs in local NGOs, umbrella groups, and collectives. The CNDH and NURC have been tamed in a similar way (Reyntjens and Vandeginste 2005, 120–21).

Umbrella structures provide a clear example of the above-mentioned strategies of management and control. They are usually thematically organized (PROFEMME for women's groups; Collectif des ligues et associations de défense des droits de l'homme au Rwanda [Collective of Alliances and Leagues for the Defense of Human Rights in Rwanda, CLADHO] for human rights organizations; IBUKA ["Remember"] for survivor groups) and are a common feature of Rwandan civil society. These structures provide an unfortunate thread of continuity between past and present. Structures, often established to protect members against repression, are widely perceived now to have been co-opted by the current government. Hierarchical in organizational culture, many are led by people who act as mouthpieces of the government. As such, they become "monitoring and control devices," used to "prevent an independent civil society from emerging" (INGO, development, interview). A Civil Society Platform, formed in 2004 as a kind of über-umbrella structure designed to group all civil society organizations together for the purposes of dealing with the government, serves a similar function (Front Line 2005, 28–30).

For those NGOs and civil society actors that step out of line, and are thereby categorized by the government as being "against us," there is a price to pay. On several occasions, the Rwandan government has cracked down on, suspended, and expelled NGOs and their staff, notably in 2003 and 2004 (Front Line 2005; Kimonyo et al. 2004, 46–47, 59; Reyntjens 2004, 184, 197n74). Local human rights organizations such as LIPRODHOR have been targeted repeatedly. Preceding the 2003 elections, a Parliamentary Commission, set up to investigate the alleged "divisionist" ideology of the Hutu opposition party, the Mouvement démocratique républicain (Democratic Republican Movement, MDR), accused LIPRODHOR of receiving funds from the international community with a view to supporting a divisionist and ethnic campaign in favor of the MDR. In 2004 a further Parliamentary Commission on Genocide Ideology investigated the assassination of several genocide survivors in Gikongoro province, and the alleged prevalence in Rwanda of a "genocide ideology." The commission report contained a wide-ranging attack on civil society and recommended the dissolution of five Rwandan NGOs, including LIPRODHOR. Among the concerns raised by these developments is that use of the label "divisionist" and accusations of spreading genocidal ideology are being used to curb political opposition and even just dissent, as well as ordinary human rights activities (e.g., awareness raising about international human rights law). Those INGOs criticized in the second commission report were mainly development agencies engaged in rights-based work and building the advocacy capacity of local NGOs: CARE International, Trócaire, and Norwegian People's Aid (NPA). Attacks on civil society continue in various guises.[4]

One could conclude, with Reyntjens (2004, 185), that "'civil society' is controlled by the regime." This is too sweeping a conclusion. While a synthesis of the dark side of Rwanda is very dark indeed, there remain occasional spaces created by electoral politics, decentralization policies, development initiatives (such as the PRSP [Poverty Reduction Strategy Paper] process), and the dependence of the government on other actors, which, on occasion, can be exploited by donors and civil society. The problem is that these spaces are ad hoc and personalized, rather than based on institutional relationships between society and the state in which individuals and groups can demand access to rights as citizens (Unsworth and Uvin 2002, 9).

Engaging with Policy Processes in Rwanda

Both the *gacaca* courts and land reform are difficult to summarize briefly. The former is the largest experiment ever conducted in post-atrocity justice. *Gacaca* courts are a significantly modified, local conflict-resolution mechanism mobilized by the government to help deal with the enormous number of post-genocide suspects (see Rettig, chap. 12, and Webster, chap. 11, both this volume). As such, they constitute an important component of post-conflict state building. Participation and transparency were key to the legitimacy of the process and to the protection of human rights, given the absence of other fair trial provisions, such as the right of an accused to legal counsel (HRW 2008, chap. 5). Procedures were amended repeatedly in an attempt to make an unmanageable problem manageable. In March 2009 the Service national des juridictions gacaca (National Service of Gacaca Jurisdictions, SNJG) announced that in total more than 1.5 million cases had been completed by the *gacaca* courts (*New Times* 2009).

Land-tenure systems in Rwanda are characterized by legal pluralism (customary and colonial, unwritten and written), regional differences, and great complexity. Population pressure and conflict-related displacement accentuate the challenges, as does the fact that Rwanda has never previously had a coherent land policy or law. The central concern of the ongoing land reform process is to provide security of tenure through registering land and granting official titles (see Huggins, chap. 16, this volume). Granting value to land is seen as a way of generating investment, transactions (in a land market), and tax revenue, which will in turn, it is argued, increase land value and public funds. Other objectives include reining in land fragmentation and promoting plot consolidation, equality and nondiscrimination in access to land, and optimizing land management and productivity. Underlying these somewhat neutral-sounding phrases is a more radical, and risky, vision of a privatized, market-driven, modernized, and mechanized agricultural sector (see Ansoms, chap. 15, this volume). A community-led registration exercise is envisaged, using three phases (public information, plot identification/adjudication, final record). The plan is to roll out the reforms across the whole of Rwanda by 2013.

Land reform and *gacaca* policy processes have been marathons rather than sprints, the former began in 1996 and the latter in 1998. The purpose here is not to detail the policy process as this has been done eloquently elsewhere (on land reform, see Musahara and Huggins 2005; on *gacaca*, see Waldorf 2010). In this chapter I focus on whether civil society has been effective in engaging in these policy processes, with the latter conceived as potential micropolitical processes and institutional arrangements through which new civil society-state relationships can be negotiated.

Rwanda is a hard case for NGOs and civil society actors: while the internal freedoms of democracy are lacking, so are the external support structures that often assist resistance to authoritarian rule. Certain models of advocacy—such as Keck and Sikkink's "boomerang" model, in which local NGOs bypass their own governments and seek out international allies to bring external pressure to bear (Keck and Sikkink 1998, 12–13)—lack purchase. The reason for this is that states and intergovernmental agencies, in particular, have mainly preferred to support the post-genocide Rwandan government. That said, some of the challenges faced by NGOs in Rwanda are common to civil society attempts to inform policy processes elsewhere, for example the need to decide between or combine insider and outsider strategies. The former is designed to forge partnerships with policymakers and power holders while the latter prioritizes channels, which put external pressure on these actors (Fitzduff and Church 2004, 168).

Civil Society Effectiveness

Civil society effectiveness hinges on three main issues: (1) strategies for engaging with a complex state; (2) an ability to navigate the transition from policymaking to policy implementation, in particular engaging with local politics and power relations at the implementation phase; and (3) internal organizational dynamics and the external relationships forged by civil society in a difficult political culture.

Engagement with the State

Two main strategies have been used by civil society agents to engage with a complex state: role combination and shifting register. These are both ways of attempting to rework the traditional tension in state-civil society relations between collaboration/partnership and advocacy/critique, in an attempt to develop a more textured and productive relationship.

With regard to role combination, many development INGOs have adopted a rights-based approach to development, which moves away from more traditional service delivery and related-capacity building toward, among other things, a greater stress on advocacy and nurturing capacity for advocacy (CARE, NPA, Trócaire). Similarly, human rights agencies were engaged in capacity-building work, such as training *gacaca* judges, as well as more conventional monitoring. Alongside *gacaca* monitoring, PRI worked with the Ministry of Internal Security (MININTER), providing training to prison guards and prison-based court clerks, in addition to supporting the implementation of a software program to improve prisoner file management. Coming from different directions, therefore, diverse actors are trying to find ways of combining a plate of activities and developing layered relationships with a complex state, which is simultaneously strong (many argue authoritarian) and weak, in the sense that it is dependent on external assistance. This is in part a strategic choice, as less controversial activities potentially create space for more controversial interventions (INGOs, development and human rights, interview). Such developments are also linked to international trends in INGO operations and development discourse (see Gready and Ensor 2005; Uvin 2004), as well as to the challenges posed by transitional contexts for NGOs.

Moving on to shifts in register, NGOs and INGOs in Rwanda have often worked hard to try to build trust and momentum with specific personalities and departments in government. It is clear from interviews with both government officials and civil society representatives that the former resent any sense that different messages or reports are being sent to, say, foreign government ministries and donors, preferring that the government be the first recipient and gatekeeper. Quiet diplomacy or "offscreen engagement," in contrast to "policymaking as political activism," is the mode of exchange preferred by the government and many, especially Rwandan, civil society actors (Rwandan staff members, INGOs, development, interview). However, it should also be noted that such an approach carries with it the very real danger, and sometimes even intent, of co-option and marginalization. LANDNET's work with former land minister Patricia Hajabakiga and the Ministry of Land (MINITERE) is a good example of careful nurturing. But it also ultimately faced difficult choices about whether and when to shift register, from one set of interlocutors to another, from one way of working to another. Such a strategy is risky: Will it produce positive outcomes? Will these outcomes outweigh the negative repercussions of undermining trust and momentum with one's core interlocutor?

LANDNET shifted register on two occasions in 2004. At a point when MINITERE and the then land minister wanted the policymaking process to be over and policy implementation to commence, LANDNET felt there was still work to be done, and, as the MINITERE door to influence closed, it circumvented its main policy interlocutor and pushed open two other doors. Both of these incidents are part of LANDNET folklore, and were recounted by a number of interviewees. These actions were consistent with a proactive philosophy: that there is space for civil society but you have to demand it, nobody is going to bring it to you (local NGO, development, interview).

First, when the land policy and law were being debated by the cabinet, LANDNET wrote a letter to the president, copied to all cabinet members, and secured a meeting with the president's economic adviser. A prime mover in the drafting of the letter talked of the care involved: "It took hours and hours, days and days, to frame the letter in a conflict-sensitive way" (Rwandan staff member, INGO, development, interview). Second, in August 2004, LANDNET made use of a U.S. Agency for International Development (USAID) Parliamentary Strengthening Program—which included a desire to increase civil society input into Parliamentary Standing Committee hearings—to do just that when land reform was discussed. Members of LANDNET believe these interventions led to further modifications of the land policy and law, and represent a landmark example of civil society advocacy in Rwanda (terms such as "unprecedented" and "pioneering" were used). But these actions also contributed to a deterioration in relations with MINITERE. One interviewee said that in response to the aforementioned letter, the convener of LANDNET was "chewed out" for forty-five minutes by the then land minister, who saw it as an attempt to "get one up on her" (INGO, development, interview). Relations have moved on with the appointment of a new land minister, but this experience with shifting register provides a valuable insight into entry points into the state, and some of the costs accompanying their exploitation.

Engaging with the Local

As a further subcategory of engagement with a complex state, the importance of local government and local power dynamics in rendering policy prescriptions a reality is key, especially as policymaking folds into policy implementation. Pottier (2002, 179) kicks off his treatment of land reform with the observation that "policy *implementation* is more likely than not to be a matter of policy *interpretation*." Using the repossession of temporarily vacated land, women's land rights, and villagization as case studies, he demonstrates how implementation, and what policy actually comes to mean in reality, is crucially molded by local power dynamics and moral discourses. What this meant in the new Rwanda was that Tutsi returnees seemed often to be favored. In short: "legal entitlement is one thing, lived reality another" (ibid., 190). While the literature on Rwanda flits between seeing local authorities as "enforcers" and as "interpreters," their key role in determining what land reform and *gacaca* polices mean in reality is beyond question, as is the divide between the RPF (at national and local levels) and the rural society that informs these processes.

The importance of local government and politics is clearer in the *gacaca* trials where the implementation phase has been completed. First, the election of judges was skewed, in that local officials often nominated candidates, and many of those candidates were involved in local administration. Second, during the information-collection phase, the government delegated this task to local administrators, rather than the participatory process originally envisaged, even though this was at no stage legally authorized. Third, local officials and SNJG agents have wielded influence in the categorization and re-categorization of accused persons. Finally, as levels of participation in *gacaca* trials fell, local officials and *gacaca* judges started to use persuasion and even force to guarantee attendance (e.g., closing shops, rounding up people, fining late arrivals and absentees). Given that community participation and transparency were central to the legitimacy of the process and to the protection of human rights, these modifications in the implementation phase seriously undermined *gacaca*'s credentials (HRW 2008, chap. 5; Waldorf 2010).

In both these case studies, local application loops back into policy reform and amendments in a dynamic that often perpetuates the tussle for control among the various relevant policy actors. Negotiating the indivisibility of policymaking and policy implementation is a key challenge for civil society seeking to impact on policy processes, and for both civil society and the state as they realign their respective roles. For civil society, it will involve being articulate in the grammar of local contexts and an ability to engage with government at all levels.

Beyond Civil Society as Part of the Problem?

Finally, effectiveness depends on keeping a difficult political environment at a distance, and not allowing it to rebound negatively on internal organizational dynamics or external relationships. Both LANDNET and PRI have struggled organizationally with long, attritional policy processes. At the policymaking–policy implementation cusp, both experienced crises.

Following the publication of the land law in September 2005, LANDNET planned a conference to discuss implementation. At this point the government essentially closed LANDNET down using very strong language, such as "betrayal."[5] Arguably this deterioration in relations was a continuation from the "register shifting" episodes of 2004. LANDNET's record of advocacy success in the policymaking period is under some threat as land reform enters the implementation phase.[6]

First of all, LANDNET faces considerable internal, structural problems. Charges include a lack of broad-based participation and commitment beyond the Steering Committee; insufficient rural, grassroots engagement; overly centralized control; concerns over inadequate organizational structures, internal transparency and democracy; and divisions between INGOs and NGOs. Organizational guidelines for LANDNET's general assembly, steering committee, and coordination agency were developed in an often acrimonious attempt to address some of these issues. But the essential challenge now is whether the network structure that served the advocacy phase well is suited to the challenges of implementation.[7] Second, the network took time to recover from the breakdown of its relations with MINITERE. A meeting between the LANDNET Steering Committee and the then minister in January 2006 appeared to slightly ease relations, although the message that committee members took away from the meeting varied considerably. One important LANDNET source stated that the government still did not want the network to take actions without seeking the Ministry's approval. It is too early to tell what impact the appointment of a new minister will have on LANDNET-government relations, but early signs are promising.

Furthermore, the network lacks a long-term strategic plan and is in danger of being marginalized. Government and the Department for International Development (DFID) sources concurred that to facilitate implementation LANDNET and civil society should assist with tasks such as community mobilization, local consultations, training, and information dissemination—a somewhat modest service-delivery agenda. The DFID road-map team, while stating that their door is open to civil society, emphasized its fragile capacity, its lack of grassroots connections, and that it has not come forward to suggest what role it could play or areas where it might have comparative advantage (members of the DFID road-map team within MINITERE, interview; Rurangwa, then director of lands, MINITERE, interview).[8]

For *gacaca*, the problems associated with the transition from policymaking to implementation were equally profound. PRI's relationship with the government essentially broke down. The organization even resorted to asking the government to propose research topics it was interested in, but received no response. This fits into a pattern: "the government leaves us be, but ignores us, which is a problem for our mandate." One interviewee stated that dialogue between the SNJG and justice NGOs in general had "failed, totally stopped" (INGO, human rights, interview). Government officials disagreed, stating that such a judgment was "very unfair": "We might have a difference in what dialogue breaking down means. You may tell me something and it is not accepted, and you say dialogue has broken down. I do not believe everything civil society says is right. After listening we can say no" (Busingye, then secretary general, Ministry of Justice, interview). There is a general sense that the space for civil society influence shrank as *gacaca* entered the implementation phase. Here, as with land reform, the government wanted civil society to move on, and essentially to sensitize (explain *gacaca* and the laws to the population) and also to monitor the courts (Domitilla Mukantaganzwa, executive secretary, SNJG; Martin Ngogo, then deputy prosecutor general, interview). In 2006 PRI underwent a wholesale review of its work in Rwanda, with local staff feeling that they were not a pure research institute and their policy impacts had been very modest. After the review, PRI stayed on, providing an invaluable resource to donors and researchers but, as with LANDNET, struggling to overcome a profoundly difficult relationship with the government.

Conclusion

Rwanda is a difficult context for civil society organizations and NGOs to operate. Effectiveness is predicated on the ability to continue to engage with a complex state, without being co-opted by it. Role combination (attempting to balance advocacy and partnership) and shifting register (between strategies, between different interlocutors within the government, between government and donors) are tactics that have had some success. Engagement needs to be sustained beyond policymaking to policy implementation, and beyond central government to donors and local government and power structures to optimize impact. Finally, effectiveness depends on not allowing the tensions and culture of a difficult working environment to rebound negatively on internal organizational dynamics or external relationships. Overall, however, micropolitical processes and institutional arrangements through which civil society–state relationships can be negotiated remain ad hoc and determined by the state. Without institutionalized, transparent means by which civil society and citizens can engage with the state (such as the Parliamentary Strengthening Program of USAID), it is difficult to see how Rwanda can move beyond familiar patterns and encounters.

Notes

The research for this chapter formed part of a larger Economic and Social Research Council (ESRC) funded project based at the Institute of Commonwealth Studies, University of London. This chapter is a revised version of NGPA Research Paper 32 (January 2009) and an article published in *African Affairs* 109, no. 437 (2010): 637–57. The analysis that follows draws on fieldwork undertaken in Rwanda in March 2006 and July 2007; all of the cited interviews took place in Kigali. NGO interviewees are referenced by organization type (international NGO [INGO] or local NGO; development or human rights). A similar format is used for donors. This is to protect the anonymity of sources. Government officials are referenced by name.

1. The major players in the justice sector are PRI, Avocats sans frontières (ASF), RCN Justice and Démocratie, and the Danish Institute for Human Rights.

2. This distancing process worked in both directions: one of the local human rights NGOs stated that they had withdrawn from their international counterparts so as to better collaborate with government.

3. Commentaries on civil society participation in policy processes in Rwanda include those on the constitution-drafting process and referendum in 2003 (Kimonyo et al. 2004, 15–16, 20, 22–23, 29; Reyntjens 2004, 185–86), the PRSP process (GoR 2002; Mutebi et al. 2003, 260–61, 269–70), and the New Partnership for Africa's Development (NEPAD) African Peer Review Mechanism (APRM 2006; Jordaan 2007; LDGL 2007, 10–17).

4. On "divisionism" and "genocide ideology," and the four Parliamentary Commissions on these topics between 2003 and 2008, see HRW (2008, chap. 7) and Waldorf, chap. 2, this volume.

5. MINITERE stated that "all land related activities for the network should stop until further advised by MINITERE." Cited in the minutes of the LANDNET Steering Committee meeting, held on January 17, 2006.

6. A number of interviews have been drawn on to compose this section.

7. For example, greater numbers and international NGO membership provided some security and added volume to civil society's voice, helped develop the complementary capacities of members, built the advocacy capacity of local NGOs, and allowed for presentation of the right "face" in external relations.

8. From November 2005, DFID funded a team in MINITERE, which ran field trials in four districts—essentially a pilot phase—to devise a strategic road map.

References

African Peer Review Mechanism (APRM). 2006. "Country Review Report of the Republic of Rwanda." June. www.eisa.org.za/aprm/pdf/Countries_Rwanda_APRM _Report.pdf.

Backer, David. 2003. "Civil Society and Transitional Justice: Possibilities, Patterns and Prospects." *Journal of Human Rights* 2, no. 3: 297–313.

Bell, Christine, and Johanna Keenan. 2004. "Human Rights Nongovernmental Organizations and the Problems of Transition." *Human Rights Quarterly* 26, no. 2: 330–74.

Carothers, Thomas. 2002. "The End of the Transition Paradigm." *Journal of Democracy* 13, no. 1: 5–21.

Crocker, David A. 2000. "Truth Commissions, Transitional Justice, and Civil Society." In *Truth v. Justice: The Morality of Truth Commissions*, edited by Robert Rotberg and Dennis Thompson, 99–121. Princeton, NJ: Princeton University Press.

Fitzduff, Mari, and Cheyanne Church. 2004. "Lessons Learned in Conflict-related Policy Engagement." In *NGOs at the Table: Strategies for Influencing Policies in Areas of Conflict*, edited by Mari Fitzduff and Cheyanne Church, 165–74. Lanham, MD: Rowman and Littlefield.

Front Line. 2005. "Front Line Rwanda: Disappearances, Arrests, Threats, Intimidation and Co-option of Human Rights Defenders 2001–2004." March. http://www .frontlinedefenders.org/files/en/FrontLineRwandaReport.pdf.

Government of Rwanda (GoR). 2002. "Poverty Reduction Strategy Paper (2002– 2005)." National Poverty Reduction Programme, Ministry of Finance and Economic Planning. June. http://www.imf.org/external/np/prsp/2002/rwa/01/063102.pdf.

Gready, Paul, and Jonathan Ensor, eds. 2005. *Reinventing Development? Translating Rights-based Approaches from Theory into Practice*. London: Zed Books.

Human Rights Watch (HRW). 2008. "Law and Reality: Progress in Judicial Reform in Rwanda." July 25. http://www.hrw.org/node/62098.

Jordaan, Eduard. 2007. "Grist for the Sceptic's Mill: Rwanda and the African Peer Review Mechanism." *Journal of Contemporary African Studies* 25, no. 3: 331–53.

Keck, Margaret E., and Kathryn Sikkink. 1998. *Activists beyond Borders: Advocacy Networks in International Politics*. Ithaca, NY: Cornell University Press.

Kimonyo, Jean-Paul, Noël Twagiramungu, and Christopher Kayumba. 2004. "Supporting the Post-Genocide Transition in Rwanda: The Role of the International Community." Democratic Transition in Post-Conflict Societies Project, Working Paper 32. http://www.clingendael.nl/publications/2004/20041200_cru_working _paper_32.pdf.

Ligue des droits de la personne dans la région des Grands Lacs (LDGL). 2007. "Critical Review of the African Peer Review Mechanism Process in Rwanda." January. http:// www.afrimap.org/english/images/report/APRM%20Rwanda%20ENG.pdf.

Musahara, Herman, and Chris Huggins. 2005. "Land Reform, Land Scarcity and Post-conflict Reconstruction: A Case Study of Rwanda." In *From the Ground Up: Land*

Rights, Conflict and Peace in Sub-Saharan Africa, edited by Chris Huggins and Jenny Clover, 269–346. Pretoria: Institute for Security Studies.

Mutebi, Frederick Golooba, Simon Stone, and Neil Thin. 2003. "Rwanda." *Development Policy Review* 21, no. 2: 253–70.

New Times. 2009. "*Gacaca* Courts to Close in June." March 12.

Pottier, Johan. 2002. *Re-Imagining Rwanda: Conflict, Survival and Disinformation in the Late Twentieth Century*. Cambridge: Cambridge University Press.

Penal Reform International (PRI). 2006. "Monitoring and Research Report on the *Gacaca*: Information-gathering during the National Phase." June. http://www .penalreform.org/publications/reports/gacaca/rep-ga8–2006-infogathering-en.pdf.

Republic of Rwanda (RoR). 2003. Constitution. May 26. http://www.mod.gov.rw/ IMG/doc/Constitution_of_the_Republic_of_Rda.doc.

Reyntjens, Filip. 2004. "Rwanda, Ten Years On: From Genocide to Dictatorship." *African Affairs* 103:177–210.

Reyntjens, Filip, and Stef Vandeginste. 2005. "Rwanda: An Atypical Transition." In *Roads to Reconciliation*, edited by Elin Skaar, Siri Gloppen, and Astri Suhrke. Lanham MD: Lexington Books.

Unsworth, Sue, and Peter Uvin. 2002. "A New Look at Civil Society Support in Rwanda?" Draft paper, Tufts University. October 7.

Uvin, Peter. 1998. *Aiding Violence: The Development Enterprise in Rwanda*. West Hartford, CT: Kumarian Press.

———. 2004. *Human Rights and Development*. Bloomfield, CT: Kumarian.

Waldorf, Lars. 2010. "'Like Jews Waiting for Jesus': Posthumous Justice in Postgenocide Rwanda." In *Localizing Transitional Justice*, edited by Rosalind Shaw and Lars Waldorf, 183–202. Stanford: Stanford University Press.

Part II

International and Regional Contexts

6

Aid Dependence and Policy Independence

Explaining the Rwandan Paradox

EUGENIA ZORBAS

Introduction

Rwanda is a poor, land-locked, aid-dependent country with few natural resources, unstable neighbors, and a post-genocide legacy of physical and psychological damage (see Collier 2007). This context makes the Government of Rwanda's economic and social development all the more impressive. Over the past decade, the Government of Rwanda has won praise and trust from its main donors for these achievements and for managing aid efficiently. By 2008, donors were funding nearly 50 percent of the government budget through general budget support (GBS)—a more mature form of aid.[1]

During this same period, however, the Government of Rwanda also carried out a number of policies, which caused donor concern. Moreover, high annual growth rates have subsided and problems of acute income inequality and top-down authoritarian governance—which predate the current regime and mirror the pre-1994 period—have resurfaced. Despite this uneven record, the Government of Rwanda continues to receive important aid flows from a

Table 6.1. Levels of Official Development Assistance (ODA) as a percentage of Rwanda's Gross National Income (GNI), post-emergency phase, 2000–2007

	2000	2001	2002	2003	2004	2005	2006	2007
ODA (USD millions, current prices)	321.4	304.5	358.2	334.93	489.56	573.93	585.77	711.94
As percentage of GNI (USD, current prices)	18.48	18.07	20.21	19.22	25.32	24.33	19.96	20.84

Source: Organisation for Economic Co-operation and Development (OECD)/Development Assistance Committee (DAC) and UN Statistical Division.

Note: Rwanda is heavily dependent on aid: the threshold for high aid dependence is typically around 10 percent of GNI.

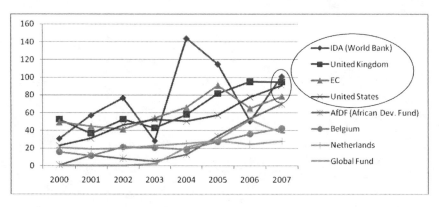

Figure 6.1 Top donors to Rwanda in post-emergency period, 2000–2007
Source: OECD/DAC, figures in USD millions.
Note: Ranked by total Official Development Assistance (ODA) disbursements.

handful of big donors, especially the United States, the United Kingdom, the World Bank, and the European Commission (see table 6.1 and fig. 6.1).

This chapter explores why the Government of Rwanda continues to receive such steadfast support from these donors. It lays out four factors that explain this paradox of aid dependence coupled with policy independence: (1) genocide guilt and exceptionalism, (2) the government's donor-friendly language and positioning, (3) the desire for African success stories, and (4) domestic support for the Rwandan Patriotic Front (RPF) across the political spectrum in the United Kingdom and United States. The chapter also discusses the few notable exceptions when donors imposed or threatened negative conditionality, most strikingly in the context of Rwandan activity in the Democratic Republic of Congo (DRC). Finally, the chapter shows how Rwanda fits into the broader development debates.

Support despite Apprehension

The RPF has matched, and even surpassed, donor expectations on several counts. Rwanda has had high growth rates, which averaged more than 10 percent per year between 1994 and 2004 and about 5 percent per year since then. In terms of social development, the Government of Rwanda is on target to achieve at least two Millennium Development Goals: universal free education by 2015, and promoting gender equality.[2] It has become known as the "Singapore of Africa" for a civil service largely free of corruption. The Government of Rwanda's push to modernize and diversify the economy is in line with the prescriptions advanced by Paul Collier (2007) in his influential book *The Bottom Billion*. The government has also recognized the importance of integration into wider regional markets, joining the Common Market for Eastern and Southern Africa (COMESA) in 2004, the Eastern African Community (EAC) in 2007, and promising to send a delegate to the Communauté économique des pays des Grands Lacs (Economic Community of the Great Lakes Countries, CEPGL) in 2009.

Despite this positive record, the Government of Rwanda has also implemented major policies, which have caused donor unease and even criticism. For example, nearly all the donors that were providing funding for shelter programs in the late 1990s (including the United States, the Dutch, and the Germans) raised concerns with the *imidugudu* (villagization) policy of resettling populations in government-selected sites. The concern arose because the Government of Rwanda had not informed them that their shelter funds were being redirected to villagization, because of bad experiences in other countries such as Ethiopia and Tanzania, which had tried similar schemes, and because they were receiving reports from implementing partners that people were being forcibly resettled (HRW 2001). Later on, during the inception phase of *gacaca* (community courts designed to try hundreds of thousands of genocide-related cases), several donors were reputedly very uneasy over the lack of assurances that the courts would meet international human rights standards (Christian Aid 2004). Later still, during the 2003 presidential and parliamentary elections, several donors voiced repeated concerns that the Government of Rwanda's vague accusations of divisionism and genocide ideology had a possible "intimidating impact" (European Union 2004). Most recently, in April 2009, several ambassadors openly expressed their "deep regret" after the Government of Rwanda announced the suspension of the British Broadcasting Corporation's (BBC) Kinyarwanda radio program for "unacceptable speech" (*New York Times* 2009).[3]

Donors publicly voiced concerns over these and other policy decisions, but they did not mount any coordinated or sustained effort. Overall aid flows were not impacted, and the Government of Rwanda did not significantly change course. *Imidugudu* construction slowed, but remained formal policy. *Gacaca* courts received significant support from donors even as concerns over due process remained unresolved. Genocide ideology was made a vaguely defined criminal offense in 2008. Last, the suspension of the BBC Kinyarwanda program was lifted, but the threat remained.[4]

The Genocide Association

Some of Rwanda's independence vis-à-vis its top donors is inextricably linked to the genocide. References to the 1994 genocide help the RPF assert more control over aid priorities in three interrelated ways. First and most obviously, they elicit strong feelings of guilt among major Western donors—even many years afterwards: "We decided to withdraw from Rwanda at that time [1994] and it is well known that the positions left behind . . . where many Tutsi had gathered around the blue helmets, they were left there to be killed. We don't feel comfortable with that. This feeling perhaps plays a role too, in our development cooperation programs" (Western diplomat, interview, May 2009). Another major Western donor representative explained: "Rwanda has a traumatized history, we feel some responsibility for taking our eyes off the ball" (interview, May 2009). As these quotes suggest, donor representatives frequently accept the West's "guilt" for the genocide.

Second, genocide references help bestow and cement an "exceptional" status on Rwanda while discouraging critical thinking as to why such an exception should be maintained (or for how long). Donors consider that Rwanda is in "post-traumatic convalescence" and that "the ordinary rules of state-building and democracy" should not apply (USAID/Rwanda 2004, 32). Donors further believe that Rwanda should be exempt from normal vetting rules for access to certain types of aid instruments. In the case of the Netherlands, Rwanda was added to its "partner countries" list despite "some governance systems that were not up to scratch and that would usually not have allowed Rwanda to access 'partner country' status. . . . Rwanda is considered a special case" (interview, April 2006). The amount of assistance Rwanda receives is also exceptional.

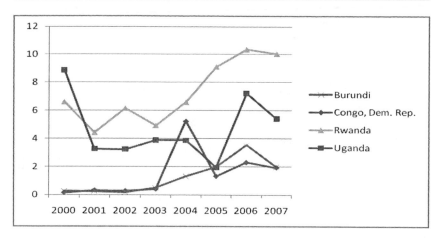

Figure 6.2. UK Official Development Assistance (ODA) per capita flows for Uganda, Rwanda, DRC, and Burundi, 2000–2007
Source: OECD/DAC, UN population estimates, figures in USD.

Figure 6.2 illustrates the extent to which British Official Development Assistance (ODA) flows to Rwanda are above those directed toward other countries in the region. The Department for International Development (DFID) admits that "these figures are higher than Rwanda's population and level of poverty might suggest" (DFID 2003, 17).[5]

Third, references to the genocide during the two Zaire/DRC military campaigns (in 1996–97 and in 1998–2002) caused donors to accept nearly all the RPF's asserted security concerns. Though many of these concerns were originally legitimate, the role of Rwanda as aggressor in DRC was continually dismissed. Only when the RPF began using language in 2004 indicating an intent to reinvade DRC did Rwanda's top bilateral donor and closest international supporter, the UK, intervene.

Asserting Ownership and Indispensability

The RPF has emphasized its policy independence since taking power in 1994—several years before ownership, harmonization, and aid effectiveness became common parlance among development practitioners. Indeed, the RPF already distrusted the international community due to its record in 1994 and its initial delay in providing financial support for the RPF government (JEEAR 1996). Though most donors eventually reversed this practice and now generously fund the Government of Rwanda, government representatives continue to state regularly that the government and no one else should decide how the country will be run. A donor representative remarked on this point that there is "an element of 'we know better' and 'you have no moral authority.' And it is hard to disagree with them" (interview, April 2006).

The RPF's early rhetoric was angry and sometimes featured anti-Western tones. But the language used by government representatives has progressively been refined to include donor-pleasing development terminology. In a 2007 speech to the UK Conservative Party, President Kagame explained:

> To realize our development vision, we . . . must substitute external conditionality . . . with effective domestic policies—knowing what we need to do and articulating this clearly and consistently to our development partners. This requires that, among other things, we learn to say "no" to donors whenever their priorities do not align with our development objectives.

Kagame's language—efficiency, partnership, alignment, national development objectives—mirrors closely that of the 2005 Paris Principles on Aid Effectiveness (HLFAE 2005).

This type of rhetoric, when coupled with the RPF's achievements, invites considerable and genuine admiration from donors. There is a sense that the RPF leadership is hardworking, professional, ambitious, even if the country remains hobbled by important capacity-shortages (partly as a result of the genocide). As one donor representative remarked, "It [Rwanda] has a very capable elite which is very determined and you can see this as a good thing—they've basically created a modern state from nothing" (interview, April 2006). Another said: "it is an excellent experience to work with them, they are serious people. . . . Despite some rhetoric which is not always West-friendly, their determination to diminish aid dependency and to empower Rwandans is donor-pleasing" (interview, May 2009). The RPF leadership is described as "enlightened" and "progressive" (interviews, June and July 2005) as well as "active and dynamic" (interview, May 2009). President Kagame's stated aspiration of progressively phasing out aid altogether has also been interpreted positively. One Western diplomat even stated that "they [the Government of Rwanda] could go without our aid [today] if they had to" (interview, May 2009)—an implausible claim given Rwanda's sheer dependence on aid.[6]

Donors tend to view the RPF as indispensable for development. This is partly because most donors simply do not know how to decode the Rwandan sociopolitical context, let alone figure out what impact their development programs are having. As one donor candidly admitted, "Reconciliation is so complex and it is difficult for us to know what is going on, it's difficult for us to distinguish ethnic groups or even socioeconomic groups!" (interview, April

2006). Uvin concurs: "The large majority of the international community has not the faintest idea what really happens in Rwanda outside of the top level of the state" (Uvin 2003). Another, perhaps equally significant handicap is that of language: "a huge problem we [in the diplomatic community] have is that no one, no one understands Kinyarwanda" (Western diplomat, May 2009).

The RPF's record of achievement, rhetoric of ownership, and perceived indispensability partly account for the Memorandum of Understanding (MoU) signed by the UK and Rwanda in 2006 (DFID 2006). The MoU guarantees that the UK will disburse at least £46 million per annum over ten years, with two-thirds going to general budget support (GBS) and part of the remaining one-third to sector budget support (SBS, earmarked to a particular ministry). A Western donor explained: "This was the first time the UK had ever signed such an agreement—guaranteeing such predictability—with any development partner. . . . It is indicative of a fair amount of trust." The same interviewee further clarified: "This means that, although the Government of Rwanda has to discuss what they will do with that money with the UK, it is really up to them to decide what they want to do with this approximately £30 million [in GBS]" (interview, May 2009).

Development as the Western Strategic Interest

Except for Belgium, the former colonial power, which sees Central Africa as right at the top of its foreign policy agenda, the United States, the UK, and even the European Commission have no real interests in Rwanda. One Western diplomat summarized it as follows: "We have no strategic interests here, and negligible commercial interests, so we are really centred on the development programme, which actually makes for an easy relationship" (interview, May 2009). Another Western diplomat said, "Our relationship is very one-sided, we just give them a lot of money, that's it" (interview, May 2009).

The absence of strategic and commercial interests has meant that the development cooperation program itself has become the principal strategic interest for big donors. All the donors I interviewed insisted that their support to Rwanda was not unconditional: "We are accountable to our Parliament and to our public. Our assistance is based on a shared set of principles: democracy, respect for human rights, aid being channeled to the poorest" (interview, May 2009). However, several expressed their desire to see this development cooperation continue: one of the Western donor representatives underscored repeatedly that aid is used "efficiently" and that it was a "very satisfying experience" to work with the Government of Rwanda, as one gets "results" (interview, May 2009). According to De Lorenzo (2008, n.p.), this makes sense because "politically, the donors need success stories as much as the recipients need the aid."

Indeed, some donors defended Rwanda's record against critics. One major donor representative described those critics as using a double standard: "Rwanda is heavily under the spotlight because Kagame is seen as quite a capable leader. There is a much lower bar for other African states, like the DRC for example. . . . Nigeria too. If they have the slightest success, they are applauded, whereas Rwanda gets a lot of scrutiny" (interview, May 2009). In addition, donors gave a selective reading of Rwanda's record. Typically donor representatives mentioned the Government of Rwanda's big achievements such as security, economic growth, low corruption, and progress toward universal primary education, but omitted the increasing economic disparities characterizing both urban and rural Rwanda. This omission was particularly glaring in my 2009 interviews because a series of studies had been widely circulated by then. A 2007 United Nations Development Programme (UNDP) report showed Rwanda's Gini coefficient (a common measure of income inequality) "almost doubling over the last twenty years" and further showed that "in two out of five provinces, as well as in urban areas outside of Kigali, the depth of poverty has actually increased since 2001 . . . meaning that the average poor household in these areas is worse off today than it was five years ago" (UNDP 2007, 17). For the other three provinces, the decrease in the depth of poverty had been "negligible" (ibid.). These studies deserve particular attention because they show that development is once again failing the vast majority of the poor, as their quality of life stays the same or actually worsens. What is more, inequality is a quantifiable indicator of the political and socioeconomic exclusion and frustration, or structural violence, which Uvin (1998) argued characterized pre-1994 Rwanda and helped authorities recruit for and execute the genocide.

Domestic Politics in the United States and Britain

A fourth element in explaining the aid dependence/policy independence paradox has to do with bilateral donors' domestic political constellations. The UK and the United States are Rwanda's most important bilateral donors in the post-1999 period. The UK had no presence in Rwanda prior to 1994, and the United States had a drastically smaller one. They were drawn to Rwanda after the genocide, and as a result a broadly sympathetic view of the RPF prevails across their political spectrums. "The UK is remarkable by the fact that Rwanda has support across the UK Parliament," said one Western diplomat. He continued:

This is not the case with the Dutch or Belgians. Also, the UK doesn't have a large Rwandan Diaspora community which itself exerts pressures on Parliaments and is often quite critical of the government in Kigali. Lastly, the Catholic Church has a tense relationship with Rwanda. Some Catholic (political) parties and church groups tend to be more critical of Rwanda as a result. This is simply not a factor in the UK. (interview, May 2009)

The same applies for the United States, where both Democrats and Republicans support the Government of Rwanda.

By contrast, the Dutch cut support to Rwanda twice—during the presidential and parliamentary elections in 2003 and after the publication of a UN report detailing Rwandan support for a Congolese rebel group in 2008. Both times, the suspension of aid was not so much a reaction to developments on the ground in Rwanda as it was a response to political pressure from the Dutch Parliament resulting from vocal media and civil society groups. In 2003 there was a feeling that the embassy had been pushed into action: "Rwanda is heavily debated in the Netherlands. . . . The Dutch Parliament is more interested in Rwanda than any other donor country" (Western diplomat, April 2006). In this vein, another Western diplomat explained: "We are humble civil servants to our capitals, our parliaments, our publics . . . we all represent governments which are very much under the control of our Parliaments. This was very much the case for the Dutch when they cut their aid [in December 2008]" (interview, May 2009).

The (Partial) Exception of Congo

The RPF enjoys strong donor financial support even as it carries out some policies, which donors deem problematic. There have been exceptions. As mentioned above, the Dutch cut their planned aid for Rwanda's National Election Commission by half. Although symbolically important, there was little follow-through or impact: Dutch aid monies increased almost every year since 2003 (see fig. 6.1), and the lack of political space in 2003 was followed by an arguably worse climate of fear and intimidation in 2004 (Front Line 2005). Moreover, the amount of Dutch aid concerned was relatively negligible ($300,000), and no other donors followed suit.

The UK's withdrawal of one quarter of its GBS to Rwanda in late 2004 was more important than Dutch action the year before.[7] The UK is Rwanda's closest bilateral ally, not only financially but in various diplomatic and economic fora: the UK publicly supported Rwanda's application to join the Commonwealth, for example. The UK's actions engendered very practical repercussions for the Government of Rwanda: in 2004, the UK was providing approximately 10 percent of the Government of Rwanda's budget via general budget support (Purcell, Dom, and Ahobamuteze 2006, 36, 173). Why did the UK take this important and highly unusual step of openly applying negative conditionality? A UK representative in Rwanda explained:

A shared principle on which our aid is premised is that of regional security. Here, we had some problems in 2004, when the Rwanda–Democratic Republic of Congo relationship rapidly deteriorated and Rwanda announced openly that it was contemplating renewed military intervention in DRC. The UK withdrew one quarter of its GBS at that stage. As this intervention never took place, relations normalised [and disbursements resumed] fairly quickly. (interview, May 2009)

Why does the DRC matter in a way that Rwandan elections do not? There is a consensus among the international community that the main threat to the financial and diplomatic capital invested for the reconstruction and development of Rwanda is regional instability (Purcell, Dom, and Aho-bamuteze 2006, para. S5). There is also agreement that peace in the DRC and the (re-)establishment of state authority are the linchpins for this stability. The Government of Rwanda therefore crosses a red line for donors when it is seen as openly meddling in eastern Congo. The UK has even reserved the right to reduce, interrupt, or terminate aid to Rwanda if "the Government of Rwanda is in significant violation of human rights or other international obligations, es-pecially those relating to regional peace and security" (DFID 2006, para. 6.1).

Rwanda appears to have learned the lessons of 2004. In the second half of 2008, Laurent Nkunda, a Congolese Tutsi warlord widely considered Rwanda's proxy, attacked civilian populations in eastern DRC, causing a renewed hu-manitarian crisis. These attacks received significant international media cover-age, which were detrimental to Rwanda's image. The Government of Rwanda successfully preempted UK action when it intensified bilateral relations with DRC, arrested Nkunda, and launched joint military operations with the Congolese Army against the Forces démocratiques de libération du Rwanda (Democratic Forces for the Liberation of Rwanda, FDLR), a Rwandan Hutu militia, some of whose members participated in the 1994 genocide. Virtually overnight, the Government of Rwanda recast itself from a destabilizing to a peacemaking force. As a result, the publication of a UN report in December 2008 that documented Rwandan support to Nkunda's militia was no longer seen as relevant. The report did prompt the Dutch and the Swedes to suspend their (much smaller) GBS programs. Yet, as one diplomat stated, "The basis on which those two donors made their decision has been overtaken by events as Rwanda and DRC forged close bilateral ties and launched joint operations in eastern DRC. It is a bright new dawn in DRC" (interview, May 2009, referring to UN 2008).[8]

Still, the DRC is only a partial exception to the overall trend of donors sticking by Rwanda. In 2004 only the UK and Sweden suspended disbursements. In 2008 only the Dutch and the Swedes did—out of the more than twenty-five bilateral and multilateral aid programs in Rwanda. What accounts for this lack of coordination among the major European donors and the United States, who are considered like-minded? Here, answers are unconvincing and technical in nature: different aid mechanisms and different budgetary cycles apparently precluded coordinated action. When asked why his institution did not follow the Dutch and Swedish example in 2008, a major donor representative explained: "We were not at that point at the budgetary cycle where a disbursement was due, so the opportunity to make such a decision did not arise" (interview, May 2009). Asked why other donors did not follow the Dutch in cutting some of their funding to the 2003 elections, a Western diplomat stated: "We did not fund the presidential elections directly" (interview, April 2006). However, this same diplomat then conceded that "we did fund the parliamentary elections," which were held virtually simultaneously as the presidential elections and were also criticized by the EU observers. Intentionally or not, the end result is "mixed messages from donors," which "provide the government with considerable space for maneuver" (Hayman 2007, 20).

Conclusion: Rwanda and the Development Status Quo

Since the end of the Cold War and the proliferation of intrastate conflicts, the mandate of international development assistance has expanded to encompass conflict prevention (DFID 2009, chap. 4; Duffield 2001). To achieve the now doubly important development outcomes of welfare *and* peace, the concept of aid effectiveness became preeminent in the 2000s. The 2005 Paris Declaration set forth the central tenets: ownership of development priorities by aid recipients, alignment, and harmonization of donors behind these priorities, mutual accountability, and predictable aid. In this vein, GBS becomes the aid instrument of choice, allowing aid dollars to be channeled directly through central government systems, not disparate individual ministries or NGOs.

But the basically technocratic approach to development enshrined in the Paris Declaration stands in sharp contrast to what were supposed to be the lessons that development practitioners learned from the 1994 Rwandan genocide. Uvin argued that it was precisely a technocratic and apolitical conception of development that led donors to contribute to the structural violence that made the genocide possible. A more principled definition of development, which included formerly off-limits areas such as good governance, justice and the rule of law, and human rights was therefore put forward. This profound redefinition of development—initially referred to as a "rights-based approach" but now usually captured under the term "good governance"—has ultimately done little to change how development is practiced in Rwanda.

There are several reasons for this. First, operationalizing concepts such as good governance, rule of law, or human rights is difficult. Though it is easy to tell when governance is bad or when rights are violated, progress is more difficult to measure. Second, despite the importance laid on forging genuine development partnerships, the power imbalance between donor and recipient governments has not fundamentally changed. Prickly aid recipients, like the Government of Rwanda, continue to denounce foreign interventionism, breaches of sovereignty, and lack of moral authority when rights violations or bad governance are raised. Indeed, Kagame regularly lambasts "this attitude that is based on ignorance and arrogance . . . from those who would argue that they know better than Rwandans what is good for them" (Kagame 2009b). Third, the Government of Rwanda is active in influencing ongoing discussions of how development should best be practiced. President Kagame will serve as an advisor to the World Bank's 2011 World Development Report to "advance global thinking" on the "links among conflict, security, governance, and development" (*New Times* 2009). The Government of Rwanda is also considered to be at the forefront of the aid effectiveness debate, particularly when it comes to ownership of aid strategies.[9] This was most recently reflected when the Government of Rwanda spearheaded its own annual Joint Governance Assessment reports between donors and the Government of Rwanda in 2008 (RoR 2008).

In looking at the evolution of development debates since the mid-1990s, it seems that donors are not so much forgetting past lessons from pre-genocide Rwanda as having difficulty coming to grips with how to actually implement them. The international aid architecture—specifically the power relations between aid-disbursing and aid-recipient governments as well as between recipient governments and their citizens—has not changed. For the reasons cited in this chapter, the Government of Rwanda can largely continue to define and pursue its own preferred development strategy, which does not fundamentally improve the lot of the poor and vulnerable nor does it alter the conditions of structural violence. This represents a failure of development in its mandates for both welfare and peace.

Notes

1. General Budgetary Support is normally considered appropriate only for governments that show promising poverty-reduction policy frameworks and the capacity to use resources effectively. It allows for aid monies to be channeled directly to the overall budget of the central government usually with minimal limitations on the use of these funds. It is considered an "ideal," more effective form of aid than project-by-project funding because it is designed to reduce transaction costs while improving aid predictability and strengthening local ownership and government capacity.

2. In 2008, Rwanda became the first country to have a majority of female parliamentarians in its national assembly.

3. The program, which was timed to coincide with the fifteenth commemoration ceremonies, included an interview with the exiled former prime minister Faustin Twagiramungu, who, along with several others, criticized the Government of Rwanda for preventing victims of Rwandan Patriotic Army (RPA) massacres from mourning their loved ones. The RPA was the former military wing of the then-rebel RPF, which became the nucleus of a new national army, the Rwanda Defense Forces (RDF).

4. BBC (and Voice of America) had already been accused of divisionism in a 2004 parliamentary commission report.

5. These large aid flows are at times referred to as the "genocide credit" (Reyntjens 2004).

6. President Kagame has paid lip service to progressively phasing out development aid to African countries altogether, as per the thesis of Dambisa Moyo's 2009 book, *Dead Aid*. He conceded though that the five-year phase-out plan called for in *Dead Aid* is "aggressive" (Kagame 2009a).

7. Sweden withheld GBS disbursements in the last quarter of 2004, also citing DRC-related political tensions.

8. Predictably perhaps, Kagame responded to the Dutch and Swedish action as follows: "Africa must wake up to the continued arrogance of the rich nations. . . . The people of Rwanda should be ready to survive in any circumstance including the absence of aid. These people who cut aid like the Dutch and the Swedes are just supporting my argument" (quoted in *Afrol News* 2008).

9. In fact, this ownership is shared jointly with donors (Hayman 2009).

References

Afrol News. 2008. "Sweden Suspends Aid to Rwanda." December 18. http://www.afrol .com/articles/32047.

Armon, Jeremy. 2007. "Aid, Politics and Development: A Donor Perspective." *Development Policy Review* 25, no. 5: 653–56.

Christian Aid. 2004. *"It's Time to Open Up": Ten Years after the Genocide in Rwanda*. London: Christian Aid.

Collier, Paul. 2007. *The Bottom Billion: Why the Poorest Countries Are Failing and What Can Be Done about It*. Oxford: Oxford University Press.

De Lorenzo, Mauro. 2008. "The Rwandan Paradox: Is Rwanda a Model for an Africa beyond Aid?" http://www.aei.org/publications/filter.all,pubID.27476/pub_detail.asp.

Department for International Development (DFID). 2003. "Rwanda: Country Assistance Plan 2003–2006." London, February. http://www.dfid.gov.uk/pubs/files/caprwanda.pdf.

———. 2006. "Memorandum of Understanding between the Government of the United Kingdom of Great Britain and Northern Ireland and the Government of the Republic of Rwanda." London, February 13. http://webarchive.nationalarchives.gov.uk/+/http://www.dfid.gov.uk/pubs/files/rwanda-mou-2006.pdf.

———. 2009. "Eliminating World Poverty: Building Our Common Future." London, July. http://www.dfid.gov.uk/documents/whitepaper/building-our-common-future-print.pdf.

Duffield, Mark R. 2001. *Global Governance and the New Wars: The Merging of Development and Security*. New York: Zed Books.

European Union. 2004. "Declaration by the Presidency on Behalf of the European Union on the Statement of the Rwandan Government to the Parliamentary Report on Genocidal Ideology." 13110/04 (Presse 285). Brussels, October 6. http://europa.eu/rapid/pressReleasesAction.do?reference=PESC/04/114&format=PDF&aged=1&language=EN&guiLanguage=en.

European Union Election Observation Mission (EU EOM). 2003. *Rwanda: Election presidentielle 25 Août 2003; Élections législatives 29 et 30 Septembre, 2 Octobre 2003* (final report). Brussels: European Union.

Front Line. 2005. "Front Line Rwanda: Disappearances, Arrests, Threats, Intimidation and Co-option of Human Rights Defenders 2001–2004." March. http://www.frontlinedefenders.org/files/en/FrontLineRwandaReport.pdf.

Hayman, Rachel. 2007. *"Milking the Cow": Negotiating Ownership of Aid and Policy in Rwanda*. Oxford: University College Global Economic Governance Program.

———. 2009. "From Rome to Accra via Kigali: 'Aid Effectiveness' in Rwanda." *Development Policy Review* 27, no. 5: 581–99.

High Level Forum on Aid Effectiveness (HLFAE). 2005. "The Paris Declaration on Aid Effectiveness and the Accra Agenda for Action." http://www.oecd.org/dataoecd/11/41/34428351.pdf.

Human Rights Watch (HRW). 2001. "Uprooting the Rural Poor in Rwanda." May 1. http://www.hrw.org/legacy/reports/2001/rwanda/.

Joint Evaluation of Emergency Assistance to Rwanda (JEEAR). 1996. "The International Response to Conflict and Genocide: Lessons from the Rwanda Experience." March. http://www.grandslacs.net/doc/0742.pdf.

Kagame, Paul. 2009a. "Africa Has to Find Its Own Road to Prosperity." *Financial Times*, May 2.

———. 2009b. "Official Liberation Day Speech." July 4. http://paulkagame
.com/2010/index.php?option=com_content&view=article&id=85%3Aliberation
-day-kigali-4-july-2009&catid=34%3Aspeeches&Itemid=56&lang=en.

Moyo, Dambisa. 2009. *Dead Aid: Why Aid Is Not Working and How There Is a Better
Way for Africa.* New York: Farrar, Straus and Giroux.

New Times. 2009. "Kagame Named Member of 2011 World Bank Advisory Council."
September 29.

New York Times. 2009. "Rwanda Suspends BBC Radio Service." April 25.

Paris, Roland. 2004. *At War's End: Building Peace after Civil Conflict.* New York: Cambridge University Press.

Purcell, Ray, Catherine Dom, and Gaspard Ahobamuteze. 2006. "Rwanda Country
Report." *Joint Evaluation of General Budget Support 1994–2004.* May. http://www
.bmz.de/de/publikationen/reihen/evaluierungen/gemeinschaftsevaluierungen/GBS
_Rwanda.pdf.

Republic of Rwanda (RoR). 2008. "Rwanda: Joint Governance Assessment." August 3.
http://www.minaloc.gov.rw/IMG/pdf_JGA_PGF_23-09-08.pdf.

Reyntjens, Filip. 2004. "Rwanda, Ten Years On: From Genocide to Dictatorship."
African Affairs 103, no. 411: 177–210.

United Nations (UN). 2008. "Final Report of the Group of Experts on the Democratic
Republic of the Congo." S/2008/773. December 12. http://www.undemocracy
.com/S-2008-773.pdf.

United Nations Development Programme (UNDP). 2007. "Turning Vision 2020 into
Reality: From Recovery to Sustainable Human Development." http://hdr.undp
.org/en/reports/nationalreports/africa/rwanda/rwanda_2007_en.pdf.

U.S. Agency for International Development (USAID)/Rwanda. 2004. "Integrated
Strategic Plan 2004–2009." Vol. 1. January 9. http://www.usaid.gov/rw/our_work/
for_partners/usaidrwandaintegratedstrategicplan2004-2009.pdf.

Uvin, Peter. 1998. *Aiding Violence: The Development Enterprise in Rwanda.* West Hartford, CT: Kumarian Press.

———. 2003. "Wake Up! Some Personal Reflections and Policy Proposals." Unpublished report. http://fletcher.tufts.edu/faculty/uvin/pdfs/reports/wakeup.pdf.

7

Funding Fraud?

Donors and Democracy in Rwanda

RACHEL HAYMAN

Introduction

Filip Reyntjens robustly criticized the European Union Election Observer Mission (EU EOM) report on Rwanda's August 2008 legislative elections as "a fake report on fake elections" (Reyntjens 2009). In the 2008 elections the Rwandan Patriotic Front (RPF) officially won 78.76 percent of the vote. However, some members of the EU Observer Team (although not in the official report) estimated that the RPF actually received 98 percent of the votes but reduced their totals to make the outcome appear more plausible (ibid.). Reyntjens asserted that the EU's failure to condemn electoral fraud sent a message to the Rwandan government that "impunity remained ensured" (ibid.). Similarly, he accused the international community of naïveté after the 2001 elections (Reyntjens 2001), and called the legislative and presidential elections of 2003 "a cosmetic operation for international consumption" (Reyntjens 2004). Reyntjens is not alone in voicing concerns about donor responses to these elections (see for example Uvin 2001, 2003; ICG 2002; HRW 2003, 2009).

Such criticism is all the more troubling when one realizes that these same donors funded the "fake report" and the "fake elections" as well as a host of democracy promotion efforts. This chapter attempts to explain the discrepancy between donor rhetoric and programing around good governance and their acceptance of the outcome of these elections. This chapter first reviews donor assistance for democratization and sketches how this has changed over time. It then examines how donors engage with government on governance and democracy issues, and how donors understand the type of political system emerging in Rwanda.

Governance, Democracy, and Donors

Governance and democracy, and the role that international actors can play in promoting them, have featured highly in development literature and the discourse of donor agencies, international institutions, and NGOs since the early 1990s. This was linked to the changing geopolitical climate, but also to the growing conviction that better governance, both administrative and political, is necessary for aid effectiveness. The list of what is necessary for good governance continues to grow to such an extent that "it may be difficult to identify a desirable condition or action that is *not* conducive to good governance" (Grindle 2004, emphasis in original). The concept of governance consequently covers a vast array of institutional and political structures and policies. Conceivably, all donor activity can now be seen as laying the groundwork for the establishment of a society based on liberal democratic principles, be it through developing the economy, improving education and social service provision, or supporting better governed institutions.[1] Indeed, Brown (2005) finds that assistance to sectors such as education or health or private sector growth, which appear quite unrelated to democracy, may have the greatest knock-on impact.

Within this array of broad governance-related actions, it is possible to identify activities more specifically targeted at influencing political transformation. Aid for democracy promotion can be defined in both broad and narrow terms. For example, Zuercher, Roehner, and Riese (2009a) provide a broad perspective on democracy assistance, covering support for elections and the political process, rule of law, institutional infrastructure, civil society and media, and civil-military relations. Kumar and de Zeeuw, on the other hand, consider democracy assistance as one element of a package of instruments that may be used for democracy promotion, including dialogue and diplomacy, sanctions and embargoes, and even military intervention. For them, democracy assistance refers to the funds, expertise, and material provided to "foster domestic groups, initiatives, and institutions that are working for a more democratic society" (Kumar and de Zeeuw 2006). Carothers (1999) outlines a fairly standard package of donor interventions that are linked to the promotion of a particular model of democracy, which rests upon elections, state institutions, and civil society. This reflects the widely accepted definition of democracy, which hinges on periodic genuine elections in which citizens choose their leaders, and political and civil liberties that permit citizens to participate freely and openly in political life (Carothers 1999, 91).

Numerous analyses have been conducted on the prospects for democratization in post-conflict societies.[2] These build on the dominant belief that democracy, including elections, can guarantee peace in post-conflict societies. However, the evidence remains inconclusive: premature election processes in post-conflict societies can sometimes bring about greater insecurity (see Brown 2005; Collier 2009). Empirically, "hybrid" regimes, such as competitive authoritarian regimes, emerge more frequently after conflict than fully fledged democracies (see Carothers 2002; Diamond 2002). The role that external actors can play in post-conflict democratization has also come under scrutiny. As Zuercher et al. (2009a, 2009b) highlight, the real impact that external actors can have upon democratization processes is poorly understood and under-researched. Earlier studies asserted that international actors "can only help and prod—nothing more" (Kumar and de Zeeuw 2006, 7).

Funding Everything and Nothing: Promoting Democracy in Rwanda

Governance and democratization have constituted an important dimension of relations between Western donors and Rwanda over the past twenty years. External demands for democracy fed into the civil war in Rwanda from 1990 to 1994, when pressure was placed on the Habyarimana regime to liberalize the political system. Donor support for this process was minimal, both in terms of positive conditionality to encourage democratization and negative conditionality to counter the rise of extremism (see Uvin 1998; Kimonyo et al. 2004; Hayman 2009b). Following the 1994 genocide, democracy promotion became an inherent part of the recovery and longer-term development strategy.

The post-conflict era can be divided into roughly three periods in relation to donor support for democratization: 1994–1998, 1999–2003, and 2004 to the present day. During the first period, Rwanda could still be described as being in an emergency phase. There was still insecurity in some parts of the country and much of the aid flowing was under emergency and rehabilitation programs. No elections were held, and aid that can be categorized as largely in support of the democratic process primarily consisted of funding for institutional infrastructure, security, and the justice sector. The second phase saw the development and consolidation of an electoral process. The national legislative and presidential elections, which were initially to be held in 1999, were put back another four years. In 1999 the first local elections were held, followed in 2001 by district-level elections (see ICG 2002). In 2003 there were national elections (parliamentary and presidential) following the adoption of a new constitution by referendum (RoR 2003). While no support was given for the 1999 local elections, many donors provided logistical, technical, and financial support for the constitutional referendum and election process of 2002–3. The third phase captures shifts in donor provision of support after the 2003 elections, through the 2008 parliamentary elections, and culminating with the 2010 presidential elections. What has become more prominent recently is donor concern with strengthening accountability between citizens and government at all levels, and strengthening the capacity of civil society to demand this accountability.

These shifts in focus over the fifteen years since the civil war are evident within donor programs. For example, in the European Commission (EC) program of 1995–2000, the good governance budget concentrated on supporting the macroeconomic framework, decentralization and institutional capacity, as well as justice and the rule of law. The 2002–7 program saw some support for the election process, institutional capacity building, and strengthening civil society. The 2008–13 Country Strategy Paper emphasizes the priority that will be accorded to human rights and good governance, including consolidating democracy through building capacity in the National Electoral Commission and the Parliament (EC 2003, 2007).

In relation to overall budgets and development priorities, funding for democracy promotion is often minimal, piecemeal, and too short term. Administrative governance, such as strengthening public financial management systems and building the capacity of the bureaucracy, has tended to take precedence.[3] An increasing number of donors are providing aid as general or sector-specific budget support (GBS or SBS), a sign of increased confidence in the public accountability mechanisms of the state and confidence in the developmental agenda of the government.

There seems to be an emerging trend toward supporting accountability between citizens and government and strengthening civil society. For example, a $10 million program, funded by the United Kingdom and executed by the United Nations Development Programme (UNDP) over the 2007–11 period, is aimed at promoting "the development of a responsive and accountable state, a state which enters into a social contract with its citizens, listens to citizens' voice, allows itself to be held accountable for the way it develops its policies and delivers its services, and a state which protects and upholds the rights of all" (see UNDP n.d.). It is doing this by providing technical assistance to parliamentary commissions, supporting the establishment of a parliamentary radio, building capacity in the Ombudsman's Office, as well as carrying out work on corruption, human rights promotion and protection, conflict management work with civic groups, electoral civic education, and media campaigns. According to one UK representative, this recognizes that there needs to be better dialogue between the Rwandan government and its citizens, which requires institutions with a credible voice.[4]

In addition, the United States has injected new funds for governance as part of making Rwanda a "threshold country" under the Millennium Challenge Corporation in 2007. Rwanda did not qualify for full compact status because it scored poorly on voice and accountability, and civil liberties and political rights. The $24.7 million three-year program is aimed at improving these areas of weakness. Programs began in mid-2009, focusing on police accountability, media strengthening, judicial independence, and strengthening national civil society organizations.[5]

Assessing Governance and Democracy

Another recent shift in democracy promotion in Rwanda is the Joint Governance Assessment (JGA). This reflects a broader trend internationally where various reports and indices have been created to capture governance issues within individual countries, across regions, and comparatively across the world. More recently, these have come to include external assessments carried out by donors and research institutes, peer-based assessments such as the African Peer Review Mechanism (APRM 2006), and self-assessments (Rakner and Wang 2007). Rwanda's JGA was developed with a team of consultants between mid-2007 and mid-2008, and formally endorsed by the government in September 2008. The JGA is an agreed framework among Rwanda and its donors for analyzing governance in Rwanda, which includes benchmarks, indicators, and targets for improvements (RoR 2008).[6] This initiative arose out of frustration within the government about international assessments and expectations of governance: their allegedly "limited grounding in objective evidence and analysis" (ibid.) and the seemingly arbitrary changes in comparative scores over consecutive years.[7] There was also a desire for a context-specific analysis, which recognized the core governance issues of relevance to Rwanda, such as the importance of security, the challenges of justice, and the need to build reconciliation and trust.

The JGA is aimed at "joint ownership and constructive discussion in order to improve the quality and usefulness of dialogue around issues of good governance" (RoR 2008, 2).[8] It represents a compromise between the very different perspectives and interests of the actors involved in preparing it. Indeed, between the initial drafts and the final version there were tensions, notably over the consultancy team's analysis of history and governance needs. Perhaps as a consequence, the language of the document is very careful in terms of making judgments around democracy. Though the JGA defines political rights as "the right of citizens to engage in political processes and to change their government and elected representatives through democratic means" (ibid., 35), most of its emphasis is on getting the balance right between competition and unity. While it is accepted that "with time greater political competition between and within political parties will emerge" (ibid., 18), the current priority is to promote inclusive government, based on "consensual rather than adversarial politics" (ibid., 15).

This language reflects a mistrust of Western-style democracy among the political elite and the broader populace. This mistrust is partly based on the violence and instability that attended the introduction of a multiparty system in the early 1990s. Some people fear that competitive democracy could easily become divisive and ethnic-based.[9] The government is expanding citizen participation in political processes through decentralization and policy consultation, but this is directed from the executive and very controlled. Reading between the lines of the JGA and its indicators, one can observe different views about how more competition should be introduced and at what pace. Donors evidently want to gauge how the government is seen to be performing by the populace. They also want more transparency, accountability, and responsiveness, better-run elections, more space for (legitimate) political competition, and more independent oversight of party registration and accounts. This links back to the increased interest of several donors in improving accountability and enhancing ways in which citizens feel they have a voice.

The JGA covers a wide range of governance issues, including state capability (ensuring security, rule of law, and provision of services), accountability (so the public can hold politicians and civil servants to account), responsiveness (including participatory mechanisms to promote government policy response to changing demands from society), fairness, inclusiveness (nondiscrimination), and legitimacy (state institutions should be widely accepted across society). A "monitoring framework" was established, which is to be reviewed annually. This includes forty-five indicators against which performance can be assessed. In October 2009, discussions were just beginning on how to go about the first review; they were focused on preparing a public perceptions survey. The delay was partly attributed to a loss of momentum during government restructuring, but also to problems around the availability of baseline information against which to assess progress. While the JGA represents an important development for dialogue on governance issues, it has serious limitations. As the JGA's outside consultants acknowledged:

It was difficult to move the discussion beyond a consideration of the working of formal institutions to examine the underlying structural political factors and informal power relationships that many governance professionals, including the [consultants], regard as being of fundamental importance. This reflected the limitations of the terms of reference, the preference given to easily measurable indicators, and the sensitivity of some of the issues raised by political economy analysis. Consequently, the final report adopts a rather technocratic view of good governance, and focuses its recommendations on reform options for improving formal institutions. (Williams et al. 2009, 6)

To be truly useful for measuring governance progress the indicators will need to be tightened up. The document provides little indication of what constitutes good or poor performance, and which key targets might trigger a response (or application of conditions) from donors. For example, there are only three indicators for political rights: citizens' ability to discern differences among political parties, elections declarations by independent observers, and publishing of financial statements of political parties (RoR 2008, 38). One difficulty will be that different groups of elections observers can come to contrasting conclusions, as the experience of the 2003 elections showed (Kimonyo et al. 2004). There is also no indication of what improvements might be necessary in response to criticisms from election observers. The challenges presented by the JGA highlight the larger issues around democratization in Rwanda.

Naïveté or Realism? Donor Reluctance to Apply Democratic Conditionality

Donor reactions to the discrepancy between the official results of the 2008 elections (where the RPF officially won 78.76 percent of the vote) and the apparently real figure (98 percent) were muted. The EU EOM report did not state this point overtly but did highlight a lack of transparency in the process of consolidating the results, as well as flagging up concerns around the sealing of ballot boxes and the prevention of multiple voting (EU EOM 2008). Likewise, the 2008 U.S. human rights report stated that the elections, while peaceful, were "seriously marred," and it quoted the Civil Society Election Observation Mission findings that it was impossible to confirm the accuracy of consolidated results (U.S. Department of State 2009). Donor officials did not react publicly to these concerns, either immediately afterward or following the release of the EU EOM report.

Are donors then "naïve" about the political situation in Rwanda, and are they sending the wrong message through their assistance for democracy promotion, as Reyntjens asserts? In August 2008, shortly before the parliamentary elections, I asked several donor representatives whether they thought Rwanda could be considered a democracy. Respondents were careful to avoid giving a direct answer. Many recognized that there was a risk of authoritarianism, and they had genuine concerns about political space and civil liberties. Several used the word "controlled" to describe the political system. Moreover, different donor representatives before and after the 2008 elections said that they felt the time was not right for fully competitive elections in Rwanda. This was justified with reference to Rwanda's historical context and with concerns about future insecurity and potentially renewed conflict. At the same time, several respondents stated that Rwanda was "going in the right direction."

There is also a general consensus that the Rwandan government responds better to a soft approach based upon constructive dialogue, rather than criticism.[10] The Rwandan government is renowned for its outspoken responses to criticism, especially on issues that touch upon questions of national security and governance. For example, the first draft of the JGA was greeted with hostility from the government. Likewise, when Rwanda was only granted threshold status for the Millennium Challenge Corporation, President Kagame is alleged to have stated that he did not care if Rwanda ever acquired compact status. As a U.S. Agency for International Development (USAID) official observed, the government is unlikely to comply with donor demands unless they see it as being in their own interests (interview, USAID, August 2008).

Donors have generally been reluctant to apply conditionality to Rwanda in respect of democratic change, although this has happened on a few occasions. Repressive measures against opposition voices in the run-up to the 2003 elections did cause serious concern among donors, and several threatened to reduce aid. In the end, only the Netherlands actually withheld promised funding, although disbursements from the EC and UK were delayed (Kimonyo et al. 2004; Hayman 2008, 2009a).[11] Since the 2003 elections, donors have expressed concerns about political developments, notably in relation to government crackdowns on "genocide ideology" (Hayman 2006, 2009a). The APRM report for Rwanda criticized democratic progress in the country (APRM 2006). Governance issues have affected the ways in which some donors provide aid. For example, the Netherlands did not provide general budget support (GBS) until 2007 because of parliamentary concerns about human rights and democracy.[12] However, negative conditionality over democracy and elections has not been carried out in a coherent and consistent fashion. Although some donors froze aid and issued critical reports in the wake of the 2003 elections, several others were quick to offer congratulations to the government on its democratic achievement.

Even though governance, including democracy, is important to donors, this is not the only—or even the main—priority of most donors. As Human Rights Watch's 2009 report states: "International donors, generally satisfied by the prospect of economic development, said little about election irregularities or human rights abuses" (HRW 2009). Economic development, poverty reduction, and attaining the Millennium Development Goals (MDGs), are much higher core priorities of most Organisation for Economic Co-operation and Development (OECD) donors in Rwanda. Governance is considered necessary to achieve these aims, but democracy per se is not essential. One donor representative said that political concerns only came into the equation when they affected the bigger picture of donor attention, such as the MDGs, or if they triggered domestic pressure in the donor country.

The 2008 legislative elections need to be seen in this light. For all the flaws highlighted by the EU EOM, there were no major incidents that caused serious concern. The 2010 presidential elections might have been another matter. Dutch and Swedish GBS was frozen in December 2008 because of Rwanda's alleged actions in the DRC, and neither country intended reversing these decisions until toward the end of 2010, that is, after the elections. In September 2009, donors were already looking toward these elections. Funding was in place through a pooled fund administered by the National Electoral Commission, and donors were hoping that certain recommendations from the EU EOM report of 2008 would be addressed, notably around a more transparent consolidation of the results. However, donors also expected the buildup to the elections to be tense with ethnicity debates hard to avoid.

This indeed proved to be the case. On August 9, 2010, Paul Kagame was reelected president with 93 percent of the vote. The run-up was tense, with extensive evidence of harassment of opposition voices (see Longman, chap. 1, and Sebarenzi, chap. 22, this volume). Yet the elections themselves were reported by various observer missions as well run. A number of western donors expressed concerns, but there was no evidence by August 2010 to suggest that aid flows were going to be affected.

Conclusion: "Good Enough" Democracy?

The donors' lack of response to evidence of electoral fraud in the 2008 elections is not surprising. Nor should we expect anything different following the 2010 presidential elections. Donor support for Rwanda in the post-conflict period has included a standard package of democracy-promotion measures that shifted over time from a focus on institutions to concerns for state-citizen accountability. Yet there is little sign that donors have come any closer to developing a clear strategy. Aid has been patchy in many areas of democracy promotion, and there is limited coherence among donors about its relative importance in relation to other activities.

Overall, Rwanda's key donors consider the country to be moving sufficiently in the right direction on democracy to qualify for continuing support. Aspects of Rwanda's governance resonate with some donors, notably its emphasis on "national unity and reconciliation," institution building, technocratic competence, and anticorruption. Donors would like to see the government less afraid of allowing legitimate political dissent, but, in the meantime, they appear willing to accept "good enough" democracy.[13] Rwanda's donors are very unlikely to use negative conditionality to push for greater democratic transformation at any point in the near future. For a start, there is limited evidence of this happening elsewhere in Africa (Brown 2005). Furthermore, political conditionality rarely has the desired effect; in fact, it can be counterproductive in undermining the democratic process itself (Uvin 2004).

From my discussions, donors in Rwanda do not appear naïve to the underlying political problems in Rwanda, but they get caught up in the development success story that Rwanda represents (at least, on the surface). But the tacit approval they are giving to Rwanda's "good enough democracy"—with its repression of political competition in the interests of unity—risks entrenching a political system that may ultimately undermine the government and donors' development endeavors. This has some worrisome parallels to donor complicity before the genocide as described in Uvin (1998), a book that is read by the vast majority of donor representatives I have come across in Rwanda. If donors are serious about supporting Rwanda to become more open and democratic, then they need to make sure that their approaches to governance and democracy are clear, coherent and consistent (both internally and among themselves), and sufficiently long-term to leave a lasting impact.

Notes

This chapter is based on research that was supported by the Economic and Social Research Council (UK), Free University Berlin (External Democracy Promotion in Post-Conflict Zones project), and Oxfam America. It was written prior to the August 2010 presidential elections, but I subsequently added some comment on those elections at the end of the chapter.

1. On different definitions of governance, see Stokke (1995, 23); Burnell (1997); Weiss (2000); Crawford (2001); Masujima (2004); and Taylor (2004).

2. For a useful overview of this literature, see Zuercher et al. (2009a).

3. For a detailed overview of donor support for governance and democracy, see Hayman (2008).

4. Interview, Department for International Development (DFID), Kigali, August 2008.

5. Information sources: http://www.usaid.gov/missions/rw/our_work/about_usaid/about.html; interviews, USAID, Kigali, August 2008; personal communication.

6. The JGA does not replace or override commitments contained in other agreements such as bilateral Memorandums of Understandings (MoUs) between donors and the Rwandan government.

7. Examples of these assessments include Burnet (2007); Kaufman, Kraay, and Mastruzzi (2008); Marshall and Jaggers (2007); and the "Freedom in the World" reports produced annually by Freedom House.

8. JGA's definition of governance draws on UNDP's definition (see RoR 2008, 7).

9. For more detailed analysis of these conceptions of democracy in Rwanda, see Kimonyo et al. (2004); IRDP (2005); Hayman (2008, 2009b).

10. In fact, there is some evidence that coherent diplomatic pressure can have an impact. The withdrawal of Rwandan troops from the DRC in 2002 was apparently brought about through diplomatic pressure. Behind-the-scenes diplomatic pressure in early 2009 apparently influenced the decision by the Rwandan government to enter into talks with Kabila and engage in a joint military operation in eastern DRC.

11. The elections went ahead as scheduled, with the government using internal and private resources. Shortly before the 2008 legislative elections, the president of the National Electoral Commission stated that the experience of 2003 had taught the government to rely on its own resources and that elections would proceed with or without donor support (*New Times* 2008).

12. Both the Netherlands and Sweden halted GBS to Rwanda in December 2008 following a UN report that accused the Rwandan government of supporting anti-government forces in the DRC. By September 2010 this aid had not been resumed.

13. This borrows from Grindle's (2007) argument that a realistic approach would be to focus on "good enough governance."

References

African Peer Review Mechanism (APRM). 2006. "Country Review Report of the Republic of Rwanda." June. www.eisa.org.za/aprm/pdf/Countries_Rwanda_APRM _Report.pdf.

Brown, Stephen. 2005. "Foreign Aid and Democracy Promotion: Lessons from Africa." *European Journal of Development Research* 17:179–98.

Burnell, Peter J. 1997. *Foreign Aid in a Changing World*. Buckingham: Open University Press.

Burnet, Jennie E. 2007. "Freedom House: Countries at the Crossroads—Rwanda." http://www.freedomhouse.org/uploads/ccr/country-7259-8.pdf.

Carothers, Thomas. 1999. *Aiding Democracy Abroad: The Learning Curve*. Washington, DC: Carnegie Endowment for International Peace.

———. 2002. "The End of the Transition Paradigm." *Journal of Democracy* 13, no. 1: 5–21.

Collier, Paul. 2009. *Wars, Guns and Votes: Democracy in Dangerous Places*. London: Bodley Head.

Crawford, Gordon. 2001. *Foreign Aid and Political Reform: A Comparative Analysis of Democracy Assistance and Political Conditionality*. Basingstoke: Palgrave.

Diamond, Larry. 2002. "Thinking about Hybrid Regimes." *Journal of Democracy* 13, no. 2: 21–35.

European Commission (EC). 2003. "République Rwandaise—Communauté européenne: Document de stratégie de coopération et Programme indicatif pour la période 2002–2007." http://ec.europa.eu/development/icenter/repository/print _rw_csp_fr.pdf.

———. 2007. "Republic of Rwanda—European Community Country Strategy Paper and National Indicative Programme for the Period 2008–2013." http://ec.europa .eu/development/icenter/repository/scanned_rw_csp10_en.pdf.

European Union Election Observer Mission (EU EOM). 2008. "Final Report: Legislative Elections to the Chamber of Deputies, 15–18 September 2008." http://www .eueomrwanda.org/EN/Final_Report.html.

Grindle, Merilee S. 2004. "Good Enough Governance: Poverty Reduction and Reform in Developing Countries." *Governance* 17:525–48.

———. 2007. "Good Enough Governance Revisited." *Development Policy Review* 25:553–74.

Hayman, Rachel. 2006. "The Complexity of Aid: Government Strategies, Donor Agendas and the Coordination of Development Assistance in Rwanda 1994–2004." PhD diss., University of Edinburgh.

———. 2008. "External Democracy Promotion in Post-Conflict Zones: Evidence from Case Studies—Rwanda." Working paper. Free University Berlin.

———. 2009a. "Rwanda: Milking the Cow; Creating Policy Space in Spite of Aid Dependence." In *The Politics of Aid: African Strategies for Dealing with Donors*, edited by Lindsay Whitfield, 156–84. Oxford: Oxford University Press.

———. 2009b. "Going in the 'Right' Direction? Democracy Promotion in Rwanda since 1990." *Taiwan Journal of Democracy* 5, no. 1: 51–75.

Human Rights Watch (HRW). 2003. "Preparing for Elections: Tightening Control in the Name of Unity." May 8. http://www.hrw.org/en/node/77843.

———. 2009. "World Report 2009: Rwanda Country Summary." http://www.hrw.org/en/world-report-2009/rwanda.

International Crisis Group (ICG). 2002. "Rwanda at the End of the Transition: A Necessary Political Liberalisation." November 13. http://www.grandslacs.net/doc/2555.pdf.

Institut de recherche et de dialogue pour la paix (IRDP). 2005. "Democracy in Rwanda." December. http://www.irdp.rw/docs/democracy.pdf.

Kaufmann, Daniel, Art Kraay, and Massimo Mastruzzi. 2008. "Governance Matters VIII: Aggregate and Individual Governance Indicators 1996–2007." World Bank Policy Research Working Paper 4654. http://papers.ssrn.com/sol3/papers.cfm?abstract_id=1424591.

Kimonyo, Jean-Paul, Noël Twagiramungu, and Christophe Kayumba. 2004. "Supporting the Post-Genocide Transition in Rwanda: The Role of the International Community." Democratic Transition in Post-Conflict Societies Project, Working Paper 32. http://www.clingendael.nl/publications/2004/20041200_cru_working_paper_32.pdf.

Kumar, Krishna, and Jeroen De Zeeuw. 2006. "Democracy Assistance to Postconflict Societies." In *Promoting Democracy in Postconflict Societies*, edited by Jeroen De Zeeuw and Krishna Kumar, 1–21. Boulder, CO: Lynne Rienner.

Marshall, Monty G., and Keith Jaggers. 2007. "Polity IV Country Report 2007: Rwanda." http://www.systemicpeace.org/polity/polity4.htm.

Masujima, Ken. 2004. "'Good Governance' and the Development Assistance Committee: Ideas and Organizational Constraints." In *Global Institutions and Development: Framing the World?*, edited by Morten Boas and Desmond McNeill, 151–63. New York: Routledge.

New Times. 2008. "Rwanda: Donors to Release Election Funds Today." May 29.

Rakner, Lise, and Vibeke Wang. 2007. "Governance Assessments and the Paris Declaration." CMI Issues Paper Prepared for the UNDP Bergen Seminar, September 2007. R 2007:10. http://www.cmi.no/publications/file/2747-governance-assessments-and-the-paris-declaration.pdf.

Republic of Rwanda (RoR). 2003. Constitution. May 26. http://www.mod.gov.rw/IMG/doc/Constitution_of_the_Republic_of_Rda.doc.

———. 2008. "Rwanda: Joint Governance Assessment." August 3. http://www.minaloc.gov.rw/IMG/pdf_JGA_PGF_23-09-08.pdf.

Reyntjens, Filip. 2001. "Again at the Crossroads—Rwanda and Burundi, 2000–2001." *Current African Issues* 24:1–25.

———. 2004. "Rwanda, Ten Years On: From Genocide to Dictatorship." *African Affairs* 103, no. 411: 177–210.

———. 2009. "Rwanda: A Fake Report on Fake Elections." http://hungryoftruth
.blogspot.com/2009/01/rwanda-fake-report-on-fake-elections.html.

Stokke, Olav, ed. 1995. *Aid and Political Conditionality.* London: Frank Cass.

Taylor, Ian. 2004. "Hegemony, Neoliberal 'Good Governance' and the International
Monetary Fund: A Gramscian Perspective." In *Global Institutions and Development:
Framing the World?*, edited by Morten Boas and Desmond McNeill, 124–36. Lon-
don: Routledge.

United Nations Development Programme (UNDP). n.d. "Democratic Governance."
http://www.undp.org.rw/Democratic_Governance.html.

U.S. Agency for International Development (USAID). 2002. "First Annual Report, FY
2002." October 31. http://pdf.usaid.gov/pdf_docs/PDABXII5.pdf.

U.S. Department of State. 2009. "2008 Human Rights Report: Rwanda." February 25.
http://www.state.gov/g/drl/rls/hrrpt/2008/af/119019.htm.

Uvin, Peter. 1998. *Aiding Violence: The Development Enterprise in Rwanda.* West Hartford, CT: Kumarian Press.

———. 2001. "Difficult Choices in the New Post-Conflict Agenda: The International
Community in Rwanda after the Genocide." *Third World Quarterly* 22:177–89.

———. 2003. "Wake Up! Some Policy Proposals for the International Community in
Rwanda." Unpublished report. http://fletcher.tufts.edu/faculty/uvin/pdfs/reports/
wakeup.pdf.

———. 2004. *Human Rights and Development.* Bloomfield, CT: Kumarian Press.

Weiss, Thomas G. 2000. "Governance, Good Governance, and Global Governance:
Conceptual and Actual Challenges." *Third World Quarterly* 21:795–814.

Williams, Gareth, Alex Duncan, Pierre Landell-Mills, Sue Unsworth, and Tim Sheehy.
2009. "Carrying out a Joint Governance Assessment: Lessons from Rwanda." Policy
Practice Brief 5. January. http://www.thepolicypractice.com/papers/15.pdf.

Zuercher, Christoph, Nora Roehner, and Sarah Riese. 2009a. "External Democracy
Promotion in Post-Conflict Zones: A Comparative-Analytical Framework." *Taiwan
Journal of Democracy* 5, no. 1: 1–26.

———. 2009b. "External Democracy Promotion in Post-Conflict Zones: Evidence
from Case Studies." *Taiwan Journal of Democracy* 5, no. 1: 241–59.

8

Waging (Civil) War Abroad

Rwanda and the DRC

FILIP REYNTJENS

Introduction

The wars in the Democratic Republic of Congo (DRC) and the entire Great Lakes region are the consequence of a unique combination of factors, chief among them the collapse of the Zairian/Congolese state and the territorial extension of neighbors' civil wars (see Reyntjens 2009). This chapter deals with the way in which the Rwandan conflict was—and still is—fought out in the DRC. When Rwanda, hiding behind a Zairian "rebellion," invaded in 1996, it was faced with a genuine security concern. The regime change in Kinshasa, engineered by a formidable regional coalition, did alleviate that concern, but relations with the new regime soured rapidly, and Rwanda (and Uganda), hiding behind a new "rebellion" created in Kigali, again invaded in 1998. The security rationale gave way to a logic of exploitation of natural resources and to a larger geopolitical design aimed at establishing a Rwandan space of political and military control in eastern DRC.

In the course of its military campaigns and political interference in the DRC, the Rwandan Patriotic Front (RPF) has exported practices used since it invaded Rwanda in 1990: these include a proactive, often arrogant behavior founded on a sense of entitlement, astute information management, a military way of dealing with political space, and a profound disrespect for human life. Rwanda's aggressive behavior has further exacerbated ethnic antagonism, and even contributed to a process of ethnogenesis, pitting two nonexistent ethnic groups, "Bantu" and "Hamites," against each other. As has happened inside Rwanda, the regime's practices have led to a dangerous level of structural violence in eastern DRC.

From Dealing with Refugee-Warriors to Regime Change in Kinshasa

Although the Rwandan civil war formally ended with the RPF's victory in July 1994, the flight of the defeated army (Forces armées rwandaises [Rwandan Armed Forces, FAR]), the militia, and more than one million civilians to Zaire exported the conflict. When the FAR entered Zaire in July 1994, they were only partly disarmed, and some of the weapons and ammunition seized were later resold to them by the Forces armées zaïroises (Zairean Armed Forces, FAZ). Until mid-1996, military equipment continued to reach them in the Goma region, despite an embargo decreed by the UN Security Council. These "refugee-warriors" (see Zolberg et al. 1989, 278) were not just the passive beneficiaries of international assistance but also actors in their own right with a clear goal in mind: they intended to recapture power in Rwanda. For a number of these Rwandans in "humanitarian sanctuaries" (Rufin 1996, 27), this objective probably included finishing an unfinished job: the genocide.

The instability caused by the presence of Rwandan refugees was not limited to eastern Zaire. From the beginning of 1995, the western *préfectures* (provinces) of Rwanda (Cyangugu, Kibuye, and Gisenyi) increasingly became the theater of raids and infiltration. Although these insurrectionist activities were initially of low intensity, the Rwandan Patriotic Army (RPA) had a great deal of trouble containing them and the number of civilian victims grew constantly. Clearly the situation that developed just a few kilometers across its borders was Rwanda's affair, and a vital one at that.

The United Nations High Commissioner for Refugees (UNHCR) maintained refugee camps that were both too large and too close to the Rwandan border because it erroneously believed there would be a rapid return of the refugees.[1] When the Zairian government asked the UN to move the refugees away from the border by resettling them in the former military training centers of Irebu, Lukandu, and Kongolo, this was refused because of the "high cost" of the operation. In addition, no effort was made to separate the civilian refugees from the armed elements among them. Moreover, the strong control of populations, very typical of Rwanda, was exported to the camps, where the refugees were organized into cells, sectors, municipalities, and *préfectures* and tightly "administered."

In a speech on February 19, 1995, then vice president Paul Kagame set the tone by stating: "I wholeheartedly hope that these attacks take place! Let them try! I do not hide it. Let them try." During the same period he confirmed candidly to the journalist François Misser that "if another war must be waged, we shall fight in a different fashion, elsewhere. We are prepared. We are ready to fight any war and we shall contain it along the border with Zaire" (Misser 1995, 121). Officials from the United States and the Netherlands, two countries close to the Rwandan regime, confirmed that they had to dissuade Kagame on several occasions from breaking the abscess of the Rwandan refugees in Zaire the hard way.[2] During a visit to the United States in August 1996, one month before Rwanda invaded Zaire, Kagame told the Americans that he was about to intervene, the more so since intelligence showed that the ex-FAR were preparing a large-scale offensive against Rwanda from Goma and Bukavu.[3] Faced with the obvious unwillingness or inability of the international community to tackle this problem, Kigali's patience clearly reached its limits. It is revealing that Rwanda was the only country that refused to sign a nonaggression pact among the Central African states at a summit held in Yaounde from July 8 to July 10, 1996. Despite all the warning signals, on September 1, 1996, the UN Security Council lifted the arms embargo imposed on Rwanda during the 1994 genocide, thus giving it a free hand at a crucial moment.

Under the guise of the "Banyamulenge rebellion" and later the "AFDL rebellion," both engineered in Kigali, the objectives and involvement of Rwanda became clear immediately after the beginning of the war in September.[4] The threats emanating from the refugees were addressed by the combination of their physical elimination, forced repatriation, and their move farther west, far from the Rwandan border. The mechanism was the same everywhere: the camps were heavily shelled, which caused many casualties and forced the refugees out. By early November, the Rwandan border was secured by a buffer zone stretching from Uvira to Goma. The role of Rwanda during this phase was key, and the "rebellion" in the Kivus was in reality an extension of the Rwandan civil war. When Belgium stated publicly in early 1997 what everyone knew, namely that thousands of Rwandan soldiers were fighting alongside the rebellion, this nevertheless met with an acerbic rebuttal. Despite all the evidence, Rwanda denied throughout the war having one single soldier in Zaire.

These denials soon proved hollow when Kagame himself unveiled the public secret in an interview in the *Washington Post* on July 9, 1997 (Pomfret 1997c). He said that "the Rwandan Government planned and directed the rebellion," that "Rwandan forces participated in the capture of at least four cities," and that "Rwanda provided training and arms for (the rebel) forces even before the campaign to overthrow Marshal Mobutu began last October." Kagame added that it would have been "more suitable if Congolese rebels had done most of the fighting," but they were not "fully prepared to carry it out alone." There is probably a great deal of hindsight in what he says, because Rwanda's initial concern was the security threat posed by the refugee camps. Regime change in Kinshasa came on the agenda much later, when Angola entered the fray against Kinshasa in early 1997.[5] But once it had become an attainable objective for the regional coalition supporting the Alliance des forces démocratiques pour la libération du Congo-Zaïre (Alliance of Democratic Forces for the Liberation of Congo-Zaire, AFDL), Rwanda played a prominent role and has continued interfering in Congolese politics ever since.

Massacring Civilians

Despite the many obstacles put in its way by Laurent Kabila's regime after the AFDL seized power in Kinshasa, a UN investigative team managed to produce a report, which Secretary-General Kofi Annan submitted to the Security Council on June 29, 1998. The report concluded that the RPA had committed large-scale war crimes and crimes against humanity. It went further by suggesting that genocide might have occurred. However, this needed additional investigation: "The systematic massacre of those (Hutu refugees) remaining in Zaire was an abhorrent crime against humanity, but the underlying rationale for the decision is material to whether these killings constituted genocide, that is, a decision to eliminate, in part, the Hutu ethnic group" (UN 1998, para. 96). This report, along with other extensive documentation, outlined a number of consistent patterns and practices by Rwanda, which are briefly summarized in the following paragraphs.[6]

Attacks against Refugee and Concentration Camps

The RPA systematically shelled numerous camps in South and North Kivu, where massacres were also committed with light weapons. Thousands of refugees, most of them unarmed civilians, were killed. These attacks continued and intensified as the refugees moved westward. The largest massacres occurred between Shabunda and Kingulube, at Shanji, Walikale, Tingi-Tingi, Kasese, and Biaro, and finally between Boende and Mbandaka. The report of a UN joint mission referred to information it received concerning

134 sites where atrocities had been committed (UN 1997). At the end of May 1997, when the AFDL had taken control of the whole country, the United Nations Commission on Human Rights (UNCHR) found that 246,000 refugees were unaccounted for. On July 8, 1997, the acting United Nations High Commissioner for Human Rights (UNHCHR) stated that "about 200,000 Hutu refugees could well have been massacred." After detailed calculations, Emizet arrives at a death toll of about 233,000 (Emizet 2000, 173–79).

It would be fastidious to describe or even simply enumerate the many massive and focused killings. However, the nature and the extent of this tragedy can be illustrated with two examples. In mid-March 1997, survivors from massacres in the area of Tingi-Tingi, who numbered approximately 135,000, set up camp near the villages of Biaro and Kasese on the rail line between Ubundu and Kisangani. Around mid-April, journalists and humanitarian agencies were denied access beyond mile 26 (km 42) of the rail line from Kisangani. The refugees were then out of reach of assistance or protection. On April 17, between two hundred and four hundred "search and destroy" elements of the RPA landed in Kisangani and were dispatched to the south and then, across the river, deployed to the camps.[7] Between April 21 and 25, the camps were attacked by RPA and AFDL military. The number of victims probably exceeded 10,000; 2,500 of them were children in a severe state of malnutrition. When assistance finally arrived, soldiers escorted the starving, sick, and exhausted survivors to Ubundu, 45 miles to the south, an area in turn declared a no-go zone. Reporters later visiting Biaro heard the sound of a digging machine requisitioned a week earlier by the rebels, but they were prevented from proceeding any further, supposedly for reasons of security. Congolese soldiers and civilians said there was an "open air incinerator." A Belgian entrepreneur running a logging operation in the area confirmed this information to this author. A soldier told a photographer working for Associated Press that "there is much work to do, digging up the bodies and burning them. When the UN eventually comes to investigate, there will be no evidence" (AP 1997).

The second example is the sequel to the first. About 45,000 survivors of the Kasese-Biaro carnage continued their trek westward. The RPA/AFDL elements chasing them made a detour to cut off the refugees at Boende. A phased massacre then began between Boende and Mbandaka. Thousands were killed in Boende, on the road and, finally, in Mbandaka itself. The Mbandaka massacres are particularly incriminating for the RPA/AFDL, because the killings took place in front of numerous local residents who were profoundly shocked by the cruelties committed against inoffensive civilians. The cross-checking of sources suggests that the number of victims in southern Equateur is about 15,000.

As early as November 26, 1996, in a communiqué concerning a massacre in Chimanga, Amnesty International mentioned the separation of men and women/children by AFDL forces, after which the men were killed. In his report of January 28, 1997, UN Special Rapporteur Roberto Garretón found that "many witnesses . . . underline the habit of the AFDL to separate men from women and children. The fate of the latter is generally known, but no news is heard from the former." According to UN sources, RPA's "Commander Jackson" admitted that it was his job to kill Hutu refugees, adding that all the male refugees were members of the Interahamwe militia responsible for the 1994 genocide of the Tutsi (Pomfret 1997b). Médecins sans frontières (Doctors without Borders, MSF) found that by March–April 1997 these gender distinctions were no longer made: women and children were exterminated too. A commander confirmed to MSF that "all those who are in the forest are considered to be the enemy" (MSF 1997, 7).

Indeed it is striking that the massacres became more widespread and systematic at the time of the Biaro-Kasese episode. It is likely that this was the moment the Rwandan authorities decided that repatriation was no longer a viable option, as an insurrection inside the country started to expand, particularly in the northwest. Kigali realized that the civil war had been re-imported with the returnees in the autumn of 1996. The only avenue remaining then became pure and simple extermination.

Humanitarian Assistance Withheld or Used to Locate Refugees

On a number of occasions, rebel forces and their Rwandan allies made it impossible to get humanitarian aid to starving, exhausted, and sick refugees, either by blocking access to them or by relocating them out of reach of assistance. As early as November 1996, humanitarian agencies were denied access to the area around Goma, which was declared a military zone. A similar decision was taken in Bukavu, where access was made impossible beyond a 20-mile radius around the town; even within that radius, freedom of movement was severely restricted.[8] During a press conference at the UN in November 1996, Secretary-General Boutros-Ghali claimed that "two years ago, the international community was confronted with the genocide of the Tutsi by weapons. Today we are faced with the genocide of the Hutu by starvation" (OAU 2000, 212). Six months later, his successor Kofi Annan accused the rebels of organizing a "slow extermination" of the refugees in the Kisangani area (IPS 1997).

Distribution of aid was also used to locate refugees. After humanitarian organizations discovered refugee concentrations, the AFDL/RPA would then declare the area a military zone with prohibited access. When the humanitarian agencies were eventually allowed back in, the refugees had disappeared. This strategy used so-called facilitators, designated by the AFDL, who were supposedly in charge of liaison with the aid organizations, but who, in reality, directed the "rebel" forces to the refugee concentrations. In April, Rwandan refugees and village chiefs in South Kivu asked the UNHCR and the International Committee of the Red Cross (ICRC) to end the search for refugees, because they feared that these operations exposed both the refugees and certain Zairian groups to attacks by AFDL and RPA troops. In mid-May 1997 the ICRC decided to stop accepting the use of facilitators.

Involvement of the RPA

In most cases, the massacres were committed by the RPA, and perhaps by their Congolese Tutsi allies, but much less so by the AFDL per se. Kabila's aim was the overthrow of Mobutu, and he had no particular interest in the extermination of the Rwandan refugees, or at least the unarmed elements among them. An RPA colonel, interviewed in Goma by John Pomfret of the *Washington Post*, candidly admitted that the military campaign in Zaire had a dual objective: to take revenge against the Hutu and ensure the security of Rwanda (Pomfret 1997a). A Tutsi official at the Congolese Ministry of the Interior told the same reporter that the Rwandan troops and their Congolese allies had been given authorization to attack the Hutu refugees, provided that they contributed to the overthrow of Mobutu (ibid.).

The operations of the RPA in the Kisangani and Boende-Mbandaka regions clearly targeted the refugees who became the object of an extermination project. Many sources mentioned military who spoke Kinyarwanda and/or who wore uniforms donated to the RPA by Germany. Names of Rwandan officers were cited, but the fact that they used their (real or fake) first names renders their identification difficult. However, it is possible to establish that the following were implicated: James Kabarebe, currently the Rwandan minister of defense; Godfrey Kabanda, and Jackson Nkurunziza (alias Jack Nziza), nicknamed "The Exterminator" (HRW 1997; McGreal 1997). Congolese General Gaston Munyango, officially the AFDL regional commander, had no real power (Pomfret 1997a).

Exploiting Congolese Resources

As a result of decades of Mobutist misrule, the Congolese state had virtually disappeared, and this hardly changed after Laurent Kabila came to power. The void left by the state was filled by other, nonstate actors. Some of these—like nongovernmental organizations (NGOs), churches, local civil society, or traditional structures—assumed some functions abandoned by the state, but other less benign players also seized the public space left by the retreating state: warlords, (ethnic) militias, and "entrepreneurs of insecurity" from both Congo and neighboring countries.[9] This void explains not only the extreme weakness in battle of the Zairian/Congolese army, which was the mirror of the collapsed state, but also why a small country like Rwanda was able, without much of a fight, to establish extraordinary territorial, political, and economic control over its vast neighbor. What Achille Mbembe has called the "satellization" of entire provinces by (much) smaller but stronger states was accompanied by the emergence of new forms of privatized governance (Mbembe 2001, 92–93).

There is a strong link between the privatization of public space and the criminalization of states and economies in the region. A UN panel set up in 2001 published a number of increasingly detailed reports on the criminal practices of "elite networks," both Congolese and from neighboring countries, and identified elements common to all these networks. They consisted of a small core of political and military elites, business people, and in the case of the occupied territories, rebel leaders and administrators. Members of these networks cooperated to generate revenue and, in the case of Rwanda, institutional financial gain. They derived this financial benefit from a variety of criminal activities, including theft, embezzlement, diversion of "public" funds, undervaluation of goods, smuggling, false invoicing, nonpayment of taxes, kickbacks to officials, and bribery (UN 2002).

Nowhere is this as clear as in the case of Rwanda, a small and very poor country devoid of natural resources, but with an elite needing to maintain a lavish lifestyle and possessing a large and efficient army.[10] In 2000 the revenue collected by the RPA in the DRC from the mineral coltan alone was believed to be US$80–100 million, roughly the equivalent of official Rwandan defense expenditure (which stood at US$86 million) (Sénat de Belgique 2003, 72). In a similar vein, the UN panel found that in 1999–2000, "the RPA must have made at least US$250 million over a period of 18 months" (UN 2001, para. 130). Stefaan Marysse calculated that the total value added of diamond, gold, and coltan plundered in the DRC in 1999 amounted to 6.1 percent of Rwanda's GDP, and to 146 percent of its official military expenditure (Marysse 2003, 88).[11] The Kigali economy, which is virtually disconnected from the Rwandan economy as a whole, was largely dependent on mineral and other extraction in the DRC (as well as on international aid).[12]

Pillaging the Congo not only allowed the Rwandan government to beef up the military budget in a way that was invisible to the donor community, but it also bought much needed domestic elite loyalty.[13] The Rwandan military and civilian elites thus benefited directly from the conflict.[14] Indeed the UN panel noted a great deal of interaction between the military apparatus, the state (civil) bureaucracy, and the business community. It found that the RPA financed its war in the DRC in five ways: (1) direct commercial activities, (2) benefits from shares it held in companies, (3) direct payments from the Rassemblement Congolais pour la Démocratie–Goma (Congolese Rally for Democracy, RCD–Goma), (4) taxes collected by the "Congo Desk" of the Rwandan External Security Organization (ESO) and other payments made by individuals for RPA protection of their businesses, and (5) direct uptake by soldiers from the land (UN 2001, para. 126).[15] In sum, the Congolese funded their own occupation by neighboring countries' armies. Local coltan diggers were even forced out of the market in 2001–2, when Rwanda used its own forced labor, in the form of prisoners "imported" from Rwandan jails (UN 2002, para. 75).

After officially withdrawing its troops from the DRC in September 2002 as a result of discreet but intense international pressure, Rwanda changed tactics by seeking alternative allies on the ground and sponsoring autonomist movements, in order to consolidate its long-term influence in eastern Congo and make the most out of the Kivu region (ICG 2003). Even after its official withdrawal, Rwanda maintained a clandestine military presence in the DRC.[16] The unpublished part of the UN panel's final report of October 2003 (UN 2003) is particularly revealing in this respect. At the request of the panel this section was to remain confidential and not to be circulated beyond the members of the Security Council, as it "contains highly sensitive information on actors involved in exploiting the natural resources of the DRC, their role in perpetuating the conflict as well as details on the connection between illegal exploitation and illicit trade of small arms and light weapons" (Kassem 2003). The findings showed an ongoing presence of the Rwandan army in the DRC. It had, the panel found, continued shipping arms and ammunition to the Kivus and Ituri, provided training, exercised command, supported North Kivu Governor Eugène Serufuli's militia, and manipulated ex-FAR/Interahamwe by infiltrating Rwanda Defense Forces (RDF, the new name of the RPA since 2002) officers into them. The "Rwanda Network" was considered by the panel "to be the most serious threat to the Congolese Government of National Unity. The main actor in this network was the Rwandan security apparatus, whose objective it was to maintain Rwandan presence in, and control of, the Kivus and possibly Ituri" (UN 2003, sec. 5, para. 2). Cuvelier (2004) has shown how the support of Rwanda for the rebel Rassemblement Congolais pour la Démocratie (RCD) heralded a growing cooperation between business people, politicians, and high-ranking military on both sides of the border.

Waging (Civil) War Abroad

The establishment of the Société minière des Grands Lacs (Great Lakes Mining Company, SOMIGL) and of the Congo Holding Company (CHC) were instruments set up by the rebel group and Rwanda to get as much financial benefit as possible out of the international interest in Kivu's natural resources. Two Rwandan companies with close links to the RPF and the army, Rwanda Metals and Grands Lacs Metals, were key in the organization of the Congolese commercial ventures of the Kigali regime (Cuvelier 2004, 85). Rwandan support for dissident forces went on throughout 2004, while the DRC was engaged in its delicate and fragile political transition. A later UN panel was concerned that "the territory of Rwanda continues to be used for recruitment, infiltration, and destabilization purposes" (UN 2005, para. 185), and it observed a "residual presence" of the RDF in North Kivu (UN 2005, paras. 199–200). As will be seen later, Rwandan support for insurgent groups in the DRC continues up to the present day.

Interfering in Zairian/Congolese Politics

Rwanda was instrumental in the creation of Zairian/Congolese rebel movements on two occasions. The attack on the refugee camps in 1996 was hidden behind the rebellion of the Banyamulenge first, and of the AFDL later. The Banyamulenge leader Manassé Ruhimbika (2001, 55) confirmed what other sources say: "In mid-October 1996 . . . following the instructions of Rwanda, Laurent Kabila and other Congolese, Ngandu Kisase, Nindaga Masasu, Déogratias Bugera, and Joseph Rubibi met in Kigali in the office of Colonel James Kabarebe to launch the AFDL." In order to avoid the blame that this was an external aggression, it was necessary to put forward a truly "Zairian" leadership. Not being Tutsi nor coming from the Kivu region, Laurent Kabila fit the profile. The Ugandan president Yoweri Museveni later explained that it was he who introduced Kabila to Kagame after the RPF's victory (*Monitor* 1999).

Just as in 1996, the "rebellion" that started on August 2, 1998, received a name and showed visible leadership faces after the outbreak of the war. Only on August 12, ten days into the war it was supposed to have initiated, did the "rebellion" receive a name, RCD. It was clear from day one that it was masterminded in Kigali, and moreover that it was endorsed by the Americans: "The United States accepted Rwanda's national security rationale as legitimate. We also recognized that the RCD was a proxy, directed in many respects from Kigali" (Gribbin 2005, 283). During the early days of the war, the United States knew that the RPA had again invaded the DRC. A Rwandan source told Ambassador Gribbin that "Rwanda would withdraw, once a responsible regime was installed (in Kinshasa)" (Gribbin 2005, 279), and Kagame directly told him that "Rwanda felt honor bound to support (the Banyamulenge mutiny) on grounds of ethnic solidarity, but also to rectify the error of putting Kabila in power" (Gribbin 2005, 280).[17] The support of the United States was taken for granted to such an extent that Bizima Karaha, Kabila's former foreign minister who joined the new "rebellion," told Gribbin: "Ambassador, we are here again for another green light" (ibid., 281). In addition to the security rationale, Rwanda also justified its intervention on humanitarian grounds: for example, at the end of August, the Rwandan minister Patrick Mazimhaka accused Kabila of launching a genocide against Congolese Tutsi and warned that Rwanda "would be drawn into the war . . . if the killing of Tutsi is not stopped" (DPA 1998, quoted in Longman 2002, 131).[18] Coming from the Rwandan regime, with its specific and tragic background, this kind of argument was difficult for the international community to challenge given the constant reminders of its failure to intervene in 1994.

The extraterritorial Rwandan civil war did not end with the succession of Laurent Kabila by his son Joseph in January 2001 nor with the Pretoria agreement of July 30, 2002, which provided for the withdrawal of the Rwandan army. Although Rwanda had pulled out most of its "visible" troops by September 2002, it maintained a clandestine residual presence, particularly in North Kivu, in order both to address the security threat posed by the Hutu rebels operating there and to continue the exploitation of Congolese resources it badly needed. The Congolese peace talks led the remnants of the FAR, which had fought alongside Kabila, to regroup and to move back to the east, where they started operating as the Forces démocratiques de libération du Rwanda (Democratic Forces for the Liberation of Rwanda, FDLR) in 2000–2001 (see Rafti 2006). The FDLR remained a destabilizing factor even though Rwanda succeeded in brokering some desertions of FDLR commanders who were incorporated into the RDF and even though there were several splits in the FDLR leadership. Indeed, although it was no longer a genuine military threat for Rwanda,[19] it offered the regime in Kigali the pretext to intervene in eastern DRC, which may well be the reason why Rwanda and the RCD–Goma "have for several years hindered efforts by MONUC to disarm and repatriate Rwandan rebel combatants in Congo" (HRW 2004). From 2003 to 2006, Rwanda regularly threatened to intervene, and it did so on several occasions, sometimes directly and sometimes by proxy.

Next to the FDLR, the other major threat to stability in the Kivus came from a number of Tutsi officers who, during the months following the signing of the DRC political accord in Sun City in early 2003, refused to accept their appointments in the new national army. Among them was General Laurent

Nkunda, who stood accused of involvement in the massacre of civilians in Kisangani in May 2002. He claimed that he would not be safe in Kinshasa, but it appears that Rwanda persuaded the renegade officers to refuse integration (ICG 2005, 5), and the link between Kigali and the insurgents soon became clear. A first incident occurred in Bukavu in February 2004 and again, on a larger scale, in May–June, when Nkunda and Colonel Jules Mutebutsi briefly captured the town, thoroughly looting it and leaving several hundred combatants and civilians dead in the process. A UN panel found evidence of Rwanda "aiding and abetting" the two officers' mutinous forces (UN 2004, paras. 65–67). The violations by Rwanda of the sanctions regime were both direct and indirect: it exercised a degree of command and control of Mutebutsi's troops, allowed the use of its territory as a rear base for military operations, participated in the—partly forcible—recruitment of troops, and supplied weapons and ammunition (ibid.). Kigali clearly misread the international mood and the reaction of its usual backers (chief among them the United States and the UK), who refused new attempts to derail the Congolese peace process and made this clearly known to the Rwandan regime. Under strong international pressure, Nkunda was forced to withdraw from Bukavu on June 10.

This adverse military development also meant that the RCD–Goma lost most of its political and military hold on South Kivu, which made it all the more determined to retain control over North Kivu, its last bastion of power (HRW 2005, 5–6). From then on, insurgent activity concentrated on North Kivu, and despite the Bukavu setback, Rwanda continued to support the insurgents in a covert, and sometimes overt, fashion. For example, it openly approved Nkunda's argument that his military actions were necessary to protect the Tutsi. On June 15, 2004, Rwanda's then foreign minister Charles Murigande stated that "if General Nkunda has intervened to attempt to halt (genocide), his intervention was probably justified" (AFP 2004a). On November 24, 2004, Kigali warned that it was about to attack the FDLR on Congolese territory, but the UN peacekeeping force Mission des Nations Unies en république démocratique du Congo (United Nations Organization Mission in the Democratic Republic of the Congo, MONUC) reacted vehemently: "The United Nations cannot accept this kind of threat and the reaction from the international community will be very firm" (AFP 2004b). An additional MONUC brigade was then deployed to North Kivu (*Financial Times* 2004a). At the beginning of December, MONUC nevertheless found that Rwandan troops had crossed the border, barely ten days after Kigali committed itself in Dar es Salaam to respect the territorial integrity of the DRC. Several other reports and satellite imagery obtained by the United Nations showed a considerable RDF presence in the Rutshuru, Walikale, and Lubero areas. They attacked villages, burned down houses, and killed civilians. A Rwandan-Congolese joint verification mission later confirmed that Rwandan troops had been present in the DRC but said reports of burned villages had been exaggerated (HRW 2005, 13).

Despite all the evidence, the Rwandan government's reaction was blunt denial, as usual: Kagame's special envoy Sezibera stated that "[a]ll reported sightings of Rwandan troops in the DRC are false . . . Rwanda does not have any troops (in the DRC)" (BBC News, December 3, 2004, quoted in Barouski 2007, 179). The United States, the UK, and the European Union (EU) again firmly warned Rwanda against any intervention in the DRC. On December 7 the UN Security Council ordered it to withdraw the forces it might have in eastern Congo. Later, UN sources also found that Nkunda's troops had received weapons and support from Rwanda (*Financial Times* 2004b; *Independent* 2004), which allowed them to stave off an offensive by the government army and to consolidate their hold on a widening part of North Kivu. As a result of the fighting, more than 100,000 civilians were again displaced. With elections still scheduled for 2005 at the time, this was a major threat to the political transition.

The UN Group of Experts stated in January 2005 that "Rwanda continues to be used for recruitment, infiltration, and destabilization purposes," for example, with Nkunda openly enlisting youngsters in Kiziba refugee camp (Rwandan Kibuye province) (UN 2005, paras. 185–92). The group was "cognizant of the presence of RDF soldiers in North Kivu [and] aware that Rwanda continues to retain a covert residual presence" in the DRC (ibid., paras. 199–200). Although Kigali dismissed the charge in its usual style, even the United States and the UK had now become wary of their protégé's persistent threats and lies.[20]

On August 25, 2005, Nkunda again threatened to relaunch the war, barely a day before the UN Group of Experts issued a new report, which stated that the Congolese government "should use all necessary measures to locate him and address the issue of his ongoing impunity." In September the Congolese general military prosecutor issued international arrest warrants against Nkunda and Mutebutsi for "the creation of an insurrectional movement, war crimes, and crimes against humanity." However, this did not deter Nkunda, who during the autumn of 2005 and in early 2006 benefited from many desertions of Kinyarwanda-speaking soldiers who were previously integrated in the Forces armées de la république démocratique du Congo (Armed Forces of the Democratic Republic of the Congo, FARDC, name of the new Congolese government army). With the elections nearing, Nkunda launched a fresh offensive in January 2006, gaining sizeable territory and uprooting tens of thousands of civilians. There were again strong suspicions that Rwanda delivered arms and equipment in preparation for the attack, and that RDF soldiers participated in the fighting (Barouski 2007, 220–22).[21]

This interference continues. On December 12, 2008, the UN Group of Experts found that, despite Rwandan denials, Kigali continued to offer financial and military support to Nkunda's militia, the Congrès national pour la défense du peuple (National Congress for the Defense of the People, CNDP) (UN 2008). The Rwandan government predictably denounced the "dangerous inaccuracies and outright lies" contained in the report, which had "malicious" objectives and which was filled with accusations "resulting from hearsay, perceptions, and stereotypes" (GoR 2008). As always, it was the others' fault: the UN and the international community "have failed to neutralize the persistent threat" posed by the FDLR, and they should "boldly acknowledge and confront their own failures and weaknesses" (ibid.). Even some of Kigali's best friends had had enough, though: upon publication of the report, the Netherlands and Sweden suspended part of their budget aid, and the UK considered following suit. This threat forced Rwanda into a charm offensive: it abandoned (and even arrested) Nkunda and neutralized the CNDP during a joint operation with the Congolese army in January–February 2009. While this operation, dubbed *Umoja Wetu* ("Our Unity") by the Rwandans, pleased the donors, it had a paradoxical outcome, as the RDF operation eliminated (at least for the time being) its ally (the CNDP) but left its enemy (the FDLR) largely unaffected. *Umoja Wetu* also legitimized Rwanda's interference in Congolese affairs, as well as having, once again, disastrous humanitarian consequences. In addition, the threat of sanctions by its Western sponsors did not deter Kigali from continuing to offer covert support to rebel movements in eastern DRC, including the Bisogo wing of the Forces républicaines fédéralistes (Federalist Republican Forces, FRF) in South Kivu up to 2009.[22]

Conclusion

The degree of political, military, and economic influence exercised by Rwanda over its vast neighbor is truly astonishing, coming from such a small and intrinsically poor country. This influence, achieved through the force of arms, was possible only on the territory of a collapsed state like Zaire/Congo. The RPF's entire background and experience, first in Uganda and later in Rwanda, made it rely on a military mode of managing political situations and spaces. Indeed the RPF leadership has gone from war to war and from one military victory to the next, ever since Kagame joined Museveni's "originals" in 1981. Authoritarian rule and the practice of massive human rights violations, both in Rwanda and the DRC, were allowed to emerge, at least in part, by the tolerance of the international community. Indeed, the Rwandan regime constantly tested the limits of that tolerance and realized that there were none. So, it crossed one Rubicon after the other. Protected by powerful allies (the United States and the UK in particular), shielded from criticism by the "genocide credit" it astutely exploits, and emboldened by a sense of impunity for its crimes, the regime felt it could afford almost anything. The consequences for millions of ordinary citizens in the Great Lakes region have been, and still are, devastating.

Notes

1. This belief was shared by the Zairian authorities who signed several agreements (e.g., on October 24, 1994, January 27, 1995, September 25, 1995, and December 20, 1995) with the UNHCR and/or Rwanda on measures supposed to incite the refugees to return home. Applying the December 1995 accord, Zaire undertook the "administrative closure" of the camps of Kibumba and Nyangezi in February 1996.

2. The EU special representative for the Great Lakes Region, Aldo Ajello, confirmed this information to me.

3. According to Robert Gribbin, then U.S. ambassador to Kigali, Kagame had already told him in March 1996 that "if Zaire continues to support the ex-FAR/ Interahamwe against Rwanda, Rwanda in turn could find anti-Mobutu elements to support," adding that "if the international community could not help improve security in the region, the RPA might be compelled to act alone" (Gribbin 2005, 144–45).

4. As will be discussed later, the AFDL's leader, Laurent Kabila, was handpicked by the Rwandan regime.

5. Rwanda, Uganda, and Burundi were initially mainly interested in neutralizing rebel forces operating from Zairian soil, by creating a buffer zone along their borders. This did not solve the problem of Angola, whose rebel movement Union for the Total Independence of Angola (UNITA) was supported by Mobutu's cronies. It is Angola that persuaded the regional coalition to take the "rebellion" to its ultimate conclusion, i.e., the ouster of the Mobutu regime.

6. Facts described here are not individually referenced, as they appear in several sources and because this would create a confusing accumulation of notes. A full list of sources for these events can be found in Reyntjens (2009, 287–90).

7. It is interesting to note that this RPA "cleansing team" arrived just two days after a visit to Kasese and Biaro by Dr. Ephraïm Kabayija, advisor in the Rwandan president's office and chairman of a commission for the repatriation and reintegration of refugees, who was invited by the UNHCR, which wished to convince the Rwandan government to accept refugee repatriation by air rather than overland. Kabayija was thus able to exactly identify the refugees' location. If he transmitted their whereabouts to the RPA, then he played the same role as "facilitators" did elsewhere in eastern Zaire

(see below). Kabayija subsequently became a minister in the Rwandan government, and he is currently a provincial governor.

8. This technique is similar to the one used by the RPF in Rwanda in 1994: on many occasions the areas where the RPA committed massacres were declared "military zones" with prohibited access (Desouter and Reyntjens 1995).

9. The expression "entrepreneurs of insecurity" (Perrot 1999) refers to rational makers of cost-benefit analyses, who realize that war, instability, and absence of the state are more profitable than peace, stability, and state reconstruction.

10. Indeed, just like eighteenth-century Prussia, post-1994 Rwanda has been called an army with a state, rather than a state with an army. In the Kivus, the Rwandan army was nicknamed "Soldiers without borders," a wink to the international nongovernmental organization (INGO) Médecins sans frontières (Doctors without Borders).

11. This percentage of Rwanda's GDP may seem a modest figure, but in light of the structure of the Rwandan economy, it is gigantic. Indeed in that same year, the production of export crops (mainly coffee and tea) only accounted for 0.4 percent of GDP (IMF 2004, 80).

12. This is what Jackson calls the "economization of conflict": a process whereby conflicts progressively reorient from their original goals (in the case of Rwanda, securing its borders) toward profit, and through which conflict actors capitalize increasingly on the economic opportunities that war opens up (Jackson 2002, 528).

13. Of course, it was not really invisible, but the international community preferred to turn a blind eye to these practices. U.S. Ambassador Gribbin, for one, candidly acknowledged this reality: "Rwanda had discovered during the first war that war in Congo was relatively cheap—even profitable. . . . [W]ell connected Rwandans . . . could seize opportunities . . . to accumulate wealth" (Gribbin 2005, 282–83).

14. Marysse adds that "as military spending . . . was limited as a condition for access to financial flows provided by the Bretton Woods institutions, . . . wartime plunder has helped finance the conflict" (2003, 89). He denounced the "ostrich policy" of a number of bilateral donors and the International Financial Institutions, which, by continuing to fund the invading countries (Rwanda and Uganda) in the knowledge that their aid is fungible, indirectly supported the continuation of the war.

15. The "Congo Desk" had an office called "Production," which oversaw the economic aspects of Rwandan operations in the DRC.

16. Many civil society sources in North and South Kivu reported Rwandan troop movements, and MONUC openly suspected the presence of the Rwandan army on Congolese soil (see, for instance, IRIN 2003).

17. This was a surprising statement, coming from the leader of a regime pretending to fight ethnic considerations.

18. In this short sentence, Mazimhaka managed to lie twice: the Rwandan army was already in the DRC, and the anti-Tutsi pogroms in 1998 started after the beginning of the war, indeed as a reaction to it.

19. According to the UN Group of Experts, in 2007 only around 6,000 FDLR fighters remained in the DRC (UN 2007).

20. Army spokesman Col. Patrick Karegeya said of the accusation: "We are not surprised because that is the usual UN trend. Where they have no facts, they have to falsely create their own" (Reuters 2005).

21. A useful update on the Kivu crisis can be found in HRW 2007. For an excellent and full treatment of the Nkunda story, see Stearns 2008.

22. According to reliable information gathered during a field trip by the author in South Kivu in June 2009.

References

Agence France-Presse (AFP). 2004a. "Intervention des dissidents en RDC: 'Probablement justifiée,' selon Kigali." AFP 15/06/2004. Kigali, June 15.

———. 2004b. "UN Warns Rwanda against Launching Attacks in DR Congo." Kinshasa, November 24.

Associated Press (AP). 1997. "Kabila's Soldier Shows Mass Graves." Kisangani, May 22.

Barouski, David. 2007. "Laurent Nkundabatware, His Rwandan Allies, and the Ex-ANC Mutiny: Chronic Barriers to Lasting Peace in the Democratic Republic of the Congo." February 13. http://www.ias.uni-bayreuth.de/resources/africa_discussion_forum/07-08_ws/LKandexANC.pdf.

Cuvelier, Jeroen. 2004. "Réseaux de l'ombre et configurations régionales: Le cas du commerce du coltan en République Démocratique du Congo." *Politique Africaine* 93:82–92.

Desouter, Serge, and Filip Reyntjens. 1995. "Rwanda: Les violations des droits de l'homme par le FPR/APR: Plaidoyer pour une enquête approfondie." Antwerp: University of Antwerp, Centre for the Study of the African Great Lakes Region. http://www.grandslacs.net/doc/1341.pdf.

Deutsche Presse-Agentur (DPA). 1998. "Foreign Troops in Congo Fighting: Rwanda Levels Genocide Charges." August 28.

Emizet, Kisangani N. F. 2000. "The Massacre of Refugees in Congo: A Case of UN Peacekeeping Failure and International Law." *Journal of Modern African Studies* 38, no. 2: 163–202.

Financial Times. 2004a. "UN Sends Congo Troops East as Rwanda Threatens Raid." November 25.

———. 2004b. "UN Evidence Suggests Rwanda Role in Congo." December 17.

Government of Rwanda (GoR). 2008. "Statement by the Government of Rwanda on the Report of the UN Group of Experts on the Democratic Republic of the Congo." Kigali, December 15.

Gribbin, Robert E. 2005. *In the Aftermath of Genocide: The U.S. Role in Rwanda.* New York: iUniverse.

Human Rights Watch (HRW). 1997. "What Kabila is Hiding: Civilian Killings and Impunity in Congo." December 1. http://www.hrw.org/en/reports/1997/10/01/what-kabila-hiding-0.

———. 2004. "Democratic Republic of Congo: Civilians at Risk During Disarmament Operations." December 29. http://www.hrw.org/legacy/backgrounder/africa/drc1204/drc122804.pdf.

———. 2005. "Democratic Republic of Congo: Civilians Attacked in North Kivu." July 12. http://www.hrw.org/en/reports/2005/07/12/democratic-republic-congo-civilians-attacked-north-kivu.

———. 2007. "Renewed Crisis in North Kivu." October 22. http://www.hrw.org/en/reports/2007/10/22/renewed-crisis-north-kivu-0.

Independent. 2004. "Rwanda Threatens to Reignite Africa's Bloodiest Conflict." December 17.

International Crisis Group (ICG). 2003. "The Kivus: The Forgotten Crucible of the Congo Conflict." Brussels, January 24. http://www.unhcr.org/refworld/docid/3efde7f34.html.

———. 2005. "The Congo's Transition Is Failing: Crisis in the Kivus." Brussels, March 30. http://www.unhcr.org/refworld/docid/425e8ac74.html.

International Monetary Fund (IMF). 2004. "Rwanda: Selected Issues and Statistical Appendix." IMF Country Report No. 04/383. December. http://www.imf.org/external/pubs/ft/scr/2004/cr04383.pdf.

Inter Press Service (IPS). 1997. "United Nations Warns of Problems in Repatriating Refugees." New York (UN), April 28.

Integrated Regional Information Networks (IRIN). 2003. "DRC: MONUC Denounces Obstruction of Verification Mission in East." Nairobi, October 29. http://ww.irinnews.org/Report.aspx?ReportID=46949.

Jackson, Stephen. 2002. "Making a Killing: Criminality and Coping in the Kivu War Economy." *Review of African Political Economy* 29:517–36.

Kassem, Mahmoud. 2003. "Letter Dated 20 October 2003 from Mahmoud Kassem, Chairman of the Panel, to UN Secretary-General Kofi Annan." October 20.

Longman, Timothy. 2002. "The Complex Reasons for Rwanda's Engagement in Congo." In *The African Stakes of the Congo War*, edited by John F. Clark, 129–44. New York: Houndsmills, Palgrave Macmillan.

Marysse, Stefaan. 2003. "Regress and War: The Case of the DR Congo." *European Journal of Development Research* 15, no. 1: 75–99.

Mbembe, Achille. 2001. *On the Postcolony.* Princeton, NJ: Princeton University Press.

McGreal, Chris. 1997. "Digging up Congo's Killing Fields." *Weekly Mail and Guardian,* July 25.

Misser, François. 1995. *Vers un nouveau Rwanda? Entretiens avec Paul Kagame.* Brussels: Luc Pire.

Monitor. 1999. "Africa: Museveni Explains Great Lakes' Crisis." June 1.

Médecins sans frontières (MSF). 1997. "Forced Flight: A Brutal Strategy of Elimination in Eastern Zaire." May 16. http://www.grandslacs.net/doc/1202.pdf.

Organization of African Unity (OAU). 2000. "Rwanda: The Preventable Genocide." Addis Ababa, July 7. http://www.africa-union.org/Official_documents/reports/Report_rowanda_genocide.pdf.

Perrot, Sandrine. 1999. "Entrepreneurs de l'insécurité: La face cachée de l'armée ougan-
daise." *Politique Africaine* 75:60–71.

Pomfret, John. 1997a. "Massacres Became a Weapon in Congo's Civil War." *Washington Post*, June 11.

———. 1997b. "Congo Leader Bars Helping U.N. Probes." *Washington Post*, June 19.

———. 1997c. "Defense Minister Says Arms, Troops Supplied for Anti-Mobutu Drive." *Washington Post*, July 9.

Rafti, Marina. 2006. "South Kivu: Sanctuary for the Rebellion of the Democratic Forces for the Liberation of Rwanda." Discussion Paper 2006-5. University of Antwerp, Institute of Development Policy and Management. http://ideas.repec .org/p/iob/dpaper/2006005.html.

Reuters. 2005. "Rwanda Dismisses UN Reports on Congo Arms Violation." Nairobi, January 25.

Reyntjens, Filip. 2009. *The Great African War: Congo and Regional Geopolitics, 1996–2006.* New York: Cambridge University Press.

Rufin, Jean-Christophe. 1996. "Les économies de guerre dans les conflits internes." In *Economie des guerres civiles*, edited by François Jean and Jean-Christophe Rufin, 19–59. Paris: Hachette.

Ruhimbika, Manassé. 2001. *Les Banyamulenge, Congo-Zaïre, entre deux guerres.* Paris: L'Harmattan.

Sénat de Belgique. 2003. "Rapport fait au nom de la commission d'enquête 'Grands Lacs' par MM. Colla et Dallemagne." Session 2002–3. No. 2-942/1. February 20. http://www.senate.be/www/?MIval=/publications/viewPub.html&COLL=S&LEG =2&NR=942&VOLGNR=1&LANG=fr.

Stearns, Jason K. 2008. "Laurent Nkunda and the National Congress for the Defence of the People (CNDP)." In *L'Afrique des grands lacs: Annuaire 2007–2008*, edited by Stefaan Marysse, Filip Reyntjens, and Stef Vandeginste, 245–67. Paris: L'Harmattan.

United Nations (UN). 1997. "Report of the Joint Mission Charged with Investigating Allegations of Massacres and Other Human Rights Violations Occurring in Eastern Zaire (Now Democratic Republic of the Congo) since September 1996." A/52/942. July 2. http://www.unhcr.org/refworld/docid/3ae6aec24.html.

———. 1998. "Report of the Secretary-General's Investigative Team Charged with Investigating Serious Violations of Human Rights and International Humanitarian Law in the Democratic Republic of the Congo." S/1998/581. June 29. http://www .undemocracy.com/S-1998-581.pdf.

———. 2001. "Report of the Panel of Experts on the Illegal Exploitation of Natural Resources and Other Forms of Wealth of the Democratic Republic of the Congo." S/2001/357. April 12. http://www.undemocracy.com/S-2001-357.pdf.

———. 2002. "Final Report of the Panel of Experts on the Illegal Exploitation of Natural Resources and Other Forms of Wealth of the Democratic Republic of the Congo." S/2002/1146. October 16. http://www.undemocracy.com/S-2002-1146 .pdf.

———. 2003. "Final Report of the Panel of Experts on the Illegal Exploitation of Natural Resources and Other Forms of Wealth of the Democratic Republic of the Congo." S/2003/1027. October 23. http://www.undemocracy.com/S-2003-1027.pdf.

———. 2004. "Report of the Group of Experts Submitted Pursuant to Resolution 1533 (2004)." S/2004/551. July 15. http://www.undemocracy.com/S-2004-551.pdf.

———. 2005. "Report of the Group of Experts Submitted Pursuant to Resolution 1552 (2004)." S/2005/30. January 25. http://www.undemocracy.com/S-2005-30.pdf.

———. 2007. "Report of the Group of Experts Submitted Pursuant to Resolution 1698 (2006)." S/2007/423. July 18. http://www.undemocracy.com/S-2007-423.pdf.

———. 2008. "Final Report of the Group of Experts on the Democratic Republic of the Congo." S/2008/773. December 12. http://www.undemocracy.com/S-2008-773.pdf.

Zolberg, Aristide R., Astri Suhrke, and Sergio Aguayo. 1989. *Escape from Violence: Conflict and Refugee Crisis in the Developing World*. New York: Oxford University Press.

9

Bad Karma

Accountability for Rwandan Crimes in the Congo

JASON STEARNS and FEDERICO BORELLO

In recent years, a lively debate has developed over whether the international community should privilege peace or justice during efforts to end conflicts, or whether the need for such a trade-off exists in the first place. In the Democratic Republic of the Congo (DRC), diplomats have consistently erred on the side of caution, shying away from justice mechanisms for fear that such moves could undermine the fragile peace process (Carayannis 2009, 12; Davis and Hayner 2009). As such, the Congo is something of an anomaly in peace processes in which the United Nations has played a major role: there has been only a politicized and barely functional truth commission, a handful of minor trials before military courts, and several high-profile but relatively marginal prosecutions by the International Criminal Court (ICC).[1] The 2010 publication of a UN "mapping report" drew media and diplomatic attention to the lack of accountability for war crimes and crimes against humanity committed during the two Congo wars of 1996–97 and 1998–2002 (UNHCHR 2010b).

In this chapter, we examine successive efforts at accountability in the DRC, focusing on Rwanda.[2] We argue that a tougher stance against impunity by Rwanda early on could have prevented Kigali's continued support of armed groups in the eastern Congo since the 2002 peace deal. It also would have served to address anti-Tutsi sentiment, one of the initial reasons for Rwandan military involvement with its neighbor.

The Roots of Rwandan Involvement in the Congo

Rwanda's involvement in the Congo initially had two main causes. The first, and best known, was the refugee crisis following the 1994 genocide (see Reyntjens, chap. 8, this volume). The second, more long-term, cause is linked to the presence of more than a million Hutu and Tutsi in the eastern Congo, whose history has long been intertwined with that of Rwanda. Since at least the eighteenth century, the Kivus were the spillover basin for conflicts within Rwanda. Tens of thousands fled expansionist wars between rival princely states, flocking to the highlands of what is today North and South Kivu. Migrations increased dramatically under Belgian colonial rule. After 1937 the Belgian administration in Congo encouraged the immigration of more than a hundred thousand peasants from Rwanda to work in plantations and mines, mostly located in the southern highlands of North Kivu. Tens of thousands of educated, wealthier Rwandans joined them following civil strife in Rwanda around the time of independence in 1962. By 1990 over half a million descendents of Rwandan immigrants lived in North Kivu (Pabanel 1991, 34).

Members of the Tutsi elite were successful in business and owned a majority of land in the highlands, having benefited from former Zairean president Mobutu's largesse. This favoritism fueled hostility against the Rwandophone community. During the transition to multiparty democracy, which began in 1990, Mobutu encouraged local ethnic divisions, especially in the Kivus and Katanga, so as to defuse opposition to his own rule. Rwandophones were barred from participating in the National Sovereign Conference, which had been assembled to draft a new constitution and pave the way for elections. Mobutu also launched a pre-electoral process of identifying citizens who would be eligible to vote, which targeted the Hutu and Tutsi communities.[3]

The first wave of violence was triggered by interethnic killings in Ntoto (North Kivu) in March 1993, which involved members of the Hunde, Nyanga, Hutu, and Tutsi communities. During the following months, militias killed hundreds, perhaps thousands of civilians (Amnesty International 1993; Mararo 1997, 33–35). The situation was complicated by the civil war in neighboring Rwanda. Starting in the late 1980s, the Tutsi-led Rwandan Patriotic Front (RPF) recruited adherents and fighters among the Tutsi population of North Kivu, where it found fertile ground for its call for a state where Tutsi would be accepted and safe. Likewise, the ruling party of then Rwandan president Juvénal Habyarimana had close ties to Hutu organizations in North Kivu, which supplied the Rwandan army with recruits. The end of the genocide in Rwanda threw copious amounts of fuel on this fire as up to a million Hutu refugees and soldiers streamed across the border into Zaire.

In South Kivu, by contrast, there is only a very small, remote Tutsi community called the Banyamulenge living on the high plateau overlooking the eastern flank of Lake Tanganyika. There, ethnic tensions were initially less severe. However, Congolese politicians opportunistically resorted to ethnic hate speech in the early 1990s (Jackson 2006, 100–103). The national legislature published a 1995 report concluding that the Banyamulenge were not Congolese, and a local administrator gave the community an ultimatum to leave the country. These tensions were exacerbated as hundreds of Rwandan-trained Banyamulenge soldiers infiltrated the high plateau in preparation for a Rwandan-backed invasion in June and July 1996. Locals reacted by hunting down Congolese Tutsi, killing hundreds and forcing thousands to flee.

The First Congo War: Aftershocks of the Genocide

The 1996 invasion by the Alliance des forces démocratiques pour la libération du Congo-Zaïre (Alliance of Democratic Forces for the Liberation of Congo-Zaire, AFDL), which was largely under the command of the Rwandan Patriotic Army (RPA), exacerbated the local violence. In South Kivu, the AFDL, which included many Banyamulenge, took revenge for earlier violence against Tutsi by massacring hundreds of civilians deemed to have supported the pogroms (UNCHR 1996; personal interviews). In North Kivu, the insurgents systematically rounded up and killed Congolese Hutu who had supported Habyarimana's regime.

The worst violence, however, was reserved for the Rwandan Hutu refugees. Between 500,000 and 650,000 Hutu returned to Rwanda in the early days of the war, leaving somewhere between 320,000 and 600,000 fleeing west into the jungle along with remnants of the army and militias that had perpetrated the 1994 genocide (Emizet 2000; Prunier 2009).[4] According to numerous reports, the RPA, together with AFDL troops, hunted the refugees down and massacred tens of thousands of them (HRW 1997; Nabeth et al. 1997; Umutesi 2004; see also Reyntjens, chap. 8, this volume). Casualty figures range widely between 60,000 and 300,000 (Prunier 2009).

The massacres of Rwandan refugees and Congolese civilians were carried out mostly by troops under the direct or indirect command of the RPA. On numerous occasions, the RPA and AFDL demonstrated that they had good command and control over their troops, and could punish them when deemed necessary. Numerous soldiers were publicly executed but mostly for individual abuses (murder, rape, and robbery), not for the systematic massacres (HRW 1997; personal interviews). Congolese eyewitnesses who buried the victims or who worked in the refugee camps at the time reported Rwandan officers methodically organizing the massacres. A Belgian priest who witnessed the massacres in Mbandaka told a foreign journalist: "The soldiers acted as if they were just doing their job, following orders. They didn't seem out of control" (Nickerson 1997).

Our interviews with Congolese soldiers who were part of these operations confirm both the extent of the massacres as well as the involvement of high-ranking Rwandan officers. The motive for these killings is not clear. Many of the Congolese soldiers interviewed, including some Congolese Tutsi, believe the motive was revenge. Other scholars, such as Alison Des Forges, thought the RPF was trying to prevent another Rwandan refugee diaspora that would return one day to threaten the regime, much as the RPF had done (personal interview, 2007).

It was not just the Rwandan government that tarred all the refugees with the brush of genocide. On January 21, 1997, Robert E. Gribbin, the U.S. ambassador in Rwanda, wrote a confidential code cable to Washington with the following advice:

We should pull out of Tingi-Tingi [refugee camp] and stop feeding the killers who will run away to look for other sustenance, leaving their hostages behind. . . . If we do not we will be trading the children in Tingi-Tingi for the children who will be killed and orphaned in Rwanda. (French 2009)

Prominent journalists, like Philip Gourevitch (1998), also unfairly stereotyped the refugees as collectively guilty of genocide.

A First Push for Accountability

The refugee massacres focused the international spotlight on the Congo and prompted the first major accountability efforts. In March 1997 the United Nations High Commissioner for Human Rights (UNHCHR) asked Special Rapporteur Roberto Garretón, who had been working in Zaire since 1994, to investigate allegations of refugee massacres. Following a visit to eastern Congo in late March, he reported that allegations of serious violations were credible and recommended that the commission deploy an investigative team (UNCHR 1996).

After Laurent Kabila, the leader of the AFDL, came to power in May 1997, the United Nations launched the "Amega Commission," which took its name from the Togolese judge appointed as head of the team. The commission had a clear mandate to investigate gross violations of human rights and international humanitarian law committed in the DRC since March 1, 1993, "in order to establish facts and responsibilities in gross violations" (UN Secretary-General 1998). The commission faced harassment and obstruction by Laurent Kabila's government but was nonetheless able to document the massacres of unarmed refugees by AFDL troops from North Kivu to Mbandaka between November 1996 and May 1997. It also found that Congolese Hutu civilians were massacred in several villages, apparently for aiding the refugees. The commission concluded that these massacres constituted crimes against humanity and possibly genocide.

Throughout 1997, investigations into the massacre of refugees constituted the main focus of international engagement with the new government in Kinshasa. To their credit, donors refused to provide much-needed funds due to its refusal to cooperate. U.S. Secretary of State Madeleine Albright even visited Kinshasa in December 1997 to lobby for further investigations. The international press ran a series of chilling articles on these massacres in mid- to late 1997 (French 1997; French and McKinley 1997; McKinley 1997). International nongovernmental organizations (INGOs) also published a number of reports. However, Laurent Kabila was constrained by his alliance with the Rwandan government, which had provided much of the military momentum behind his victory. Furthermore, Rwanda controlled sections of the security forces in Kinshasa: most strikingly, Colonel James Kabarebe, the former commander of Kagame's presidential guard, was then chief of staff of the Congolese army. Despite this, international pressure centered on Kinshasa and not Kigali, as diplomats were reluctant to pressure a Rwandan government that was battling an insurgency and insisting that the Congo was a sovereign government and that the refugee crisis came under that country's jurisdiction.

The Second Congo War: A Continental War, Brutal Counterinsurgencies

The second Congo war (1998–2003) brought an abrupt end to those investigations and triggered a new succession of massacres. The war was actuated when Laurent Kabila asked his Rwandan allies to leave the country, prompting Kigali, and then Kampala, to help create new rebel movements in the eastern DRC. Again, the main dispute was between Kinshasa and Kigali, though seven other countries were subsequently drawn in to support one or the other side. In response to the new rebellions, Laurent Kabila's government supplied weapons and training to allied militias in the Kivus. The Congolese army shipped tons of weapons to both the Mai-Mai militia and the Forces démocratiques de libération du Rwanda (Democratic Forces for the Liberation of Rwanda, FDLR), which included remnants of the former Rwandan army and militia that had fled Rwanda after the genocide.[5] This proxy insurgency on the cheap was effective, as it tied down the RPA and its ally, the Rassemblement Congolais pour la Démocratie (Congolese Rally for Democracy, RCD), in the Kivus, but it had a devastating effect on the local population.

The humanitarian impact for the Congolese was worse than during the first war. Millions of civilians were displaced and hundreds of thousands killed and raped by members of all armed groups. The pattern for these abuses was set by the Kasika massacre that took place in August 1998 in South Kivu. A ragtag militia from the Nyindu community ambushed a column of mixed RPA and Congolese rebels, killing several high-ranking officers. Unable to locate the attackers, the RPA retaliated against the local community, massacring hundreds of civilians (UNCHR 1999; HRW 1999; personal interviews). Similar incidents took place across eastern Congo over the next several years. The Mai-Mai and FDLR were also guilty of mass abuses, especially when they left the narrow confines of their ethnic groups and tried to deter local populations from supporting the RCD. In the eastern towns of Shabunda and Kindu, for example, Mai-Mai militia raped thousands of women, accusing them of collaborating with the RCD (HRW 2002).

As in the first war, there was considerable opposition to what most communities perceived as a Tutsi-led aggression. Anti-Tutsi rhetoric flourished and, in the early days of the war, led to pogroms against Tutsi civilians in Kinshasa and the massacre of hundreds of Tutsi in army camps throughout the country (HRW 1999). This violence was one of the stated motivations for Rwandan intervention, although the FDLR's increasingly serious insurgency in northwestern Rwanda was initially the main reason. As the war progressed, Rwanda also became more and more economically invested in the conflict, earning hundreds of millions of dollars from the minerals trade and taxation rackets (UN 2001, 2003; Prunier 2009).

Throughout the second war, calls for bringing suspected perpetrators to justice were ignored. Human rights concerns were pushed to the margins, relegated to the human rights division of the UN peacekeeping mission (Mission des Nations Unies en république démocratique du Congo [United Nations

Organization Mission in the Democratic Republic of the Congo, MONUC], created in 1999) and UN special rapporteurs. The more the peace process advanced, the more accountability was seen as an obstacle to further progress. "We already had very little leverage on the various belligerents," one American diplomat said. "We didn't want to compromise that further with excessive demands" (personal communication, 2003). For example, when RCD troops massacred more than 150 civilians in Kisangani in May 2002 and over fifty others in Walungu in April 2003, MONUC and diplomats did not press for the RCD officers, whose identities were known, to be brought to justice for fear that it would deter the RCD from joining the transitional government in Kinshasa. In private, MONUC's leadership often seemed to view accountability as a nuisance that obstructed political solutions, rather than as a further means of pressuring the parties (personal communication, 2005).

Documenting Abuses during the Transition: Don't Rock the Boat

All the major belligerents signed the Global and Inclusive Accord in Pretoria on December 17, 2002, which led to the creation of a transitional government six months later. The peace deal sprang largely out of a regional dynamic. Rwanda, Uganda, Angola, Zimbabwe, and Congo were tired of a war that had depleted their budgets and tainted their credibility abroad. One might have thought that the 2002 peace deal would have jump-started mechanisms against impunity. Ironically, however, the peace deal only further buried accountability efforts. "Our approach was all carrot and no stick," one American diplomat involved in the peace talks said. "That left little room for accountability" (personal communication, 2003).

The spirit of inclusiveness, the leitmotif of the transition, blocked attempts to hold leaders accountable for past violence. As part of the peace agreement's power-sharing formula, former rebel groups were allotted positions in key institutions that they could fill with any member of their own group. No effort was made to vet suspected criminals, and several people suspected of very serious abuses found themselves in powerful positions in the government and army. General Gabriel Amisi, one of the RCD commanders allegedly responsible for the massacre of civilians in Kisangani in May 2002, was promoted to become commander of the army's land forces. General Mustafa Mukiza, a commander allegedly responsible for massacres carried out in the Central African Republic in 2002, was promoted to become head of a military region.

Yerodia Ndombasi, who incited anti-Tutsi pogroms in Kinshasa in August 1998, became vice president.

The transition also saw a resurgence of violence in the Kivus, the crucible of the conflict since 1993. Participants in the peace process consistently used violence as a parallel means of gaining leverage in the transitional government and protecting their interests. As there was little threat of being held accountable, such warlordism became a ubiquitous political tool. Two militias in particular threatened the country's stability: the Rwandan Hutu militia, the FDLR; and a new Congolese Tutsi militia, the Congrès national pour la défense du peuple (National Congress for the Defense of the People, CNDP). The CNDP was created in 2004 under the leadership of General Laurent Nkunda. The emergence of the CNDP was in large part due to the unaddressed concerns of the Rwandan government and the local Tutsi elite after the RCD, which had controlled almost a third of the country during the 1998–2003 war, won only around 4 percent of votes in the 2006 elections. With the RCD's marginalization, these interest groups were left without leverage to protect their security, political, and economic interests. Nkunda stepped in to fill that role (Stearns 2008; UN 2008, paras. 59–60). The CNDP has been backed by Rwanda and the local Tutsi community, as well as by some RCD officials. The fighting that flared up persistently in North Kivu between the CNDP and the FDLR between 2006 and 2009 was the worst the country had seen since the height of the war; thousands of civilians were killed or raped and more than a million were displaced.

Rwanda, the Congo, and the West

Throughout the transition period, the international community set up a false dichotomy: stability versus accountability. Whereas transitions in Sierra Leone and East Timor were seen as propitious moments for vetting and prosecutions, diplomats in the Congo did not want to "rock the boat" (HRW 2005). There were several reasons for this. First, violence in the Congo was perceived within a political and historical context that justified Rwanda's actions. Some diplomats viewed the RPF's role in the Congo through the prism of the genocide (see Zorbas, chap. 6, this volume). When Clare Short, then the UK secretary for international development, was asked in the House of Commons about UK aid to Rwanda being misused for war in Congo, she shifted the conversation to "the forces of the genocide, which are trying to get back into Rwanda to complete the genocide" (House of Commons 2001). This emphasis on the genocide made it difficult for donors who had done nothing to prevent the 1994 massacres and then failed to dismantle the ex-FAR's grip on the refugee camps to reproach the Rwandan government for its actions in the Congo.[6]

A second reason for donors' reluctance to pressure Kigali for accountability was the lack of information. Rumors and conspiracy theories always abounded in the region, with little proof to back them up. This was accentuated by the Rwandan army's strict control over information flows. As Nick Gowing (1998) argued in his analysis of the AFDL war:

The Great Lakes crisis of late 1996 to mid-1997 illustrates how unwittingly both the Humanitarian Community (HC) and media were thwarted and misled by what might arguably be labelled a new, undeclared doctrine of information control drawn up by the new generation of leaders across Central and Eastern Africa.

"We just didn't know what was going on," the U.S. special envoy Howard Wolpe suggested, because "most of the reports about abuses were coming from the Catholic Church and we didn't know what to make of them" (personal interview, 2008). When nongovernmental organizations (NGOs) or UN investigators brought charges against the Rwandan government, its skilled diplomats always replied with demands for proof. The many unfounded allegations made by Congolese authorities and NGOs, often tainted by anti-Tutsi sentiment, did not make matters easier. It was only in 2002, after a series of UN reports and investigations found Rwanda motivated as much by profit as by self-defense, that donors began asking difficult questions and, crucially, threw into question further International Monetary Fund (IMF) disbursements. Another UN report in 2008, which revealed Rwandan support to Nkunda, led to the suspension of budgetary support from Sweden and the Netherlands and also contributed to pressure on Kigali to arrest him.

In part, this lack of information and the veiled nature of Rwandan involvement in the Congo makes it difficult for ICC prosecutors to pursue crimes committed by Rwanda after the ICC's mandate began in July 2002. Since that date, there have been several massacres carried out by armed groups linked to Kigali—in particular Nkunda's CNDP.[7] Although ICC prosecutors are investigating some of these crimes against humanity, they have their hands full with other investigations and have had difficulties obtaining sufficient evidence to prove Nkunda's guilt, let alone Rwanda's involvement (personal interview, 2009).

Finally, and perhaps decisively, diplomats in Congo feared that a push for accountability could destabilize the fledgling government. In Kinshasa, diplomats did not condition billions in aid on any action against impunity (HRW 2005). Thus, human rights considerations were decoupled from the peace process, just as Rwanda and Uganda were partly de-linked from the conflict in the Congo. Donor aid—largely from the United Kingdom, the United States, and international financial institutions—supplied over half of Rwanda's budget and more than a third of Uganda's throughout the war in the Congo. That clearly signaled Rwanda and Uganda that their involvement and crimes in the Congo would not have serious consequences. "You never have hard, documentary proof for these allegations," a former British diplomat said. "On the other hand, we had invested so much in rebuilding Rwanda—did we want to give that all up on the basis of rumors?" (personal interview, 2007).

The Mapping Exercise

In September and October 2005, UN soldiers were led by local villagers to several mass graves in Rutshuru, about fifty miles (80 km) north of Goma in North Kivu province. Human remains were visible, and local villagers told UN investigators that Hutu civilians, allegedly massacred in 1996, were buried there. This discovery was a reminder that past crimes had not been dealt with, and the story quickly hit the international media. The Congolese government dispatched military investigators, though their interest quickly waned.

The UN, however, felt that it had to act. The province was becoming more violent, and top officials at UN headquarters—including Secretary-General Kofi Annan, who had closely followed the various human rights investigations in the Congo since 1996—felt that the moment had come to make a more concerted push for accountability. The initial idea was to reactivate the Amega Commission, but it soon became clear that changes needed to be made, as another bloody regional war had occurred in the ten years since that commission's withdrawal. Lengthy internal discussions meant that it took almost three years to see the creation of the "justice mapping exercise." The mapping team was given an ambitious, three-pronged mandate. First, it would catalogue the most serious violations of human rights and international humanitarian law that had occurred between March 1993 (the same start date given to the Amega Commission) and June 2003 (the beginning of the transition). Its second objective was to evaluate the capacities of the Congolese judicial system to deal with violations uncovered by the team. Finally, the team was to make recommendations on transitional justice measures to assist the Congolese government in dealing with such abuses. The mapping exercise constituted the first international comprehensive probe into the two wars' most egregious abuses. It was also intended to jump-start the process of transitional justice in the Congo.

The team operated under a tight schedule and budget for about ten months, and deployed staff to all provinces. No in-depth investigation was required of the team, and a nonjudicial standard of evidence was adopted to corroborate information. Nonetheless, field teams confirmed all the incidents included in its final report with at least two independent and reliable sources (usually eyewitnesses). Previously reported events were confirmed and many new abuses uncovered.

The Mapping Report and Rwanda's Reaction

The mapping team presented its report to the UNHCHR in June 2009. More than a year later, in August 2010, the report was leaked to *Le Monde* amidst allegations that the Rwandan government was pressuring the UN to edit or quash the report (Châtelot 2010). Though the leaked report accused a wide range of governments and rebel groups of serious violations, its most controversial—and most publicized—claim was that the RPA and AFDL's "systematic and widespread attacks" in 1996 and 1997, "which targeted very large numbers of Rwandan Hutu refugees and members of the Hutu civilian population, resulting in their death, reveal a number of damning elements that, if they were proven before a competent court, could be classified as crimes of genocide" (UNHCHR 2010a, para. 517). The draft report acknowledged that "certain elements could cause a court to hesitate to decide on the existence of a genocidal plan," including the repatriation of tens of thousands of Rwandan Hutu refugees to Rwanda and the separation (and consequent survival) of Rwandan Hutu women and children (ibid.). Still, the report concluded that "it seems possible to infer a specific intention on the part of certain AFDL/ APR commanders to partially destroy Hutus in the DRC, and therefore to commit a crime of genocide, based on their conduct, words and the damning circumstances of the acts of violence committed by the men under their command. It will be for a court with proper jurisdiction to rule on this question" (ibid., para. 518).

Not surprisingly, the Rwandan government reacted fiercely to the leaked report. A government spokesman stated, "It is immoral and unacceptable that the UN, an organisation that failed outright to prevent genocide in Rwanda . . . now accuses the army that stopped the genocide of committing atrocities in the Congo" (Kezia-Musoke 2010). The government subsequently issued a lengthy critique of the draft report's methodology and findings (RoR 2010). It accused the report of promoting the "double genocide theory" (ibid., 6, 27), which it described as "part of a political agenda seeking to absolve those who committed the 1994 genocide and to undermine the developments that have taken place in Rwanda by claiming that there is no difference between those who committed the genocide and those who stopped it" (ibid., 6n1). In its response, the government also stated that the "return of millions of refugees to Rwanda is entirely inconsistent with the supposed finding [i.e., of possible genocide]" (ibid., 5). Finally, the government implicitly invoked the peace versus justice debate in denouncing the "dangerous and irresponsible attempt by the Report to undermine the peace and stability attained in the Great Lakes region" (ibid., 3–4).

The Rwandan government also threatened to withdraw its approximately three thousand soldiers from the UN and African Union peacekeeping mission in Darfur if the UN went forward with official publication of the leaked report. This was not the first time the government had tried to block international accountability for its crimes. Congo filed a case against Rwanda before the International Court of Justice (ICJ), alleging genocide among other crimes. Rwanda refused to consent to the court's jurisdiction, invoking its reservation to Article IX of the Genocide Convention (which empowers the ICJ to hear disputes between states over the Convention). As Judge Rosalyn Higgins and four other ICJ judges wrote in their concurring opinion, "It must be regarded as a very grave matter that a state should be in a position to shield from international judicial scrutiny any claim that might be made against it concerning genocide. A State so doing shows the world scant confidence that it would never, ever, commit genocide" (ICJ 2006, para. 25). Rwanda also pressured the UN into suppressing the 1994 Gersony Report that documented the RPA's killings of Rwandan civilians in 1994 (Des Forges 1999, 728–32; French and Gettleman 2010) and blocked the International Criminal Tribunal for Rwanda (ICTR) from indicting any RPA soldiers for war crimes or crimes against humanity committed in 1994 (see Peskin, chap. 10, this volume).

The UNHCHR responded to the leak by postponing official publication of the mapping report to October 1, 2010, in order to give Rwanda and other states mentioned in the report an opportunity to submit comments (UNHCHR 2010c). In late September, following a quick visit by UN Secretary-General Ban Ki-Moon to Kigali to meet Kagame, Rwanda lifted its threat to withdraw its peacekeepers from Darfur—reportedly in exchange for the UN's agreement not to immediately refer the mapping report for judicial action (French and Gettleman 2010). The final, published report did not differ significantly from the leaked version, though it did add more detail about the law on genocide and the evidence that might lead a court to find genocide (UNHCHR 2010b, paras. 510–22). Still, the report's conclusion about Rwanda's crimes is highly damning:

The scale of the crimes and the large number of victims, probably several tens of thousands . . . are illustrated by the numerous incidents listed in the report (104 in all). The extensive use of edged weapons (primarily hammers) and the apparently systematic nature of the massacres of survivors after the [refugee] camps had been taken suggests that the numerous deaths cannot be attributed to the hazards of war or seen as equating to collateral damage. The majority of the victims were children, women, elderly people and the sick, who were often undernourished and posed no threat to the attacking forces. . . . The pursuit lasted for months, and on occasion, the humanitarian assistance intended for them was allegedly deliberately blocked, . . . thus depriving them of resources essential to their survival. Thus the apparent systematic and widespread attacks described in this report reveal a number of inculpatory elements that, if proven before a competent court, could be characterized as crimes of genocide. (ibid., 31).

Conclusion

The UN mapping report is possibly the last opportunity to jump-start accountability processes for the war crimes, crimes against humanity, and possibly genocide committed in the Congo between 1993 and 2003. Indeed, the mapping team was tasked with formulating transitional justice options for the country. The report recalled that the 2002 peace agreement had proposed an ad hoc international criminal tribunal for Congo and a Truth and Reconciliation Commission (TRC). After assessing the strengths and weaknesses of those options (and others), the report recommended three specific transitional justice mechanisms: (1) a special mixed (i.e., national-international) chambers within the Congolese judiciary, much like the War Crimes Chamber in Bosnia (UNHCHR 2010b, paras. 1043–46); a new TRC that would avoid the errors of the earlier commission (ibid., paras. 1065–72); and a national reparations program (ibid., paras. 1097–1124). Some Congolese and international human rights NGOs have voiced support for a special mixed chambers (ibid., para. 1043; HRW 2010b, 3).

There are two key rationales for seeking accountability for the crimes documented by the mapping team. First, as the report itself recognizes, impunity for those past crimes creates a permissive environment for new crimes. Ken Roth, the executive director of Human Rights Watch (HRW), stated: "Many of the patterns of abuse against civilians documented by the UN team continue in Congo today, fed by a culture of impunity. Creating a justice mechanism to address past and present crimes will be crucial to ending this cycle of impunity and violence" (HRW 2010a). If the international community had put more pressure on Rwanda early on, it might have deterred its subsequent support for militias such as the CNDP. For example, a December 2008 report by the UN Group of Experts (UN 2008) put substantial diplomatic pressure on Rwanda, which responded by arresting Nkunda (see Zorbas, chap. 6, this volume).

Second, the occupation of eastern Congo by Rwandan troops and Tutsi-led militias has done inestimable damage to communal relations in the Kivus. Tens of thousands have been killed in the name of ethnic self-defense. In the absence of neutral law enforcement, each ethnic group has created its own militia to protect its interests. The resulting security dilemma has, ironically, created even greater security hazards for the Tutsi community as it fans anti-Tutsi sentiment and genocide revisionism. As a result, some Congolese Tutsi, especially from the Banyamulenge community, have come to denounce Kigali's interference in Congolese affairs, saying it has exacerbated the discrimination against them (*Economist* 2004). A mixed chambers and a serious TRC could serve as a forum to debate past injustices, particularly in relation to the violence perpetrated both against and by the Congolese Tutsi community. In discussions with community leaders in rural areas in the Kivus, it is striking how little each community knows about the abuses suffered by "enemy" communities. Thus the Bembe and Fuliro continue to see the Tutsi only as aggressors, and vice versa. Each group focuses on its own wounds. This creates fertile ground for recruitment by opportunistic warlords and politicians. It is also likely to encourage cross-border conflict as anti-Tutsi diatribes in the Congo influence politics in neighboring Rwanda and Burundi.

Once again, however, regional dynamics risk relegating justice and accountability to the sidelines in the name of "higher goals." In November 2008, President Joseph Kabila (who succeeded his father in 2001) launched negotiations with the Rwandan government after finally realizing he would not be able to defeat the CNDP militarily. After several months, a deal was reached that allowed Rwanda to deploy troops in the Kivus to attack the FDLR. In exchange, Rwanda arrested Nkunda and ordered his commanders to integrate into the Congolese army. This radical realignment of military alliances—with Kinshasa and Kigali joined together against their former respective allies, the FDLR and the Nkunda faction of the CNDP—was greeted warmly by donors.[8] The main fault line of the Congolese conflict, the Kigali-Kinshasa axis, had finally been addressed, and for the first time in over a decade, the two countries seemed to be working toward common goals. Many of the underlying problems—the prevalence of anti-Tutsi sentiment in the Kivus, the return of forty thousand Congolese Tutsi refugees home from Rwanda, the distribution of economic and political power in North Kivu—have not been solved, and the new joint operations against the FDLR have caused immense displacement and humanitarian suffering. But this thaw will condition diplomats' attitude toward the mapping report. There will probably be little appetite for any prosecution of the crimes documented by the mapping report, as it would not only target high-ranking members of the Congolese armed forces but also those across the border in Rwanda. Such prosecutions will likely be seen as throwing this realignment off course.

Notes

1. By contrast, a variety of justice mechanisms have been used to consolidate peace in Rwanda, Kosovo, Bosnia, East Timor, Sierra Leone, Liberia, and Haiti, including international tribunals, mixed domestic-international tribunals, truth commissions, and vetting.

2. This is not meant to diminish the responsibility of other actors, such as Uganda and Angola.

3. There are many communities in the Congo that straddle its borders and whose members have cross-border family ties and activities, including the Kongo (DRC-Angola-Congo/Brazzaville), the Lunda (Congo-Angola), the Nande (Congo-Uganda), and the Zande (Congo-Sudan).

4. Médecins sans frontières (Doctors without Borders, MSF) conducted a survey of refugees who had survived the trek across the DRC into neighboring Congo-Brazzaville (Nabeth et al. 1997). In its relatively small sample, MSF found that 17.5 percent of people in their families had made it, 20 percent had been killed, and a further 60 percent had disappeared. If the survey was representative, then at least 60,000 refugees were killed. A UN investigation led by Roberto Garretón (UNCHR 1996) received reports of 8,000 to 12,000 people killed in the eastern Congo alone. Kisangani Emizet (2000) estimates that 233,000 refugees were killed, using as a baseline the number of refugees in the camps and then drawing on reports of refugee returns until 1997.

5. The Army for the Liberation of Rwanda (ALIR) changed its name to FDLR in 2000 after the U.S. government placed ALIR on the terrorist watch list.

6. As long as the ex-FAR (and later the FDLR) were active, it was difficult for donors to criticize the Rwandan government for heavy-handed tactics in hunting them down. This was especially true in the 1997–1999 period, when the ex-FAR waged an insurgency in northwestern Rwanda that displaced tens of thousands. Donors also remained silent as the Rwandan military killed thousands of civilians during its counter-insurgency operations in that region.

7. Examples include the massacre of civilians by the Congolese army and Nkunda's troops during the siege of Bukavu in May 2004; the systematic rape of civilians by

the CNDP in Rutshuru in January 2007; and the massacre of over 150 civilians by the CNDP in Kiwanja in November 2008.

8. Rwanda continued to support the CNDP faction led by Bosco Ntaganda, who has been indicted by the ICC for war crimes, until 2008.

References

Amnesty International. 1993. "Zaire: Violence against Democracy." AFR 62/011/1993. September 16. http://www.amnesty.org/en/library/info/AFR62/011/1993.

Carayannis, Tatiana. 2009. "The Challenge of Building Sustainable Peace in the DRC." Centre for Humanitarian Dialogue. Geneva, July. http://www.hdcentre.org/files/DRC%20paper.pdf.

Châtelot, Christophe. 2010. "Afrique: L'ONU ne veut pas laisser impunis dix ans de massacres en RDC." *Le Monde*, August 27.

Davis, Laura, and Priscilla Hayner. 2009. "Difficult Peace, Limited Justice: Ten Years of Peacemaking in the DRC." International Center for Transitional Justice. New York, March. http://www.ictj.org/static/Africa/DRC/ICTJDavisHayner_DRC_DifficultPeace_pa2009.pdf.

Des Forges, Alison. 1999. *Leave None to Tell the Story: Genocide in Rwanda*. New York: Human Rights Watch.

Economist. 2004. "Congo: The Battle Lines Are Redrawn, Again." June 10.

Emizet, Kisangani N. F. 2000. "The Massacre of Refugees in the Congo: A Case of UN Peacekeeping Failure and International Law." *Journal of Modern African Studies* 38, no. 2 (2000): 163–202.

French, Howard W. 1997. "Refugees from Congo Give Vivid Accounts of Killings." *New York Times*, September 23.

———. 2009. "Kagame's Hidden War in the Congo." *New York Review of Books*, September 24.

French, Howard W., and James C. McKinley. 1997. "Hidden Horrors: Uncovering the Guilty Footprints along Zaire's Long Trail of Death." *New York Times*, November 14.

French, Howard W., and Jeffrey Gettleman. 2010. "Dispute over U.N. Report Evokes Rwandan Déjà Vu." *New York Times*, September 30.

Gourevitch, Philip. 1998. *We Wish to Inform You That Tomorrow We Will Be Killed with Our Families: Stories from Rwanda*. New York: Farrar, Straus and Giroux.

Gowing, Nick. 1998. "Dispatches from Disaster Zones: New Challenges and Problems for Information Management in Complex Emergencies: Ominous Lessons from the Great Lakes and Eastern Zaire." Paper presented at the "Dispatches from Disaster Zones" conference, London, May 27–28.

House of Commons. 2001. "Ministerial Meeting." *Hansard Debates*, series 6, vol. 375 (November 21). http://hansard.millbanksystems.com/commons/2001/nov/21/ministerial-meeting.

Human Rights Watch (HRW). 1997. "Zaire: Transition, War and Human Rights." April 1. http://www.hrw.org/legacy/reports/1997/zaire/.

————. 1999. "Democratic Republic of Congo: Casualties of War: Civilians, Rule of Law, and Democratic Freedoms." February 1. http://www.unhcr.org/refworld/docid/3ae6a7f64.html.

————. 2002. "The War Within the War: Sexual Violence Against Women and Girls in Eastern Congo." June 20. http://www.hrw.org/node/78573.

————. 2005. "Elections in Sight: 'Don't Rock the Boat'?" December 15. http://www.hrw.org/en/reports/2005/12/15/elections-sight.

————. 2010a. "DR Congo: UN Report Exposes Grave Crimes." October 1. http://www.hrw.org/en/news/2010/10/01/dr-congo-un-report-exposes-grave-crimes.

————. 2010b. "Tackling Impunity in Congo: Meaningful Follow-up to the UN Mapping Report." October 1. http://www.hrw.org/node/93228.

International Court of Justice (ICJ). 2006. "Joint Separate Opinion of Judges Higgins, Kooijmans, Elaraby, Owada, and Simma." *Armed Activities on the Territory of the Congo (Democratic Republic of the Congo v. Rwanda)*. ICJ Reports, February 3, pp. 65–70. http://www.icj-cij.org/docket/files/126/10441.pdf.

Jackson, Stephen. 2006. "Sons of Which Soil? The Language and Politics of Autochthony in Eastern D.R. Congo." *African Studies Review* 49, no. 2 (September): 95–123.

Kezia-Musoke, David. 2010. "Rwanda Says Leaked U.N. Report Malicious." *Reuters*, August 27.

Mararo, Bucyalimwe. 1997. "Land, Power and Ethnic Conflict in Masisi (Congo-Kinshasa), 1940s–1994." *International Journal of African Historical Studies* 30, no. 3: 503–38.

McKinley, James C. 1997. "Machetes, Axes, and Rebel Guns: Refugees Tell of Attacks in Zaire." *New York Times*, April 30.

Nabeth, Pierre, Alice Croisier, Mirdad Pedari, and Jean-Herve Bradol. 1997. "Acts of Violence against Rwandan Refugees." *The Lancet* 350, no. 9091: 1635.

Nickerson, Colin. 1997. "Refugee Massacre Unfolds in Congo." *Boston Globe*, June 6.

Pabanel, Jean-Pierre. 1991. "La question de la nationalité au Kivu." *Politique Africaine* 41:32–40.

Prunier, Gérard. 2009. *Africa's World War: Congo, the Rwandan Genocide and the Making of a Continental Catastrophe*. Oxford: Oxford University Press.

Republic of Rwanda (RoR). 2010. "Official Government of Rwanda Comments on the Draft UN Mapping Report on the DRC." September 30. http://www.ohchr.org/Documents/Countries/ZR/DRC_Report_Comments_Rwanda.pdf.

Stearns, Jason K. 2008. "Laurent Nkunda and the National Congress for the Defence of the People (CNDP)." In *L'Afrique des grands lacs: Annuaire 2007–2008*, edited by Stefaan Marysse, Filip Reyntjens, and Stef Vandeginste, 245–67. Paris: L'Harmattan.

Umutesi, Marie-Beatrice. 2004. *Surviving the Slaughter: The Ordeal of a Rwandan Refugee in Zaire*. Madison: University of Wisconsin Press.

United Nations (UN). 2001. "Report of the Panel of Experts on the Illegal Exploitation of Natural Resources and Other Forms of Wealth of the Democratic Republic of the Congo." S/2001/357. April 12. http://www.undemocracy.com/S-2001-357.pdf.

———. 2003. "Report of the Panel of Experts on the Illegal Exploitation of Natural Resources and Other Forms of Wealth of the Democratic Republic of the Congo." S/2003/1027. October 23. http://www.undemocracy.com/S-2003-1027.pdf.

———. 2008. "Final Report of the Group of Experts on the Democratic Republic of the Congo." S/2008/773. December 12. http://www.undemocracy.com/S-2008-773.pdf.

United Nations Commission on Human Rights (UNCHR). 1996. "Report on the Situation of Human Rights in Zaire, Prepared by the Special Rapporteur, Mr. Robert Garretó [sic], in Accordance with Commission Resolution 1996/77." E/CN.4/1997/6/Add.1. September 16. http://www.unhchr.ch/Huridocda/Huridoca.nsf/TestFrame/41d835da0825b80f80256656003bfb06?Opendocument.

———. 1999. "Report on the Situation of Human Rights in the Democratic Republic of the Congo, Submitted by the Special Rapporteur, Mr. Roberto Garretón, in Accordance with Commission Resolution 1998/61." E/CN.4/1999/31. February 8. http://www.unhchr.ch/Huridocda/Huridoca.nsf/0/8e3dbacbae51ce608025674600 34073d?OpenDocument.

United Nations High Commissioner for Human Rights (UNHCHR). 2010a. "Democratic Republic of the Congo, 1993–2003: Report of the Mapping Exercise Documenting the Most Serious Violations of Human Rights and International Humanitarian Law Committed within the Territory of the Democratic Republic of the Congo between March 1993 and June 2003." August draft.

———. 2010b. "Democratic Republic of the Congo, 1993–2003: Report of the Mapping Exercise Documenting the Most Serious Violations of Human Rights and International Humanitarian Law Committed within the Territory of the Democratic Republic of the Congo between March 1993 and June 2003." Unofficial translation from French original. Final report, October 1. http://www.ohchr.org/Documents/Countries/ZR/DRC_MAPPING_REPORT_FINAL_EN.pdf.

———. 2010c. "Statement by the High Commissioner for Human Rights Navi Pillay." October 1. http://www.ohchr.org/Documents/Countries/ZR/HC_Statement _on_Release_EN.pdf.

United Nations Secretary-General. 1998. "Letter from the Secretary-General on the Mandate of the Team, Referred to in the Final Report of the Amega Commission." S/1998/581. June 29. http://www.undemocracy.com/S-1998-581.pdf.

Part III

Justice

10

Victor's Justice Revisited

Rwandan Patriotic Front Crimes and the Prosecutorial Endgame at the ICTR

VICTOR PESKIN

Introduction

Founded on the principle that all victims of atrocity have a right to justice, contemporary international war crimes tribunals are mandated to prosecute individual suspects from all sides of an armed conflict. This mandate sets these institutions apart from the victor's justice paradigm of the Allied-run Nuremberg and Tokyo military tribunals. Today's tribunals, of course, are different from those of Nuremberg and Tokyo because they are not operated by the winners of particular armed conflicts. But this difference does not immunize today's tribunals from being effectively controlled by the winning side. A victorious state may, on its own or in conjunction with international allies, thwart a tribunal's prosecution of the state's atrocities. Whereas the Yugoslavia and Sierra Leone tribunals have sought prosecutions from all sides, the Rwanda tribunal has not. As the International Criminal Tribunal for Rwanda (ICTR) nears the end of its mandate, it has yet to indict a single Rwandan Patriotic Front (RPF) suspect implicated in the nongenocidal massacres of Hutu civilians in 1994. If moving beyond victor's justice is so fundamental, why has this not occurred at the ICTR? Specifically, why have successive ICTR chief prosecutors not indicted RPF suspects?

Answering these questions requires addressing the political and legal factors that have shaped the decision of the ICTR prosecutors to forgo targeting RPF suspects. While none of the four ICTR chief prosecutors has issued RPF indictments, each one has approached the RPF question differently. This chapter pays particular attention to the different approaches of three prosecutors and their relationship with the RPF-led government. The first prosecutor, Richard Goldstone (1994–96), focused on securing the cooperation of a testy Rwandan government and avoided opening the volatile issue of investigating the RPF. Carla Del Ponte's tenure at the ICTR (1999–2003) was marked by her vocal and ultimately unsuccessful confrontation with Kigali over her bid to investigate RPF crimes. Hassan Jallow's tenure (2003–present) has been markedly conciliatory toward the Rwandan government. Initially, Jallow was largely silent on the RPF issue, refusing to say whether he would issue RPF indictments. In 2008 he reached an "understanding" with the Rwandan government to forgo tribunal indictments if it conducted a fair trial of RPF suspects who had been under ICTR investigation (Jallow 2008, 11). In seeking an arrangement that suited the interests of the Rwandan government, Jallow has sought to avoid becoming the target of Kigali's wrath and to avert the political crisis that might arise if he tried to prosecute the RPF. At first glance, Jallow's approach appears to resemble the International Criminal Court's (ICC) notion of complementarity in which it prosecutes only if a domestic legal system is unable or unwilling to do so. However, Jallow has abdicated the ICTR's responsibility to ensure that individuals from all sides of the Rwandan conflict face international trial for violations of international humanitarian law.

Moving beyond the victor's justice paradigm at the ICTR proved particularly difficult because of the strategic opposition of the Rwandan government. This opposition has been bolstered by three factors. First, the Tutsi-led RPF government has garnered significant international backing for its self-declared status as representative and rescuer of Tutsi victims of the 1994 genocide. Second, the government has likened calls for RPF prosecutions to genocide denial and genocide ideology (Article 19 2009; HRW 2008, 92). Finally, the government has intimidated the tribunal by blocking prosecution witnesses from testifying in genocide trials.

RPF Massacres: In the Shadow of Genocide

In the wake of the 1994 genocide, there has been considerable scrutiny of the international community's failure to intervene. In this context, the RPF's massacres in 1994 (the period of the ICTR's jurisdiction) have received little attention. Some of the most popular accounts of the Rwandan genocide, such as Samantha Power's (2002) Pulitzer Prize–winning book on genocide, make no mention of RPF crimes. A number of observers who acknowledge RPF crimes downplay their magnitude by echoing the Rwandan government's claim that these were isolated revenge killings carried out by aggrieved RPF soldiers. This claim has been an enduring one—Philip Gourevitch repeated it in his May 2009 *New Yorker* article (Gourevitch 2009, 46)—despite the fact that Alison Des Forges and Human Rights Watch's (HRW) investigative work have shown it to be false. In her seminal 1999 book on the Rwandan genocide, Des Forges documented extensive massacres by the well-disciplined RPF that belie its claims of isolated revenge killings. She estimated that the RPF killed approximately twenty-five thousand to thirty thousand Hutu during 1994 (Des Forges 1999, 692–735). As Des Forges concluded, "Revenge killings by soldiers—or other crimes of passion—as well as the unintentional killings of civilians in combat situations could never account for the thousands of persons killed by the RPF between April and late July 1994" (Des Forges 1999, 734).

In the immediate aftermath of the genocide, accounts of RPF crimes were politically volatile. A United Nations High Commissioner for Refugees (UNHCR) investigation, which found evidence that the RPF had killed twenty-five thousand to forty-five thousand Hutu civilians from April to August 1994, was never publicly released (Des Forges 1999, 728). The suppression of the so-called Gersony report (ibid., 726)—done at the highest levels of the UN and endorsed by key U.S. officials—started a pattern of international acquiescence toward RPF crimes both in Rwanda and in the eastern Democratic Republic of Congo (DRC) (see Reyntjens, chap. 8, and Stearns and Borello, chap. 9, this volume). Despite the fate of the Gersony report, a UN Commission of Experts recognized the widespread RPF massacres in its 1994 report (see UNHCR 1994). In light of that report, the Security Council mandated the tribunal to prosecute serious violations of international humanitarian law committed by all sides of the conflict—not simply the genocide committed by the Hutu extremists.

Richard Goldstone and the Question of Gravity

The ICTR's first chief prosecutor, Richard Goldstone, took no steps to prosecute the RPF. When I interviewed Goldstone in 2003, he affirmed the principle that individuals from all sides of an armed conflict should be prosecuted for international humanitarian law violations. However, Goldstone stated that he had discretion not to prosecute where the crimes of one side were not sufficiently grave. This, he asserted, was the case with RPF crimes:

I wouldn't have issued an indictment against [Bosnian Muslims at the ICTY (International Criminal Tribunal for the Former Yugoslavia)] for the sake of . . . saying what an even-handed chap I am. I think crimes have to be of the magnitude that justify doing it. . . . We didn't have enough resources to investigate all the nines and the tens. And the RPF, who acted in revenge, were at ones and twos and maybe even fours and fives. (Peskin 2008, 189)

Goldstone's explanation is problematic on two grounds. First, he uncritically accepted the RPF's claim of revenge killings. Second, he ignored the fact that the RPF killed significantly more civilians than the Bosnian Muslims had. Thus, Goldstone's decision not to pursue the RPF needs to be understood in the larger context of the nascent tribunal's strained relationship with the RPF-led government.

Although Kigali had asked the Security Council to create a tribunal, the Rwandan government cast the sole vote against it, objecting to plans to locate the tribunal outside Rwanda and the prohibition on the death penalty for convicted *génocidaires*. The government's displeasure with the new tribunal left Goldstone anxious to ensure that Rwanda would provide the necessary cooperation for the ICTR to function. Without enforcement powers of their own, contemporary international tribunals are reliant on states for cooperation. However, the ICTR is much more dependent on a single state than any other tribunal: Rwanda can bring proceedings to a halt by preventing Rwandan witnesses from traveling to the ICTR and by blocking prosecutors and investigators from visiting Rwanda. By contrast, no one state in the former Yugoslavia can shut down the ICTY's work because that tribunal (like the ICC) operates simultaneously in several states. Thus, when the Milošević government in Serbia refused to cooperate with the ICTY in the 1990s, the tribunal turned to the Tudjman government in Croatia, which provided some cooperation.

Goldstone was keenly aware of the ICTR's vulnerability. During his tenure, the ICTR clashed with the Rwandan government over who would gain custody of key genocide fugitives arrested outside Rwanda. In the interest of maintaining good relations, Goldstone allowed Rwanda to try Froduald Karamira—which led to his speedy trial, conviction, and execution—even though the Hutu extremist could have been an important source of information for prosecuting other top genocide suspects at the ICTR.

Goldstone's successor, Louise Arbour, recognized the need to investigate the RPF cases. Arbour, who served as chief prosecutor of the ICTR and ICTY from 1996 to 1999, reportedly expressed concern that such investigations could lead to retribution against her Kigali-based investigators (Peskin 2008, 190). Toward the end of her tenure, Arbour quietly opened a preliminary probe into RPF crimes. It was Carla Del Ponte, the ICTR's third chief prosecutor, who would pursue the RPF file with the most vigor.

Carla Del Ponte and the Rise and Fall of the "Special Investigations"

For Del Ponte, the path to prosecuting RPF suspects was strewn with political obstacles. Just two months after she took up her post at the ICTR in 1999, Del Ponte faced a crisis that jeopardized the tribunal's future. The government had suspended cooperation to protest a ruling by the ICTR Appeals Chamber to release Jean-Bosco Barayagwiza, a notorious genocide suspect, to remedy violations of his due process rights. Only when the Appeals Chamber reversed its decision in early 2000 and announced that Barayagwiza would stand trial did the government resume cooperation. This incident made clear that continued cooperation was contingent on the tribunal not antagonizing the regime.

Nonetheless, in December 2000, Del Ponte announced a full-fledged investigation of RPF crimes. Then, in April 2002, she publicly criticized the Rwandan government for failing to fulfill both its promise and its international legal obligation to cooperate with her "special investigations" (Peskin 2008, 194). Further, she declared that she would issue the first RPF indictments by the end of 2002. What ensued in the following months was a high-stakes battle pitting Del Ponte against a government determined to keep the international tribunal focused exclusively on prosecuting Hutu genocide suspects. Del Ponte had hoped that public criticism of Rwandan noncompliance would bring the sort of international backing she was beginning to receive in her quest for cooperation from Serbia, Croatia, and Bosnia. But it soon became apparent that the international politics of cooperation was very different for Rwanda than for the Balkans. Specifically, American and British backing of the Rwandan government outweighed their legal obligation to support the tribunal's quest for cooperation from Kigali.

Rwanda did not sit by as Del Ponte criticized its noncompliance in spring 2002. The government launched an offensive that sought to "counter-shame" the tribunal for its real and alleged shortcomings (Peskin 2008, 195). In that way, the government strategically avoided the issue of RPF investigations.

When Del Ponte showed no sign of dropping her investigations, the government turned up the heat. In early June 2002 the government instituted burdensome travel requirements that effectively blocked Tutsi genocide survivors from traveling to Arusha to testify in ongoing genocide trials. Without those prosecution witnesses, trials quickly ground to a halt. Under international pressure, the government relented and allowed witnesses to travel to Arusha in August. Although witness travel resumed, Kigali had gained the upper hand: Del Ponte did not issue the promised indictments at the end of 2002.

The government subsequently took its opposition a step further by pressing the UN to remove Del Ponte from her post as ICTR chief prosecutor. Stunningly, the Security Council complied in August 2003. After intense lobbying from the Rwandan government and quiet backing from London and Washington, the Security Council did not renew Del Ponte's four-year term as the ICTR's prosecutor (although it kept her on as the ICTY's prosecutor), and it created a separate prosecutor for the ICTR. UN Secretary-General Kofi Annan and Western diplomats maintained that these decisions were driven by a need to increase efficiency in order to meet new Security Council deadlines for closing both tribunals. But Del Ponte was not given the choice of which post to retain. Furthermore, the timing of the Security Council's action left it open to the charge that it sacrificed Del Ponte to placate Rwanda and forestall RPF indictments. Del Ponte viewed the loss of her post at the ICTR as "a political decision" (Peskin 2008, 221). As she told me in a December 2003 interview: "What I know is that the United States [and Britain] didn't want . . . RPF indictments" (ibid.). In the same interview, Del Ponte stated that she lacked sufficient evidence to bring indictments. Yet, key tribunal insiders have contradicted that assessment, saying she did have enough evidence to issue and sustain indictments (ibid., 223). It remains an open question whether she chose not to indict because of political pressure.

Hassan Jallow's Prosecutorial Endgame and the Domestic Compromise

The high drama surrounding Del Ponte's dismissal from the ICTR showed the limits of prosecutorial independence and the obstacles to moving beyond victor's justice. In the years since her departure, the issue of RPF indictments has largely faded from view. Where Del Ponte was adversarial, her successor, Hassan Jallow, has been conciliatory. He has shown little interest in risking the type of confrontation with Kigali that seems to have cost Del Ponte her job.

Even while he kept observers guessing about his intentions, Jallow showed an unwillingness to prosecute the RPF. First, he appeared to endorse the RPF's self-portrayal as being above reproach by qualifying "allegations" of RPF crimes with the claim that the RPF "waged a war of liberation . . . putting an end to the genocide" (Jallow 2005, 156). Second, he has essentially argued that the Security Council's completion strategy for the tribunal diminishes the time and resources to pursue RPF prosecutions (Jallow 2004, 6). In 2004 the Security Council set deadlines (since extended) for completing trials and appeals at the ICTR and ICTY. In so doing, it called on prosecutors to ensure that any additional indictments "concentrate on the most senior leaders suspected of being the most responsible for crimes within" their jurisdictions (ibid.). That same year, Jallow reinterpreted that Security Council resolution as excluding RPF crimes: he claimed erroneously that it had "dictated" a prosecutorial strategy "to concentrate on those bearing the greatest responsibility for the genocide, the leaders of the genocide" (ibid.).

In June 2008, Jallow informed the Security Council that he had reached agreement with the Rwandan government for a Rwandan military court to try four RPF suspects implicated in the June 1994 massacre of the archbishop of Kigali, twelve clergy, and two others—a case that had been investigated by Del Ponte's special investigations team. Jallow told the Security Council that his office would monitor the trial and reassert the tribunal's primacy if the Rwandan proceedings did not meet international standards.

The idea of dispensing with the volatile RPF issue by handing off a single case to Rwanda did not originate with Jallow. On the contrary, the domestic prosecution option had long been advocated by the Rwandan government and its most powerful allies, the United States and Britain. Late in Del Ponte's ICTR tenure, American and British officials pushed this course of action to derail her high-profile bid to indict RPF suspects. In a May 2003 meeting in Washington, then U.S. Ambassador-at-Large for War Crimes Richard Pierre-Prosper pressed Del Ponte to sign an agreement that would transfer a case to Rwanda for domestic trial. Although she balked, this Washington plan eventually became Jallow's endgame solution to the RPF problem.

In handing over this case to Rwanda, Jallow likely hoped for a sympathetic international response based on the new norm of complementarity embodied in the ICC. Under this norm, the ICC functions as a court of last resort, prosecuting only when a state is unable or unwilling to do so itself. In fact, there is little common ground between Jallow's and the ICC's criteria for determining a state's readiness to undertake its own prosecutions. Jallow's deference to the Rwandan government contrasts sharply with ICC chief prosecutor Luis Moreno-Ocampo's assessment of state willingness and capacity to prosecute Darfur atrocities and postelection violence in Kenya. Against Jallow's protracted, five-year wait before handing over the RPF case to Rwanda, Moreno-Ocampo's complementarity assessment was expeditious: it took the ICC approximately twenty-one months to determine that the Sudanese courts had failed to demonstrate a genuine willingness to pursue cases under ICC scrutiny (Peskin 2009, 668). In Kenya, Moreno-Ocampo has also moved relatively quickly to determine the government's unwillingness to prosecute suspects implicated in the violence (ICC 2009). Rwanda's five-year delay would have been more than enough evidence at the ICC of a state's unwillingness or inability to undertake a credible domestic prosecution.

The extraordinary nature of Jallow's compromise is brought into relief when we compare it not only to the ICC's complementarity but to the ICTY, which operates under the same rules as the ICTR. The ICTY has indeed allowed the states of the former Yugoslavia to prosecute cases under tribunal indictment or scrutiny in their domestic courts. But before entrusting those less important cases to states, the ICTY had first gotten their cooperation in prosecuting the most important cases at the ICTY.

For the Rwandan government, a domestic prosecution has served its interests by thwarting high-profile tribunal indictments and prosecutions, which could have tarnished its international legitimacy.[1] In October 2008 a Rwandan military court concluded its case against the four RPF suspects charged with the massacre of the clergy. The brief trial resulted in light sentences for two junior RPF officers (who admitted to the killings) and the acquittal of two higher-ranking ones (HRW 2009a).[2] The trial was problematic on several grounds. First, while there appears to be strong evidence that the massacre constituted a crime against humanity, the suspects were prosecuted on the lesser charge of war crimes (HRW 2009b). Second, evidence suggests that the massacre was ordered by RPF commanders, but the trial steered clear of prosecuting senior RPF officials (ibid.). Third, evidence and testimony at trial served to reinforce the government's long-standing claim that the massacre was a spontaneous act of violence by aggrieved RPF soldiers (ibid.). For these reasons, this domestic RPF trial appears to have done more to obscure than reveal the true responsibility for that crime.

In June 2009, Jallow ruled out the possibility that his office would retry the case, saying that the trial had been "properly conducted" (Jallow 2009). By contrast, HRW, which had closely monitored the trial, called it "a political whitewash and a miscarriage of justice" (HRW 2009a). A year earlier, Alison Des Forges had issued an HRW report that concluded "political considerations have made it virtually impossible for victims of crimes by RPF soldiers to receive justice" (HRW 2008, 4).[3] Jallow's endorsement of the Rwandan proceedings is made more unconvincing given that ICTR judges, as well as British, French, and German courts, had refused to transfer genocide cases to Rwanda out of concern for the fairness of its legal system. It goes without saying that those genocide cases are less politically sensitive than the RPF case.

Jallow asserted that his decision was based solely on legal considerations, and especially "on the availability of credible evidence" (Jallow 2009). He further explained that his office lacked sufficient evidence to issue its own indictments (ibid.). That strongly suggests that Rwanda withheld the evidence that enabled it to bring its own prosecution (however flawed). In effect, then, Jallow's transfer of the case rewarded Rwanda for its noncooperation with the prosecutor's special investigations.

Conclusion

Regardless of the actual integrity of the domestic trial, the deeper issue is that Jallow's transfer of the case keeps RPF crimes in the shadows by sidestepping international prosecution. Jallow has evaded his legal duty to prosecute the RPF. While hailing the ICTR's mission to replace "a culture of impunity with one of accountability," Jallow has effectively granted impunity to the RPF (Jallow 2007). The UN Group of Experts and leading human rights researchers and advocates such as Alison Des Forges recognized that RPF crimes were grave enough to be tried internationally. Although Jallow has not directly contested the public evidence implicating the RPF in widespread massacres, in his single-minded efforts to maintain Rwandan cooperation, he has left the impression that such crimes do not rise to international importance.

Compromise and negotiation are inherent to the contemporary tribunals' pursuit of international justice given their lack of enforcement powers to compel state cooperation. As a result, prosecutors have tried to leverage cooperation by offering concessions to states. Although prosecutorial bargaining is central to the operation of international justice, it is frequently obscured from public view. Indeed, chief prosecutors maintain a posture of non-negotiable rectitude to maintain their legitimacy as legal actors immune to political expediency. Thus, Jallow argues that the non-issuance of RPF indictments, the transfer of the RPF case to Rwanda, and the endorsement of the Rwandan proceedings should be regarded as acts of prosecutorial independence rather than of acquiescence to the Rwandan government. But he cannot escape the perception that his prosecutorial choices are shaped by the tribunal's fragile relationship with, and enduring dependence on, the Rwandan government.

Notes

I thank Scott Straus and Lars Waldorf for inviting me to participate in a 2009 University of Wisconsin–Madison conference in honor of Alison Des Forges as well as to contribute to this volume. I am indebted to Lars and Scott for their insight and editing of this chapter. Parts of this chapter are informed by Lars's research on the Rwandan judiciary, which he presented at the Madison conference. I am also particularly grateful to Harvey Peskin and Eric Stover for extensive comments on earlier drafts of this chapter.

1. This, in turn, might have triggered unwelcome media and diplomatic scrutiny into the government's repression at home and its widespread but overlooked human rights violations in DRC. See French 2009, 44–47.

2. On appeal, the eight-year sentences for the junior officers were reduced to five years.

3. While the government points to figures showing that it prosecuted thirty-two RPF soldiers between 1994 and 1999, all of these cases were for "crimes of revenge" rather than crimes against humanity or war crimes. The fourteen convicted defendants received relatively light sentences. See HRW 2008, 90.

References

Article 19. 2009. "Comment on the Law Relating to the Punishment of the Crime of Genocide Ideology of Rwanda." London, September. http://www.article19.org/ pdfs/analysis/rwanda-comment-on-the-law-relating-to-the-punishment-of-the-crime -of-genocid.pdf.

Des Forges, Alison. 1999. *Leave None to Tell the Story: Genocide in Rwanda.* New York: Human Rights Watch.

French, Howard W. 2009. "Kagame's Hidden War in the Congo." *New York Review of Books,* September 24.

Gourevitch, Philip. 2009. "The Life After." *New Yorker,* May 4.

Human Rights Watch (HRW). 2008. "Law and Reality: Progress and Judicial Reform in Rwanda." July. http://www.hrw.org/sites/default/files/reports/rwanda0708_1 .pdf.

———. 2009a. Letter to the Prosecutor of the International Criminal Tribunal for Rwanda Regarding the Prosecution of RPF Crimes. May 26. http://www.hrw.org/ node/83536.

———. 2009b. Letter to ICTR Chief Prosecutor Hassan Jallow in Response to his Letter on the Prosecution of RPF Crimes. August 14. http://www.hrw.org/ en/news/2009/08/14/letter-ictr-chief-prosecutor-hassan-jallow-response-his-letter -prosecution-rpf-crime.

International Criminal Court (ICC). 2009. Office of the Prosecutor. "Request for Authorisation of an Investigation Pursuant to Article 15: Situation in the Republic

of Kenya." Submitted to Pre-Trial Chamber 2. November 26. http://www.icc-cpi
.int/iccdocs/doc/doc785972.pdf.

Jallow, Hassan B. 2004. "The OTP-ICTR: Ongoing Challenges of Completion."
Guest Lecture Series of the ICC Office of the Prosecutor. November 1.

———. 2005. "Prosecutorial Discretion and International Criminal Justice." *Journal
of International Criminal Justice* 3:145–61.

———. 2007. "Justice after Genocide: The Challenges of the Criminal Tribunal for
Rwanda." Speech to the University of Lund. January 31.

———. 2008. "Statement at the 5904th Meeting of the United Nations Security Council." S/PV.5904. June 4. http://www.securitycouncilreport.org/site/
c.glKWLeMTIsG/b.3974145/.

———. 2009. Letter from Hassan B. Jallow to Kenneth Roth. June 22. http://www
.hrw.org/en/news/2009/08/14/letter-ictr-chief-prosecutor-hassan-jallow-response
-his-letter-prosecution-rpf-crime.

Peskin, Victor. 2008. *International Justice in Rwanda and the Balkans: Virtual Trials and
the Struggle for State Cooperation.* New York: Cambridge University Press.

———. 2009. "Caution and Confrontation in the International Criminal Court's Pursuit of Accountability in Uganda and Sudan." *Human Rights Quarterly* 31:655–91.

Power, Samantha. 2002. *"A Problem from Hell": America and the Age of Genocide.* New
York: Basic Books.

United Nations High Commissioner for Refugees (UNHCR). 1994. "Summary of
UNHCR Presentation before Commission of Experts." October 10. http://rwandinfo
.com/documents/Gersony_Report.pdf.

The Uneasy Relationship between the ICTR and *Gacaca*

DON WEBSTER

Introduction

My first encounter with Alison Des Forges was pretty grim. This was more than a decade ago, and I was packing up my apartment in New York to move to Kigali, Rwanda, where I would begin work with the United Nations International Criminal Tribunal for Rwanda (ICTR) as a prosecuting trial attorney. I had managed to get hold of a documentary film on the Rwandan genocide, and I played it in a nonstop loop for two or three days while I reduced my personal belongings to my travel allowance of two suitcases. Alison was one of the talking heads in this seemingly interminable film, and, by my tenth viewing, her narrative began to take shape in my mind. It was an immersion that I thought would prepare me for the work ahead. Several months later, in my office in Kigali, a colleague mentioned in passing that Alison was in the building. I immediately stopped what I was doing and searched until I found her. It was almost as if she had walked out of the frame of that documentary: she was just as understated and sharply perceptive as she had appeared on screen. And thus began a professional and personal collaboration that enriched my work and my life at the ICTR for the next ten years.

My last encounter with Alison was in late December 2008 when I accompanied her to an event at New York University Law School. The crowd glowed with admiration for the Rwandan delegation, the guests of honor. Alison was surprisingly quiet throughout, but as soon as the event was over, she jumped up and approached the Rwandan minister of justice, who must have played some role in her exclusion from Rwanda. She extended her hand, saying, "I welcome you to my country, Mr. Minister; that's a courtesy that your government is refusing to extend to me." And there he was, cornered by a diminutive, gray-haired woman whose grace and calm locked him in direct confrontation. Within earshot of all his admirers she requested a meeting, and when he mentioned his busy schedule, she offered to wait for him in the breakfast room at his hotel the next day because "everybody needs breakfast." Of course, he acquiesced, but it came as no surprise to learn from Alison that the minister never showed up to breakfast. That was Alison: indomitable and ever hopeful.

In this chapter, I examine the intersection between the Rwandan criminal justice system and the ICTR from my vantage point as the lead prosecutor in the *Karemera et al.* trial.[1] I will start by providing some background on the *Karemera* trial and explain why I initially thought *gacaca* (community courts) could provide us with helpful evidence for the prosecution. Then, I describe two ways in which *gacaca* actually provoked unexpected challenges in our case.

The *Karemera et al.* Case

The *Karemera et al.* trial involves three high-level civilian authorities, all of whom were senior officials in President Juvénal Habyarimana's Mouvement républicain national pour la démocratie et le développement (National Republican Movement for Democracy and Development, MRND), the political party that substantially ruled Rwanda from 1975 to 1994. All three also played a role in the Interim Government that took power during the first week of April 1994 and that we on the prosecution side view as having led Rwanda down the path of genocide in 1994. The three defendants are Edouard Karemera, minister of interior in the Interim Government; Matthieu Ngirumpatse, the MRND president and an advisor to the Interim president; and Joseph Nzirorera, the MRND national secretary and, by July 1994, president of the Interim National Assembly.

I began working in the ICTR Office of the Prosecutor in January 1999. At that pivotal period in the tribunal's history, the indictment against these three defendants was a bit tattered and forlorn because it had been ripped out of a much more comprehensive indictment against *Bagosora and 29 others* (what we called the *Global* indictment). This *Global* indictment was meant to create a megatrial that would tackle the pyramidal structure of political authority during the genocide. It was our attempt at the ICTR to create a trial and a historical record of the Rwandan genocide that would approach the monumentality of the Nuremberg prosecutions. The key defendants were these senior MRND party officials along with Colonel Théoneste Bagosora and the rest of the military high command who conceived and implemented genocide as a strategy of war against the Rwandan Patriotic Front (RPF). The lesser, though equally essential, defendants were local leaders of the Interahamwe militias (Hutu paramilitary groups) that ordered and coordinated killings across Rwanda, and in between were the various *préfets* (governors) and *bourgmestres* (mayors) who embodied state authority at the local level. This trial against thirty defendants would demonstrate how political and military authority filtered down to the killing fields.

The tribunal did not confirm the *Global* indictment. The confirming judge rejected it on procedural grounds in March 1998, and the Appeal Chamber confirmed his decision. Thus, prevented from launching a megatrial, we reassembled the shards of the *Global* indictment through successive motions for joinder: instead of *Bagosora and 29 others*, we would have a military trial, a government trial, a media trial, and so on. Undaunted, we even attempted to join the seven defendants on the original *Karemera et al.* indictment (then referred to as Government I) with the four defendants of *Bizimungu et al.* (then dubbed Government II), along with the joint indictment of Jean de Dieu Kamuhanda and Augustin Ngirabatware, and the single indictment against Eliezer Niyitegeka, in order to create a slightly lesser megatrial against the entire Interim Government. In other words, the prosecution attempted a "second bite of the apple" to create a monumental trial but on a lesser scale. This too foundered on the rock of judicial intransigence. The Trial Chamber rejected the prosecution's joinder motions in August 1999 and eventually severed a few of the defendants, so that *Karemera et al.* now proceeded against only three of the seven original indictees.

At the heart of the *Global* indictment was the former Interim prime minister, Jean Kambanda, who pleaded guilty to genocide and confessed his knowing and willing participation in a genocidal conspiracy as titular head of the Interim Government. He had cooperated extensively with the prosecution, providing more than eighty hours of recorded interviews that laid bare the dynamics of the genocidal enterprise. His information also led to the arrest of other suspects. He was anticipated to be the central prosecution witness at trial. Unfortunately, however, he denounced his guilty plea and withdrew his cooperation after being given the maximum sentence of life imprisonment in September 1998. I was part of the prosecution team that opposed his appeal of that sentence in 1999. In common law jurisdictions, a guilty plea and an agreement to cooperate with the prosecution motivates leniency from the court and a reduced sentence. That did not happen here, so the initial optimism that was buoyed by Kambanda's promised evidence soon gave way to frustration. And it is at this troubled juncture that developments in Rwanda's criminal justice system started to raise hopes.

Gacaca's Initial Appeal

By 1999, Rwanda's ever swelling prison population presented a daunting challenge to the fledgling RPF government (see Tertsakian, chap. 13, this volume). Most of the arrests resulted from simple denunciations by those who had survived the genocide. How were trials to be organized for more than 120,000 genocide suspects with Rwanda's meager resources, especially given the competing priorities of securing its western border with the DRC and reorganizing its devastated polity and economy? There was scarcely the means to count and identify the prison population, much less to enforce international standards of due process. Against this backdrop, the idea of an innovative, alternative strategy to mete out justice on the hills made a great deal of sense to me.

I was a bit leery of the rather strident criticism offered up so quickly by Alison when the proposals for *gacaca* first emerged. As a lawyer schooled in the pragmatism of New York City's criminal courts at the height of the "crack wars," *gacaca* held promise by encouraging plea bargains and reduced sentences, which could alleviate prison overcrowding. Rwanda's prisons were populated by those foot soldiers of the genocide who did not have the means or political connections to be evacuated to Europe or fly off to West Africa. These former *bourgmestres, conseillers,* and militiamen who had been chased back into Rwanda after the second Congo war could possibly provide the evidence against the national political leaders on our ICTR indictments—if properly motivated.

The tension between Rwanda and the ICTR had subsided somewhat, and a spirit of cooperation was beginning to take hold by late 2000 (see Peskin 2008; Peskin, chap. 10, this volume). The time was ripe to investigate Rwanda's prisoners for credible evidence and the Ministry of Justice (MINIJUST) was now willing to give us access to the prisons. But there was a new, equally compelling reason: we had lost our key witness in Kambanda. So, what better way to find new evidence than the previously untapped reserve of participants at the base and middle of the criminal hierarchy.

Investigators were permitted to visit prisons throughout Rwanda. Potential witnesses were initially screened by prison authorities, and those who expressed their willingness to confess and who seemed likely to have had some contact with the ICTR defendants were placed at our disposal. The prisoners made signed statements to investigators, and those who were credible and relevant became the basis for new indictments. Later on, some of those prisoners were called to testify for the prosecution at trial, including the *Karemera et al.* trial. The ICTR has a very expansive pretrial disclosure regime, and the judges proved willing to enforce that even more broadly in our trial. As a result, we were required to obtain and provide copies to the defense of all prior statements that these prisoners had made to Rwandan judicial authorities.

Gacaca's Undermining of ICTR Prosecution Witnesses

To comply with the Trial Chamber's disclosure orders, we made consistent efforts to procure charge sheets, prior statements, confessions, guilty pleas, trial judgments, and appeal judgments, both from the *gacaca* jurisdictions and from the ordinary courts. Aside from the logistical challenge, what we quickly discovered is that cases often lacked finality in Rwanda. *Gacaca* repeatedly gave new life to old charges, and a witness's testimony at the ICTR appeared to feed back into *gacaca* in Rwanda, generating new cases and stoking the flow of documentation that then reentered our litigation at the tribunal.

Let me illustrate this by discussing what has happened in *Karemera et al.* In our trial, several former Interahamwe gave evidence that one of the defendants collaborated with military authorities to train, arm, and mobilize these MRND party youth to attack the local Tutsi population, which was characterized as "the enemy" or "accomplices of the enemy." These prisoner-witnesses initially denied their crimes when they were first denounced and arrested—something that was then documented in their initial interviews with the local prosecutor. Several years later, as they started to confess in *gacaca*, they gave piecemeal accounts of their crimes. But *gacaca* requires prisoners to give a full account of their crimes and to identify co-perpetrators.[2] In listing their co-perpetrators, they mutually accuse each other. So, the accumulation of confessions breeds additional accusations, which in turn generate additional confessions. All this documentation makes its way to defense teams at the ICTR in pretrial disclosures, and the defense puts it to good use in cross-examining these former Interahamwe witnesses, who then admit, deny, or explain these additional accusations against them. The defendants at the ICTR may then filter that new information back to Rwanda through friends and family members, which then results in renewed accusations against these witnesses in *gacaca*. After all, the ICTR defendants' friends and family participate in *gacaca* as members of the community or even as judges. So, here we have the odd circumstance where there may even be an identity of interest between the ICTR defendants, who have axes to grind against co-perpetrators who testified against them, and Tutsi genocide survivors, who are loathe to see their former assailants released back into their midst for simply having pleaded guilty.

Both the defendants in Arusha and the genocide survivors in Rwanda want these confessed criminals to be punished anew and repeatedly, the former for giving prosecution evidence against them, and the latter for their crimes in 1994. The situation is then compounded when these prisoner-witnesses are actually released from prison but then face re-arrest and re-incarceration on new *gacaca* charges. This revolving door of justice sours them against the ICTR, which they (rightly or wrongly) assume has contributed to these new accusations in *gacaca*. Their vulnerability and frustration makes them susceptible to manipulation, and that has led to another recent development: prisoner-witnesses recanting evidence that they previously gave at the ICTR. All this undermines our ability to establish reliable prosecution evidence from these co-perpetrators. What initially offered such great promise as a wellspring of new evidence from confederates of the ICTR defendants has actually become highly problematic for us.

Gacaca's Distortion of the Historical Record

Sadly, *gacaca* has also distorted the historical record of the genocide that ICTR prosecutions helped to build. This happened in two ways. First, the actions of our defendants—and the role of political elites more generally—in organizing and implementing the genocide at the local level has been obscured by testimonies in *gacaca*. This is especially the case when prisoner-witnesses recant their testimony for the reasons described earlier. Second, and perhaps more damagingly, *gacaca* has upended findings by the ICTR and has even countermanded acquittals in Rwanda's national courts. The informal *gacaca* courts have managed to assume ultimate authority for genocide prosecutions in Rwanda, supplanting the authority of the conventional courts. In fact, *gacaca* has become the highest court of the land. Those suspects in local and regional leadership positions were supposed to be judged exclusively by the ordinary courts, whose formal proceedings could ensure fuller accountability. Yet some of these suspects were convicted by *gacaca* after having been acquitted by ordinary courts. This not only results in individual travesties of justice, but it also profoundly distorts our historical record of the genocide.

Again, I want to draw on an example from the *Karemera et al.* case. We called two witnesses to testify for the prosecution who had offered essentially the same testimony several years earlier in the *Akayesu* trial. In September 1998, Jean-Paul Akayesu, a former *bourgmestre* in Gitarama, became the first person convicted for genocide by an international court. Both witnesses gave substantially consistent accounts of the same events in the *Akayesu* trial, even though one testified for the prosecution and the other was called by the defense. Both testified as free men, but, as fate would have it, both were arrested in Rwanda after testifying in the *Akayesu* trial. By the time they returned to Arusha to give evidence in the *Karemera* trial, one had been summarily released (without any adjudication) while the other remained—and still remains—in custody in Rwanda. He is really the object of my concern. This particular witness, like Akayesu, was a *bourgmestre* in Gitarama, a prefecture dominated by the Mouvement démocratique républicain (Democratic Republican Movement, MDR) party, the main opposition party, during the years leading up to the genocide.

Generally speaking, the south-central prefectures of Butare and Gitarama were opposed to the MRND, which was dominant in the northwest of the county. The political competition between the south and the north, and between the MDR and the MRND, was woven into the escalating and radicalizing currents that erupted in mass atrocity in April 1994. When the civil war restarted in Kigali on April 7 after the downing of President Habyarimana's plane, Gitarama's authorities organized roadblocks to prevent Interahamwe from Kigali from extending their killing campaign southward into their province. The Interahamwe had not been well established in Gitarama because it was a stronghold of the MDR; in fact, Silas Kibwimana, a notorious Interahamwe leader, was chased out of Gitarama at one point because hostility to the MRND and its youth wing was so entrenched there.

Initially, the Gitarama authorities were able to contain sporadic violence and deter Interahamwe incursions. But when the Interim Government abandoned Kigali on April 12 and established temporary headquarters just outside the town of Gitarama, it literally destroyed the bulwark that had kept the Interahamwe at bay. Presidential guards, soldiers, and Interahamwe militiamen accompanied the Interim Government into Gitarama, and their presence bolstered the forces of disorder. When Gitarama's *préfet* called a meeting of his *bourgmestres* to organize and reinforce security measures on April 18, Prime Minister Kambanda insisted on addressing the group. Kambanda, along with several other Interim Government ministers and national party leaders, exhorted the *bourgmestres* to follow the government's program. This appears to have been the only documented encounter between national civilian authorities and local administrative authorities where the Interim Government's policy was so explicitly expounded.

After this meeting, Akayesu and several other *bourgmestres* who had previously tried to contain the violence fell into line with the Interim Government and gave the Interahamwe full berth. Akayesu's change of heart after the April 18 meeting is the basis for his conviction. Eventually, the Interahamwe killed a *bourgmestre* who had continued to resist. Several others who resisted the killing managed to survive by deftly keeping up appearances of solidarity with the Interim Government while selectively and strategically resisting its demands, or simply by hiding. Our prosecution witness in the *Akayesu* and *Karemera et al.* trials belongs to this latter group.

After testifying in *Akayesu*, he was arrested and charged with genocide, but after almost a decade in prison, the local prosecutor was unable to substantiate any of the accusations against him. The prosecutor general issued a memorandum ordering his release, but that was stopped short by order of a *gacaca* court. This *bourgmestre* was eventually sentenced by a *gacaca* court to thirty years of imprisonment. He confessed his criminal responsibility for the killings of Tutsi in his locality for having failed, as an administrative authority, to protect them. That his authority was undermined by the Interim Government and the Interahamwe was immaterial. Nor was the *gacaca* court obliged to prove a case against him as he confessed. His empty case file was never scrutinized because his conviction was based entirely on his plea, yet it was the very paucity and unreliability of the accusations against him that had led the prosecutor general to dismiss his case before *gacaca* intervened to prevent his release.

Presumably, the local prosecutor had resources to investigate as fully as any *gacaca* court, with access to the same witnesses and with even more sophisticated means of accessing and assessing the evidence. Yet *gacaca* intervened to undo what the conventional justice system had achieved: a just disposition of this case. It also came to my attention that another former *bourgmestre*, who had been living and working in Gitarama unperturbed by the criminal justice system for almost fourteen years, suddenly found himself accused for the first time in *gacaca*, and then convicted and sentenced in absentia. He had never been accused by local prosecutors.

Here, we have a very disturbing development where the informal mechanisms of *gacaca* are now undoing the justice meted out by the formal judicial system: *gacaca* has trumped the ordinary courts. It is bad enough that this places possibly innocent people in legal jeopardy, but what is worse is that *gacaca*'s condemnation of anyone who held any position of authority during 1994 risks undermining our ability to create a reliable historical record of the genocide. The Rwandan genocide was *politicized*, and reflected and incorporated regionalist tensions. Gitarama is a compelling example of this. But *gacaca* is creating a historical erasure by significantly diminishing the credibility of those witnesses who testified about the Interim Government's dismantling of resistance to its genocidal campaign. This increasingly discredited evidence is what helped us demonstrate how the Interim Government actually implemented its genocidal policy—something that is important not only for securing convictions but also for clarifying the historical record. An unvarnished account of the Rwandan genocide would reveal mid-level, regional authorities who were ambivalent or coerced, or who were insufficiently noble to die as martyrs, as well as those who were intermittent opportunistic adventurers. Even so, there were those in positions of authority who resisted the Interim Government's genocidal campaign, a fact that is seemingly incompatible with *gacaca*.

Conclusion

Gacaca's ability to circumvent the formal dispositions of courts of supposedly greater competence, and its tendency to subsume, dominate, or trump the authority of lawyers, prosecutors, and judges in the ordinary courts, takes us back to the very issues that fueled Alison's concerns at its inception. As Alison argued, *gacaca* did not have sufficient due process mechanisms to ensure fairness, was easily manipulated by the authorities or by the local community, was diffuse and interminable, and eclipsed review. These deficiencies compromised not only its capacity to dispense justice for the genocide but also its ability to complement the more formal procedures of Rwanda's conventional courts and our international criminal tribunal.

While *gacaca* has opened a floodgate of information from perpetrators to lay bare the modalities of the killing campaign, it may obscure more fundamental issues: how local authorities implemented policies received from national leaders, or how those policies were, in certain instances, selectively resisted or compromised at the local level; or how the genocidal campaign escalated in relation to the extension of the war. These are important variables for a regime of individual criminal accountability, which is ultimately the objective of any system of criminal adjudication: the individuation of responsibility. And it is at this juncture that we pause and await the final judgment in *Karemera et al.*, a case against national leaders that is heavily reliant on evidence from co-perpetrators and mid-level regional authorities. Their occasionally complicit, ambiguous, tentative, and complicated alliances with our ICTR defendants will challenge the trier of fact, and *gacaca* seems to have made that fact-finding enterprise even more daunting.

Notes

This essay builds on my comments at the conference "Reconstructing Rwanda: Fifteen Years after Genocide, a Tribute to Alison Des Forges," organized by the Institute of Commonwealth Studies in London on March 20, 2009. The views expressed here do not represent the ICTR; they simply reflect my tentative and still evolving thoughts. At the time of writing, this case is ongoing so I can only discuss matters that are in the public domain and that will not compromise the case. It may be interesting to come back to my discussion here in another few years, after a final judgment in the case, to see to what extent my thoughts were misdirected or prescient. In July 2010, Joseph Nzirorera, one of the three co-accused jointly charged in this case, died suddenly while in the final phase of the presentation of his defense case. In fact, he was in the middle of his cross-examination as one of the last defense witnesses. Since it was Nzirorera who relied most heavily on *gacaca* records to challenge the prosecution's case, it is unclear how extensively the ICTR Trial Chamber will delve into the interplay between *gacaca* records and witness testimony to assess the evidence for final judgment of the remaining two defendants.

1. *Prosecutor v. Karemera et al.*, ICTR-98-44-T. The pleadings in the case are available at http://www.unictr.org.

2. If a *gacaca* confession is subsequently judged to be incomplete or inaccurate it can be rejected, but quite often the *gacaca* guilty plea is the first, or the only, record of the prisoner's wrongdoing given the absence of formal indictments for many accused.

Reference

Peskin, Victor. 2008. *International Justice in Rwanda and the Balkans: Virtual Trials and the Struggle for State Cooperation.* New York: Cambridge University Press.

12

The Sovu Trials

The Impact of Genocide Justice on One Community

MAX RETTIG

The way forward, I believe, is to make sure that justice is actually seen, felt, and understood by those who need it most: the people of the community.

> Former U.S. ambassador and ICTR prosecutor Pierre-Richard Prosper

Reconciliation is impossible. Reconciliation means nothing to the people of Sovu.

> Male genocide survivor, Sovu, December 2006

Already we have reconciliation today. We share everything.

> Female farmer, Sovu, November 2006

Introduction

Since 1994 the international community and Rwanda have conducted four types of trials to render justice for the 1994 Rwandan genocide: international trials at the United Nations–sponsored International Criminal Tribunal for Rwanda (ICTR) in Arusha, Tanzania; transnational trials in Belgium, Canada, Switzerland, the Netherlands, and most recently Finland; military and civilian trials in Rwanda's domestic courts; and a vast network of community courts called *gacaca*. Not enough is known about how Rwandans themselves view these trials. Quantitative data gauging Rwandan attitudes toward genocide trials is scant, out of date, and in some cases suspiciously positive given the range of problems the trials have experienced.[1] We are left to wonder which trials, if any, have contributed to truth, justice, and reconciliation.

Sovu, in southern Rwanda, provides a unique opportunity to begin to answer this question. This small rural community is one of very few places to have been implicated in all four types of trials. On June 12, 2001, the trial of the so-called Butare Six began before the ICTR. The defendants allegedly led the campaign of genocide that swept Butare Prefecture, which includes Sovu. Also in the dock in Arusha was Aloys Simba, a retired Rwandan military colonel who orchestrated the violence in Butare and neighboring Gikongoro Prefecture. Only three days before the Butare trial began, Sisters Gertrude and Kisito from the Sovu convent were sentenced by a Belgian jury to fifteen and twelve years, respectively, for betraying refugees who had sought safety in the convent and for supplying the gasoline used to incinerate Tutsi refugees at the Sovu health center. Chief Adjutant Emmanuel Rekeraho, the leader of the genocide in Sovu and Simba's deputy, provided written testimony against the nuns. After the ICTR declined to prosecute Rekeraho, he was tried and sentenced to death by a Rwandan military tribunal; his sentence was commuted to life when Rwanda abolished the death penalty. Finally, Sovu's *gacaca* courts, meeting weekly, adjudicated hundreds of cases of accused *génocidaires*.

Drawing on qualitative and quantitative evidence collected during ten months of fieldwork in Sovu in 2006 and 2007, this chapter reveals how four types of genocide trials have impacted one Rwandan community. This chapter uses the reconstruction of social trust as one of the principal metrics for all four types of trials. Of course, trials may aim to achieve other important goals, including sanctioning those responsible for wrongdoing, creating a historical record of past abuses, and establishing the rule of law. However, social trust is key to the long-term security and stability of the community. Furthermore, reconciliation was a stated goal of the ICTR, the trial of Sisters Gertrude and Kisito, and *gacaca*.

Certain clear trends emerge from this study. Sovu residents do not consider themselves well informed about international trials, transnational trials, or Rwanda's military tribunals. As a result, they expressed uncertainty about the utility of those trials in promoting local reconciliation. While residents are intimately familiar with *gacaca*, their views about the community trials are mixed, even contradictory. Despite some favorable public opinion data, *gacaca* also exposed—and perhaps deepened—conflict, resentment, and ethnic disunity in Sovu. In addition, lies, half-truths, and silence limited *gacaca*'s contribution to truth, justice, and reconciliation.

As stated, this chapter explores each of the four types of genocide trials and Rwandans' perceptions of them. But first, for context, it is important to understand the dynamics of the genocide and its legacy in Sovu.

Sovu: The Genocide and Its Legacy

Sovu is a rural community near Butare town, Rwanda's intellectual capital and second largest city.[2] It lies in the country's southern region, not far from Burundi, in what was known in 1994 as Butare Prefecture. Before the genocide, it was one of the most ethnically mixed areas of Rwanda, and political moderates held considerable power there. In 1994, Butare had the only Tutsi *préfet* (governor) in the country. He and other officials in Butare Prefecture opposed the violence that erupted after President Juvénal Habyarimana's assassination on April 6. For nearly two weeks, the violence largely spared Sovu as Hutu and Tutsi men, together, fended off attacks launched by violent extremists from the neighboring community.

On April 17, 1994, the extremist government removed the Butare *préfet* from power. That same day many of Sovu's Tutsi women and children began to gather at the local health center for safety. Two days later, on April 19, the interim president and prime minister traveled to Butare to deliver a message: all men should be prepared to "work"—a euphemism for "kill." Soon thereafter, moderates lost control of Sovu. Rekeraho, president of the local Mouvement démocratique républicain (Democratic Republican Movement, MDR) party and an adherent of MDR-Power, removed Sovu's moderate *conseiller* (sector head) and installed a more "cooperative" replacement. Rekeraho reported to Aloys Simba, who the ICTR later sentenced to twenty-five years for his role in the genocide as head of civil defense for Butare and Gikongoro Prefectures. Rekeraho also met frequently with Sylvain Nsabimana, the new *préfet* of Butare and a defendant in the Butare trial. Just two days before the first large-scale massacres were perpetrated in Sovu, Rekeraho and Nsabimana traveled together to see where Tutsi refugees had assembled.

In Sovu, as elsewhere, the genocide occurred in two main phases. Although there were sporadic episodes of violence as early as April 18, the first major massacre began in the morning hours of April 22. Civilians and militias attacked refugees at the health center with machetes, guns, clubs, and grenades.[3] That afternoon, several hundred Tutsi were burned alive when the health center's garage was set ablaze, the doors barricaded shut, and the flames ignited with gasoline supplied by Sisters Gertrude and Kisito. By the end of April 23, as many as eight thousand were dead, among them refugees whom Sister Gertrude, as the mother superior, had forced out of the religious compound.

In the second phase, civilians and militias searched for Tutsi who had escaped the initial massacres. During this period, Rekeraho and his deputy continued to train militias to carry out the killings and man roadblocks at key areas in Sovu. Three days after the initial massacre, Sister Gertrude forced thirty Tutsi refugees to leave the convent; they were subsequently killed. Then, in early May, Sister Gertrude wrote a letter to the authorities in Butare, urging them to remove the remaining refugees from the convent so that daily spiritual activities could "resume in peace" (Des Forges 1999, 537). The refugees, mostly relatives of Tutsi nuns, were handed over to the communal police and most, if not all, were killed. Once families had been driven from their homes or killed, looters appropriated their cattle and crops. Rape and sexual mutilation were used as tools of genocide in Sovu, just as they were in other areas of the country.

Throughout the genocide, Rekeraho drove along the paths of Sovu to exhort Hutu men to "work." Most complied, although according to Rekeraho and local residents, not all of those who manned roadblocks or made night rounds actually killed anyone and no Hutu in Sovu was killed for refusing to participate in the genocide. However, Hutu who hid Tutsi may have had their cattle expropriated (interview with Rekeraho, May 2007).

As the Rwandan Patriotic Front (RPF) advanced toward Sovu, Hutu fled to Gikongoro Prefecture in large numbers. Allegedly, the RPF killed an unknown number of Hutu civilians in Sovu in the weeks and months following the genocide, and some Sovu residents reportedly were killed in the infamous massacre at the Kibeho internally displaced persons camp in 1995. Few prosecutions have been initiated against members of the RPF in response to allegations of wrongdoing. Sovu residents spoke of these incidents in private, always unprompted, and with considerable anguish.

Socioeconomic and political realities bind Sovu residents together on Rwanda's densely populated hills. Yet Sovu's demographics reveal the deep social dislocation caused by the genocide and civil war. More than 80 percent of those who live in Sovu today fled their homes in 1994, and at least 57 percent of Sovu residents lost a close family member due to violence between 1994 and 2007. Sovu's adult population is roughly 30 percent male and 70 percent female— even more skewed than the national average. Part of the reason for this disparity lies in the fact that as of June 2007, between two hundred and three hundred people from Sovu were in prison on genocide charges. In all, some 70 percent of Hutu in Sovu had a family member in prison. In addition, several dozen men from Sovu fled the area in recent years, reportedly to escape *gacaca*. Finally, one-fifth of all adult women are widows. Despite such dramatic social upheaval, the community's ethnic composition—roughly 20 percent Tutsi and 80 percent Hutu—has remained largely unchanged since 1994, owing to the influx of Tutsi returnees and the imprisonment of Hutu men.

Despite this legacy, some positive social trends can be observed. Respondents rejected the notion that interethnic marriage leads to social problems, embraced the idea that people must learn to live together regardless of their ethnicity, and disavowed the use of violence as a legitimate method of dispute resolution. A *cabaret* (bar) in Sovu is likely to be filled with both Hutu and Tutsi. More than 95 percent of Sovu residents reported having shared a drink with a member of another ethnic group within the month prior to the interview; two-thirds of the 95 percent said that they did so out of friendship. Furthermore, roughly half of all adults in Sovu have a family member from the other ethnic group. Large majorities in both surveys say that security and access to education have improved since 1994. Statements meant to gauge social isolation—such as "There would be fewer problems if children married someone from their own ethnic group" and "In Sovu, prisoners and survivors usually do not mix"—elicited largely negative responses. While the first survey revealed that 15 percent of survivors and 3 percent of nonsurvivors prefer to go to someone from their own ethnic group for help, those figures dropped to 10 percent and 0 percent, respectively, in the second survey. The statement "I prefer to buy things from a shopkeeper of my own ethnicity" drew laughter (only 2 percent responded affirmatively). Socioeconomic realities appear to trump ethnic division in Sovu.

Despite steady economic growth nationally since 1994, Sovu remains poor. Roughly 90 percent of all adults in Sovu rely on subsistence agriculture, and more than 80 percent report a monthly income below twenty dollars. The vast majority of adults have had little opportunity to receive an education; only one-third of adults completed primary school, with only 2 percent completing secondary school.

Research Methods and Design

To give Rwandans their rightful place in the debate over genocide trials, I carried out a ten-month, multimethod study of Sovu. I attended *gacaca* weekly for ten months (from September 2006 through June 2007), administered two public opinion surveys at a six-month interval, and conducted dozens of additional semistructured interviews.[4] Those interviewed included groups of survivors, family members of prisoners, prisoners themselves, local officials, *gacaca* judges, and finally Rekeraho and his deputy, Jean-Baptiste Kamanayo, both of whom are widely seen as the principal orchestrators of the genocide in Sovu. I also researched the local dynamics of the genocide through trial transcripts and secondary sources.

Discrepancies between the data and observations—and within the data itself—reflect the difficulty of conducting public opinion research in Rwanda. According to Filip Reyntjens, Rwandans tend to communicate "strategically" (de Vulpian 2004, 82). Before responding to a question, Rwandans may consider the personal consequences: Does the person posing the question have authority over me? Can this person help me or hurt me? Can they arrest me, have me fired, or even kill me? (ibid., 82). In my research, several interviewees expressed fear that they would be punished for expressing opinions contrary to government policies. One woman said, "Do not show my answers to the authorities. They would condemn me" (interview, May 2007). This phenomenon introduces an element of uncertainty into whether the data accurately reflect public opinion and underscores the importance of relying on both qualitative and quantitative evidence.

This study purposely focuses on one Rwandan community. The results, therefore, do not necessarily represent the Rwandan experience as a whole. However, they should not be dismissed as exceptional. Taking the example of *gacaca*, some variation in the way the courts operated from one community to the next is natural. However, many of the same trends and phenomena observed by Avocats sans frontières (Lawyers without Borders, ASF) and Penal Reform International (PRI) throughout the country are mirrored in Sovu. Incomplete confessions, poor training for the judges, and difficulty in achieving a quorum all have proved problematic in Sovu just as ASF and PRI have shown them to be elsewhere. Sovu is a representative community in other respects, too. Like most Rwandan communities, Sovu is rural and its demographics closely resemble national averages. Furthermore, once the genocide began in Sovu, it followed roughly the same course as in other parts of the country: the balance of power shifted from moderates to extremists, an initial wave of massacres was perpetrated, followed by killings on a smaller scale and the displacement of Hutu when the RPF took control. Thus, while Sovu may not represent the national experience writ small, it is not an outlier.

International, Transnational, and Military Trials

The international, transnational, and military trials largely failed to capture the attention of Sovu residents. The ICTR's outreach efforts fell woefully short in Sovu, the Belgian government did no outreach aside from the investigation, and the military trial of Rekeraho and Kamanayo, which took place in nearby Butare town, was attended by very few Sovu residents.[5]

Perhaps as a result, Sovu residents expressed uncertainty as to whether any of these trials had contributed to local reconciliation.

The Butare Six trial is one of the longest-running, most expensive trials in the history of international criminal justice (including more than seven hundred trial days).[6] Yet 94 percent of respondents said they were "not informed" or "not well-informed" about the ICTR. This fact is perhaps surprising because it was the removal of moderates from the government and the installation of radicals—like members of the Butare Six—that allowed the genocide to begin in Sovu. The trial of Aloys Simba also could have been expected to generate local interest as he was Rekeraho's immediate superior. Yet a substantial percentage of Sovu residents expressed uncertainty when asked whether the punishments at the ICTR are "fair compared to those at *gacaca*" (48 percent), whether the ICTR is fair to all groups (45 percent), and whether the ICTR contributed to reconciliation in Sovu (45 percent).

The numbers are strikingly similar for the 2001 trial of Sisters Gertrude and Kisito—the first trial under Belgium's universal jurisdiction law. Although the trial generated significant media attention both in Belgium and internationally, 88 percent of Sovu residents said they were "not well-informed" or "not informed" about the landmark trial. Only 20 percent of residents said that they had heard radio reports about the trial, while one-third said that they received news about the trial from neighbors. Perhaps as a result, "uncertain" was the most common response to questions about the trial's impact on local reconciliation (49 percent), whether the trial was fair to all groups (62 percent), and whether the punishments handed down were fair compared to the sentences at *gacaca* (62 percent).[7]

While the military trial of Rekeraho and Kamanayo garnered only slightly more attention, public opinion about the trial was more positive. The men—sentenced to death and life imprisonment, respectively—faced trial in a large hall in Butare town, only a few miles from Sovu. However, few people from Sovu reportedly attended the trial, and a substantial majority (80 percent) said they are either "not well-informed" or "not informed" about the trial. Despite that fact, respondents expressed positive views about the trial's impact in Sovu. Majorities said that the trial had contributed to justice (60 percent) and reconciliation (57 percent).

Gacaca Trials

Gacaca brought more people to trial and exposed more about how the genocide was perpetrated at the local level than the ICTR, transnational trials, and the Rwandan courts combined. Yet public opinion about *gacaca* is decidedly mixed and some evidence suggests that *gacaca* may have fuelled conflict in the community.

Several indicators, including the pace of the trials, the number of released prisoners, and some public opinion data, tell an encouraging story about *gacaca*. In Sovu the *gacaca* courts pronounced fifty-five verdicts between September 2006 and June 2007, including "innocent" verdicts for thirteen accused, many of whom had been wrongfully imprisoned for over a decade. In addition, *gacaca* judges accepted twenty-five confessions and released those who had confessed from prison to perform community service. Asked whether *gacaca* was going well, 73 percent replied favorably in the first survey and 88 percent responded favorably in the second.[8] The statements "*Gacaca* will bring peace to Rwanda" and "I have confidence in *gacaca*" drew the support of 78 and 85 percent of respondents, respectively, in the first survey and more than 90 percent each in the second.[9] A majority (57 percent) of survivors and returnees say that *gacaca* adequately addresses their problems, including reparations and insecurity; a larger majority (84 percent) of nonsurvivors say that *gacaca* adequately addresses the problems facing prisoners and their families, including poverty and false accusations.[10]

Notwithstanding these positive indicators, one woman told me, "It is not at all clear who is telling the truth at *gacaca*" (interview, May 2007). More than 70 percent of nonsurvivors and 90 percent of survivors and returnees concurred, saying that people tell lies at *gacaca*. In addition, the accuracy and completeness of confessions almost always were challenged. That fact is particularly troubling because confessions were intended to encourage perpetrators to apologize, reveal how loved ones had died, and reintegrate perpetrators into their communities by allowing them to perform community service in lieu of lengthy prison sentences. Yet almost as a rule, survivors and other community members questioned the completeness of the confessions. Nearly 40 percent of the time, judges deemed the confessions incomplete and imposed prison terms at or near the maximum—on average, twenty-five years.

Sovu residents also used *gacaca* as a forum for settling old disputes. A plurality of Sovu residents reported that "people in the community feel afraid or anxious on the day of *gacaca*" and that "people do not attend *gacaca* because they are afraid of being accused." According to the survey data, conflicts over land and housing grew more frequent as *gacaca* continued. In the first survey, 54 percent of nonsurvivors reported that conflicts over land and housing had improved since 1994, but 51 percent of survivors and returnees said the opposite. In the second survey, 44 percent of nonsurvivors and only 20 percent of survivors and returnees reported an improvement. One-quarter of respondents said that "on the day of *gacaca*, there are problems or disputes within families," and just over 30 percent of respondents said that "as a result of *gacaca*, there are incidents such as intimidation, disputes between families, theft, or even violence."

Conflicts over land, property, and marital infidelity spurred false accusations. One woman appeared before *gacaca* in May 2007, twelve years after she first went to prison on charges that she murdered her husband during the genocide. After a two-day trial, it became clear that a dispute over the deceased's coffee plantation had prompted the accusation. The defendant was exonerated, but she has not been able to recover the land or the home that she was to inherit from her late husband. In another case, a man accused his brother of making false accusations. The brother who stood accused had slept with the other's wife only a week after the marriage ceremony. *Gacaca* provided an opportunity for payback. Although the judges eventually exposed the underlying conflict, such false accusations have made it more difficult for *gacaca* to reveal the truth about what happened in 1994.

Of course, lies are told in courtrooms around the world. But lies and half-truths posed a particularly grave threat to the success of *gacaca* because lies erode a key goal of *gacaca*: rebuilding social trust. In addition, unlike Western legal systems, *gacaca* was administered by judges who are not trained jurists, and limited procedural safeguards are in place to protect defendants from lies. *Gacaca* trials also relied exclusively on witness testimony. Yet because the trials took place more than a decade after the events, memories were often unreliable.

The silences and omissions that were omnipresent at *gacaca* were as damaging as the lies and half-truths. For example, although the surveys did not collect attitudinal data about the exclusion of alleged RPA (Rwandan Patriotic Army) crimes, dozens of people in the community raised the issue spontaneously.[11] In one woman's words:

Hutu were killed after 1994. Some were shot in the camps; others in their homes. RPA soldiers killed people in Sovu and Maraba and in the camps. People were taken away from their families and they never came back. There should be justice for the crimes committed by the *Inkotanyi* [RPA] in 1994, 1996, and 1997. Some survivors even came with the *Inkotanyi* to kill people in the camps and in homes. (interview, May 2007)

Such selective justice may have undermined reconciliation and detracted from public trust in the RPF government.

In addition, the practice of *ceceka* (Kinyarwanda for "keep silent") compromised *gacaca*. *Ceceka* represents an implicit pact by which Hutu agree not to give testimony against other Hutu. A prisoner from Sovu, who maintained his innocence, defined *ceceka* as "saying nothing if you are Hutu. For example, let's say I am going to trial. I go to testify, and Hutu will stay quiet while the survivors speak. But it is the Hutu who saw what happened; the Tutsi were hiding" (interview, March 2007). Two-thirds of Sovu residents said that "*ceceka* keeps people from speaking the truth at *gacaca*." As a result, the evidentiary burden shifts to survivors, yet their ability to testify is limited by the fact that many survivors are alive today precisely because they were hiding during the genocide; thus they are unlikely to have witnessed atrocities outside of their own experiences. In addition, because nonsurvivors make up the vast majority of Rwandan citizens (roughly 80 percent in Sovu), their participation was critical.

While the practice of *ceceka* blocked the flow of inculpatory testimony, exculpatory testimony—that is, testimony separating the truly guilty from the wrongfully accused—was also difficult to obtain. More than 60 percent said that "people are afraid of defending the accused." Nonsurvivors feared that if they defended the accused, they would be accused themselves. A woman whose husband was in prison said that nonsurvivors "keep quiet just because what we say is not considered as true. . . . We sometimes say this person did this and not this, and when we see that they [survivors and the judges] do not believe us, we keep quiet" (interview, March 2007). A second woman, also a nonsurvivor, echoed the first: "Survivors are the only ones who speak. Truly, there is no freedom of expression at *gacaca* for ordinary people who have family in prison" (interview, March 2007). Overall, 41 percent of respondents agreed that "there are people or groups whose voices are not considered at *gacaca*."

Some people in the community suggested that there is a third silence: the silencing of nonsurvivors who served as judges during deliberations. A prisoner described this phenomenon: "No one would believe you if you speak against the survivors. . . . Because they work with survivors, Hutu [judges] are afraid and say nothing" (interview, March 2007). Other people in the community made similar—or even graver—accusations about the judges. Two former *gacaca* judges said that the benches are packed so that every panel of judges is majority Tutsi. I could not test these claims, but their very existence speaks to a lack of confidence in *gacaca*.[12]

These problems, plus the strain of weekly genocide trials on the community, are almost certainly part of the reason that 99 percent of respondents said they "wish *gacaca* would finish soon so that the community could move on." The Sovu *gacaca* courts missed several deadlines set by the government because of its large caseload and slow pace. By tripling the number of courts and meeting as many as three times per week, the local authorities were able to bring *gacaca* to its conclusion in Sovu by June 2009.

Security, Interethnic Relations, Authority, and Reconciliation

Encouraged by the perception that Rwanda is stable, donors have given considerable foreign aid to rebuild the country, support the legal system, and combat poverty and poor health. However, as a male genocide survivor in Sovu told me, "There is a difference between peace and security. Today we have security, not peace" (interview, December 2006). A breakdown in the government's control, he suggested, could leave space for a return to violence. Conversations with members of the community echoed this assertion. A man imprisoned since September 1994 and accused of participating in the massacres at the Sovu health center warned of future violence: "Hatred is gaining another dimension and *gacaca* is causing family conflicts. Children whose parents are in jail will always ask where their daddies are. They will prepare revenge" (interview, March 2007). Such ideas, combined with a lack of political freedom and an underlying perception that poverty is growing worse (57 percent in the first survey and 68 percent in the second), could lead to instability.

Despite general agreement that security has improved since 1994, several incidents revealed that conflict persists. In February 2007, one survivor who testified regularly at *gacaca* woke up to find her crops uprooted. After learning about the incident, local officials rounded up between forty and fifty nonsurvivors from the area and announced a collective punishment: they would all pay the woman for the destroyed crops. When the police arrived from Butare, the group was told to lie on the ground and were beaten with branches (interviews, April 2007; HRW 2007). Four months later, in a separate incident, a group of so-called bandits broke into the home of an elderly couple, beat them, destroyed their crops, and stole a few meager belongings. The man recovered, but his wife died at the hospital several days later. Some in the community insisted it was a coincidence that the man had been called to testify at *gacaca*; others suspected that the "robbery" was linked to his testimony. In late 2007 the teenage daughter of a prominent survivor, a former *gacaca* judge who testified in Belgium and almost every week at *gacaca*, died of what people in the community call "poisoning."

People in the community said that poisonings are directed against those who testify against genocide suspects. Nearly one-third of respondents said that there have been more incidents of poisoning since *gacaca* started. In addition, survivors reported feeling intimidated while giving testimony at *gacaca*. A female survivor told me, "When survivors give testimony, people look at them with hate, as if they could even kill them" (interview, December 2006). Eighty percent of Sovu residents said that theft of crops and property has grown worse since 1994. One man, a nonsurvivor, explained, "There are many prisoners and these are the ones who are supposed to be working, so the women are alone at the house and they must work for their kids and to bring food to the prisoners. The kids stay at home and are not well looked after, and they are very poor. These are the ones who steal" (interview, May 2007).

Many Sovu residents expressed the view that ethnic harmony is little more than a veneer. When asked about interethnic relations, a secondary school student said, "I could say that relationships between groups are good, but really we do not meet. They [survivors] stay in the [new housing settlement] and others stay up here in our homes" (interview, December 2006). Another interviewee put it this way: "We live well together, but in the huts it is different. A person who brings food to a family member in prison has anger and pain. And survivors still have pain. They pretend they don't but it is still in their hearts" (interview, December 2006).

Distrust between nonsurvivors and survivors was also evident. According to a female nonsurvivor, "Because of *gacaca*, people in the community do not trust each other" (interview, November 2006). While the majority of nonsurvivors said that trust in the community has increased since 1994 (60 percent in the first survey and 54 percent in the second), survivors and returnees were less sure (47 percent in the first survey and 39 percent in the second). Some responses indicated that beyond separation and distrust, outright animosity remained in the community. One Hutu woman told me, "In their hearts, people know who they are and they should keep their identity. They should know who to mix with" (interview, December 2006)

Although more than two-thirds of Sovu residents said that reconciliation is taking hold, considerable evidence suggests that *gacaca* has not significantly reduced mutual distrust in the community. A Hutu woman who was married to a Tutsi man in 1994 reported being menaced because she saw who killed her husband and children. On the subject of community relations she said, "Reconciliation? Impossible. They killed my husband and ten of my children under my very eyes and I am supposed to take them back? I do not want to reconcile with them. I want them to let me die in peace" (interview, May 2007). Another woman said, "There is no reconciliation today because there are still conflicts. When we pass each other on the path, we do not even say hello to each other" (interview, March 2007). Finally, several people in the community identified the end of *gacaca* as the point where reconciliation can begin: "Maybe there can be reconciliation when *gacaca* finishes" (interview, May 2007).

Conclusion

After a robust legal response featuring four distinct types of genocide trials, it is critical to recognize shortcomings as well as successes. Important lessons can be drawn from the Sovu trials, lessons that may inform future responses to mass atrocity.

Where domestic legal systems have been destroyed or where domestic trials would prove too incendiary, international and transnational trials can bring alleged perpetrators to justice. But policymakers should be skeptical of the capacity of international and transnational trials to promote local reconciliation, particularly when outreach efforts are inadequate. Where domestic systems are up to the task, they can play an important role in doing justice, exposing truth, and promoting reconciliation. The military trial of Rekeraho and Kamanayo had the narrowest aim—namely, to punish two men whose guilt was never much in doubt. In achieving that goal, it appeared to garner the approval of Sovu residents, who reported that the trial contributed to justice and reconciliation.

Whether *gacaca* has sewn the seeds of reconciliation or of renewed discord may not be known for some time. *Gacaca* adjudicated hundreds of cases in Sovu and dozens were released from prison after confessing their crimes. However, the trials also revealed deep social fissures in the community. While *gacaca* has brought new facts to light in some cases, the contested nature of the trials obscured the truth. Sovu residents failed to participate openly and honestly, and the trials faltered as a result. Policymakers would be wise to consider whether social trust has been adequately reconstructed *before* turning to community tribunals for criminal prosecution.

Notes

This chapter is a revised version of an article published in *African Affairs* 51, no. 3 (2008): 25–50. It does not necessarily represent the views of the U.S. Government or the U.S. Department of State.

1. Gacaca does not comply with international human rights norms regarding fair trials (ISHR 2009, 4). Judges are inadequately trained to handle serious legal questions and control often unwieldy proceedings (African Rights 2003). Fear of reprisals blocks the free flow of testimony (ASF 2007). Massacres of Hutu civilians by some members

of the rebel Rwandan Patriotic Army are off-limits for *gacaca*; as a result, members of the Hutu ethnic majority may perceive *gacaca* as an exercise in victor's justice (Amnesty International 2002). The inclusion of property crimes meant that *gacaca* courts heard over one million cases, raising the concern that *gacaca* has imposed collective guilt on the Hutu majority (Waldorf 2006, 422–34). Finally, and perhaps most worrisome for a system of participatory justice, the population often is unmotivated to attend trials and give testimony (PRI 2005).

2. The narrative presented in this section is based on interviews conducted by the author with Sovu residents and prisoners in 2006–7, *gacaca* observations, Rwandan court documents related to the trial of Emmanuel Rekeraho and Jean-Baptiste Kamanayo, and ICTR court documents related to the Butare Six trial and the trial of Aloys Simba.

3. Sovu residents and lawyers for Sisters Gertrude and Kisito referred loosely to civilian killers as Interahamwe, but Rekeraho told me that Sovu did not have any Interahamwe—the youth militia from the Mouvement républicain national pour la démocratie et le développement (National Republican Movement for Democracy and Development, MRND) party. Rather, Rekeraho provided military-style training to members of the youth wing of the MDR party and others.

4. According to figures obtained by my research team from the Huye Sector office in September 2006, 2,879 people in Sovu are at least eighteen years old and thus are eligible to attend *gacaca*. This group formed the target population. With a team of trained Rwandan research assistants, I administered 505 survey questionnaires: 250 in November–December 2006 and 255 in May 2007. With a 95 percent confidence interval, this leaves a sampling error of 5.9 percent for communitywide data. Breakdowns in the data between survivors and returnees and nonsurvivors are not representative. To collect a sample, my team and I visited every other house in the jurisdiction of Sovu's *gacaca* court, where we randomly selected one adult member of the household to participate in the survey. We skipped every other house to avoid oversampling a particular subset of the population, which is somewhat geographically segregated. Some questions for the two surveys were based on those administered by Longman, Pham, and Weinstein (2004, 206–25). In the first survey, less than 1 percent of total interviewees refused to participate. Just over 1 percent of total interviewees stopped the interview early, in all cases because of emotional stress. In the second survey, 3 percent of total interviewees refused to participate or could not be located. Less than 1 percent of total interviewees stopped the interview early, this time because they felt uncomfortable answering questions about ethnicity without express permission from local authorities. To protect interviewees from possible retaliation I have withheld their names, although few specifically requested anonymity.

5. Alison Des Forges and Timothy Longman similarly reported that, aside from the small urban elite, most Rwandans had little knowledge of the ICTR's work (Des Forges and Longman 2004, 56).

6. The trial, which opened in 2001, was still going on in August 2010.

7. Both Gertrude and Kisito are on conditional release at the Benedictine abbey in Maredret, Belgium, after serving roughly half of their sentences.

8. A somewhat countervailing trend is that the percentage of respondents who "strongly agree" that *gacaca* is going well dropped 13 percentage points from the first survey to the second.

9. These figures are consistent with earlier findings. For example, a public opinion survey conducted in early 2002, after the election of *gacaca* judges but before the courts had begun to function, found that 83 percent of Rwandans had confidence in *gacaca* (Longman, Pham, and Weinstein 2004). In an earlier survey, 53 percent of respondents said they were "highly confident" that *gacaca* would promote a lasting peace (Ballabola 2001). A third survey, conducted in 2003 by Rwanda's National Unity and Reconciliation Commission (NURC), revealed some skeptical attitudes toward *gacaca* but still was generally positive (NURC 2003).

10. In Rwanda today, it is not acceptable to ask an individual's ethnicity. For the purposes of this chapter, survivor and returnee were defined based on responses to the question, "Do you consider yourself a genocide survivor?" However, I reserved the right to change the attribution based on additional information. Generally, a survivor is defined as any person who was targeted during the genocide. All Tutsi who lived in Rwanda in 1994 and some Hutu fit this definition. "Returnees" are Rwandan Tutsi who returned to Rwanda after July 1994. "Nonsurvivors" are Hutu who lived in Rwanda in 1994 and who were not targeted during the genocide. However, other definitions of survivor exist. Several Sovu residents who do not fit within the above definition have told me that they consider themselves survivors. One man told me, "We are all survivors" (interview, December 2006).

11. I did not ask questions related to alleged RPF crimes because my research assistants feared government retaliation and because my ability to conduct research depended on permission of local and national authorities. However, interviewees often raised the subject themselves.

12. Phil Clark argues that *gacaca* provided a forum for communities to engage in constructive dialogue (Clark 2007, 801). During some *gacaca* sessions in Sovu, the public appeared to participate openly. However, that was not the norm.

References

African Rights. 2003. "Gacaca Justice: A Shared Responsibility." January.

Amnesty International. 2002. "Gacaca: A Question of Justice." AFR 47/007/2002. December. http://www.amnesty.org/en/library/info/AFR47/007/2002.

Avocats sans frontières (ASF). 2007. "Monitoring des juridictions gacaca: Phase de jugement—Rapport analytique no. 2, Octobre 2005–Septembre 2006." http://www.asf.be/publications/Rapport_analytique_GacacaII_FR.pdf.

Ballabola, Stella. 2001. "Perceptions about the Gacaca Law in Rwanda: Evidence from a Multi-Method Study." *Cahiers du Centre de Gestion des Conflits* 3:112–13.

Clark, Phil. 2007. "Hybridity, Holism, and 'Traditional' Justice: The Case of the *Gacaca* Courts in Post-genocide Rwanda." *George Washington International Law Review* 39:765–837.

Des Forges, Alison. 1999. *Leave None to Tell the Story: Genocide in Rwanda*. New York: Human Rights Watch.

Des Forges, Alison, and Timothy Longman. 2004. "Legal Responses to Genocide in Rwanda." In *My Neighbor, My Enemy: Justice and Community in the Aftermath of Mass Atrocity*, edited by Eric Stover and Harvey Weinstein, 49–68. New York: Cambridge University Press.

de Vulpian, Laure. 2004. *Rwanda, un genocide oublié? Un procès pour mémoire*. Brussels: Éditions Complexe.

Human Rights Watch (HRW). 2007. "'There Will Be No Trial': Police Killings of Detainees and the Imposition of Collective Punishments." July 23. http://www.hrw.org/en/reports/2007/07/23/there-will-be-no-trial.

International Service for Human Rights (ISHR). 2009. "Rwanda: Third Report." Human Rights Committee, 95th Session, March 18–19. *Treaty Body Monitor*, April 20. http://www.ishr.ch/document-stuff/browse-documents/doc_download/330-ishrs-report-on-examination-of-rwanda-hrc-march-09.

Longman, Tim, Phuong Pham, and Harvey Weinstein. 2004. "Connecting Justice to Human Experience." In *My Neighbor, My Enemy: Justice and Community in the Aftermath of Mass Atrocity*, edited by Eric Stover and Harvey Weinstein, 206–25. New York: Cambridge University Press.

National Unity and Reconciliation Commission (NURC). 2003. "Opinion Survey on Participation in Gacaca and National Reconciliation." Kigali, January.

Penal Reform International (PRI). 2005. "Integrated Report on Gacaca Research and Monitoring: Pilot Phase January 2002–December 2004." http://www.penalreform.org/.

Waldorf, Lars. 2006. "Rwanda's Failing Experiment in Restorative Justice." In *Handbook of Restorative Justice: A Global Perspective*, edited by Dennis Sullivan and Larry Tifft, 422–34. London: Routledge.

13

"All Rwandans Are Afraid of Being Arrested One Day"

Prisoners Past, Present, and Future

CARINA TERTSAKIAN

Introduction

In August 2008 I visited Kigali to meet a number of people who had been released after many years in prison, and, for a few days, I saw the world through their eyes. It was a snapshot of a strange, baffling world, one where these former prisoners seemed to have no real place. Kigali had been completely transformed during the period the prisoners had spent in prison. I remembered the words of prisoners I had met several years earlier who had tried to anticipate what life would be like outside the prison walls. "Here in prison, it's another world," one of them told me. "After ten years, we have been overtaken." Another stated: "We felt we were about to be sent to a completely different country." Once released, they found the country more changed than they could have imagined. Many points of reference have disappeared, and some places have literally become unrecognizable. Some former prisoners, describing their period in prison as a kind of time warp, recognize that the onus is on them to adjust to the new realities. Like all other Rwandans racing to keep up with the speed of change, they find ways of coping. But the more profound political changes that the government engineered in Rwandan society may be more difficult to accept.

Seventeen years after the genocide, the situation of prisoners and former prisoners in Rwanda remains a controversial and unpopular subject. Some observers and critics still express indignation at the suggestion that we might try to approach the plight of individuals accused of genocide with any degree of compassion. Among these critics are seasoned journalists, academics, and even human rights workers, some of whom have witnessed the conditions in Rwanda's prisons firsthand. The acute suffering experienced by tens of thousands of prisoners and the prolonged denial of justice have failed to move international opinion. The horror of the genocide, coupled with the shame at the international failure to stop it, has led to such a sharp polarization of views that there is little room for nuance or complexity in our reactions. The Rwandan genocide, almost more than any other event in recent history, has created a blind spot in our collective and individual response to human suffering and has obscured objective realities. This blind spot is perhaps the greatest challenge to genuine reconstruction and democratization in post-genocide Rwanda.

The unacknowledged abuses suffered by prisoners are likely to have consequences for the success of the government's reconstruction efforts and for the long-term prospects of reconciliation. What Rwanda's prisoners and former prisoners think and do is not a peripheral matter. It affects a significant proportion of the Rwandan population: not only these individuals themselves, but the next generation. Children who have seen their parents imprisoned for years without justice have grown up harboring feelings of ethnic victimization. Unless these problems are addressed, they will continue to undermine Rwanda's social and ethnic cohesion, and threaten the country's future unity.

What Makes Rwanda's Prisons Unique

Those who planned the 1994 genocide in Rwanda made sure that responsibility for the killings was carried by as many people as possible: tens of thousands, maybe hundreds of thousands, of Hutu were actively involved.[1] The huge number of perpetrators meant that in the aftermath of the massacres, it became very difficult to pinpoint who had killed and who had not. Rwandans say that at the local level, everyone knows exactly who did what during the genocide. But the truth has sometimes been hard to find, and one of the lasting legacies of the genocide has been the destruction of trust and certainty: on the surface, any Hutu might have been a killer, and any Hutu is therefore a suspect.

As a result, the prisons in Rwanda are unique in several fundamental ways. First, there is the sheer number of prisoners. At its peak, around 1998, the prison population reached about 130,000.[2] Almost everyone you meet in Rwanda has at least one and probably several relatives or acquaintances in prison. They may not mention this unless asked—not out of shame but because it has become part of the normal fabric of life. Second, because of these numbers, there is the extraordinary level of overcrowding. The Rwandan prisons in toto are one of the most extreme experiences of mass human confinement in recent history, though they have rarely been recognized as such. Representatives of organizations who have worked in prisons in many different countries have described the conditions in Rwanda's prisons as unparalleled. Third, there is the gravity of the crimes attributed to most prisoners. The vast majority stand accused of genocide.[3]

The fourth aspect is the social composition of the prison population. Few of Rwanda's prisoners have the stereotypical profile of criminal offenders. Most are ordinary men and women from a wide range of social and professional backgrounds, who had never set foot in a prison before. A whole society is living behind the prison walls, from rich government officials to poor peasants and everything in between. While most prisoners come from rural backgrounds (reflecting the makeup of the Rwandan population), an unusually high proportion are "intellectuals"—a term Rwandans use to refer to those with a good level of education. The result of this mix of backgrounds is a hugely diverse, vibrant, skilled, and complex prison population. Finally, Rwandan prisons differ from those in other countries in terms of their internal organization. Prison staff rarely penetrate the prisoners' living quarters. The prisons are almost entirely run by the prisoners themselves, reinforcing the sense of a complete and closed world.

An Overview of the Prisons from 1994 to 2009

From July 1994 on, tens of thousands of people were arrested across the country at an astonishing speed and incarcerated in prisons that quickly filled to several times their capacity. Prisoners literally lived on top of one another, with no room to lie down, no room to sit and, at times, no room to even stand. As the blocks filled up, prisoners had to sleep in the kitchens, in the showers, in the toilets. Thousands slept in the courtyards outside, without shelter. Men, women, young children, the elderly, and the sick—all were thrown in together. Diseases were rife. The overcrowding was so extreme, and the facilities so poor, that it could take several hours for a prisoner to reach the toilet. Thousands died as a direct of result of these conditions. A former prisoner described how at night prisoners formed a long line, resting their heads between each other's legs. If someone wanted to turn over, they all had to turn over at the same time. "People used to die," he recounted, "sometimes ten in one day. If they died at night, the body would stay there until the next day. When we turned over at night, we would turn the dead person over too." He was one of only three survivors from a group of seventy-four arrested in 1995.

It was in large part thanks to the International Committee of the Red Cross (ICRC) that a much larger number of prisoners did not die. The ICRC provided food, water, blankets, medical care, and hygiene equipment to the prisons. It also registered prisoners. Most important of all, the ICRC could watch and report on the treatment of prisoners.

Many of these prisoners had nothing in their case files and had been arrested on blanket accusations of "genocide" without any investigation. Many may well have been guilty but had not had a chance to defend themselves or even hear the charges against them. Many others were innocent. Thousands of arrests were carried out arbitrarily and indiscriminately, particularly between 1994 and 1999. Some denunciations were made in good faith by people who had witnessed killings during the genocide, but others were motivated by the desire to settle personal scores. For many ordinary Rwandans, as well as for the government, this was an opportunity to get rid of perceived enemies and rivals. The overwhelming majority of people arrested in these circumstances remained in prison for years—in some cases, more than a decade—without charge or trial.

In 2004 I spent several months talking to prisoners in different prisons in Rwanda, listening to their descriptions of the inhuman conditions and absence of justice as they spent year after year waiting for even a basic hearing (see Tertsakian 2008). While the prison population had declined to 85,500—still more than 1 percent of the country's population—prison conditions remained shocking. Little more than fifteen inches (40 cm) was the standard width of the living space of each prisoner. There were no cells, just row after row of wooden planks, on bunklike structures. Hundreds of prisoners still slept outside, under the sun and the rain. There were severe food shortages and long lines for water and for the showers. In several prisons, minors were still detained with adults. Family visits lasted only three minutes. To any outsider, these conditions were intolerably cruel. Yet, ten years on, I found they had been accepted as normal and barely worthy of comment. Even some of the prisoners seemed to have gotten used to them. It was only when they started talking that the full extent of their suffering, as well as their bitterness and trauma, became apparent.

Between 2005 and 2009, the prison system began evolving in a broadly positive direction, though there have been setbacks and new human rights concerns. The number of prisoners dropped through a combination of large-scale releases and community service known as Travaux d'intérêt général (TIG). *Gacaca* turned out to be a double-edged sword: it prompted releases but also resulted in new denunciations and new arrests.[4] Prisoner numbers dropped to around 70,000 at the end of 2005, then shot up again, reaching 98,000 in June 2007. The government responded by expanding TIG and the prison population decreased again.[5]

In 2007 Rwanda abolished the death penalty, and hundreds of prisoners on death row had their sentences commuted to life imprisonment. But a new, alarming provision was introduced: prisoners serving a life sentence for genocide would not be entitled to "any kind of mercy, conditional release or rehabilitation" unless they had served at least twenty years in prison. In addition, they were to be held in isolation, or solitary confinement.[6] Facilities for isolating thousands of prisoners simply do not exist in Rwanda, so by 2009 this provision had not yet been applied. However, with the modernization of several prisons, it is conceivable that isolation cells could be created.

By 2009 the government's management of the prison system had improved and the administration had become increasingly streamlined.[7] Building on a 2006 law for the organization of the National Prisons Service and a national prison plan—which includes a schedule for prison closures, construction of new prisons, and work facilities up to 2020—the government introduced a series of improvements. These include a more professionalized and better-trained prison staff, and ambitious plans for all official data on prisoners' cases to be centralized in a new computerized program.[8] In early 2009, minors were gradually transferred from various detention facilities and grouped together in designated prisons, where they are held separately from adults. Now, most families will have to travel huge distances to visit their children in these prisons.

In August 2009 the prison population stood at around 61,000. Yet living conditions were still difficult and most of the prisons remained extremely crowded: they were at around 140 percent of total capacity. Prisoners reported that most aspects of their daily life remained unchanged. Also, new restrictive rules had been introduced: the frequency of visits was reduced from once a week to twice a month, and visitors were prohibited from bringing food to the prisons, unless they could produce a medical certificate for the prisoner.

Shifts in Government Policy

For several years after the genocide, the fate of Rwanda's prisoners was bottom of the list of government priorities. Given the scale of popular participation in the genocide, the fact that large numbers of people were arrested was not surprising. Rwanda lacked appropriate mechanisms and trained personnel to gather evidence and sift the guilty from the innocent. Yet these factors do not explain or excuse the government's lack of concern when hundreds, even thousands, of prisoners started dying. The government passed that off as an inevitable consequence of the genocide.

Many Rwanda observers have tried to divine the government's motivation for continuing to arrest such great numbers of people when it was clear that it would never have the capacity to process their cases, and in the full knowledge that many of those arrested were innocent. Furthermore, prison conditions were so extreme that it was obvious that many prisoners were likely to die before their cases got anywhere near a court. The generous interpretation was that the government lacked the capacity to cope with the consequences of the genocide. At the other end of the spectrum, there were those who believed that the new government was pursuing a policy of vengeance, imprisoning as many Hutu as possible, regardless of their guilt or innocence, and that the likely deaths of thousands of Hutu prisoners suited its political agenda. In reality, government officials held different views, but those who wanted to improve prison conditions were sidelined. Gambling on the guilt of the international community for failing to stop the genocide, hardliners rightly calculated that arbitrary arrests and prison conditions were unlikely to adversely affect Rwanda's relationship with foreign donors, no matter how many prisoners died.

As the years passed, however, the cost of keeping such a large proportion of the country's population in prison became too high for the Rwandan government, particularly as the ICRC dramatically scaled down its assistance. The only option was to start releasing prisoners. In 1998 the government announced that it would start releasing the old and the very sick, as well as those without case files. Between three thousand and four thousand prisoners from these categories were released, and a further three thousand in 2001 and 2002. In January 2003, in advance of presidential and parliamentary elections, President Paul Kagame announced a wider-ranging program of releases that saw approximately twenty-four thousand released over a three-month period. Those released include prisoners who had confessed to their participation in the genocide and had already served their sentence in pretrial detention.

The confessions system was at the heart of the government's policy on releases, which, together with TIG, has dramatically reduced the prison population since 2005. As part of its strategy to reduce the burden on the justice system, the government set up a program to encourage prisoners to confess to the crimes they committed during the genocide. If their confessions were accepted, they could be released or benefit from a reduced sentence. For a confession to be valid, however, prisoners had to describe not only what they did during the genocide but also what others did. If they did not denounce others, their confessions were not admissible. The government's barely concealed ulterior motive was to demonstrate that as many people as possible participated in the genocide. In this way, the bulk of the Hutu population was "proved guilty," not through any process of trial but by self-incrimination.

A range of means were deployed to encourage prisoners to confess, including various forms of pressure, coercion, and bribery (see Tertsakian 2008, 395–423). These methods certainly helped the government reach its target of getting large numbers of confessions, but there were huge casualties too: justice, truth, and the fate of thousands of innocent people in prison. The confessions program turned the principle of justice on its head: it resulted in a situation where people guilty of the most terrible crimes walked free, while many who were innocent remained in prison. One prisoner summed up the situation as follows: "I wonder: is it a crime not to have killed? Or is having killed the best way of getting out of prison?"

Prisoners fabricated confessions just in order to qualify for release. They took responsibility for crimes they had not committed, implicated others in crimes they may not have committed either, invented incidents that never took place, confessed to killing people who were still alive. Numerous deals were struck; guilt and innocence were bought; truth did not even enter into the bargain. Some prisoners were driven to confess only by the fear that others would denounce them in their confessions. Others confessed to crimes their relatives or friends may have committed, to protect the real perpetrators, who were still free. The truth became more and more elusive, until the confessions lost their very meaning.

Looking back over these shifts in government policy over the last fifteen years, it is apparent that developments in the prison situation have been motivated by political as much as practical considerations. In the years immediately following the genocide, the government was very reluctant to contemplate large-scale releases. Memories of the genocide were too fresh, and some feared that the security threats posed by the insurgency in the northwest of the country might be heightened by the release of thousands of prisoners accused of genocide.[9] In subsequent years the security threats receded, and the government consolidated its political grip on the country, in large part through systematic repression. In such an environment, the release of thousands of prisoners no longer seemed such a threatening prospect. Having successfully

"Afraid of Being Arrested One Day"

neutralized all meaningful opposition, the government could safely assume that released prisoners, most of them deeply traumatized by their experience of imprisonment, would keep their heads down and not cause any problems, at least for the foreseeable future.

The Legacy of the Prison Crisis

In 2008 and 2009 I tracked down some of the former prisoners I had met in prison in Kigali four or five years earlier. In the villages and on the hills, former prisoners may be easily identifiable. But in Kigali they blend in, invisible, except to each other. Yet they are everywhere, like an army of ghosts. I spent an afternoon with a former prisoner. In the first two hours, we met about eight other former prisoners on the streets of Kigali, just by chance. They recognized him, came to greet him, and embraced him. Most had not seen him since his release three years earlier. Even the waiter in the cafe where we stopped to have a drink had been in prison with him. After each of these encounters, he would summarize their cases for me: "That one was in prison for thirteen years," or "he used to live in block 3," or "his brother was sentenced to death," and other such details. These people were defined by their imprisonment, but only to the initiated. When I asked him about each of their stories, he recounted them with such precision—names, dates, locations—that it was as if he was talking about his own life. The unnatural proximity in which prisoners are forced to live means that they all know the most intimate details of each other's lives, and they do not forget them.

These chance encounters on the streets of Kigali should have been moments of happiness, and in some respects they were, but most of these people seemed ill at ease in their new environment. It was as if they did not quite know what to do with themselves. I remembered what one former prisoner had told me a few years earlier, after his release: "We are always afraid of going back in there. . . . It frightens us. We are not free."

Released prisoners in Rwanda are always afraid of being re-arrested. That fear is well founded and still rules their lives from day to day. The fear was accentuated by the *gacaca* trials, in which even prisoners who had been tried and acquitted by the regular courts found themselves re-arrested, sometimes on the same charges. Many former prisoners lived in dread, waiting to be summoned by their local *gacaca* court, unable to predict what would happen if they were suddenly faced with new, or old, accusations. Watching the ease with which witnesses and judges were corrupted only heightened their anxiety. Beyond the anxieties of individual prisoners, this fear has led to a deeper, moral confusion and uncertainty, which runs throughout Rwandan society. One prisoner told me: "All Rwandans are afraid of being arrested one day. . . . Innocent people are no longer even sure they are innocent."

Just as prisoners were at the bottom of the government's list of priorities in the years following the genocide, so former prisoners remain at the bottom of the pile today. Despite much talk of reconciliation and reintegration, there is nothing to help guide them in their new world. Politically and socially, they are disenfranchised. There is no recognition of the hardships they have suffered and, correspondingly, no support for them whatsoever. There are no counseling services, or at least none that they feel able to use, as they tend to assume that these are reserved for genocide survivors; there is no help in the form of training or coaching to enable them to find work and reintegrate into society.

Many prisoners and former prisoners, as well as their families, harbor feelings of bitterness and resentment at the suffering they endured in prison, at the denial of justice for so many years, and at the continuing failure by the government, and society as a whole, to recognize the wrong that was done to them. One prisoner told me: "The government has created a system of vindictiveness in people's hearts."[10]

It is tempting to think that the worst of Rwanda's prison problem is over. In some respects, the immediate crisis has passed, if we define it in terms of life-threatening conditions or the number of unprocessed case files. But the legacy of the prison crisis cannot be disposed of so easily, and the crisis itself cannot be reduced to statistics. Rwanda's prisoners are individuals with their own history, with memories, with lives to lead, and with a contribution to make to the reconstruction of their country. Many have been left wondering where they belong in contemporary Rwanda.

The treatment of prisoners over the last seventeen years throws a long shadow over the new Rwanda. The grievances of prisoners and their families relating to years of unlawful imprisonment have still not been addressed, and there is no sign that the government intends to address them in the near future. Furthermore, the fact that thousands of prisoners were left to die in silence between 1994 and 1999 remains one of several dark chapters of the post-genocide years for which no one has been held to account.

Notes

1. Straus estimates the number of perpetrators at 175,000–210,000 (Straus 2006, 115–18).
2. This is an approximate total, which nongovernmental organizations (NGOs) working in the prisons used as an unofficial estimate at the time. Official figures were

slightly lower. No one knows exactly how many prisoners were held during this period, as statistics were unreliable and did not include the hundreds or possibly thousands held in unofficial or secret detention centers.

3. At the end of 2004, around 90 percent of Rwanda's prisoners were accused of genocide. Following large-scale releases from 2005 on, the proportions have evened out. In July 2009, according to Rwandan government statistics, just over half (38,000) were accused of genocide, while the rest (23,260) were accused of common crimes.

4. For information about *gacaca*, see reports published by Penal Reform International (PRI) and Avocats sans frontières (ASF), and Rettig, chap. 12, this volume. For information about prisoners' own system of *gacaca*, introduced inside the prisons, see Tertsakian 2008, 364–66.

5. For information on TIG, see PRI 2007. There has been a tendency to portray TIG as the equivalent of prisoner releases. In reality, a sizeable proportion of prisoners carrying out TIG have done so in camps, which, in some respects, can be compared to open-air prisons. The work involves physically demanding labor, such as stonecutting and construction.

6. The exceptions are prisoners transferred from the International Criminal Tribunal for Rwanda (ICTR) or extradited to Rwanda from other countries.

7. The ICRC had gradually reduced its assistance since 2000, and especially after 2005. The results were mixed, with prisoners complaining that the government was not fulfilling its side of the bargain. By 2008–9, the government appeared to have gained better control, though prisoners still complained about the provision of food and medical care.

8. The system was developed by PRI. After a long period of preparation, this database was set up in the prisons in January 2009. Prison staff began using it during the course of the year, but as of August 2009 it was not fully operational.

9. The period 1996–99 was marked by attacks against Tutsi civilians by armed groups composed of individuals who had taken part in the genocide. These attacks were met with a brutal counterinsurgency operation by the Rwandan army, targeting not only the insurgents but also Hutu civilians accused of collaborating with them. Many Hutu prisoners accused of genocide were perceived as sympathetic to the aims of the insurgents.

10. Not all former prisoners feel this way. Some, especially the younger ones, have adopted a more pragmatic attitude and are trying to resume a range of activities, almost as if nothing has happened, finding it convenient, perhaps, that this painful episode of their lives remains unacknowledged. They allow themselves to be swept along, like everyone else, in the frantic pace of change—learning English, teaching themselves how to use computers, applying for jobs, trying to fit in.

References

Amnesty International. 2002. "Gacaca: A Question of Justice." AFR 47/007/2002. December. http://www.amnesty.org/en/library/info/AFR47/007/2002.

Penal Reform International (PRI). 2004. "From Camp to Hill: The Reintegration of Released Prisoners." Research Report on the Gacaca 6. London, May. http://www.penalreform.org/files/rep-ga6-2004-released-prisoners-en_o.pdf.

———. 2007. "Community Service (TIG) Areas of Reflection." Monitoring and Research Report on the Gacaca. March. http://www.essex.ac.uk/ARMEDCON/story_id/000875.pdf.

Straus, Scott. 2006. *The Order of Genocide: Race, Power, and War in Rwanda*. Ithaca, NY: Cornell University Press.

Tertsakian, Carina. 2008. *Le Château: The Lives of Prisoners in Rwanda*. London: Arves Books.

Part IV

Rural Reengineering

14

High Modernism at the Ground Level

The Imidugudu *Policy in Rwanda*

CATHARINE NEWBURY

Land is the source of powerful emotions as well as critical resources in contemporary Africa. As Issa Shivji reminds us, land issues constitute an important "terrain of democratic struggles in Africa" (Shivji 1996, quoted in Bowen 2000, 210). Therefore state-sponsored efforts to reshape the rural landscape test the legitimacy of postcolonial governments, and often illustrate the dynamics of (and the possibilities for) democratic participation. But at a more fundamental level the politics of land merits our attention because millions of people depend directly on access to land for their very subsistence. Where the perceived responsibilities of the government for economic development—sometimes defined by outside financial agencies, sometimes encouraged by internal initiatives—potentially compromise access to land on the part of rural residents, tension often arises.

In the past twenty years, many countries in Africa have engaged in efforts to revise land policies and laws; land issues remain volatile in Côte d'Ivoire, Kenya, Zimbabwe, South Africa, and many other states. In contemporary Rwanda, land issues are particularly sensitive and not only because of the country's recent history. First of all, Rwanda remains one of the most densely populated countries in Africa and simultaneously one where more than 80 percent of the population is rural—reflecting one of the lowest urbanization rates in Africa. Therefore most people rely directly on agrarian output for their material survival. Second, there is deepening inequity in land access, with large holdings and microholdings (as well as landlessness) both increasing. At the same time, Rwanda is a country that has seen successive waves of people returning from diverse historical layers of migration. These returning refugees often advance claims to particular land plots, formerly their own, with the result that many plots have overlapping claims embedded in histories of flight. Finally, Rwanda's current administration rests on fragile legitimacy and is characterized by increasingly narrow ethnic composition. Thus, land reconfigurations defined from above may be doubly incendiary.

Also significant are ambitious new agrarian policies promoted assertively by the post-genocide government in Rwanda. These policies, designed to commercialize production and encourage regional specialization in crops that grow best in particular regions, regulate what rural producers can grow in some regions of the country, when they should plant, and how they may market their crops. The policies often entail substantial coercion and are resented by rural people because of the threat to their food security and the harsh penalties for noncompliance (Ansoms 2009; Huggins 2009; Ingelaere 2007).

In such a highly charged political terrain, Rwanda's leaders might have been expected to take a gradualist, consultative approach to changing land policy, one that would have encouraged broad-based participation and given real voice to the concerns of diverse constituencies, including rural producers. This chapter attempts to understand why that did not happen in post-genocide Rwanda. It focuses on *imidugudu*, a government-sponsored program of villagization to replace the traditional Rwandan residence pattern of scattered homesteads.[1] But villagization was not new to African political history. In Africa and beyond, such policies have had disastrous consequences. The following discussion explains why the Rwandan government pushed ahead with villagization despite these histories and explores whether Rwanda will be able to avoid the fate faced by those earlier programs.

High Modernism and Villagization

The *imidugudu* project was conceived by the state and its agents with little input from the population and justified through the use of a "high modernist" discourse. James Scott's *Seeing Like a State* provides uncanny insights into understanding the nature of the political processes at work. Scott's study, which includes the case of villagization in Tanzania during the 1970s, identifies "a pernicious combination of four elements in these large-scale forms of social engineering that ended in disaster" (1998, 4). The four elements underlying such schemes include the following:

- A bureaucratic state concerned with the administrative ordering of state and society, and attempting to make the social landscape legible;
- A "high modernist" ideology involving uncritical belief in the possibilities for the comprehensive planning of human settlement and production;
- The presence of an authoritarian state willing to use the full weight of its coercive power to bring these designs into being; and
- A civil society that lacks the capacity to resist these plans (ibid., 4–5).

Elsewhere in Africa, villagization programs have often entailed substantial coercion, even when the program initially was meant to be voluntary. In Tanzania, Mozambique, and Ethiopia, for example, villagization was imposed through a top-down process with little prior planning, and the government lacked adequate resources to supply services and amenities to the villages (Leeuwen 2001, 625–30); high administrative costs (borne by households) often led to high social costs—a resistant peasantry. Villagization has also had negative environmental effects, through deforestation, the overuse of fields near villages, or, for individual households, the loss of access to multiple plots in diverse micro-ecologies, which served as protection against unpredictable weather patterns; for peasant households risk aversion was more important than profit maximization, and scattered landholdings were essential to that strategy. Many villagization programs saw labor shortages become more acute and production decline, because people had to travel longer distances to reach their fields from their consolidated settlements. Distance from their fields also contributed to uncertainty and concern among rural dwellers about losing their rights to land or their harvests. With consolidated settlement came increased accusations of theft and sorcery. In Tanzania, villagization generated an accelerated rural exodus to the towns during the 1970s; contrary to the cooperative ideology of *ujamaa* (the notion that development should be participatory and egalitarian, promoting the common good), opportunities for accumulation by rich peasants actually increased. Where these effects took place, villagization programs spawned resentment toward the governments that imposed them (Lorgen 1999; Scott 1998).

To illustrate his point, Scott finds instructive certain parallels between villagization in Tanzania and collectivization in the Soviet Union under Stalin. He emphasizes that the "'softer' version of authoritarian high modernism" found in Tanzania differed from policies in the Soviet Union; villagization in Tanzania did not have as far-reaching and brutal consequences as Soviet collectivization. Nevertheless, compulsory villagization in Tanzania resembled

Soviet collectivization in several significant dimensions: a common emphasis on a logic of "improvement," a shared aesthestic that highlighted visual images of order and efficiency (such as the representation of a well-ordered village) over agrarian results, and a state tendency to ignore—or dismiss—local knowledge (1998, 224). According to Scott:

Like Soviet collectives, ujamaa villages were economic and ecological failures. For ideological reasons, the designers of the new society had . . . also forgotten the most important fact about social engineering: its efficiency depends on the cooperation of real human subjects. If people find the new arrangement, however efficient in principle, to be hostile to their dignity, their plans, and their tastes, they can *make* it an inefficient arrangement. (ibid., 225)

Time and again it has been shown that bureaucratic logic is no substitute for agrarian experience.

Land and Rural Radicalism in Rwandan History

State-building that involves efforts to create "legibility" and standardization of rural peasantries—leading to greater control—have a long history in Rwanda, shaped significantly by both pre-colonial patterns of governance and colonial social engineering. A major characteristic of these patterns of governance and official discourse is that they tend to be dismissive of peasants and unresponsive to local knowledge. If anything, these aspects appear to be intensified in post-genocide Rwanda (see Ansoms, chap. 15, this volume; Ansoms 2008, 2009; Musahara and Huggins 2005; Huggins 2009; Ingelaere 2007; Pottier 2006). Similarly, although a "high modernist" ideology of development so attractive to decision makers is not new to Rwanda, it has gained an assertive ascendance with the post-genocide government.

Under Belgian rule the colonial state in Rwanda intruded significantly in rural production. From the 1930s, many rural producers were required to grow coffee for export and forced to cultivate certain food crops resistant to drought, as part of an anti-famine program. The rural population was also mobilized to drain marshes, construct terraces, and dig anti-erosion ditches. Altogether these measures constituted a massive labor commitment, which fell most heavily, and in many areas exclusively, on Hutu. By the end of the colonial period, the rural landscape was significantly stratified by wealth; most of the wealthy benefited from employment by the state. Those chiefs and subchiefs who formed the lower levels of the colonial administration and who had the wherewithal to hire—or command—labor for their fields were able to benefit from expanding cash-crop production, such as coffee. By no means were all Tutsi wealthy and powerful, but since all the chiefs and most of the subchiefs were Tutsi, ethnicity was an important perception in rural stratification (C. Newbury 1988; Newbury and Newbury 2000).

As independence approached, struggles over access to land fueled rural radicalism during the political competition of the 1950s: when the Visiting Mission from the UN Trusteeship Council visited Rwanda in 1957, they encountered peasants lining the roads with placards reading: "nos champs s'il vous plaît" (our fields, please). After independence in 1962, land remained a nexus of local conflicts, but the ethnic dimension of these tensions radically shifted. In each commune the *bourgmestre* (chief magistrate, normally Hutu) presided over distribution of the land of Tutsi who had fled various episodes of ethnic violence from 1959 through 1964; the beneficiaries, for the most part, were Hutu. With population growth and concomitant pressures for more agricultural land, there was a gradual conversion of former pasturage to cultivation. The numbers of cattle per capita declined, while small livestock such as goats and pigs increased (Bézy 1990, 22–23; Nzisabira 1995). Still, cattle remained an important signifier of prestige and wealth. Population growth during the 1970s and 1980s also contributed to growing land scarcity. Increased pressures on land in the north and central regions led to significant internal migration toward less densely settled areas in the east and southeast of Rwanda, where land was more available but agriculture more risky because of irregular rainfall (Olson 1994). By the 1980s a gathering rural crisis was evident in distress sales of land and more numerous and more intense conflicts over land rights (André 1998).

Increasing immiseration of the rural population and a growing gap between rich and poor contributed to the delegitimation of the Second Republic, led by Juvénal Habyarimana (C. Newbury 1992). In the late 1980s and early 1990s, rural resentments boiled to the surface. Land access and agrarian policies more generally were not the only issues, but these were at the root of many grievances. Many rural producers found themselves unable to make ends meet, while corruption and accumulation increased among some high government officials.[2] One indication of the decline in government legitimacy was a significant drop in attendance at public meetings called by commune authorities. Another was resentment over unpaid communal labor for public works (*umuganda*). From 1988, rural producers in some areas destroyed their coffee trees to show their anger at government agricultural policies (de Lame 1996). Because postcolonial governments had retained colonial regulations making it illegal to interplant food crops with coffee trees (or to cut down coffee trees), uprooting coffee trees reflected resistance to government regulations. It also served as a form of withdrawal from the international commodity markets; many people preferred to grow bananas. Unlike coffee, yields from banana groves can be turned into banana beer for which there is an assured local market; income from a banana grove is spread more evenly throughout the year, whereas income from the coffee harvest comes only once a year; and bananas are not subject to the vagaries of the export market.[3]

By the 1980s, landlessness affected certain categories of people particularly harshly. Where pressure on available land was especially intense, young people (especially young women) and the very poor were more likely than others to be excluded from access to land. There is also evidence that where men bought land for themselves, they normally would not divide such land among their sons and did not follow the practices associated with lineage land held under customary rules; those who obtained land through purchase rejected claims based on custom (André 1998).

Although land scarcity was not the cause of the genocide, access to land was nonetheless manipulated by people connected with the state-organized genocide (D. Newbury 1999).[4] As Alison Des Forges pointed out, those who participated in gangs that attacked Tutsi sometimes were rewarded with land. Rural *bourgmestres* took the fields of Tutsi who had been killed and distributed these to Hutu for cultivation. In particular, leaders of militia bands apparently received greater benefits than others in the allocation of land (Des Forges 1999, 299–300). In fact, one of the reasons for compiling lists of those killed was to determine if their deaths left land vacant—or if there were remaining family members who had also to be killed to make that so. Yet during the genocide, distribution of property that had belonged to Tutsi, as well as booty looted from development projects, schools, and hospitals, gave rise to disputes among Hutu. Most of those involved in such conflicts "fought not over money but over land, cattle, or crops" (ibid., 299). Conflict over land was not always ethnic; class was also a consideration. For example, in the northwest (and possibly elsewhere), the violent events of the genocide provided opportunities for militias to attack not only Tutsi but also Hutu who had larger landholdings than others on their hill (André and Platteau 1998).

The post-genocide government therefore inherited a complex land matrix whose layered contours had been formed over many decades. The complexity of land claims was daunting. But the strong sense of mission on the part of the Rwandan Patriotic Front (RPF) and a belief that it knows what is best for the population have led the leaders to claim that they can modernize the country more effectively and more rapidly than the previous post-colonial regimes; indeed they are proud to have achieved as much as they have in only seventeen years of post-genocide rule. In fact, what may have been seen by some as an impediment became an asset: since key decision makers are returnees from exile and therefore relative newcomers to Rwanda, many had never lived in Rwanda—at least not as farmers—and therefore they could be guided by their planning unencumbered by the realities on the ground. When the *imidugudu* policy was introduced in 1996, most of these leaders had only limited knowledge of local dynamics, let alone of local ecologies. Rwanda is also a highly authoritarian state, in which the military plays an important role; assisted by infusions of grants and loans from donors, the state commands substantial coercive power, and civil society was prostrate after the genocide. Therefore Scott's components of the culture of high modernism were all in place: a highly bureaucratic state apparatus, a belief in the need for social engineering, an authoritarian political culture, and a disorganized civil society lacking the capacity to influence policy collectively.

Many civil society groups have subsequently reemerged or been created, and some of these organizations have made valiant efforts to participate in debates over reconstruction and development. But on issues of villagization there are strong constraints to vigorous involvement by civil society in Rwanda. The most important is the fact that the *imidugudu* policy was initially defined as a security issue; when it comes to security the limits to dissent permitted by the government are narrow. Second, the legacy of Rwanda's deeper culture of politics encourages compliance with the powerful and discourages open dissent. Third, the post-genocide government has successfully extended the reach of the state into many of Rwanda's church groups, human rights organizations, and other associations (see Longman, chap. 1, this volume; Longman, forthcoming).

The *Imidugudu* Policy

After the genocide, the Rwandan government was faced with the challenge of providing places to live for the hundreds of thousands of "old-case returnees"—those who fled in the early 1960s or early 1970s, often the allies (or charges) of the RPF now in power. Many of these people, who are mostly Tutsi, initially occupied the houses and expropriated the land of people who had died or fled; some of them actually reclaimed their former residences, others simply took whatever land was convenient. Significant additional pressures occurred with the 1996–97 return from Tanzania and Congo of about 1.5 million "new-case" returnees—mostly Hutu who had fled from Rwanda in 1994. The government first decided that construction of houses for the Tutsi repatriates should take place in villages—as a practical matter, as a security measure, and to promote development goals.[5] But this practice was expanded into a policy to cover all new housing construction. Aid was tightly controlled: donors who provided assistance for "shelter" were allowed to build only in specified villages or in places near a road designated by a *bourgmestre*.

In 1999 the Ministry of Land (MINITERE) announced that "the ultimate objective of the government is to enable the entire rural population to live in the grouped settlements" (HRW 2001, 85). The Rwandan government argued that the policy had four main advantages:

- Grouping houses in villages brings the population close to roads, facilitates provision of water and other services, and improves people's access to schools and health clinics;
- Villagization permits more rational use of land since housing can be constructed on less fertile land, and the broad enclosures typical of rural Rwanda households can be reduced in size;
- Villagization can encourage income-earning activities for residents; and
- Villagization will provide better security for people and property (ADL 2000, 5).

Because the central government defined villagization as a security issue and mandated that it should be implemented throughout the country, it was difficult to debate with government officials the relative merits and disadvantages of such a policy. "Security" touched on psychological perceptions as well as empirical realities—and was the monopoly of the state. Rwandans hesitated to question villagization openly, for such opposition could be—and often was—interpreted as unwillingness to recognize the losses, trauma, and fears of genocide survivors. Despite skepticism about the policy among many internal and international organizations, most donors nevertheless went ahead with "shelter" programs, based on villagization schemes (Hilhorst and van Leeuwen 1999; Van Hoyweghen 1999, 2000).[6]

On occasion, expatriates voiced their concern, noting the patterns of government-directed villagization elsewhere in Africa, which invariably have involved force, problems with implementation, and decline of agricultural productivity. At one point, the minister of lands responded, "Rwanda cannot and should not base its rural development and settlement planning on comparison to other countries where similar programs have failed" (Leeuwen 2001, 632). Rwandan officials also countered skepticism with explanations based on a high modernist ideology that promised future development benefits. I heard Rwandan government officials state that rural Rwandans living in scattered settlement patterns are primitive and that moving them into villages is a way to make them more modern and developed. In addition, some compared *imidugudu* to primary education, a policy innovation in the 1930s that was initially resisted but is now widely accepted.

Beyond official pronouncements, when one takes a closer look at the implementation of the *imidugudu* policy over time, several patterns are evident. Between 1996 and 1999, most of the population in the southeast (formerly Kibungo Prefecture) and northeast (then Umutara Prefecture) was required to move into houses built along roads or in villages. Officials in these areas promoted villagization because of the need for housing and land to accommodate returnees, and for security against guerilla incursions in areas near the border. In 1994, Kibungo and parts of Umutara had lost about two-thirds of their previous population as a result of the genocide; many people were killed and hundreds of thousands of others (mostly Hutu) fled to Tanzania. Meanwhile, after the genocide, large numbers of repatriates ("old-case" refugees, mainly Tutsi) moved into these same areas from Uganda, Tanzania, and Burundi; they took up residence wherever they could find space. Therefore, when the new-case Hutu refugees returned to Kibungo in 1996, many of them found their houses and land occupied by old-case refugees who after the genocide had themselves returned from earlier exile. Rather than requiring the old-case refugees to cede houses to their former owners, the local authorities required everyone to move into villages. Most nongovernmental organizations (NGOs) provided assistance in building some of the *imidugudu*, but in effect most people had to build their own houses, usually with some assistance such as roofing materials provided by donor aid. By 1999, 80 percent of the population in these two prefectures lived in villages. In Kibungo, redistribution of land also occurred, as local officials instructed the former residents to divide their land with the newcomers.

In the northwest, in the then prefectures of Gisenyi and Ruhengeri, villagization followed a different pattern. During 1997 and 1998 this was a war zone, where Hutu *abacengezi* ("insurgents," or "rebels") made sporadic attacks on army installations, killed local officials, and attacked Tutsi refugees who had fled from ethnic violence in the Congo. The *abacengezi* claimed to be fighting to liberate Hutu from Tutsi oppression. But Hutu civilians in the north became the main victims of these conflicts. The Rwandan Patriotic Army (RPA) retaliated mercilessly against the civilian (Hutu) population who were suspected of providing succor and support to the guerillas. Cultivation of crops suffered, and even basic survival became difficult. Hundreds of thousands of Hutu were forced to flee; they moved to large temporary camps—each with

40,000 people or more living in unhealthy and literally deadly conditions. Thus, when the Rwandan government proceeded to implement villagization in these areas of the northwest in 1999, the policy bore a troubling similarity to the "protected villages" strategy used by armies in counterinsurgency contexts elsewhere. As one diplomat (otherwise well disposed to the Rwandan government) commented at the time, "I've talked to farmers, local officials, even some ministers, and all think this a bad idea. . . . They talk about having consulted everyone, but it is another case of the top-down approach: we think for them" (*Economist* 1999, 43). Most people had no assistance in building their houses in the *imidugudu*, and this was a particularly difficult burden for female-headed households (Burnet and RISD 2001).

It is difficult to assess the overall impact of *imidugudu* given the lack of reliable data. Human Rights Watch (HRW) estimated that 225,000 households (or just over a million people) were living in *imidugudu* at the end of 1999 (HRW 2001). Writing in 2005, two land experts put the figure at nearly 2 million people, but this was concentrated in three former provinces: 92 percent of the population in both Kibungo and Umutara, and 53 percent in Ruhengeri. In other provinces, only about 4 percent of the population was living in *imidugudu* (Musahara and Huggins 2005, 326; see also Takeuchi and Marara 2000, 29–31). A 2004 media account stated that the government had built approximately 300,000 houses as part of its *imidugudu* program (IRIN 2004).

To date, the results of *imidugudu* are disappointing: many households are worse off both in terms of housing quality and land possession. The policy failed to decrease pressure on available land holdings, and in many cases even created or deepened land conflicts. Yet the government has repeatedly reaffirmed its commitment to villagization. As one government official stated in 2004: "Despite some shortcomings in implementing this policy, the government still firmly believes that *imidugudu* represents the only feasible alternative to Rwanda's land population equation for the foreseeable future" (IRIN 2004). Various drafts of District Development Programs in mid-2007 refer to villagization as a specific policy objective. In late 2009 a prominent parliamentarian told local leaders in the Eastern Province (formerly Kibungo and Umutara provinces) that "we as Rwandans have no alternative but to live in Midugudu [*sic*]. It thus has to be every one's responsibility, to see to it that people are settled according to the acceptable norms" (Rwembeho 2009). With the reorganization and remapping of Rwanda's administrative units in 2005, the government applied the term *imidugudu* to local-level administrative units that had previously been designated as *cellules*. This shift, which may be part of a deliberate strategy, has made it difficult to differentiate between planned villages and local neighborhoods.

Views from Below

As Scott has reminded us in *Seeing Like a State*, those who would reshape the rural landscape without paying attention to what rural dwellers are doing and want to do—and the complex ways in which they have adapted to harsh, insecure environments—are likely to meet with resistance, outcomes rather different from announced goals, and often failure. This section examines how *imidugudu* has fared.

In the late 1990s, two Rwandan NGOs conducted research on villagization and voiced concerns about the way it was being implemented (ADL 1999; RISD 1999).[7] In September 1999, one of these groups, the Rwanda Initiative for Sustainable Development (RISD), sponsored a workshop in Kigali on Land Use and Villagisation in Rwanda (Palmer 1999). The tone of the workshop was cautious and respectful of government directives. For example, discussions started from the premise that "there is no alternative" to villagization. Moreover, the two surveys conducted among inhabitants of *imidugudu* were intended not to discredit the policy but to gather information that could help to improve it. Still, the workshop's conclusions and the studies' findings were unequivocal: inadequate planning and confusion about directives from the central government had led to incoherent policy regarding villagization at the local level. At that point, most of the villages lacked services and amenities, and little had been done to involve rural people in the planning, layout, and placement of villages. In some regions, people were obliged to destroy their homes and then move to a village where they had to build new houses, often with little or no assistance. And, in most cases no compensation was given to people whose land was expropriated to serve as the sites for *imidugudu*. Subsequent studies by HRW (2001) and researchers (e.g., Van Hoyweghen 1999, 2000) have reinforced those findings.

Resettlement in *imidugudu* was meant to be voluntary. A high-ranking government official gave assurances in 1997 that "no one will be forced to go along with a program of villagization" (HRW 2001, 14). But when many people proved less than willing to move, local officials used coercion: threats, fines, and even destruction of existing shelters (ibid., 14, 19–38).[8] In recent years, the government has created local *imidugudu* committees ostensibly to make implementation more participatory. Yet, policy implementation remains largely prescriptive and top-down. When some local leaders complained about the competence of the *imidugudu* committees, a parliamentarian told them to educate those committees: "You all know the required size of Mudugudu [*sic*], let them know the number of houses recommended in a particular Mudugudu for the purposes of resettling residents" (Rwembeho 2009).

Many people living in *imidugudu* became less economically secure. A key aspect of economic security involves how far a rural inhabitant's fields are located from the residence. If fields are distant, it is difficult for producers to carry out the intensive cultivation characteristic of Rwanda's agrarian system. People living in the *imidugudu* had to travel significantly farther to reach their fields and to fetch firewood than before they had moved. As one *umudugudu* resident told a journalist, "We are forced to move kilometers away to access land for cultivation. This becomes difficult for a person my age" (IRIN 2004). Time is a constraint, and so is the ability to enrich the soil with nutrients (e.g., compost from household garbage and manure from goats or other livestock). Having to travel a long distance to reach the fields reduces the time available for caring for crops, and this places a special burden on female heads of household, who are already overworked. In addition, placing farmers at a long distance from their fields exposes their crops to theft. Furthermore, it was difficult to keep goats, cattle, or other livestock in the *imidugudu* because of lack of space and lack of pasturage nearby.

Specialists familiar with agricultural production in rural Rwanda might note another concern. There is a saying that what makes banana groves thrive is "the smoke from houses"—banana trees grow best when proximate to homes, a recognition of the important role of compost and latrines in the healthy growth of banana plants, and the multiple uses of banana leaves and trunks. The banana grove surrounding a home also provides shade, protection from the wind, and a pleasing aesthetic environment. But in most *imidugudu* the house plots are too small to allow room for a garden around the house, and often inadequate space or no assistance with building materials was provided for construction of a latrine for each house. This is not something to bother a technocrat, but such cultural claims to dignity and propriety are essential to social life.[9]

A decade after the *imidugudu* policy was introduced, Des Forges observed that although "Rwandan authorities put forward the villagization policy as a way to improve the lives of ordinary Rwandans, . . . the perceptions of many residents of these settlements is that they are poorer now than they were before they moved" (Des Forges 2006, 363). In northwestern Rwanda, for example, results of a 2005 study by the Global IDP Project showed that of 192,000 families needing housing in *imidugudu*, only 12,000 had received assistance. None of the residents had sufficient land, adequate food, or the means to pay for school fees and medical care. Moreover, Des Forges noted, "As was the case with villages created in eastern Rwanda, some of the land confiscated as part of the process was later taken over by military officers. In order to stay alive, some village residents had to seek day labor on the land they used to own. Some working as laborers for others now earn only about 100 Rwandan francs" (Des Forges 2006, 362–63).

The *imidugudu* policy has reinforced social tensions around land, often along ethnic lines. A 1998 study in Kibungo Prefecture found "that people tend to interpret the programme in political and ethnical terms and this has consequences for their intentions, strategies and everyday practices" (Hilhorst and Leeuwen 1999, 36–37). Thus, RISD, the United Nations High Commissioner for Refugees (UNHCR), and HRW found that most *imidugudu* were occupied by a single ethnic group (HRW 2001, 61). HRW wrote:

The move to *imidugudu* may even have promoted ethnic segregation by disturbing previously existing housing patterns, which were often ethnically diverse. In those *imidugudu* that were ethnically mixed, the resources available to Hutu were often much less than those available to Tutsi, a difference that exacerbated tensions in some cases. (ibid., 61)

Concluding Remarks

Rwanda's ambitious *imidugudu* policy has failed in three key respects: (1) it quickly became coercive, much like the later program of *gacaca* courts (see Rettig, chap. 12, this volume); (2) it reduced economic security and quality of life; and (3) it increased social tensions, particularly along ethnic lines. These failures should have come as no surprise. Rwanda refused to heed the disastrous consequences that villagization programs have had in other African states and ignored concerns from donors, human rights NGOs, and local people. Yet, despite all this, the RPF continues to forge ahead with its high-modernist plan to reshape rural Rwanda. In the end, the ones who are paying the price—ecologically, socially, and politically—are the country's rural producers.

Notes

I am grateful to David Newbury and Lars Waldorf for helpful comments on an earlier version of this chapter. I would also like to thank several institutions that have provided generous support for my research: the Institute for Advanced Study, the Program in Agrarian Studies at Yale University, and the John D. and Catherine T. MacArthur Foundation Research and Writing Grant Program.

1. *Imidugudu* (singular, *umudugudu*) is the Kinyarwanda term used for villages, with houses built close together near or alongside a road.

2. In a term evocative of the class inequality in the society, poor rural dwellers—both Hutu and Tutsi—referred to those in power as *abaryi* (eaters) (Gasana 2000, 212; see also Bigagaza, Abong, and Mukarubuga 2002, 52).

3. Failure to mulch coffee trees adequately during the dry season was another form

of less open resistance, with an important gender dimension. Women and children were the main family members responsible for mulching the coffee plants to protect them from hot sun during the dry season. This required substantial work, often carrying leaves from banana gardens to nourish the coffee fields. Agricultural reports of the 1980s regularly voiced concern that rural people were not attending to proper mulching of coffee trees; in fact women were withdrawing their labor from an activity that brought them little benefit.

4. See also Rose (2007). Diverging from those who assume "that land scarcity in Rwanda is linked to or contributed to the genocide," Laurel Rose argues that "the genocide influenced land-grabbing during the war and continues to influence interpretations of and responses to land-grabbing after the war" (2007, 49).

5. It was also noted that the Arusha Accords of 1993 called for locating returnees from exile in villages.

6. One reason for this was the pressure to act quickly to provide humanitarian aid in the post-conflict "emergency" context. Once the emergency phase had passed, some donors began withdrawing support from the villagization program. This was partly a response to evidence that in some areas people were forced to destroy perfectly good houses to move into villages, and indications that villagization might actually erode peasants' ability to produce more food more efficiently. For a detailed discussion of donor and NGO involvement in *imidugudu*, see HRW 2001, 74–91.

7. The ADL study was based on a total of 495 interviews conducted in a sample of thirty-four *imidugudu* in sixteen communes, distributed among the ten prefectures of the country. The RISD study was based on individual interviews and focus group discussions conducted in villages of four prefectures: Kigali Rural, Ruhengeri, Gikongoro, and Butare. With particular reference to women's land rights, see Burnet and RISD 2001.

8. Since overt resistance to government policy in post-genocide Rwanda is risky, discontent is more commonly expressed through "everyday forms of resistance," what James Scott (1985) has called "weapons of the weak." For an analysis of such strategies in post-genocide Rwanda, see Thomson 1999.

9. Rwandan advocates of the *imidugudu* policy assured me that the villages that lacked latrines and space for kitchens were just poorly planned; blame was placed on expatriate donors who, these Rwandans alleged, sometimes did shoddy work and did not care about the outcome. There is considerable variability in the quality of house construction in *imidugudu* and size of house plots. But few of the villages provide sufficient space for a food garden near each house.

References

Association rwandaise pour la défense des droits de la personne et des libertés publiques (ADL). 2000. "Etude sur la situation des droits humains dans les villages *imidugudu*." January.

André, Catherine. 1998. "Terre rwandaise, accès, politique et reforme foncières." In

High Modernism at the Ground Level

L'Afrique des Grands Lacs: Annuaire 1997–1998, edited by Filip Reyntjens and Stefaan Marysse, 141–73. Paris: L'Harmattan.

André, Catherine, and Phillip Platteau. 1998. "Land Relations under Unbearable Stress: Rwanda Caught in the Malthusian Trap." *Journal of Economic Behavior and Organization* 34, no. 1: 1–47.

Ansoms, An. 2008. "Striving for Growth, Bypassing the Poor? A Critical Review of Rwanda's Rural Sector Policies." *Journal of Modern African Studies* 46, no. 1: 1–32.

———. 2009. "Re-Engineering Rural Society: The Visions and Ambitions of the Rwandan Elite." *African Affairs* 108, no. 431: 289–309.

Bézy, Fernand. 1990. "Rwanda 1962–1989: Bilan socio-économique d'un régime." Institut d'Etudes du Développement. January. http://www.uclouvain.be/cps/ucl/doc/ucl/documents/besy_rwanda.HTML.

Bigagaza, Jean, Carolyne Abong, and Cecile Mukarubuga. 2002. "Land Scarcity, Distribution and Conflict in Rwanda." In *Scarcity and Surfeit: The Ecology of Africa's Conflicts*, edited by Jeremy Lind and Kathryn Sturman, 50–82. Pretoria: Institute for Security Studies.

Bowen, Merle L. 2000. *The State against the Peasantry: Rural Struggles in Colonial and Postcolonial Mozambique.* Charlottesville: University Press of Virginia.

Burnet, Jennie E., and RISD. 2001. "Culture, Practice and Law: Women's Access to Land in Rwanda." In *Women and Land in Africa: Culture, Religion and Realizing Women's Rights*, edited by L. Muthoni Wanyeki, 176–206. Claremont, South Africa: David Philip.

de Lame, Danielle. 1996. *Une colline entre mille ou le calme avant la tempête: Transformations et blocages du Rwanda rural.* Tervuren, Belgium: Musée Royal de l'Afrique Centrale.

Des Forges, Alison. 1999. *Leave None to Tell the Story: Genocide in Rwanda.* New York: Human Rights Watch.

———. 2006. "Land in Rwanda: Winnowing Out the Chaff." In *L'Afrique des Grands Lacs: Annuaire 2005–2006*, edited by Filip Reyntjens and Stefaan Marysse, 353–71. Paris: L'Harmattan.

Economist. 1999. January 13–19.

Gasana, James K. 2002. "Natural Resource Scarcity and Violence in Rwanda." In *Conserving the Peace: Resources, Livelihoods and Security*, edited by Mark Halle, Jason Mathew, and Jason Switzer, 199–246. Winnipeg: International Institute for Sustainable Development.

Hilhorst, Dorothea, and Mathijs van Leeuwen. 1999. "*Imidugudu*, Villagisation in Rwanda: A Case of Emergency Development?" Wageningen Disaster Studies. http://www.disasterstudies.wur.nl/NR/rdonlyres/E08690FD-1923-4358-B3B4-FBA2F7734B91/25004/no2villagisationinrwandartf.pdf.

Huggins, Chris. 2009. "Agricultural Policies and Local Grievances in Rural Rwanda." *Peace Review: A Journal of Social Justice* 21, no. 3: 296–303.

Huggins, Chris, and Jenny Clover, eds. 2005. *From the Ground Up: Land Rights, Conflict and Peace in Sub-Saharan Africa.* Pretoria: Institute for Security Studies.

Human Rights Watch (HRW). 2001. "Uprooting the Rural Poor in Rwanda." May 1. http://www.hrw.org/legacy/reports/2001/rwanda/.

Ingelaere, Bert. 2007. "Living the Transition: A Bottom-Up Perspective on Rwanda's Political Transition." Discussion Paper 2007.06. Institute of Development Policy and Management, University of Antwerp. http://www.ua.ac.be/objs/00172206 .pdf.

Integrated Regional Information Network (IRIN). 2004. "Rwanda: Government Implements Low-Cost Housing for Returnees." October 5. http://www.irinnews.org/report.aspx?reportid=51581.

Leeuwen, Mathijs van. 2001. "Rwanda's *Imidugudu* Programme and Earlier Experiences with Villagisation and Resettlement in East Africa." *Journal of Modern African Studies* 39, no. 4: 623–44.

Longman, Timothy. Forthcoming. "Memory, Justice, and Power in Post-Genocide Rwanda."

Lorgen, Christy Cannon. 1999. "The Experience of Villagisation: Lessons from Ethiopia, Mozambique, and Tanzania." Oxfam-GB. January. http://oxfam.org.uk/resources/learning/landrights/downloads/fullreport.rtf.

Musahara, Herman, and Chris Huggins. 2005. "Land Reform, Land Scarcity, and Post-conflict Reconstruction: A Case Study of Rwanda." In *From the Ground Up: Land Rights, Conflict and Peace in Sub-Saharan Africa*, edited by Chris Huggins and Jenny Clover, 269–346. Pretoria: Institute for Strategic Studies.

Newbury, Catharine. 1988. *The Cohesion of Oppression: Clientship and Ethnicity in Rwanda, 1860–1960*. New York: Columbia University Press.

———. 1992. "Rwanda: Recent Debates over Governance and Rural Development." In *Governance and Politics in Africa*, edited by Goran Hyden and Michael Bratton, 193–219. Boulder, CO: Westview Press.

Newbury, David. 1999. "Ecology and the Politics of Genocide: Rwanda 1994." *Cultural Survival Quarterly* 22, no. 4: 32–36.

Newbury, David, and Catharine Newbury. 2000. "Bringing the Peasants Back In: Agrarian Themes in the Construction and Corrosion of Statist Historiography in Rwanda." *American Historical Review* 105, no. 3: 832–77.

Nzisabira, Jean. 1995. "Système du pouvoir, pression démographique et pratiques agraires au Rwanda." In *Les Racines de la Violence dans la région des Grands-Lacs*, 65–79. Brussels: Les Verts au Parlement Européen.

Olson, Jennifer M. 1994. "Demographic Responses to Resource Constraints in Rwanda." Rwanda Society-Environment Project, Working Paper 7. September. Department of Geography and the Center for Advanced Study of International Development, Michigan State University.

Palmer, Robin. 1999. "Report on the Workshop on Land Use and Villagisation in Rwanda." Oxfam-GB. October. http://www.oxfam.org.uk/resources/learning/landrights/downloads/kigali.rtf.

Pottier, Johan. 2002. *Re-Imagining Rwanda: Conflict, Survival and Disinformation in the Late Twentieth Century*. Cambridge: Cambridge University Press.

———. 2006. "Land Reform for Peace? Rwanda's 2005 Land Law in Context." *Journal of Agrarian Change* 6, no. 4: 509–37.

Rwanda Initiative for Sustainable Development (RISD). 1999. "Land Use and Villagisation in Rwanda." Paper presented at the Land Use and Villagisation Workshop, Kigali, September 20–21. Oxfam-GB. http://www.oxfam.org.uk/resources/learning/landrights/downloads/risdpap.rtf.

Rose, Laurel. 2007. "Land and Genocide: Exploring the Connections with Rwanda's Prisoners and Prison Officials." *Journal of Genocide Research* 9, no. 1: 49–69.

Rwembeho, Stephen. 2009. "MPs Advise on Rural Settlement." *New Times*, October 1.

Shivji, Issa. 1996. "Land, the Terrain of Democratic Struggles in Africa." *CODESRIA Bulletin* 4: 23–26.

Scott, James C. 1985. *Weapons of the Weak: Everyday Forms of Peasant Resistance*. New Haven, CT: Yale University Press.

———. 1998. *Seeing Like a State: How Certain Schemes to Improve the Human Condition Have Failed*. New Haven, CT: Yale University Press.

Takeuchi, Shin'ichi, and Jean Marara. 2000. "Agriculture and Peasants in Rwanda: A Preliminary Report." Joint Research Program Series 127. Institute of Developing Economies, Japan External Trade Organization. http://www.ide.go.jp/English/Publish/Download/Jrp/127.html.

Thomson, Susan. 1999. "Resisting Reconciliation: State Power and Everyday Life in Post-Genocide Rwanda." PhD diss., Dalhousie University.

Van Hoyweghen, Saskia. 1999. "The Urgency of Land and Agrarian Reform in Rwanda." *African Affairs* 98, no. 392: 353–72.

———. 2000. "The Rwandan Villagisation Programme: Resettlement for Reconstruction?" In *Conflict and Ethnicity in Central Africa*, edited by Didier Goyvaerts, 208–24. Tokyo: Institute for the Study of Languages and Cultures of Asia and Africa, Tokyo University of Foreign Studies.

15 Rwanda's Post-Genocide Economic Reconstruction

The Mismatch between Elite Ambitions and Rural Realities

AN ANSOMS

In contrast to many other African states, Rwanda has a clear vision of how it wants to achieve economic progress and poverty reduction (MINECOFIN 2000, 2002, 2007). The overall aim of the current political elite is to transform Rwanda from a "low human development" to a "medium human development" country, as defined by the United Nations Development Programme's (UNDP) Human Development Index. To accomplish this, the government is pursuing ambitious social engineering of the rural sector. First, policymakers are attempting to transform the agricultural sector into a professionalized motor for economic growth, which leaves little room for traditional smallholder agriculture. Second, they are upgrading rural life, which hides the extent of poverty and inequality. Finally, policymakers are transforming Rwanda into a target-driven society from the highest to the lowest level. Overall, these three goals fit within a top-down developmentalist agenda where the state plays a central role in reshaping the rural environment.

Top-down, state-centered governance is not new to Rwanda. Nor are the rural-urban gap, the anti-rural bias in policymaking, and the state-society cleavage specific to the post-1994 period. But the current vision and ambition of the Rwandan elite go much farther than previous attempts at reform, and are all the more problematic, given that they see no role for small-scale peasants. This chapter provides a brief overview of Rwanda's economic recovery and then describes how the post-genocide political elite differ from their predecessors. Next, I analyze how current policymakers are realizing their three social engineering goals for rural society. The chapter concludes with some of the potential shortcomings and dangers of this project.

To capture the discourse of Rwandan policymakers, I draw on twenty-six interviews conducted between May and July 2007 with persons closely involved in poverty reduction, agricultural policy, and land policy. These included officials of the three ministries centrally engaged in rural development: the Economic Development and Poverty Reduction Strategy (EDPRS) department within the Ministry of Finance and Economic Planning (MINECOFIN); the Ministry of Agriculture and Animal Resources (MINAGRI); and the Ministry of Land (MINITERE). Alongside secondary data, these interviews provide a comprehensive picture of the present rural development discourse within government circles.[1] Then I draw from multiple focus-group interviews with distinct socioeconomic categories in six rural settings. These insights from the microlevel help contextualize the (potential) impact of social engineering on the ground.

Overview of Rwanda's Economic Reconstruction

After a devastating four-year civil war and an apocalyptic genocide in 1994, Rwanda's post-conflict reconstruction has certainly been impressive in many respects. The state was rebuilt at surprising speed and has provided service delivery in education, health, and infrastructure. Economic recovery has been exceptional: after an initial postwar boom, average annual growth remained high at 7.4 percent between 1997 and 2006 (Ansoms 2005). In 2008, GDP growth even reached 11.2 percent (IMF 2009a, 2009b). On the other hand, concerns have mounted in the past few years. Economic growth has not been accompanied by significant poverty reduction. While poverty decreased in percentage terms from 60.3 percent in 2001 to 56.9 percent in 2006, poverty actually increased in absolute terms from 4.82 to 5.38 million people over these same years. Furthermore, inequality increased from a Gini coefficient of

0.47 in 2001 to 0.51 in 2006 (MINECOFIN 2002, 2007). This is particularly worrisome as high levels of inequality are correlated with increased risk of conflict (Muller and Seligson 2008). Economic progress has been particularly limited in rural areas: the benefits of economic growth remain concentrated in the hands of a small class of agricultural entrepreneurs, while the majority of Rwandan peasants confront worsening living conditions. This is illustrated by the rising Gini in the rural setting from 0.37 in 2001 to 0.44 in 2006.

Rwandan policymakers are aware that poverty and inequality are growing problems. A government report reviewing the period from 2001 to 2006 acknowledges that "because growth over this period has been accompanied by increasing inequality, this has reduced its impact on the reduction of poverty levels" (RoR 2006, 7). Nevertheless, the government is extremely sensitive to any outside criticism. A 2007 report expressed strong concern over Rwanda's limited achievements in poverty reduction (UNDP 2007). The report was signed by James Musoni, the finance minister, who was also the chairman of the steering committee that oversaw the report's formulation. Two weeks after the report's launch, Musoni publicly disavowed it, claiming he had not read the final version and accusing the Swedish editor of adding unfounded and misleading interpretations (*New Times* 2007a). This was not an isolated incident: two years earlier, the government halted a World Bank study into rural livelihoods (Ingelaere 2010).

Elite Attitudes toward the Peasantry

Following the genocide, Rwanda has been ruled by a predominantly Anglophone Tutsi elite, who grew up in exile, mostly in cities or in cattle-farming areas. After their military victory in 1994, the new elite installed themselves in Kigali. This was partly for security reasons (as the countryside was still unstable between 1994 and 1999), but it also reflected that the returnees had lost many ties to their "hills of origin" and had little incentive to go back. As a European donor representative noted: "Many of the government officials have never known the Rwandan countryside. . . . [Kigali] is where they are concentrated now; it explains why they have limited knowledge and understandings of how peasants live" (interview, May 2007).

Not surprisingly, this new Tutsi elite has very different attitudes toward the peasantry than the previous Hutu elite. President Juvénal Habyarimana's regime (1973–94) had championed Rwanda as an agrarian society; indeed, the president often "glorified the peasantry and pictured himself as a peasant" (Verwimp 2003). For example, in a speech commemorating twenty-five years of rule in 1987, Habyarimana credited farmers with making Rwanda a successful development story: "Their fabulous capacity to adapt, their pragmatism, their genius, their profound knowledge of our eco-systems that allowed them to extract an amazing degree of resources from their plots of land" (ibid., 16; Newbury and Newbury 2000, 856; Pottier and Nkundabashka 1992, 851).[2] This view and rhetoric has been wholly abandoned by the post-genocide regime. The influential Vision 2020 policy document insists that "[i]t will be necessary to formulate and implement realistic developmental policies that move beyond past delusions of viable subsistence-based agriculture" (MINECOFIN 2000, 17; RoR 2004b). The land policy takes this even farther, arguing that "the Rwandan family farm unit is no longer viable" (RoR 2004a, 16).

The new elite portray the solution to rural poverty as a matter of adopting "a good mentality." In his 2000 inaugural speech, for example, President Paul Kagame stated: "We would like to urgently appeal to the Rwandese people to work. As the Bible says, 'he who does not work should not eat'" (Kagame 2000). The president frequently states that each citizen has a responsibility to overcome her own poverty. These pronouncements have shaped how government officials view poverty. A district official in the southern province blamed the mentality of the people there for weak performance indicators:

You talk to them and you think they listen, but the people do nothing with the good advice you give them. They say "yes" because they are tired of you and your speeches, but they are never convinced. . . . They are resistant, they are really difficult. (interview, May 2007)

Similarly, the Strategic Plan for Agricultural Transformation refers to the peasantry's ignorance and resistance to productivity-enhancing measures that go beyond traditional subsistence farming (RoR 2004b, 6–17). This elite view disregards the institutional barriers that small-scale peasants face, such as land scarcity, climatic changes, crop diseases, limited options to diversify incomes, no cash reserves, and the lack of safety nets.

What Place for Small-Scale Peasants?

Many of the policymakers I interviewed advocated rapid modernization and professionalization of the agricultural sector, with a strong focus on maximizing productivity and output growth (Ansoms 2008). Indeed, the government has attempted to achieve this through several policies. First, it has pushed monocropping and regional crop specialization to realize economy-of-scale effects and expand market exchange. Peasants are encouraged to cultivate one particular crop type per plot. In addition, each region is supposed to specialize in particular crops based on bio-climatic conditions and market needs.[3] This policy takes a top-down approach: local authorities determine the crops for which the region has a comparative advantage and then guide the peasants to adopt these crops.

The proclaimed growth and pro-poor effects of monocropping and regional specialization are extremely uncertain. First, the extreme variety in soil types and climatic conditions makes it difficult for local administrators to assign the "right" crops to administratively defined regions. Second, small-scale peasants are reluctant to abandon mixed cropping because such risk-diversification enables them to cope with crop failure or uncontrollable market-price fluctuations. Finally, peasants lack bargaining power in regional markets to take advantage of the economies-of-scale effects realized through concentrating on particular crops.

Policy-imposed crop cultivation is not a recent idea. The Belgian colonial administrators and the Habyarimana government also practiced "forced cultivation." Pottier (1992) explained how agronomists and "vulgarisateurs" promoted mono-cropping (and combinations of beans and corn or soy and corn) as the only good gardening method in 1986 (the year of agricultural intensification). He pointed out the disastrous results of this top-down approach. Similarly, Newbury and Newbury (2000) critiqued such state-induced practices, which often favor technical insights on climatic conditions and land suitability over the local knowledge and abilities of the peasants themselves. They also highlighted the risk that elites redirect policies to their own benefit. Given the problematic experience with forced cultivation in the past, the current scale of crop planning, the blind belief of the administration in technical solutions, and the degree of force used during the implementation are major reasons for concern.

Most government officials among our interviewees linked the professionalization and commercialization of the agricultural sector to the necessity for larger farm units. One high-ranking official at MINITERE stated:

We will not take someone's land. The consolidation objective has the aim to intensify productivity; this is not equal to taking away land from people. When [MINAGRI] is talking about large farms, they do not mean that these farms would belong to one person. . . . Households will consolidate in terms of land use, not in terms of land ownership. (interview, July 2007)[4]

A high-ranking MINAGRI official, however, proposed more radical action to achieve larger land units:

At this point, most people are not earning because the pieces of land they have access to are too small. . . . We have to get more people off the land, as we cannot continue a system with small pieces of land. . . . When people get off the land, there will be more land in the hands of fewer people, which will allow a better planning of the system. (interview, June 2007)

Most of the interviewed officials saw no significant role for smallholders in a green revolution within the agricultural sector. This is alarming given that the rural sector is predominantly populated by "small family farms (over 90 percent of all production units) . . . with an average of less than one hectare in size, integrating polyculture—animal production systems" (RoR 2004b, 10). Furthermore, it goes against recent World Bank thinking that emphasizes the importance of smallholders for sub-Saharan Africa (World Bank 2007).

Almost all interviewed policymakers referred to the importance of the off-farm sector to absorb the existing labor surplus, which would increase further if more people are moved out of agriculture. One of Vision 2020's principal goals, cited extensively by our interviewees, is to decrease the population dependent on agricultural activities from 85 percent to 50 percent by the year 2020. Taking current population growth into account, this would mean creating 2.2 million new jobs in the off-farm sector by 2020 (Ronnås et al. 2010).

Some policymakers had an unrealistic view of the potential for off-farm employment. One stated: "We will build factories that work twenty-four hours. And this is not only in Kigali, also in other centers of economic interest" (interview, June 2007). The first Rwandan Poverty Reduction Strategy Paper (PRSP) mentioned the possibility "to leap-frog the stage of industrialisation and transform her [Rwanda's] subsistence economy into a service-sector driven, high value-added information and knowledge-based economy that can compete on the global market" (MINECOFIN 2002; *New Times* 2007b). Most interviewees had more realistic views, and hoped that agricultural growth would create employment in the off-farm sector. Nevertheless, the pro-poor character of agricultural growth is at this point extremely low and is not likely to improve with the current policies (Ansoms 2008; Twizeyimana 2009). As a result, such a trickle-down effect is doubtful given that increased income among the "lucky few" is unlikely to be reinvested in industries and services in the rural setting that result in massive employment opportunitoes to absorb the excessive labor force. An independent consultant reflected:

We should not dream. Where will we put all these people? If we would find something that could employ 40 to 60 percent of the population, at that moment we could count on a trickle-down effect. But with a range of activities that can give revenue to 2 to 5 percent of the population, we will never be able to create a trickle-down effect of which the benefits will reach the other 85 percent. (interview, July 2007)

A human rights activist made a similar point:

[If the government wants to reduce the population dependent upon agriculture from 85 to 50 percent], what will the 35 percent do? . . . The important thing is that people have viable livelihood strategies and that they can be satisfied with their lives. I do not see this happening in a context where rural policies allow for the rich to walk away with the gains of the agricultural sector, while others are increasingly excluded. I believe that the essential thing is the redistribution of the gains of growth. . . . Rural policies may strive for increased productivity and conservation of soils. But they have to be appropriate and adapted to the capacity of small peasants. (interview, May 2007)

Instead of focusing on highly productive farm units, rural policies should aim to increase productivity for large numbers of small-scale farmers. Even a modest income increase for this layer of society could enhance demand for off-farm services—and thus the demand for off-farm labor.

Upgrading Rural Life

A second ambition of the Rwandan elite is to upgrade rural life. They have done this not only through forced villagization (see C. Newbury, chap. 14, this volume) but also through banning certain economic and personal activities. For example, the government banned traditional brick-making in 2006 due to its impact on the environment (both pollution and deforestation). This had a huge negative impact for the off-farm labor force. In addition, the price of bricks and roof tiles has increased substantially. The government has re-allowed brick-baking, but only with modern ovens that are unaffordable for local entrepreneurs.

The government has also imposed modernity in terms of dress and behavior. Twizeyimana mentions the obligation to wear shoes, to be clean, use mosquito nets, adhere to the health insurance guidelines, wear school uniforms, construct toilets, make compost pits, and dry dishes on tables (instead of on the grass) (Twizeyimana 2006). Ingelaere gives a more extensive overview of "measures improving general well-being through a system of fines" (Ingelaere, chap. 3, this volume). When I visited my six field sites in June–August 2007, local inhabitants mentioned the existence of an obligation to "walk with shoes." Several people reported that on arriving at the market without shoes, local authorities took their food money to buy them shoes. In other words, it seems to be prohibited to appear poor. This cosmetic upgrading of rural life only hides the true extent of poverty and inequality in the countryside.

Social Engineering through Performance Targets

The social engineering ambitions take a very concrete form in the policymakers' eager race toward performance targets at all levels. This is driven partly by the donor community's emphasis on target-driven development. The EDPRS's sector "logframes" mention very detailed and very ambitious targets. An international donor representative cautioned that "there is a danger to focus too much on targets and not on the process. The results are important, but as important are the processes to arrive to these results" (interview, July 2007).

By July 2007 these targets were already (partly) communicated to district offices, which had to consider them when designing their District Development Plans. In addition, the district mayors have signed annual performance contracts (*imihigo*) with President Paul Kagame from 2006 on (see Ingelaere, chap. 3, this volume). The central state and local peasants see local authorities as mere implementers of national strategies without much ability to translate or reinterpret these strategies for local contexts.[5] The lack of bottom-up reflection on the usefulness of targets will become all the more problematic with the government's ambition to now expand *imihigo* up to the household level. In these contracts, households should "make vows of the achievements that they will have attained in a period of one year," which "will [be] base[d] on the government's goals meant to uplift the country's economy and the people's welfare," and which will be assessed by the local authorities (*New Times* 2007b).

Blind enforcement of national policies by local authorities can have disastrous results. In 2006, officials urged peasants in the Eastern Province to adopt monocropping and plant their crops "in rows." That autumn, local administrators in certain districts uprooted crops where peasants had not followed these instructions (Reyntjens 2007, 2). In May 2009 some peasants explained local malnutrition as the effects of a drought and the obligation to grow only corn. They were not allowed to minimize the risk of total crop failure by producing different crop types (Twizeyimana 2009).

Conclusion: Implications for Rural Policy

The Rwandan government's social engineering ambitions reflect a very top-down developmentalist agenda that leaves little room for bottom-up feedback mechanisms. In fact, there is a profound mismatch between the Rwandan elite's ambitions and the rural realities on the ground. The elite push for rapid modernization and "professionalization" of the agricultural sector risks increasing both poverty and inequality.

While agrarian change is unavoidable and even desirable in the long term, it can be achieved in a far more pro-poor way through a policy that supports smallholder agriculture. Such a policy should focus on the large mass of small-scale farmers that still have sufficient landholdings to produce for self-sufficiency in addition to some occasional surpluses. These peasants should be helped to take up a role as rural entrepreneurs. This cannot be achieved by forcing modern production techniques on them. Instead, positive incentives such as risk-reduction mechanisms (i.e., crop insurance) and safety nets should be provided. In addition, the negotiation capacity of small-scale farmers on the agricultural markets needs to be improved through a system of cooperatives that they actually control. Finally, the government can facilitate more accessible microcredit programs that would allow smallholder farmers to invest in commercial agriculture or to explore the possibility to (partially) transform themselves into nonagricultural entrepreneurs.

The government should actively stimulate a rural middle class rich enough to reinvest its profits locally, but not so rich that it reinvests in urban or foreign projects. Growth created through their hands would be more broadly based and would more easily trickle down to the remainder of rural society. The reinvestments made by a broad, rural middle class into the nonagricultural economy could indeed result in an increased demand for off-farm products and services within the local economy. This would trigger a trickle-down effect that takes on board the poorest rural categories dependent upon wage labor. At the same time, the Rwandan government could further enhance the capacity of this last group by providing training and technical education. In addition, policies should invest in safety nets that actively prevent these categories from falling into the group of chronic poor.

Notes

Parts of this chapter were previously published in *African Affairs* 108, no. 431 (2009): 289–309.

1. The majority of interviewees (seventeen) worked for the Rwandan government.

The interviews with four donors and five civil society organizations reiterate some points made in the paper, but they should not be considered fully representative.

2. However, Habyarimana's policies also displayed at times a strong anti-rural bias despite the pro-peasant rhetoric (Verwimp 2003).

3. Article 63 of the new land law specifies that productive land use "shall be based on the area's master plan and the general structure on land allocation, organization and use, and [the adoption of] specific plants certified by relevant authorities" (RoR 2005).

4. We found that peasants strongly rejected the idea of such collective land use patterns. Somewhat better-off peasants did not want their land and their production decisions linked to those less well-off. Meanwhile, poorer peasants expressed concerns that consolidation could erode their land rights. They implicitly feared what Alison Des Forges (2006) described as the "winnowing out of the chaff."

5. When I asked peasants for their opinion on specific policies, I got reactions like "one can not discuss with the state," "one can not refuse the law that is given by the state," "a peasant can not neglect the ideas of the state," "generally, the peasant is always in favor of the authorities [referring to the fact that they have no choice]." Going into more detail, one mentioned, "our own *umudugudu* coordinator has no power; and for the executive secretary (at the sector level), he might say that we are being disobedient toward the government if we protest."

References

Ansoms, An. 2005. "Resurrection after Civil War and Genocide: Growth, Poverty and Inequality in Post-Conflict Rwanda." *European Journal of Development Research* 17, no. 3: 495–508.

———. 2008. "Striving for Growth, Bypassing the Poor? A Critical Review of Rwanda's Rural Sector Policies." *Journal of Modern African Studies* 46, no. 1: 1–32.

———. 2009. "Re-Engineering Rural Society: The Visions and Ambitions of the Rwandan Elite." *African Affairs* 108, no. 431: 289–309.

Des Forges, Alison. 2006. "Land in Rwanda: Winnowing Out the Chaff." In *L'Afrique des Grands Lacs: Annuaire 2005–2006*, edited by Filip Reyntjens and Stefaan Marysse, 353–71. Paris: L'Harmattan.

Ingelaere, Bert. 2010. "Do We Understand Life after Genocide? Center and Periphery in the Construction of Knowledge in Postgenocide Rwanda." *African Studies Review* 53, no. 1: 41–59.

International Monetary Fund (IMF). 2009a. "Rwanda: 2008 Article IV Consultation, Fifth Review under the Three-Year Arrangement under the Poverty Reduction and Growth Facility." IMF Country Report 09/58. http://www.imf.org/external/pubs/ft/scr/2009/cr0958.pdf.

———. 2009b. "Rwanda: Sixth Review under the Three-Year Arrangement under the Poverty Reduction and Growth Facility." IMF Country Report 09/264. http://www.imf.org/external/pubs/ft/scr/2009/cr09264.pdf

Kagame, Paul. 2000. "Address to the Nation by H. E. Paul Kagame on his inaugura-
tion as President of the Republic of Rwanda." April 22. http://www.quabe.com/
rwanda/president/speeches/2000/speech_PRINT.html.

Ministry of Finance and Economic Planning (MINECOFIN). 2000. "Rwanda Vision
2020." July. http://www.minecofin.gov.rw/docs/LatestNews/Vision-2020.pdf.

————. 2002. "Poverty Reduction Strategy Paper" (2002–2005). National Poverty
Reduction Programme. June. http://www.imf.org/external/np/prsp/2002/rwa/01/
063102.pdf.

————. 2007. "Economic Development and Poverty Reduction Strategy, 2008–2012."
July 9. http://www.rada.gov.rw/IMG/pdf/EDPRS_Version_July_9th.pdf.

Muller, Edward N., and Mitchell A. Seligson. 2008. "Inequality and Insurgency." In
Development and Underdevelopment: The Political Economy of Global Inequality,
edited by M. A. Seligson and J. T. Passé-Smith, 155–71. 4th ed. Boulder: Lynne
Rienner.

Newbury, David, and Catharine Newbury. 2000. "Bringing Peasants Back In: Agrarian
Themes in the Construction and Corrosion of Statist Historiography in Rwanda."
American Historical Review 105, no. 3: 832–77.

New Times. 2007a. "I Didn't Read UN Report before Launch—Musoni." August 24.

————. 2007b. "Performance Contracts to Be Signed at Household Level." November 19.

Pottier, Johan, and Augustin Nkundabashka. 1992. "Intolerable Environments: To-
wards a Cultural Reading of Agrarian Practice and Policy in Rwanda." In *Bush
Base: Forest Farm*, edited by David Parkin and Elisabeth Croll, 146–68. London:
Routledge.

Republic of Rwanda (RoR). 2004a. "National Land Policy." Ministry of Land. February. http://www.minela.gov.rw/fr/IMG/pdf/National_Land_Policy.pdf.

————. 2004b. "Strategic Plan for Agricultural Transformation in Rwanda." Ministry of Agriculture and Animal Resources. October 2004. http://www.fao.org/
fileadmin/templates/nr/images/resources/pdf_documents/kagera/rwanda/rw_agr
_dev_plan.doc.

————. 2005. "Organic Law Determining the Use and Management of Land in
Rwanda, No. 08/2005 of 14/07/2005." http://www.lexadin.nl/wlg/legis/nofr/
oeur/arch/rwa/ORGANIC_LAW_N.doc.

————. 2006. "Preliminary Poverty Update Report." National Institute of Statistics Rwanda. December. http://196.44.242.24/eicv/survey0/data/docs/studies/
Master%20Report.pdf.

Reyntjens, Filip. 2007. "Chronique Politique du Rwanda 2005–2007." In *L'Afrique des
Grands Lacs: Annuaire 2005–2006*, edited by Filip Reyntjens and Stefaan Marysse,
1–19. Paris: L'Harmattan.

Ronnås, Per, et al. 2010. "Rwanda Forging Ahead: The Challenge of Getting Everybody
on Board." Employment Working Paper 62. International Labour Office, Geneva.
http://www.ilo.org/wcmsp5/groups/public/---ed_emp/documents/publication/
wcms_142908.pdf.

Twizeyimana, Albert-Baudoin. 2006. "Rwanda: La propreté à marché forcée." *InfoSud-Belgique*, June 29.

——. 2009. "Rwanda: La malnutrition ronge les campagnes." May 14. http://www.fdu-rwanda.org/fr/rwanda/detail/article/rwanda-la-malnutrition-ronge-les-campagnes/index.html.

United Nations Development Programme (UNDP). 2007. "Turning Vision 2020 into Reality: From Recovery to Sustainable Human Development." http://hdr.undp.org/en/reports/nationalreports/africa/rwanda/rwanda_2007_en.pdf.

Verwimp, Philip. 2003. "Development and Genocide in Rwanda: Political Economy Analysis of Peasants and Power under the Habyarimana Regime." PhD diss., Katholieke Universiteit Leuven.

World Bank. 2007. "Agriculture for Development." World Development Report 2008. Washington, DC. http://siteresources.worldbank.org/SOUTHASIAEXT/Resources/223546-1171488994713/3455847-1192738003272/WDR_Final.pdf.

16

The Presidential Land Commission

Undermining Land Law Reform

CHRIS HUGGINS

Introduction

Rwanda is in the midst of major land tenure reform involving significant donor support. A land policy gained cabinet approval in 2004, a land law was promulgated in 2005, and a pilot land registration project in four cellules ended in mid-2008 (NLTRP 2008). Nationwide land registration commenced in June 2009 and major changes to agricultural production have recently been effected in many parts of the country through implementation of the agricultural policy.[1] A number of recent studies have raised concerns about the potential impacts on human rights, food security, and socioeconomic stability. Critics argue that implementation of the law and policies could result in greater inequality, increased landlessness, and significant sociopolitical tensions (see, e.g., Des Forges 2006; Pottier 2006; Musahara and Huggins 2005; Ansoms 2009).

This chapter focuses on an underexamined aspect of the land question in Rwanda: the role of official government commissions in redistributing land. In particular, the chapter looks at the recent Presidential Commission on Land in Eastern Province, which offers a useful indicator of government attitudes toward land issues in Rwanda. The commission, which was established directly by President Paul Kagame and staffed by high-ranking military officers and government officials, had little oversight or influence from international donor agencies. The commission's land redistribution shows that Rwandan elites lack commitment to a transparent and equitable land reform and registration process, and are able to ignore national laws to benefit themselves and their allies.

The chapter begins with a brief discussion of how land reform is vitally important to rebuilding post-conflict states. It then explains the role of land tenure in Rwanda's conflict dynamics. Next it provides a condensed overview of the current land law and policy, and their implementation (up to October 2009). The remainder of the chapter looks at the workings of the Presidential Commission.

Land Reform in the Global South

Land tenure and land use policies are of central importance to governance and state-building in many developing countries, particularly those recovering from conflict and/or prolonged authoritarian rule (Huggins 2009b). The immediate post-conflict period is often characterized by a spate of land-grabbing by those in positions of power. Land-grabbing may exacerbate local grievances, create a climate of "winner-takes-all" politics, and threaten the long-term stability of the country. Population movements, especially forced displacements associated with conflict, often result in complex land disputes between original land users and "secondary occupants." Land laws and policies may be outdated, inappropriate, or discriminatory. Consequently, many post-conflict interventions in the land sector focus on strengthening existing dispute-resolution mechanisms at the local or national level, as land disputes usually represent the majority of cases in both customary systems and state courts. This may strengthen the "rule of law," but it also may alter the balance of power between local actors (e.g., land users, customary leaders, and local authorities) and the central state. In some cases, land reform is designed to undermine local-level "competition" to central state power and increase the extent and depth of state control (Herbst 2000).

Governments and international donors have increasingly focused on land law reform, which alters tenure systems without necessarily redistributing land (Manji 2006, 80). They often perceive land tenure insecurity as an obstacle to economic development (particularly, foreign investment) and view systematic land registration as key to improving land tenure security and resolving land conflicts.[2] However, evidence from many countries demonstrates that land registration programs cause many people who enjoyed user rights and other so-called secondary rights under customary systems to lose out while the heads of household benefit (Van Banning 2002, 345). Women, in particular, often do worse as their husbands or male relatives gain titles (Meinzen-Dick and Mwangi 2008). Studies in Central and South America suggest that land titling disproportionately benefits large-scale farmers and reinforces existing inequalities (Baranyi, Deere, and Morales 2004).

Land commissions are often established as part of broader reform efforts. Commissions vary widely in terms of their mandates, with some being given powers to expropriate landowners and redistribute land, while others are empowered only to collect information and make recommendations. South Africa's land commission has been fairly successful in restituting land to victims of forced displacement during the apartheid era (Roux 2006). After initial insistence on the "willing buyer, willing seller" model slowed restitution, the commission has now begun expropriating the land of those unwilling to sell (Huggins 2009b). In Burundi, land commissions composed of political appointees have been mandated to intervene in land disputes and establish the legal owners. In general, they have been highly corrupt and have only increased local tensions (Kamungi, Oketch, and Huggins 2005). In Kenya, the Ndung'u Commission investigated irregular and illegal allocation of land and issued a comprehensive report, identifying land grabbers and recommending major changes to the land administration system, as well as a review of title deeds (Republic of Kenya 2004). The report serves as a vital resource for those advocating justice around land, and it has provided input to the National Land Policy and the draft constitution, but few of its recommendations have been implemented because dozens of powerful politicians and civil servants would have to return stolen land and/or face prosecution. It is difficult to draw conclusions from such different contexts and experiences, but the Kenyan case demonstrates that even unimplemented recommendations can provide a useful resource for continued lobbying by civil society groups, if information is made publicly available.

Land in Rwanda

Land has long been a source of conflict in Rwanda due to the high population density and the related competition for productive land (Bruce 2007). Population density is estimated at 340 inhabitants per square kilometer, which is one of the highest rates in Africa (FAO 2006). Agriculture is the primary occupation of approximately 80 percent to 90 percent of the population (UNDP 2007; RoR 2004b). The distribution of land is highly unequal, and the Gini coefficient of land distribution has been steadily increasing: from 0.43 in 1990 to 0.594 in 2002 (Ansoms 2007; Musahara and Huggins 2005). At least 11.5 percent of the population is completely landless. Almost 30 percent of households own less than 0.2 hectares (less than 0.5 acres) of land, which is insufficient to feed their families.[3] Half of all cultivated and ranch land experiences moderate to severe soil erosion (Musahara and Huggins 2005). Soil fertility is therefore low in most areas, and agricultural productivity is limited and declining. Food insecurity is a persistent problem, particularly in the drier parts of the country, and may be negatively affected by the agricultural consolidation and commercialization policies implemented from 2007 on (Huggins 2009a). By late 2009 there were signs that serious food insecurity would soon be experienced in large parts of the country (Kagire 2009a).

Successive regimes in Rwanda have dispossessed segments of the population, often along ethnic lines. Alison Des Forges described how the German and Belgian colonial regimes backed the Tutsi monarchy's claims over land:

Chiefs and sub-chiefs representing the *umwami* [king] found it increasingly easy to exercise the right to distribute vacant land. . . . They extended this right to the broader prerogative of actually dispossessing landholders who did not obey their orders. (Des Forges 2006)

The resulting landlessness and anger at the chiefs was channeled by Hutu political leaders into violence against Tutsi at the end of the colonial period. The post-independence Hutu regime redistributed land belonging to the twenty thousand Tutsi killed and the three hundred thousand who fled during this period. After the predominantly Tutsi Rwandan Patriotic Front (RPF) invaded the country in October 1990, the Hutu regime whipped up fears that that the RPF would dispossess Hutu of their land. During the 1994 genocide,

[a]uthorities played upon both fears and hopes related to land in order to recruit participants in the genocide. On the one hand, they insisted that the Tutsi intended to re-establish the rule of the umwami and to reclaim the lands distributed to other Rwandans after the Tutsi flight in the 1960s. On the other, they promptly distributed lands vacated by the killings or flight of Tutsi, thus rewarding participants and encouraging their further involvement. Propaganda during the genocide stressed the solidarity of the Hutu majority, who were identified as people of the land. (Des Forges 2006)

Following the genocide, some Tutsi returnees engaged in land-grabbing. Some government officials (particularly in the Eastern Province) promoted ad hoc, partial expropriations of land to restitute Tutsi returnees for what they had lost—even though official policy prohibited restitution of land for those who had left Rwanda more than ten years earlier.

Post-genocide Rwanda remains susceptible to conflict over land. A conflict vulnerability assessment funded by the U.S. Agency for International Development (USAID) highlighted the importance of land issues, arguing that the government's drive to "professionalize" the agricultural sector

could become a prominent proximate cause for conflict if access to land tenure mainly benefits élites. . . . Increased tenure security for some could in fact lead to increased livelihood insecurity for others. If a segment of society were perceived as being the primary or exclusive beneficiaries of such changes, land reform could become a major focus of resentment. (Weeks, Rakita, Brown, and Munyeli 2002)

Similarly, Des Forges (2006) worried that

the land policy and land law seem likely to push a substantial number of poor farmers off the land. . . . Further impoverishment of the poor will increase the risk of conflict and given the recent history of Rwanda, such conflict is likely once again to take an ethnic coloration.

To understand the basis of Des Forges's concerns, I now discuss the land law and land policy, which herald fundamental changes in the way that land is owned and used.

Land Law and Land Policy

The 2005 Organic Land Law (RoR 2005) is very much a "framework law" that outlines the legal principles but omits the implementation mechanisms. Three key principles are mandatory land registration, land consolidation to improve economic productivity, and the requirement that landowners practice "professional" agriculture (see Musahara and Huggins 2005, 307). This essentially neoliberal model is centered on the registration of individual plots, which can be freely transacted.[4] As elsewhere on the continent, registration is justified on the basis of economic growth, with government officials maintaining that "the land titles will act as collateral for people to secure loans from banks" (Kagire 2009c). However, in contrast to the usual neoliberal model, extensive conditions are placed on ownership. The restrictions on agricultural land use, production, and marketing in many areas is reminiscent of the collectivization of 1970s Tanzania (Huggins 2009a; see C. Newbury, chap. 14, this volume).

The land law and policy were developed following a process of civil society consultation that was comprehensive by Rwandan standards. However, only a few key civil society recommendations were included in the final documents (Musahara and Huggins 2005). The land law has been followed by "secondary" legislation essential for implementation, such as the expropriation law.[5] The development of this secondary legislation has been far less participatory.[6] Most of the key legislation was developed and discussed within a relatively short period (early to mid-2006). For example, the State minister for lands verbally encouraged civil society discussion of the draft expropriation law, but the Ministry itself did not distribute the draft to civil society organizations or organize any large-scale consultation meetings with nongovernmental organizations (NGOs). In addition, local NGOs were hard-pressed to provide comments on so many technical, specialized questions within a relatively short time frame.

The National Land Tenure Reform Programme (NLTRP), funded by the UK's Department for International Development (DFID), has "set out a framework for a land reform process that secures the rights of all citizens including the poor and vulnerable, whilst also supporting national economic development and promoting environmental sustainability" (RoR 2006). Broadly, the NLTRP involves two main elements. First, it establishes a new legal and policy framework for land tenure in line with the 2005 Organic Land Law. Secondly, it "regularizes" tenure through a nationwide land registration process. In a pilot phase, landholdings in four cellules in four different provinces were registered between 2006 and 2008.[7] The government has chosen an astonishingly ambitious three to five year time frame for registering all landholdings in the country. If the national registration process is implemented too rapidly to allow rigorous external monitoring, there is a clear risk that local administrators will engage in land-grabbing. The risk is all the more real given the lack of equitable and transparent outcomes from the Presidential Commission.

The Presidential Commission on Land in Eastern Province

The Presidential Commission on Land in Eastern Province involves one of the most sensitive areas in the country as far as land disputes are concerned.[8] In parts of Eastern Province, "land sharing"—essentially a form of uncompensated expropriation—was implemented from 1996 on when Tutsi refugees returned to the country. The land was simply divided equally between the two households (usually the Hutu secondary occupant and the returning Tutsi original owner). Thus, this redistribution predominantly benefited Tutsi

(Koster 2008). Although government officials presented land sharing as voluntary, it was essentially mandated by the provincial authorities without popular consultation (see RoR 2006, 71). Former administrators stated that it was "an order" (interview with former local administrator, Kiziguro sector, Eastern Province, November 25, 2005). A United Nations High Commissioner for Refugees (UNHCR) source quoted in a study stated: "People had no choice. It's all about access to services. If you didn't do it, you would have a problem" (Bruce 2007). Those compelled to divide their property ordinarily received no compensation for the part lost. Some who refused were imprisoned (HRW 2001). The 2005 Land Law attempts to retroactively legalize land sharing, though the validity of this clause is questionable.[9] While some Rwandans have accepted land sharing, it remains a source of grievance for others (interviews, Nyagatare, Eastern Province, September 29, 2007). A government study found that land sharing remains a major cause of land disputes in Kirehe District, where in some sectors "local authorities were allegedly bribed" or gave land to close relatives (RoR 2006, 85). Unsurprisingly, the same study found that some people who lost their land "have not accepted this and still believe their land was unfairly given to others" (ibid., 93).

The other contentious land issue in this province is the acquisition of massive tracts by senior military officers, politicians, former local administrators, and other politically connected individuals (Kagame 2007; Musoni 2007). Many farms and ranches were obtained by occupying land belonging to those displaced during the genocide and civil war who have since returned. In response to a journalist's question about the role of the authorities in land-grabbing, the president stated, "Certain leaders are indeed guilty . . . I am aware of the examples you have given me of some leaders who have appropriated hectares of land. There are also some Ministers implicated" (Kagame 2007). In response to these concerns, the president established a land commission in mid-2007 to redistribute large landholdings to landless citizens.

The timing of the Presidential Commission was more than a little suspicious. As donors were investing millions of dollars and significant technical assistance in developing transparent systems for demarcating landholdings, adjudicating disputes, and involving local community members, the president created an unaccountable and non-transparent commission to redistribute some of the largest and most politically sensitive landholdings in the country ahead of the official land tenure reform process. The composition of the commission only deepened those suspicions. General Fred Ibingira, who owned an estimated 320 hectares in the province, chaired the commission.[10] Many members of the commission were senior politicians who owned large tracts of land, and some were suspected land-grabbers. The commission has not published its guidelines, its decisions, or its reports. Government officials did not respond to my efforts to obtain these documents.[11] Thus, I have had to rely largely on public statements by government officials in assessing the commission's workings.

The commission's rationale was to redistribute large landholdings, some of which had been illegally grabbed. The commission kicked off the redistribution on January 22, 2008, with General Ibingira's land. A pro-government newspaper reported that "the general and his family had 320 hectares, but now remain with 95 hectares. As provided for by the law, he retained 25 hectares, whereas seven other members of his family who shared the same farm were given 10 hectares each" (Kimenyi 2008a). There does not appear to be any legal basis for awarding 25 hectares to suspected land-grabbers and 10 hectares to their family members. Given that the average household owns just 0.6 hectares, it is easy to imagine how most of the population views grants of 10 or 25 hectares.

Local administrators were told that the commission was going to distribute landholdings larger than 25 hectares (interviews, Nyagatare Sector, Nyagatare District, February 20, 2008). Yet the commission has also targeted many people who are not large landowners. Citizens owning 10 hectares or less who have documentation to prove they bought their plots have had their land redistributed (interview with international land tenure experts, Kigali, February 26, 2008). The commission's criteria for redistributing the seized land are equally unclear. Pro-government media reported that 54,392 hectares (nearly 135,000 acres) would be redistributed—but "in the event that according to it officials find it necessary not to give out a certain piece of land, it will remain in government possession for future use" (Musoni 2008a). According to a local informant, "the authorities at [the village] level take some names off [the list of applicants] to make sure that their friends can get land. There is also corruption" (interview, *umudugudu* Gituro, Nyagatare Sector, Nyagatare District, Eastern Province, February 19, 2008).

The Presidential Commission has violated the 2007 law on expropriation. First, it does not have legal authority to carry out expropriations (RoR 2007a, art. 11). Second, it does not appear to have complied with the procedural steps for expropriations.[12] Third, it permitted a conflict of interest by expropriating the land of persons sitting on the commission. Overall, then, the Presidential Commission has undermined the rule of law and created a worrisome precedent immediately prior to a nationwide land regularization process.

Some local people are skeptical about the work of the land commission. One local opinion leader complained about the lack of public participation and the conflict of interest (interview with local opinion-leader, Kabarole,

Eastern Province, September 29, 2007). Another resident of Eastern Province with good contacts in the local administration told me that even the local authorities had complained they knew very little about the commission's activities (interview with local opinion leader from Kagitumba, Eastern Province, Nyagatare, Eastern Province, September 29, 2007).

Conclusion

The Presidential Commission on Land in Eastern Province casts serious doubt on Rwanda's commitment to following the laws and procedures for registering land claims and thus improving security of land tenure. The success of the national land registration program depends largely on the willingness of political and administrative authorities to ensure that procedures are correctly followed as the risks of injustice and corruption are high. The speed with which land registration will take place also makes independent monitoring and evaluation very difficult. The NLTRP has argued that "systematic 'people-led' land registration will work in Rwanda," but has also "stressed the need to act before local officials took things into their own hands, and technical assistance staff cautioned that a clear legal basis and stronger capacity were necessary for effective implementation" (Bruce 2007). The commission has undermined land tenure security through arbitrary decision making and a lack of transparency. Its actions confirm Des Forges's concern that "the policy and laws appear to offer more security for the prosperous and powerful, eagerly solicited for their capacity to invest, than for the majority of Rwandans who make a bare living from their plots" (Des Forges 2006).

Notes

1. The agricultural policy involves a number of components, including a shift from traditional Rwandan agricultural production techniques and crops to new commercial varieties and mono-cropping systems. An important part of this is 'regional crop specialization' and land-use consolidation (see Ansoms, chap. 15, this volume).

2. Land tenure experts increasingly acknowledge that customary tenure systems are not inherently "insecure"; instead, the "so-called insecurity of indigenous property systems is more a function of neglect and subordination in public policy and law than of their essential characteristics" (Okoth-Ogendo 2006). In many places, the state itself is the primary source of tenure insecurity, through the illegal or legally dubious conversion of customary lands to private or governmental uses.

3. The UN estimates that the average household needs to cultivate at least 0.7 hectares (1.7 acres) in order to be food secure (UNDP 2007).

4. Land will be held through long-term leasehold agreements, rather than freehold title, but active land markets can be expected to develop just as they do when land is held through title.

5. Some twenty-eight pieces of secondary legislation, ministerial orders, or other subsidiary regulations are being written in order to make the land law operational. See, for example, RoR (2007b).

6. See Gready, chap. 5, this volume, for an in-depth analysis of government/civil society relations.

7. The exercise was widely seen as a success, and was highly transparent, with site visits by interested civil society organizations.

8. Prior to the 2005 administrative reform, what is now Eastern Province was Umutara and Kibungo Provinces. Land disputes in this region are also somewhat atypical, as large parts of the province were formerly part of Akagera National Park. Sections of the park were opened up by the government for pasture and farming to accommodate returning refugees following the genocide.

9. Article 87 of the law simply states that "land sharing which was conducted from the year nineteen ninety four (1994) is recognized by this organic law."

10. Ibingira is best known as the commanding officer during the 1995 Kibeho massacre, in which two thousand to four thousand displaced persons were killed.

11. Phone calls to the Ministry of Land (MINITERE) and Land Center staff, February 18–26, 2008; e-mail communication to MINITERE officials overseeing the land distribution exercise, and the MINITERE general e-mail address, April 7, 2008; e-mail communication to MINITERE officials overseeing the land distribution exercise, and the MINITERA general e-mail address, September 2, 2008, and November 5, 2009. Rwandan land sector professionals were also unaware of the report and/or unable to obtain a copy.

12. If the National Land Commission has approved the application, the District authorities must convene a consultative meeting with the local population within thirty days after receipt of the application for expropriation. The relevant Land Commission must take a decision within a period of fifteen days after the consultative meeting with the population, at which point it convenes another public meeting and declares in public the final decision taken on the project proposal. The decision must also be announced on national radio and through state newspapers for a period of thirty days after the decision was made.

References

Ansoms, An. 2007. "Striving for Growth, Bypassing the Poor? A Critical Review of Rwanda's Rural Sector Policies." Discussion Paper 2007/02. Institute of Development Policy and Management, University of Antwerp. http://www.ua.ac.be/objs/00152940.pdf.

———. 2009. "Faces of Rural Poverty in Contemporary Rwanda: Linking Livelihood Profiles and Institutional Processes." PhD diss., University of Antwerp.

Baranyi, Stephen, Carmen Deere, and Manuel Morales. 2004. "Land and Development in Latin America: Openings for Policy Research." North-South Institute/ International Development Research Centre (IDRC), Ottawa. http://www.nsi-ins .ca/english/pdf/land_use_final_eng.pdf.

Bledsoe, David. 2004. "Republic of Rwanda Land Policy and Law, Trip Report: Findings and Recommendations." RDI/USAID/MINITERE, Kigali.

Bruce, John W. 2007. "Drawing a Line under a Crisis: Reconciling Returnee Land Access and Security in Post-Conflict Rwanda." Humanitarian Practice Group, Overseas Development Institute, London. June. http://www.odi.org.uk/resources/ download/3186.pdf.

Bureau of Democracy, Human Rights, and Labor. 2006. "Country Reports on Human Rights Practices: Rwanda, 2005." Washington, DC: U.S. Department of State.

Des Forges, Alison. 2006. "Land in Rwanda: Winnowing out the Chaff." In *L'Afrique des Grands Lacs: Annuaire 2005–2006*, edited by Filip Reyntjens and Stefaan Marysse, 353–71. Paris: L'Harmattan.

Ferguson, James. 2006. "Transnational Topographies of Power: Beyond 'the State' and 'Civil Society' in the Study of African Politics." In *Accelerating Possession: Global Futures of Property and Personhood*, edited by Bill Maurer and Gabriele Schwab, 89–112. New York: Columbia University Press.

Food and Agriculture Organization of the United Nations (FAO). 2006. "A Case Study of the Implications of the Ongoing Land Reform on Sustainable Rural Development and Poverty Reduction in Rwanda." Paper presented at the International Conference on Agrarian Reform and Rural Development, Porto Alegre, Brazil. January.

Gasasira, Charles, and Herman Musahara. 2004. "The Land Question in Kibungo Province." Centre for Conflict Management, University of Rwanda.

Herbst, Jeffrey. 2000. *States and Power in Africa: Comparative Lessons in Authority and Control*. Princeton, NJ: Princeton University Press.

Huggins, Chris. 2009a. "Agriculture Policies and Local Grievances in Rural Rwanda." *Peace Review* 21, no. 3: 296–303.

———. 2009b. "Linking Broad Constellations of Ideas: Transitional Justice, Land Tenure Reform, and Development." In *Transitional Justice and Development: Making Connections*, edited by Pablo de Greiff and Roger Duthie, 332–74. New York: Social Science Research Council.

———. 2009c. "Historical and Contemporary Land Laws and Their Impact on Indigenous Peoples' Land Rights in Rwanda." Forest People's Programme, London. http://www.forestpeoples.org/sites/fpp/files/publication/2010/05/ rwandalandrightsstudy09eng.pdf.

Huggins, Chris, and Jenny Clover, eds. 2005. *From the Ground Up: Land Rights, Conflict and Peace in Sub-Saharan Africa*. Pretoria: Institute for Security Studies.

Human Rights Watch (HRW). 2001. "Uprooting the Rural Poor in Rwanda." May 1. http://www.hrw.org/legacy/reports/2001/rwanda/.

Kabatesi, K. n.d. "What Is the Fate of Landowners?" Letter to the editor, *New Times*, undated. http://www.newtimes.co.rw/index.php?issue=13448&article=4362.

Kagame, Paul. 2007. "Presidential Press Conference, Village Urugwiro, Kigali." Broadcast on Radio Rwanda, April 20. Unofficial Human Rights Watch translation from the original Kinyarwanda.

Kagire, Edmund. 2009a. "President Happy with Land Reform." *New Times*, April 24.

———. 2009b. "Agriculture Output Could Reduce by Half Next Year." *New Times*, October 23.

———. 2009c. "U.S.$55 Million for Land Registration Exercise." *New Times*, July 11.

Kamungi, Prisca Mbura, Johnstone Summit Oketch, and Chris Huggins. 2005. "Land Access and the Return and Resettlement of IDPs and Refugees in Burundi." In *From the Ground Up: Land Rights, Conflict and Peace in Sub-Saharan Africa*, edited by Chris Huggins and Jenny Clover, 195–267. Pretoria: Institute for Security Studies.

Kimenyi, Felly. 2008a. "Share Resources, Kagame Tells Rwandans." *New Times*, January 24.

———. 2008b. "Kagame Warns Fake Land Beneficiaries." *New Times*, January 25.

Kimenyi, Felly, and Godfrey Ntagungira. 2008. "Use Land Properly—Kagame." *New Times*, September 2.

Koster, Marian. 2008. "Fragmented Lives: Reconstructing Rural Livelihoods in Post-Genocide Rwanda." PhD diss., Wageningen University.

Leckie, Scott. 2007. *Housing, Land and Property Restitution Rights of Refugees and Displaced Persons: Laws, Cases and Materials*. New York: Cambridge University Press.

Manji, Ambreena. 2006. *The Politics of Land Reform in Africa: From Communal Tenure to Free Markets*. New York: Zed Books.

Manzi, Gerald. 2007. "The Problem of Land in Eastern Province." *Umuseso* no. 288, July 20–26. Translation from the original Kinyarwanda courtesy of Human Rights Watch.

Meinzen-Dick, Ruth, and Esther Mwangi. 2008. "Cutting the Web of Interests: Pitfalls of Formalizing Property Rights." *Land Use Policy* 26:36–43.

Ministry of Land (MINITERE). 2007. "The Roadmap to Land Reform." Powerpoint slides presented at NLTRP strategic roadmap workshop, Kigali, October 3. Printed version in author's possession.

Moore, Donald. 2005. *Suffering for Territory: Race, Place, and Power in Zimbabwe*. Durham, NC: Duke University Press.

Musahara, Herman, and Chris Huggins. 2005. "Land Reform, Land Scarcity and Postconflict Reconstruction: A Case Study of Rwanda." In *From the Ground Up: Land Rights, Conflict and Peace in Sub-Saharan Africa*, edited by Chris Huggins and Jenny Clover, 269–346. Pretoria: Institute for Security Studies.

Musoni, Edwin. 2007. "Rwanda: Military, Police Team Probe Land Ownership." *New Times*, June 28.

———. 2008a. "54,000 Hectares of Land to Be Re-distributed in Eastern Province." *New Times*, January 23.

———. 2008b. "Thank You Mr. President, New Land Owners Say." *New Times*, January 25.

————. 2008c. "Land Re-distribution Exercise Resumes This Week." *New Times*, January 29.

Mutara, Eugene. 2009. "Nationwide Land Demarcation Starts Today." *New Times*, June 22.

National Land Tenure Reform Programme (NLTRP). 2008. *NLTRP Newsletter*. Issue 12, May–June.

National Unity and Reconciliation Commission (NURC). 2005. "Opinion Survey: Land Property and Reconciliation." Kigali, July.

Newbury, Catharine. 1993. *The Cohesion of Oppression: Clientship and Ethnicity in Rwanda, 1860–1960*. New York: Columbia University Press.

Ntagungira, Godfrey. 2007. "Desperate Residents Storm Nyagatare Sector Offices Over Land." *New Times*, October 23.

————. 2008a. "100 More Residents Acquire Land." *New Times*, February 15.

————. 2008b. "Twelve False Land Claimants Held." *New Times*, February 16.

————. 2008c. "Not All Re-distributed Land Was Grabbed." *New Times*, March 26.

Nyamu-Musembi, Celestine. 2006. "Breathing New Life into Dead Theories of Property Rights: De Soto and Land Relations in Rural Africa." Institute of Development Studies (IDS). http://www.ntd.co.uk/idsbookshop/details.asp?id=953.

Okoth-Ogendo, H. W. O. 2006. "Formalising 'Informal' Property Systems: The Problem of Land Rights Reform in Africa." Background paper prepared for the Commission for the Legal Empowerment of the Poor. Nairobi. http://www.undp.org/legalempowerment/reports/National%20Consultation%20Reports/Country%20Files/15_Kenya/15_4_Property_Rights.pdf.

Pottier, Johan. 2006. "Land Reform for Peace? Rwanda's 2005 Land Law in Context." *Journal of Agrarian Change* 6, no. 4: 509–37.

Republic of Kenya. 2004. "Report of the Commission of Inquiry into the Illegal/Irregular Allocation of Public Land." Nairobi, December.

Republic of Rwanda (RoR). 2004a. "National Land Policy." MINITERE. February. http://www.minela.gov.rw/fr/IMG/pdf/National_Land_Policy.pdf.

————. 2004b. "Strategic Plan for Agricultural Transformation in Rwanda." MINAGRI. October.

————. 2004c. "Activities Report, 2004." Office of the Ombudsman. (Unofficial Human Rights Watch translation from the original Kinyarwanda.)

————. 2005. "Organic Law Determining the Use and Management of Land in Rwanda, No. 08/2005 of July 14, 2005." http://www.lexadin.nl/wlg/legis/nofr/oeur/arch/rwa/ORGANIC_LAW_N.doc.

————. 2006. "Phase 1 of the Land Reform Process for Rwanda: Developing the Strategic Road Map." Land Sector Stakeholder Group Mid-Term Briefing Note. MINITERE. Kigali, September.

————. 2007a. "Law No. 18/2007 of 19/04/2007 Relating to Expropriation in the Public Interest." Ministry of Justice. http://www.minela.gov.rw/IMG/pdf/LOI_D_EXPROPRIATION.pdf.

————. 2007b. "Phase 1 of the Land Reform Process for Rwanda: Results of Preparatory Field Consultations in Four Trial Districts; March–October 2006." DFID/ HTSPE/MINITERE. Kigali, February 16. http://www.rmportal.net/framelib/ ltpr/052709/dfid-supported-rwanda-land-tenure-assessment-feb-2007.pdf.

Roux, Theunis. 2006. "Land Restitution and Reconciliation in South Africa." Paper presented at special event on Transitional Justice in South Africa, University of Cambridge, 2006. http://www.saifac.org.za/docs/res_papers/RPS%20No.19.pdf.

United Nations Development Programme (UNDP). 2007. "Turning Vision 2020 into Reality: From Recovery to Sustainable Human Development." http://hdr.undp .org/en/reports/nationalreports/africa/rwanda/rwanda_2007_en.pdf.

Van Banning, Theo R. G. 2002. *The Human Right to Property*. New York: Intersentia.

Vansina, Jan. 2004. *Antecedents to Modern Rwanda: The Nyiginya Kingdom*. Madison: University of Wisconsin Press.

Weeks, Willet, Sara Rakita, Michael Brown, and Josephine Munyeli. 2002. "Rwanda Conflict Vulnerability Assessment." Management Systems International, Washington, DC. August. http://pdf.usaid.gov/pdf_docs/PNACU962.pdf.

Williams, Rhodri C. 2005. "Post-conflict Property Restitution and Refugee Return in Bosnia and Herzegovina: Implications for International Standard-Setting and Practice." *NYU Journal of International Law and Politics* 37, no. 3: 441–553.

Part V

History and Memory

17

The Past Is Elsewhere

The Paradoxes of Proscribing Ethnicity in Post-Genocide Rwanda

NIGEL ELTRINGHAM

Introduction

Throughout three years working in "conciliation" and development consultations in Rwanda (1995–97) and during fieldwork among members of the post-genocide government in 1998, I consciously avoided introducing ethnicity into conversations. Eager to avoid reductionism and to access
nuanced understandings, I left it for the respondents to choose how ethnicity
would become a subject of discussion. This was often immediate, in response
to the opening question, "Does the 'International Community' understand
Rwanda?" Respondents, especially members of the Rwandan Patriotic Front
(RPF), would then recount a standard, de-personalized history, which maintained that ethnicity had been created, or substantially distorted, by colonial authorities, thereby disrupting a pre-colonial unity (see Buckley-Zistel
2009, 34–41; Eltringham 2004, 163–77; Vansina 2004, 134–39). This key element of the "RPF healing truth" (Zorbas 2007, 94–98) reflects Valentine
Daniel's (1997, 309–10) observation that "the nation-state promises to soothe
and heal, but its healing comforts are expressed in the language of recovery

and restoration, through an orientation toward the past." Nationalism requires a golden age, requires *restoration* and, in this sense, the RPF are true revolutionaries, seeking a return to a prior state of affairs.[1] While the "RPF healing truth" rests upon a dialogue with the past, it is, however, a past *outside* living memory, immune from the critique and detail of personal recollection. And yet, it is on such personal recollection, however selective, that individuals rely to navigate their current situation making them, in turn, immune to official, sanctioned narrative.

None of my respondents in 1998 proposed that ethnicity should, or could, be legislated out of existence. But this is what the government has subsequently promoted. The de facto proscription of ethnicity has been interpreted as a cynical attempt to mask the monopoly of political power by the Tutsi returnees (Reyntjens 2004, 187); as an effort to silence political criticism (Waldorf 2009, 109–12); as irrelevant because of available proxies whereby "Tutsi" became *rescapés* and "Hutu" became *génocidaires* (Eltringham 2004, 75–76); or as obscuring the more assiduous divide between rural and urban Rwanda (see Ansoms 2009; Newbury and Newbury 2000). The question remains, however, whether restraining the manner in which Rwandans can openly commune with their past obstructs them in "their responsibility for ensuring that the worst of the past never happens again and the best of it is salvaged and retained" (Jackson 2005, 357).

Relativising Narratives

The Rwandans I interviewed in 1998 were willing to talk about ethnicity and in a more nuanced fashion than one may expect. Here, I choose respondents who defined themselves as Tutsi. Some respondents maintained a notion of unity in ethnic diversity. For example, a government spokesman stated:

The truth is that Rwandans are one people. If you deny this, you are driven by something else. One language, territory, culture of the people, of different groupings on one hill, *secteur*, village. The same language, poetry, and dancing. Everything is the same. There is no Hutuland, Tutsiland, or Twaland. In every administrative unit, *cellule*, *secteur* you will find Batwa, Batutsi, and Bahutu. In each and every unit of administration down to the smallest, you can find this mix. (interview, Kigali, May 1998)

Many respondents adopted this impersonal, descriptive position. Others conveyed a more personal account of having to come to terms with ethnicity.

For example, an "old-case load" returnee, who worked with street children in Kigali, commented:

To be frank, when I came back from outside I thought Hutu were savages, but I met Tutsi who are even worse and I meet Hutu who are really committed to unity. You know we have extremists on both sides. Most of the street children are Hutu, which is surprising when people always say that the Hutu are killing the Tutsi. When I say we should help the orphans, people say to me, "But they are our enemies." But I say, "You have come back to this country, you have been reintegrated, why not them?" (interview, Kigali, April 1998)[2]

This returnee had revised his initial attitude to "Hutu" not by dismissing ethnicity but through experience *structured* by ethnicity. In so doing, he had re-situated ethnic identity by stripping it of a determinism he had once assumed and by transforming it from a self-evident proposition into an unstable element that, from now on, would always require his contingent assessment ("I met Tutsi who are even worse") and adjectival qualification ("we have extremists on both sides").

Of particular interest were those who shared with me their own reflective positions informed by *personal* ancestry, *personal* experience, and *personal* contemporary location. In so doing, they nuanced ethnicity in *their* past, simultaneously reframing it in *their* present:

Every time I talk with foreigners, their perception of reality is influenced by colonial times. This is the greatest misconception, this dichotomy between Tutsi as rulers and Hutu as exploited. People think every Tutsi in the past was a ruler, a member of a noble class, an aristocrat. People from outside introduce me as "Jean, he comes from an aristocratic family." But this is a very, very bad simplification, a misconception.[3] My father (and grandfather) was a Tutsi, but he wasn't a ruler. The father of my mother wasn't a ruler. My mother served with Hutu in the court of a Tutsi chief. But, even a Rwandan said to me, "You are the exception that proves the rule." So not even Rwandans understand. For these old-case load returnees there are simply two groups: Tutsi are victims, Hutu are victimizer. But, this is a simplification; not all Hutu were killing. But, for those who return from Uganda, Nairobi, Canada, etc., Hutu are simply Interahamwe [the extremist Hutu militia that carried out genocidal massacres]. The farther they come from geographically, the more simplified their image becomes, perhaps because they watch CNN. For them Hutu equals murderer and Interahamwe, Tutsi equals victim, good and so on. (interview, Kigali, May 1998)

Although this genocide survivor "hid in the bush" throughout the genocide, here he chooses neither to embrace ethnicity (denounce all Hutu) nor to dismiss ethnicity (as colonial fabrication), but to re-situate ethnicity. He does this not in relation to the vision of ethnicity found in genocide propaganda (1990–94) but in relation to a distortion he was currently witnessing among Tutsi who had returned to Rwanda after 1994. Drawing on his own biography as refracted through his social location in 1998, this survivor disrupts ethnicity and in so doing disarms ethnicity of its deterministic, binary qualities.

And yet I encountered equally nuanced commentaries among returnees. Although an old-case load returnee (a high-ranking civil servant in 1998) began by describing pre-colonial Rwanda as "a well-integrated nation split up by external forces," he continued:

In 1959 I was at school at Shyogwe and saw them attack the home of a young chief.[4] They said they were "going to work." I asked them why they were doing this. They said that if they didn't, there were five thousand people behind who would come, cut down banana trees, kill cattle and burn their houses. But this was not apartheid South Africa. Intermarriage was very common. Even as refugees in Uganda, we went to school together. I had Hutu friends at school. We were very, very close; we never fought. We were all Banyarwanda, speaking the same language. So, when they call for "reconciliation," reconciliation between who? I have to take the individual. Some Hutu, some Tutsi are wonderful. Some Hutu, some Tutsi are terrible. Therefore, if someone says to me "reconcile with Hutu," what do they mean? The Hutu feels that all Hutu are branded as killers; some extremist Tutsi just want revenge; and politicians can use divisive measures to advance both Hutu and Tutsi. But society has to be Hutu, Tutsi, and Twa as it always has been. If only the country could be brought to a point where they know the truth about themselves. What was the real cause, what was initiated, what were the objectives? We need to know the truth. (interview, Kigali, May 1998)

Although this returnee concludes with the suggestion that Rwandans need to "know the truth about themselves," this is preceded by a discussion of his own past—evoked to assist him in the challenges he faced in the present. For him, reflecting on the truth was as much a personal, as a national, need. And his search for truth was not a static reflection on a distant, de-personalized past, but a dynamic process in the present. Meditating on his personal experience in the past and observations in the present, how (and with whom) was he to reconcile in the immediate future? Ultimately, he construed ethnicity as meaningless in this personal challenge, but he achieved this only through a reflection in which ethnicity was not rejected but relativized.

These respondents were members of an urban, political elite. While anthropologists reject the exoticizing notion that the views of "ordinary" people should be privileged (see Eltringham 2006, 69–70; Nader 1972; Sluka 1999), research conducted beyond the urban elite in Rwanda (see Fujii 2009, 103–53; McLean Hilker 2009) has revealed rich insights regarding the flexible, relative quality of ethnicity. Other research has demonstrated that by reflecting on personal biography, refracted through current social location, many "ordinary" Rwandans are also choosing to re-situate ethnicity and envisage ethnic relations quite distinct from the divisive caricatures found in genocidal propaganda (see Longman and Rutagengwa 2004, 178; Zorbas 2007, 173–75).

"Urugwiro Village" and the Promise of Participation

In 1998, members of the government, including a number of my respondents, were engaged in their own meditation on the past at a series of "Saturday workshops" to study "the issue of the unity of Rwandans," held in "Urugwiro Village," the official seat of the president. The outcome was a report, "The Unity of Rwandans." After fifty-seven pages of a past populated by ethnic groups, the report concludes:

Banyarwanda must understand that maintaining themselves prisoners of their belonging to ethnic Hutu, Tutsi, and Twa groups is one of the big obstacles standing in their way to development. In fact, to remain prisoner of one's ethnic group without having any thing positive in mind, is like locking oneself up in a cave so that one cannot look outside. What matters is to live together peacefully, work together for the development of their country, so that Banyarwanda can tackle and solve their common problems, and break their narcissism and wake up to the progress the world has achieved. (RoR 1999, 58)

Rwandans, therefore, had to liberate themselves from the prison of ethnicity. Three years later even the terms "Hutu" and "Tutsi" were absent from the law punishing "Offences of Discrimination and Sectarianism" (RoR 2001), which defined the "crime of discrimination" as

when the author makes use of any speech, written statement or action based on ethnicity, region or country of origin, color of the skin, physical features, sex, language, religion or ideas with the aim of denying one or a group of persons their human rights provided by Rwandan law and International Conventions to which Rwanda is party. (art. 3)

This was followed in 2008 by the "Law Relating to the Punishment of the Crime of Genocide Ideology" (RoR 2008):

The genocide ideology is an aggregate of thoughts characterized by conduct, speeches, documents, and other acts aiming at exterminating or inciting others to exterminate people basing on ethnic group, origin, nationality, region, color, physical appearance, sex, language, religion, or political opinion, committed in normal periods or during war. (art. 2)

The laws' aspirations are, of course, legitimate (see Waldorf 2009, 102, 106–7, 118). More importantly, these laws do not, in themselves, proscribe the mention of ethnicity. And yet research (see, for example, Burnet 2008, 185; Eide 2007, 34–55) demonstrates that Rwandans interpret these laws as mostly requiring public silence regarding ethnicity.

To put this process in simple terms, members of the government, from whom these laws emanated, had themselves been free to commune with the Rwandan past in the comfort of "Urugwiro Village" and, as "The Unity of Rwandans" indicates, those present had spoken and written freely on the nature of "Hutu" and "Tutsi." As a respondent described the Saturday workshops to me, "Truth is being taught, everybody is exposed, everybody is willing to talk" (presidential advisor, interview, Kigali, June 1998). A 2006 report, "Genocide Ideology and Strategies for its Eradication" (produced by a commission established by the Senate in 2004), celebrated this open reflection:

[T]he great innovation cutting across all these achievements is the participatory approach which has always prevailed and still continues today to characterize political undertakings. It is indeed the best management tool for the aftermath of genocide and its ideology as it calls for the involvement of Rwandans in the identification and resolution of their problems. This move emerges specifically from conferences and debates that were held at Village Urugwiro from March 1997 to May 1998, bringing together Rwandans from all categories with the aim of finding solutions together to the major problems of the country. They produced many ideas which are the basis of today's great achievements. (Rwandan Senate 2006, 118)

And yet this open, participatory dialogue with the past was to be formally denied to the general population, due to popular interpretation of the 2001 and 2008 laws. For the population, the past could be revisited only in the accusatory *fora* of national and *gacaca* courts (wherein ethnicity would be ossified in the form found in genocidal propaganda; see Apuuli 2009, 17–18) or the didactic *ingando* reeducation camps (wherein ethnicity would be dismissed as colonial fabrication; see Eide 2007, 38–42; Mgbako 2005, 218–19; PRI 2004, 23–41).[5]

Members of the government had visited and consulted an impersonal, apparently static past and decided that ethnicity must remain there as irredeemable. The survivor and second returnee (who reflected on his childhood in Uganda) had visited and consulted their personal, supposedly static pasts and found therein the means to re-situate rather than dismiss ethnicity. In their orientation to the past, both members of the government and my respondents demonstrate that the past does not exist independently of our present relationship to it, that the present "replete with its own preoccupations, struggles, and interests appropriates the past" and in so doing "revises the way the past *appears* to us" (Jackson 2005, 356, emphasis in the original; see Halbwachs 1992, 49). And yet both the government and my respondents relied on the illusion that the past is a static, distinct, concurrent world that one can visit and consult. Like the narrator in L. P. Hartley's *The Go Between* (1953), they both acted as if "the past is a foreign country: they do things differently there." But, despite this illusion of the past as a fixed, concurrent, foreign country, the divergent position of the government in relation to that of my respondents demonstrates that the past is potentiality.[6] Given that research indicates ethnicity remains an overwhelming, if necessarily private, preoccupation for Rwandans (see Buckley-Zistel 2006, 138; Eide 2007, 50–53; McLean Hilker 2009; PRI 2004, 39), we must ask whether the best use of the past's potentiality is to prohibit the mention of ethnicity or, as with my respondents, actively encourage a free reflection through which ethnicity will be nuanced and relativized.

The "World of Present Experience"

To relativize ethnicity away from its supposedly inveterate, divisive connotations depends both on an individual's personal experience and the recognition that ethnicity is not the sole determining social locator in Rwanda. This is made apparent at the International Criminal Tribunal for Rwanda (ICTR), where I have been conducting research since 2005. On first appearing before the tribunal, Rwandan witnesses (both survivors and "detained witnesses") are asked to confirm details on a "personal particulars" form: name, date of birth, nationality, ethnicity, current occupation, occupation in 1994, place of birth, current address, address in 1994. Having confirmed this information, the witness is asked to date and sign the document. This composite of locators is, primarily, the means by which law makes the person a legible entity. But these are also elements that reflect, although they do not exhaust, key ways in which Rwandans identify themselves and others: age (understood socially), gender, urban or rural residence, regional provenance, class/occupation, experience of exile, ethnicity. These elements are interdependent, always suspended in a shifting relationship with contextually determined salience.

The witness is located in both the past and the present. That a person's past and present location are given natural parity testifies to the integral, mutually constitutive relationship of the past and present in the construction of the witness (and the relevance of their testimony) in the here and now. As the examples of my respondents suggest, this applies equally to Rwandans as agents who seek to construct their own selfhood and locate themselves and others through dialogue with the past. As Paul Connerton (1990, 22) says of personal memory, it figures "significantly in our self-descriptions because our past history is an important source of our conception of ourselves; our self-knowledge, our conception of our own character and potentialities." But this is a dynamic, responsive, ongoing dialogue. This is captured best by Michael Oakeshott (1933, 355): "There are not two worlds—the world of past happenings and the world of our present knowledge of those past events—there is only one world, and it is the world of present experience." What is crucial, however, is that this singularity of experience is hidden from the agent by the illusion that they are consulting a concurrent past that exists "elsewhere." This illusion is what gives the government's policy the patina of being reasonable and what reassures the survivor and returnee that their past is a solid basis for guidance.

While agents find reassurance in this illusion of a static past, in reality it brings with it great potentiality. The prime function of memory or, more correctly, what agents consider as "personal history,"

is not to preserve the past but to adapt it so as to enrich and manipulate the present. . . . Memories are not ready-made reflections of the past, but eclectic, selective reconstructions based on subsequent actions and perceptions and on ever-changing codes by which we delineate, symbolize, and classify the world around us. (Lowenthal 1985, 210)

As others have demonstrated, memory becomes a "psychological truth" responding to the needs of the present (see Laub 1992, 59–63; Portelli 1981, 100; Portelli 1985, 18; Vansina 1980, 271, 276). This is not to suggest that the sensation of two simultaneous worlds (in which a concurrent past awaits objective consultation) is false and should, or can, be eradicated. Rather, it suggests a need to appreciate that revising the way the past appears is not only inevitable but is, as the survivor and returnee demonstrate, a potential means to *relativize* ethnicity.[7] This, however, can happen only when ethnicity is openly discussed. Ethnicity must be posited if it is to be re-positioned.

Fabulation

Research (Buckley-Zistel 2006, 139–40; Fujii 2009, 76–102; Longman and Rutagengwa 2004, 169–70; Mironko 2004, 212) suggests that, from the vantage point of the present, many Rwandans underplay the role of ethnicity in the 1994 genocide. Scott Straus (2006, 134), for example, writes of his respondents (predominantly confessed perpetrators) that "most Rwandans did not participate in the genocide because they hated Tutsi as despicable 'others,' because they adhered to an ethnic nationalist vision of society, or because racist propaganda has instilled racism in them." Such a discovery, one that should reassure the Rwandan government, was, of course, only possible when ethnicity could be freely discussed. And yet Charles Mironko (2004, 193) raises the important question of whether these contemporary accounts are actually "representation of the social realities of 1994 [or] a representation of [contemporary] processes." Regarding actors reporting opinions held in the past, Jan Vansina (1980, 269) warns that

most people in a variety of cultures claim to remember opinions, both their own and those of others. All such claims are suspect. How often do people not genuinely claim as their own opinions which they took in fact from others? Moreover, one's memory cannot record every change of opinion one had held because opinions usually change gradually and often unconsciously. . . . [A] person's belief about the continuity or discontinuity of his or her opinions in the past is a core part of every personality. No one is schizophrenic enough to sort out the different strata of past opinions and their consequences. Remembrance of opinions must be distrusted unless there are strong grounds to the contrary.

If one wishes to re-create the past as if it were a distinct and concurrent world, then one must distrust emphatic remembrance of past opinions and, as Vansina suggests, seek corroboration. But if one is open to the potentiality of the past *in the present*, that the purpose of memory "is not to preserve the past but to adapt it so as to enrich and manipulate the present" (Lowenthal 1985, 210), then the inevitable fabulation of opinions (Vansina 1980, 266) becomes a means by which past divisive categories are relativized in the present. In other words, the past, as Michael Jackson (2005, 357–58) suggests, is

not imposed upon the present, but offers itself up . . . to the living as a basis for creatively comprehending their present situation and making informed choices about how it is to be addressed and lived. . . . For though the past contains the germ of antipathy, defensiveness, and violence, it also contains the possibilities of trust, openness, and reconciliation.

My respondents drew on selective and possibly fabulated aspects of their own pasts, informed by ethnicity, to find guidance on who they should trust and with whom they should reconcile in the present. Likewise, Eugenia Zorbas's (2007, 173–75) respondents expressed a desire to "to live like we lived before" in which "we had mixed marriages, we helped carry each other's sick, we shared beer" (see also Buckley-Zistel 2006, 140, 142). In these statements, ethnicity has to be present as an index by which coexistence can be envisaged and evaluated. Asked to describe what a reconciled community would look like, Zorbas's (2007, 173) respondents described a fabulated "highly partial, idyllic picture of life before the genocide." Such idealized remembrance is a form of hopeful anticipation. Anticipating an unpredictable future would be dismissed as naive, so anticipation takes place through the medium of an unalterable idealized past. If we privilege the needs of current experience, such processes are not suspect. Rather, in their current experience Zorbas's respondents act as if that past idyll is a concurrent world to be emulated in the present. Whether such emulation is successful (see Buckley-Zistel 2006, 146–47), ethnicity must be in the present world because it is present in the idealized world that Rwandans seek to emulate.

Summary

The question remains whether this natural need to salvage what is positive from the past (rather than the impossible task of envisaging a whole new existence de novo) is obstructed by the proscription of ethnicity and attendant elements of the "RPF healing truth." Like the Rwandan government, Zorbas's respondents envisage restoration, but it is not restoration of a pre-colonial unity beyond living memory (see Zorbas 2009, 134–35). Rather they salvage what was good from a personal past immediately prior to the genocide, a past in which, unlike the government's account of pre-colonial Rwanda, ethnicity was undoubtedly present and must be faced head on, relativized rather than wished away. Drawing anything good from the period 1959–94, however, contradicts a central aspect of the government's discourse, that everything after 1959 was malign (Eltringham 2004, 175–76).

Another aspect of many "salvaging" narratives is that they place responsibility on the pre-1994 urban elite for the calamity suffered by the "bas people." Research indicates that "ordinary" Rwandans place the blame for the 1994 genocide onto "les hauts résponsables," that is, the metropolitan political elite (see Buckley-Zistel 2006, 140; Hatzfeld 2005, 77–78; Longman and Rutagengwa 2004, 170, 178; PRI 2004, 37; Zorbas 2007, 224). This gives rise to a paradox. On one hand, the current government is unlikely to actively nurture an emerging sense of community cohesion that relies upon a positive image of ethnic relations prior to 1994 coupled with the denigration of a distant urban elite, a position that members of the government themselves now occupy. Indeed, Zorbas (2007, 224) suggests that in contemporary Rwanda, the "perception of central and local authorities as intrusive and coercive may actually have been a unifying factor among my grassroots respondents." On the other hand, this displacement of responsibility to a pre-1994 elite replicates the Rwandan government's own attempts to generate commonality among Rwandans by displacing responsibility to "outside" colonial forces (see Mgbako 2005, 223; PRI 2004, 35–38). Having introduced a logic of externalizing responsibility, how can the government censure the adoption of the same practice among the population, even if it results in the negative portrayal of the government itself?

The Rwandan government has called for "the involvement of Rwandans in the identification and resolution of their problems" (Rwandan Senate 2006, 118). But can this really be achieved when Rwandans feel that they cannot openly reflect on ethnicity that was, and remains, an unavoidable presence in their lives? Given that research suggests that free reflection does not inevitably result in the reiteration of the vision of ethnic identity found in genocidal propaganda, but a relativizing of ethnicity, then is an important potentiality being unnecessarily suppressed? Should the Rwandan government not take note of the survivor who observed that "in certain ways, ethnicity is like AIDS, the less you dare talk of it, the more ravages it causes" (Hatzfeld 2005, 77)?

Notes

An earlier version of this paper was presented at "Healing the Wounds: Speech, Identity, and Reconciliation in Rwanda," held at the Cardozo School of Law, New York City, March 30, 2009. Thanks to Sheri Rosenberg and Zach Pall for the invitation and hospitality. Thanks also to Lars Waldorf and Scott Straus.

1. For the political origins of the RPF, see Cyrus Reed (1996) and Dorsey (2000).

2. "Old-case load returnees" refers to, predominantly, Tutsi who fled violence in Rwanda from 1959 to 1973 (see Eltringham 2004, 38–50) and who returned to Rwanda following the 1994 genocide.

3. By the end of the 1950s the average family income of Hutu and non-elite *petits* Tutsi (90–97 percent of those designated as Tutsi) was virtually the same (Linden and Linden 1977, 226). Only about ten thousand "*elite* Tutsi" out of an estimated three hundred thousand of those designated as "Tutsi" were associated with the political class (Harroy 1984, 234; see Codere 1973, 20).

4. He is referring to the anti-Tutsi violence of what, prior to 1994, was referred to as the social revolution of 1959 (see Eltringham 2004, 38–50).

5. In 1998 a respondent who had attended a re-education camp in October 1997 told me: "The first tenet they preached every day was that it was the white people that brought tribalism, in order to 'divide and conquer.' They taught us that Tutsi are not from Ethiopia and had been here forever. Everyone knows this is not true, but we

clapped just to show we were accepting the teaching. There were no discussions. One woman, who had been a university teacher, when she asked questions was told she was wrong, that this is how history was. Another tenet was that before white people arrived, Hutu and Tutsi got along fine." Chi Mgbako (2005, 208) reports that members of the government maintain that the Urugwiro Saturday workshops and *ingando* are analogous as "participatory," when it appears; the former involved free reflection and the latter are entirely didactic.

6. As Michael Jackson (2005, 356) suggests, the past is "never one thing, but *many*; and it is characterised less by necessity than *potentiality*" (emphases in the original).

7. Of course, the very word "revise" and its derivative "revisionism" could be construed as denial. And yet we cannot avoid the fact, as Jan Vansina (1980, 266), the ethnographer and historian of Rwanda, notes, that "fabulation" is inevitable in how we make the past relevant to our present so that it concurs with our current self-image.

References

Ansoms, An. 2009. "Re-Engineering Rural Society: The Visions and Ambitions of the Rwandan Elite." *African Affairs* 108, no. 431: 289–309.

Apuuli, Kasaija Phillip. 2009. "Procedural Due Process and the Prosecution of Genocide Suspects in Rwanda." *Journal of Genocide Research* 11, no. 1: 11–30.

Buckley-Zistel, Susanne. 2006. "Remembering to Forget: Chosen Amnesia as a Strategy for Local Coexistence in Post-genocide Rwanda." *Africa* 76, no. 2: 131–50.

———. 2009. "Nation, Narration, Unification? The Politics of History Teaching after the Rwandan Genocide." *Journal of Genocide Research* 11, no. 1: 31–53.

Burnet, Jennie E. 2008. "The Injustice of Local Justice: Truth, Reconciliation, and Revenge in Rwanda." *Journal of Genocide Studies and Prevention* 3, no. 2: 173–93.

Codere, Helen F. 1973. *The Biography of an African Society, Rwanda 1900–1960: Based on Forty-Eight Rwandan Autobiographies*. Tervuren: Musée Royal de l'Afrique Centrale.

Connerton, Paul. 1990. *How Societies Remember*. Cambridge: Cambridge University Press.

Cyrus Reed, William. 1996. "Exile, Reform, and the Rise of the Rwandan Patriotic Front." *Journal of Modern African Studies* 34, no. 3: 479–501.

Daniel, E. Valentine. 1997. "Suffering Nation and Alienation." In *Social Suffering*, edited by Arthur Kleinman, Veena Das, and Margaret M. Lock, 309–58. Berkeley: University of California Press.

Dorsey, Michael. 2000. "Violence and Power-Building in Post-Genocide Rwanda." In *Politics of Identity and Economics of Conflict in the Great Lakes Region*, edited by Ruddy Doom and Jan F. J. Gorus, 311–48. Brussels: VUB University Press.

Eide, Trine. 2007. "Pretending Peace: Discourses of Unity and Reconciliation in Rwanda." Master's thesis, University of Bergen.

Eltringham, Nigel. 2004. *Accounting for Horror: Post-Genocide Debates in Rwanda*. London: Pluto Press.

————. 2006. "Debating the Rwandan Genocide." In *Violence, Political Culture and Development in Africa*, edited by Preben Kaarsholm, 66–91. Oxford: James Currey.

Fujii, Lee Ann. 2009. *Killing Neighbors: Webs of Violence in Rwanda*. Ithaca, NY: Cornell University Press.

Halbwachs, Maurice. 1992. *On Collective Memory*. Translated and edited by Lewis A. Coser. Chicago: University of Chicago Press.

Harroy, Jean-Paul. 1984. *Rwanda: De la féodalité à la démocratie (Souvenir d'un compagnon de la marche du Rwanda vers la démocratie et l'indépendance)*. Brussels: Hayez.

Hartley, L. P. 1953. *The Go-Between*. London: Hamish Hamilton.

Hatzfeld, Jean. 2005. *Into the Quick of Life: The Rwandan Genocide; The Survivors Speak*. London: Serpent's Tail.

Jackson, Michael. 2005. "Storytelling Events, Violence, and the Appearance of the Past." *Anthropological Quarterly* 78, no. 2: 355–75.

Laub, Dori. 1992. "An Event without a Witness: Truth, Testimony and Survival." In *Testimony: Crises of Witnessing in Literature, Psychoanalysis, and History*, edited by Shoshana Felman and Dori Laub, 75–92. London: Routledge.

Linden, Ian, and Jane Linden. 1977. *Church and Revolution in Rwanda*. Manchester: Manchester University Press.

Longman, Timothy, and Théoneste Rutagengwa. 2004. "Memory, Identity and Community in Rwanda." In *My Neighbor, My Enemy: Justice and Community in the Aftermath of Mass Atrocity*, edited by Eric Stover and Harvey M. Weinstein, 162–82. Cambridge: Cambridge University Press.

Lowenthal, David. 1985. *The Past Is a Foreign Country*. Cambridge: Cambridge University Press.

McLean Hilker, Lyndsay. 2009. "Everyday Ethnicities: Identity and Reconciliation among Rwandan Youth." *Journal of Genocide Research* 11, no. 1: 81–100.

Mgbako, Chi. 2005. "Ingando Solidarity Camps: Reconciliation and Political Indoctrination in Post-Genocide Rwanda." *Harvard Human Rights Journal* 18:201–24.

Mironko, Charles. 2004. "Social and Political Mechanisms of Mass Murder: An Analysis of Perpetrators in the Rwandan Genocide." PhD diss., Yale University.

Nader, Laura. 1972. "Up the Anthropologist—Perspectives Gained from Studying Up." In *Reinventing Anthropology*, edited by Dell H. Hymes, 284–311. New York: Pantheon Books.

Newbury, David, and Catharine Newbury. 2000. "Bringing the Peasants Back In: Agrarian Themes in the Construction and Corrosion of Statist Historiography in Rwanda." *American Historical Review* 105, no. 3: 832–77.

Oakeshott, Michael. 1933. *Experience and Its Modes*. Cambridge: Cambridge University Press.

Penal Reform International (PRI). 2004. "From Camp to Hill: The Reintegration of Released Prisoners." Research Report on the Gacaca 6. London, May. http://www.penalreform.org/files/rep-ga6-2004-released-prisoners-en_0.pdf.

Portelli, Alessandro. 1981. "The Peculiarities of Oral History." *History Workshop* 12, no. 1: 96–107.

———. 1985. "Oral Testimony, the Law and the Making of History: The 'April 7' Murder Trial." *History Workshop Journal* 20, no. 1: 5–35.

Republic of Rwanda (RoR). 1999. "The Unity of Rwandans—Before the Colonial Period and Under the Colonial Rule; Under the First Republic." Kigali, August. www.grandslacs.net/doc/2379.pdf.

———. 2001. "Law No. 47/2001 of 18/12/2001 Instituting Punishment for Offences of Discrimination and Sectarianism." http://www.grandslacs.net/doc/4040.pdf.

———. 2008. "Law No. 18/2008 of 23/07/2008 Relating to the Punishment of the Crime of Genocide Ideology." http://www.unhcr.org/refworld/docid/4acc9a4e2 .html.

Reyntjens, Filip. 2004. "Rwanda Ten Years On: From Genocide to Dictatorship." *African Affairs* 103, no. 411: 177–210.

Rwandan Senate. 2006. "Rwanda: Genocide Ideology and Strategies for its Eradication." Kigali, April.

Sluka, Jeffrey A. 1999. "State Terror and Anthropology." In *Death Squad: The Anthropology of State Terror*, edited by Jeffrey A. Sluka, 1–45. Philadelphia: University of Pennsylvania Press.

Straus, Scott. 2006. *The Order of Genocide: Race, Power, and War in Rwanda*. Ithaca, NY: Cornell University Press.

Vansina, Jan. 1980. "Memory and Oral Tradition." In *The African Past Speaks: Essays on Oral Tradition and History*, edited by J. C. Miller, 262–79. Folkestone: Dawson.

———. 2004. *Antecedents to Modern Rwanda: The Nyiginya Kingdom*. Madison: University of Wisconsin Press.

Waldorf, Lars. 2009. "Revisiting *Hotel Rwanda*: Genocide Ideology, Reconciliation and Rescuers." *Journal of Genocide Research* 11, no. 1: 101–25.

Zorbas, Eugenia. 2007. "Reconciliation in Post-genocide Rwanda: Discourse and Practice." PhD diss., London School of Economics and Political Science.

———. 2009. "What Does Reconciliation after Genocide Mean? Public Transcripts and Hidden Transcripts in Post-genocide Rwanda." *Journal of Genocide Research* 11, no. 1: 127–47.

18

Topographies of Remembering and Forgetting

The Transformation of Lieux de Mémoire in Rwanda

JENS MEIERHENRICH

Introduction

This chapter analyzes the vicissitudes of memory (Meierhenrich 2006; Olick 1999; Halbwachs 1992; Connerton 1989) in post-genocide Rwanda. It is culled from a larger, long-term project on the transformation of *lieux de mémoire* (Nora 1984–93, 1989), or sites of memory, that revolves around a historical and spatial analysis of all the genocide memorials, informal and otherwise, that have emerged—and sometimes vanished—in Rwanda in the last fifteen years (Caplan 2007; Cook 2006; Smith and Rittner 2004; generally, see Young 1993).[1] The transformation of the country's *lieux de mémoire* is one of the most remarkable, and insufficiently researched, developments in post-genocide Rwanda. Not only is the countryside full of such sites, but these *lieux de mémoire* have become an important bone of contention in the struggle over Rwanda's future.

Controversy has ensued over how the divided society ought to remember its loss. Disagreements exist concerning the *purpose* of remembering the genocide dead (the function of memorialization) as well as over appropriate *ways* of doing so (the forms of memorialization). For example, contemporary Rwandans disagree about whether *lieux de mémoire* should serve private or public functions. While some favor memorialization as an end in itself, others—notably some Tutsi elites who returned from exile—conceive of memorialization as a means to an end, the marketing of genocide to the international community. Furthermore, extensive field research in the countryside has revealed that survivors and other stakeholders do not agree on the question of whether to display human remains—skulls, bones, clothing, and such. There is also disagreement over whether the centralization of collective memory—in the form of state-sanctioned memorials for each district—is an appropriate way of coming to terms with the legacies of the genocide.

In an effort to understand the transformation of *lieux de mémoire* in post-genocide Rwanda, I have analyzed a wide variety of types of sites—from *massacre sites* to *burial sites* to *ceremonial sites* to *didactic sites* (to name but the most important varieties) in different parts of the country. To this end, I have brought to bear such diverse methodologies as ethnography, including visual ethnography (Collier and Collier 1986), and Geographic Information Systems (GIS) technology (Gregory and Ell 2007).

In this chapter, I focus in particular on the spatial dimensions of memorialization. For Maurice Halbwachs, the first scholar to emphasize the social character of memory, space was "a reality that endures" (quoted in Misztal 2003, 16). In a little known study, *The Legendary Topography of the Gospels in the Holy Land*, published in 1941, Halbwachs hones in on the spatial dimensions of memorialization in Jerusalem, highlighting the manner in which Jews, Romans, Christians, and Muslims over the centuries reconfigured space according to their religious beliefs. Halbwachs writes: "When one looks at the physiognomy of the holy places in successive times, one finds the character of these groups inscribed" (Halbwachs 1992, 235). In what follows, I focus on the nature of inscription in post-genocide Rwanda.

By focusing on topographies of memory, I shed light on the dynamics of memorialization in post-genocide Rwanda. A focus on the mechanisms and processes of memorialization is of critical importance for explaining and understanding the politics of state-building more generally. Surprisingly, only a few scholars and practitioners have grasped the role of memorialization in the creation and maintenance of international peace and security. As one group of scholars recently observed:

Memorialization remains an underdeveloped, or unevenly developed, field. This may be because memorials are too often understood as outside the political process—relegated to the "soft" cultural sphere as art objects, to the private sphere of personal mourning, or to the margins of power and politics. As a result[,] memorials are rarely integrated into broader strategies for democracy building. Memory sites fall between the cracks of existing policies for historic preservation, transitional justice, democratic governance, urban planning, and human rights. (Brett et al. 2007, 2)

This chapter is an effort to take memorialization seriously in the context of state-building by illustrating, in the context of post-genocide Rwanda, the exercise of power over memory (see Müller 2002). For in many respects, the transformation of Rwanda's *lieux de mémoire* is an example of the spatial control that the Government of Rwanda has been advocating, and seeking to popularize, in the countryside (Ansoms 2009, 303), initially by means of a controversial—and not infrequently coercive—villagization policy known as *imidugudu* (HRW 2001; Hilhorst and Van Leeuwen 2000), and subsequently by means of far-reaching land reform aimed at phasing out small-scale agriculture and introducing large-scale commercial farming (Des Forges 2006; RoR 2004; Pottier 2002).

The chapter is organized into three parts. The first part builds a framework for analysis. Grounded in recent advances in the burgeoning literature on remembering and forgetting, it introduces a typology of *lieux de mémoire* that highlights multiple relationships between memory and space. The second part turns from the theory of memory to its practice. It investigates the nature and meaning(s) of two very different *lieux de mémoire* in Rwanda's Bugesera region, notably the well-known Nyamata site and the largely unknown Kanzenze site. The third part concludes and considers implications.

A Typology of *Lieux de Mémoire*

For the French historian Pierra Nora, *lieux de mémoire* "are fundamentally remains, the ultimate embodiments of a memorial consciousness that has barely survived in a historical age that calls out for memory because it has abandoned it" (1989, 12). Departing from Nora, my emphasis is not just on instances of what he terms "privileged memory" but on what I call "underprivileged memory." For Rwanda's six national genocide memorials—Bisesero, Kigali, Murambi, Ntarama, Nyamata, Nyarabuye—represent but a small fraction of the hundreds, perhaps thousands, of spatial structures devoted to the commemoration of those murdered in the genocide.

In order to comprehend the insufficiently appreciated diversity of memorialization in post-genocide Rwanda, I used photography as a research tool and to date have compiled a database of more than seven thousand original research photographs of vastly different *lieux de mémoire*.[2] The vast majority of these largely informal structures, many of which appear to be more meaningful to Tutsi survivors because they are more easily accessible to them, have fallen into disrepair and are in dire need of preservation.

In the light of this field experience, my conception of the term *lieux de mémoire* is simultaneously broader and narrower than Nora's. It is broader because it encompasses sites whose creation was not immediately instrumental. In contrast to Nora, I allow for the possibility of spontaneous emergence on expressive grounds. It is narrower in that it refers to material sites only. Unlike Nora, I do not consider anniversaries, revolutionary calendars, commemorative minutes of silence, or other such immaterial phenomena to be examples of *lieux de mémoire*. My focus is solely on spatial structures, broadly conceived.

I have thus far visited and assessed, with a small research team, more than one hundred of Rwanda's *lieux de mémoire*, most of them underprivileged sites of memory. While the collected data do not yet form a basis for definitive conclusions about the contentious politics of memory in post-genocide Rwanda (Sewell 2001; Martin and Miller 2003), my initial findings offer a glimpse into the dynamics of contention over the memory of the genocide. These dynamics come into sharper relief if we distinguish between two broad types of *lieux de mémoire*, namely memorials and loci. As Paul Connerton (2009, 7) explains, "Many acts of remembering are site-specific, but they are not all site-specific in the same way."

Memorials as Lieux de Mémoire

The notion of *memorial* refers here to a *lieu de mémoire*: the product of intentional design rather than spontaneous emergence. Memorials exist for the express purposes of remembering *and* forgetting. As Connerton (2009, 29) writes, "The relationship between memorials and forgetting is reciprocal: the threat of forgetting begets memorials and the construction of memorials begets forgetting. . . . Memorials conceal the past as much as they cause us to remember it." In other words, the fact that memorials become imbued with memory is integral to their existence because memorials result from an *intentional encoding* of place.

In the case of post-genocide Rwanda, many memorials, thus defined, dot the countryside. The most prominent of these are the aforementioned six national genocide memorials, where the intentional coding of space has been most pronounced. But other *lieux de mémoire*, most of them former massacre sites, have also been turned into memorials. A considerable number of these memorials—although far from the majority—feature prominent displays of human remains: skulls and bones and femurs, neatly sorted and arranged.[3]

Loci as Lieux de Mémoire

Here, the notion of locus refers to "a place easily grasped by the memory, such as a house, arch, corner, column, or intercolumnar space. The loci or places in question can be actually perceived or they can be simply imagined" (Connerton 2009, 5). When loci become imbued with memory, this is incidental—not integral—to their existence. Loci, unlike memorials, result from a spontaneous encoding of place.

This is how loci work in the creation and maintenance of memory: "The real or imagined place or set of places functions as a grid onto which the images of the items to be remembered are placed in a certain order, and the items are then remembered by mentally revisiting the grid of places and traversing them step by step. The premise of the whole system is that the order of the places will preserve the order of the things that have to be remembered" (Connerton 2009, 5).

Having distinguished between memorials and loci, I relate both to the *types of memory* that I introduced earlier, namely privileged memory and underprivileged memory. If we integrate the two typologies, we obtain a simple two-by-two memory matrix. The matrix generates four subtypes of *lieux de mémoire*. It bears emphasizing that these subtypes are ideal typical constructions. They constitute conceptual standards against which to measure empirical reality. Put differently, empirical instantiations of *lieux de mémoire* will approximate but rarely ever fully embody any of these subtypes. As a heuristic device, the memory matrix is useful for comparing spatial forms of remembering and forgetting, in post-genocide Rwanda and elsewhere. In the remainder of this chapter, I concern myself only with two of these subtypes, namely the privileged memorial and the underprivileged locus.

A Comparative Analysis

This part focuses on the vicissitudes of memory in Rwanda's Bugesera region. I have deliberately singled out the well-known Nyamata site and the largely unknown Kanzenze site as *lieux de mémoire* for the purpose of this comparative analysis. First, by focusing on two sites that are located in close proximity to one another, I am able to hold constant geographical and other factors that invariably shaped the experience of the genocide, and thus have had an impact on the dynamics of memorialization and its discontents. Second, the two sites allow me to draw attention to the overlooked similarities and differences between memorials and loci in the memorialization of the 1994 genocide.

The particular pairing selected for analysis here—Nyamata and Kanzenze—exemplifies the upper-left quadrant and the lower-right quadrant of our imaginary matrix. I conceive of the Nyamata and Kanzenze sites as polar opposites on what we might call a "memorialization continuum" stretching from informal to formal instantiations of *lieux de mémoire*. The pairing thus makes possible an analysis of the instantiation of privileged memory in the form of a memorial (Nyamata), and of underprivileged memory in the form of a locus (Kanzenze). To be sure, the inquiry is not meant to be representative of the entire universe of Rwanda's *lieux de mémoire*. Rather, the purpose here is to highlight some aspects of the spatiality of memory—and to tentatively explore the relationship between modernization and memorialization in post-genocide Rwanda.

A Topography of Remembering: Nyamata

The *lieu de mémoire* at Nyamata, together with the memorials at Gisozi and Ntarama, ranks among the most frequently visited. Located in relatively close proximity to the capital, Kigali, the Nyamata memorial is a popular stop for foreign visitors—be they tourists or journalists—with little knowledge of the complexity of the genocide and the authoritarian regime that has ruled the country ever since.

Here, for example, is how Andrew Blum (2005), writing in the travel section of the *New York Times*, recounted his experience at Nyamata after visiting the underground crypts behind the main church where thousands of remains are stored on shelves: "The odor exempted us from the need for imagination. It relieved us of the need for understanding." And this is precisely one of the intended consequences of memorialization at Rwanda's national genocide memorials: to disable comprehension. It is in this sense that the Nyamata memorial, and *lieux de mémoire* like it, can be said to service privileged memory, that is, memory that is officially sanctioned because it is in accordance with the post-genocidal raison d'état.

Philip Gourevitch, another casual observer of things Rwandan, responded not unlike Blum when he visited, years earlier, the genocidal dead on open display at Nyarubuye. Writes Gourevitch: "[L]ooking at the buildings and the bodies, and hearing the silence of the place, with the grand Italianate basilica standing there deserted, and beds of exquisite, decadent, death-fertilized flowers blooming over the corpses, it was still strangely unimaginable. I mean one still had to imagine it" (1998, 16). It stands to reason that the vast majority of uninitiated visitors to Nyamata and Nyarubuye and sites like it will experience a shock and awe similar to that experienced by Blum and Gourevitch. By appealing to emotions rather than reason, Rwanda's national memorials keep observers at bay. It is indeed difficult to formulate critical questions about the legitimacy of the post-genocidal regime when one is face to face—both literally and figuratively—with the legacies of the genocidal regime that preceded it. By remembering the past in a very particular, macabre manner, these memorials facilitate a forgetting of the present.

The selective remembering at work in Nyamata emphasizes the violence of death and destruction. This is perhaps expected, and yet, interestingly, it is far from common if we analyze the entire universe of *lieux de mémoire* in post-genocide Rwanda. I cannot claim, at this point, to have assessed the entire universe of Rwanda's *lieux de mémoire*. However, having visited and studied up close and personal more than one hundred of them—in different shapes and sizes and in every part of the country—I can say that "Rwanda's bones" (Guyer 2009) are far less ubiquitous in the landscape and far less often a defining characteristic of the country's *lieux de mémoire* than a visit to Nyamata would lead one to think. What are the implications of this finding for understanding the dynamics of memorialization in post-genocide Rwanda?

Even a cursory analysis of the secondary literature on post-genocide Rwanda suggests that the Rwandan Patriotic Front's (RPF) "nonanthropomorphizing style of commemoration" (Guyer 2009, 163)—with its belief in the centrality of unburied, indistinguishable remains—has been enormously successful as far as marketing the genocide is concerned. For even an observer as astute as Guyer appears to have (partially) fallen prey to the RPF's instrumentalization of national genocide memorials, for she argues that "[t]he predominant strategy of memorializing Rwanda's 1994 genocide has entailed leaving massacre sites intact and displaying the bones of the dead—or, in the case of one memorial, preserving thousands of corpses in powdered lime. Far from being sanitized spaces of worked-through mourning or barren sites without clear traces of the violence that occurred there, Rwanda's genocide memorials are raw and macabre" (ibid., 157) Unfortunately, this generalization captures but a tiny slice of really existing memorialization in post-genocide Rwanda. While Guyer (ibid., 157) correctly notes that the RPF's predominant strategy has been to favor the installation of the macabre over the representation of the mundane at national memorials like Nyamata, this is not the case at most of the local and other subnational efforts at memorialization. While those instantiations of memory in the periphery, too, have been subjected (and often succumbed) to pressures from the center for conforming in their commemorative messages, the presence of skulls and bones and femurs declines significantly when one leaves behind the national genocide memorials. And even in settings where human remains do play a role (as they do, for example, at St. Peter's Church in Kibuye, or Nyange Church), they tend to be far less conspicuous.

The relative absence of human remains is not entirely surprising, for according to anthropologists, memorials like the one at Nyamata are largely foreign to Rwandan culture (see Brandstetter 2005). Notwithstanding the fact that many Rwandans do express a liking of the national genocide memorials, this may at times be the result of necessity rather than of choice. In interviews, survivors' preferences for memorials over loci were regularly associated with a sense of safety and security that only national genocide memorials were seen to be able to provide (because they tend to be more vigilantly guarded). Yet when pressed, and after having gained a modicum of their trust, a considerable number of survivors appeared to favor home burials. In fact, several respondents bemoaned the government's prohibition on private burials in the immediate vicinity of people's homes.[4]

This brings into sharp relief the relationship between modernization and memorialization, for the embrace of national genocide memorials runs counter to more "traditional" burial rites in Rwandan culture, where the "culte pour le cadavre," despite a half century of European-style colonialism and missionary zeal, is far from fully entrenched. As both Claudine Vidal (2001) and Anna-Maria Brandstetter (2005) point out, the significance of cemeteries is lost on many ordinary Rwandans who, whenever possible, try to maintain the all-important bond with the spirits of the deceased by burying them in a ritualistic but decidedly nonceremonial manner in their homes or environs. In fact, the display of human remains is thought to conjure a deceased's *umuzimu*, or ghost, the disturbance of which is believed to be powerful, even dangerous, in Rwanda's oral culture (Brandstetter 2005, 311). It is for this reason that memorials like the one at Nyamata have in some survivors instilled a "horror of dead bodies" (Vidal 2001, 16). How, then, do loci compare to memorials in the memorialization of the 1994 genocide?

A Topography of Forgetting: Kanzenze

The old Kanzenze Bridge is perhaps the country's most historically charged and disturbing piece of infrastructure. Located in the Bugesera region, on the road to Nyamata, the Kanzenze Bridge used to be a strategic crossing point of the Nyabarongo River (since renamed the Akagera). Now used only as a footbridge, the bridge looks serene, even peaceful, languishing in the sun. Yet the bridge and surrounding marshes were a horrific killing site in 1994 (see Hatzfeld 2003, 2005). From the metal frame construction, Hutu perpetrators flung Tutsi victims, dead or alive, into the muddy waters of the river below. Less than two years before that, the Hutu extremist Léon Mugesera had made a notorious speech in which he had incited genocide against the Tutsi by saying "your home is in Ethiopia . . . we will send you by the Nyabarongo so you can get there quickly" (Supreme Court of Canada 2005; see also Rikhof 2005).[5]

Today one would never know what transpired on and around the Kanzenze Bridge, on this strategically most important of all bridges crossing the Nyabarongo, some sixteen years ago. The bridge looks serene, even peaceful, but its history exemplifies the relationship between modernization and memorialization in post-genocide Rwanda.

The government recently broke ground on a new $155 million international airport to be built in the Bugesera region south of Kigali. With this megaproject in mind, the government also upgraded the road that links the city to the countryside and built a modern bridge over the Nyabarongo River at Kanzenze. Made of concrete, not metal, the new construction epitomizes the forward-looking orientation of post-genocide Rwanda. It spells reconstruction and development—modernity. The new bridge fits seamlessly into the compelling (albeit simplistic) narrative of Rwanda's "rebirth" or "dramatic recovery" that many international journalists (e.g., Kinzer 2008) as well as the new African Peer Review Mechanism (APRM 2006) have promoted.

No attention has been paid to the future of the old Kanzenze Bridge. "[M]odernity," writes Connerton, "has a particular problem with *forgetting*" (2009, 1, emphasis in original). The case of the Kanzenze Bridge, like many other *lieux de mémoire*, bears out this observation. In June 2006, François Ngarambe, president of IBUKA ("Remember"), the umbrella group for genocide survivors, called on the government to construct a memorial near the Nyabarongo River bridge, but so far his appeal has fallen on deaf ears. It remains unclear why the Rwandan government has been reticent to honor those genocide dead with an official memorial. The only formal *lieu de mémoire* that recalls the thousands of Rwandans—the presumed "invaders from Ethiopia"—whose bodies were dispatched by way of the Nyabarongo is a memorial in Namirembe, Uganda.

Conclusions

The current diversity of memorialization in Rwanda is very much a decentralized phenomenon. It has been a contingent outcome resulting, for the most part, from the spontaneous emergence of many different types of *lieux de mémoire*. This outcome contrasts sharply with the Rwandan government's centralizing projects of economic reform, political control, and genocide justice (see chapters by Ansoms, Ingelaere, C. Newbury, and Rettig, this volume). So, it is not surprising, therefore, that there has been an ever stronger emphasis on the centralization of memory in recent years. In March 2007 the Rwanda Parliament established the National Commission for the Fight Against Genocide to navigate the contentious politics of memory, and among other things "to plan and coordinate all activities aimed at commemorating the 1994 genocide" (Article 4[4], Organic Law No. 09/2007). A concerted effort has also been underway for several years now to prioritize memorials over loci in the memorialization of the genocide. While the country's six national genocide memorials and a handful of district memorials are being preserved, hundreds, if not thousands, of Rwanda's smaller *lieux de mémoire* have been languishing in various states of disrepair, slowly disappearing from sight.

Where memorialization has been pursued, it seems to have served, more often than not, the purpose of legitimating authoritarian rule rather than honoring the genocide dead. The Nyamata memorial exemplifies the Rwandan government's exercise of power over memory. By keeping the genocide "fresh," as Blum puts it, the RPF has been able to continuously pursue what I have elsewhere termed its "strategy of suffering" vis-à-vis the international community (Meierhenrich, forthcoming). In fact, leading architects of the postgenocidal order have openly acknowledged the importance of "keeping the genocide alive" (Tito Rutaremara, ombudsman of the Republic of Rwanda, interview, Kigali, September 1, 2008). In this context, genocide memorials like the one in Nyamata "justify a repressive government by presenting a spectre of past violence as a permanent future possibility, but they also serve as an instrument of repression. Whatever contestation about their legitimacy they generate, the skulls and bones leave visitors speechless" (Guyer 2009, 161). Guyer further adds that "the traumatic silence that they generate can be difficult to distinguish from the enforced silence that the regime demands and indeed operates as a supplement to it" (ibid., 162).

Instead of being preserved, many *lieux de mémoire*, especially loci like Kanzenze Bridge, vanish. Some succumb to the elements; others are being deliberately erased in the name of modernization, frequently to the dismay of survivors. Sometimes memory is being centralized: different *lieux de mémoire* are uprooted and forcibly merged. In other cases economic reconstruction demands the social destruction of *lieux de mémoire*, informal or otherwise. Recently, a large swath of Kiyovu Cya Abacyene, a densely populated residential neighborhood in Kigali, was destroyed in order to make room for a new business district. With it went many spatial structures that had recalled the atrocities of 1994 in a "taken for grantedness" manner—the very thing that makes locus "more important than the memorial . . . as a carrier of place memory" (Connerton 2009, 34).

The challenge facing post-genocide Rwanda is determining the intended and unintended consequences of memorialization, whether in the form of memorials or loci. *If* the RPF-led regime is as serious about fostering "reconciliation" (see Meierhenrich 2008) as it claims—and most of the contributors to this volume have expressed doubts that this is the case—it would be well advised to take seriously all topographies of memory. As one scholar writes in a study of vanishing traces in another post-genocidal society, "Before we plunge into yet another ocean of blood, it behooves us to reflect on the causes and consequences of previous atrocities and to finally understand that the origins of collective violence invariably lie in repressing memory and misconstruing the past" (Bartov 2007, 201).

Notes

1. For preliminary results of this project, see www.genocidememorials.org.
2. Several thousand of these photographs—as well as a series of empirical vignettes—are available at www.genocidememorials.org.
3. For studies of Rwanda's more prominent genocide memorials, see Smith and Rittner (2004); Brandstetter (2005); Cook (2006); Caplan (2007); Rugenda (2008); and Guyer (2009).
4. This is based on observational field research conducted in every province (and most districts) of Rwanda. Most of the ethnographic and interview data were collected in 2008; the rest date from 2002.
5. Mugesera's reference to Ethiopia was an invocation of the "Hamitic Hypothesis," the discredited theory that the Tutsi came from Ethiopia and hence were "foreign."

References

Ansoms, An. 2009. "Re-engineering Rural Society: The Visions and Ambitions of the Rwandan Elite." *African Affairs* 108, no. 431: 289–309.
African Peer Review Mechanism (APRM). 2006. "Country Review Report of the Republic of Rwanda." June. www.eisa.org.za/aprm/pdf/Countries_Rwanda_APRM _Report.pdf.
Bartov, Omer. 2007. *Erased: Vanishing Traces of Jewish Galicia in Present-day Ukraine.* Princeton, NJ: Princeton University Press.
Blum, Andrew. 2005. "Searching for Answers and Discovering That There Are None." *New York Times*, May 1.
———. 2007. "Planning Rwanda." *Metropolis Magazine*, November. http://www .metropolismag.com/story/20071121/planning-rwanda.

Brandstetter, Anna-Maria. 2005. "Erinnern und trauern: Über Genozidgedenkstätten in Ruanda." In *Kommunikationsräume–erinnerungsräume: Beiträge zur transkulturellen Begegnung in Afrika*, edited by Winfried Speitkamp, 219–324. Munich: Meidenbauer.

Brett, Sebastian, Louis Bickford, Liz Sivkenko, and Marcela Rios. 2007. "Memorialization and Democracy: State Policy and Civic Action." Report based on the conference held June 20–22, 2007, Santiago, Chile. http://issuu.com/flacso.chile/docs/memorialization_democracy.

Caplan, Pat. 2007. "'Never Again': Genocide Memorials in Rwanda." *Anthropology Today* 23, no. 1: 20–22.

Collier, John, Jr., and Malcolm Collier. 1986. *Visual Anthropology: Photography as a Research Method*. Albuquerque: University of New Mexico Press.

Cook, Susan. 2006. "The Politics of Preservation in Rwanda." In *Genocide in Cambodia and Rwanda: New Perspectives*, edited by Susan Cook, 281–99. New Brunswick, NJ: Transaction Publishers.

Connerton, Paul. 1989. *How Societies Remember*. Cambridge: Cambridge University Press.

———. 2009. *How Modernity Forgets*. Cambridge: Cambridge University Press.

Des Forges, Alison. 2006. "Land in Rwanda: Winnowing Out the Chaff?" In *L'Afrique des Grands Lacs: Annuaire 2005–2006*, Filip Reyntjens and Stefaan Marysse, 353–71. Paris: L'Harmattan.

Eltringham, Nigel. 2004. *Accounting for Horror: Post-genocide Debates in Rwanda*. London: Pluto Press.

Gourevitch, Philip. 1998. *We Wish to Inform You That Tomorrow We Will Be Killed with Our Families: Stories from Rwanda*. New York: Farrar, Straus and Giroux.

Gregory, Ian N., and Paul S. Ell. 2007. *Historical GIS: Technologies, Methodologies and Scholarship*. Cambridge: Cambridge University Press.

Guyer, Sara. 2009. "Rwanda's Bones." *Boundary 2* 36, no. 2: 155–75.

Halbwachs, Maurice. 1992. *On Collective Memory*. Translated and edited by Lewis A. Coser. Chicago: University of Chicago Press.

Hatzfeld, Jean. 2003. *Machete Season: The Killers in Rwanda Speak*. New York: Farrar, Straus and Giroux.

———. 2005. *Into the Quick of Life: The Rwandan Genocide; The Survivors Speak*. London: Serpent's Tail.

Hilhorst, Dorothea, and Mathijs van Leeuwen. 2000. "Emergency and Development: The Case of *imidigudu*, Villagization in Rwanda." *Journal of Refugee Studies* 13, no. 3: 264–80.

Human Rights Watch (HRW). 2001. "Uprooting the Rural Poor in Rwanda." May. http://www.hrw.org/legacy/reports/2001/rwanda/.

Kinzer, Stephen. 2008. *A Thousand Hills: Rwanda's Rebirth and the Man Who Dreamed It*. New York: Wiley.

Lemarchand, René. 1970. *Rwanda and Burundi*. New York: Praeger.

Mamdani, Mahmood. 2001. *When Victims Become Killers: Colonialism, Nativism, and the Genocide in Rwanda.* Princeton, NJ: Princeton University Press.

Martin, Deborah G., and Byron Miller. 2003. "Space and Contentious Politics." *Mobilization* 8, no. 2: 143–56.

Meierhenrich, Jens. 2006. "A Question of Guilt." *Ratio Juris* 19:314–42.

———. 2008. "Varieties of Reconciliation." *Law and Social Inquiry* 33:195–231.

———. 2009. "The Transformation of *lieux de mémoire*: The Nyabarongo River in Rwanda, 1992–2009." *Anthropology Today* 25:13–19.

———. Forthcoming. "The Political Economy of 'Lawfare': Gacaca Jurisdictions in Rwanda, 1994–2009."

Minear, Larry, and Philippe Guillot. 1996. *Soldiers to the Rescue: Humanitarian Lessons from Rwanda.* Providence, RI: Thomas J. Watson Jr. Institute for International Studies, Brown University.

Misztal, Barbara. 2003. *Theories of Social Remembering.* Maidenhead: Open University Press.

Müller, Jan-Werner. 2002. "Introduction: The Power of Memory, the Memory of Power, and the Power over Memory." In *Memory and Power in Post-war Europe: Studies in the Presence of the Past*, edited by Jan-Werner Müller, 1–35. Cambridge: Cambridge University Press.

Nelson, Robert S., and Margaret Olin. 2003. "Introduction." In *Monuments and Memory, Made and Unmade*, edited by Robert S. Nelson and Margaret Olin, 1–10. Chicago: University of Chicago Press.

Nora, Pierre. 1989. "Between Memory and History: *Les lieux de mémoire.*" *Representations* 26:7–25.

———. 1984–93. *Les lieux de mémoire.* 7 vols. Paris: Gallimard.

Olick, Jeffrey K. 1999. "Collective Memory: The Two Cultures." *Sociological Theory* 17, no. 3: 333–48.

Pottier, Johan. 2002. *Re-imagining Rwanda: Conflict, Survival and Disinformation in the Late Twentieth Century.* Cambridge: Cambridge University Press.

Republic of Rwanda (RoR). 2004. "National Land Policy." MINITERE. February. http://www.minela.gov.rw/fr/IMG/pdf/National_Land_Policy.pdf.

Reyntjens, Filip. 2004. "Rwanda, Ten Years On: From Genocide to Dictatorship." *African Affairs* 103:177–210.

Rikhof, Joseph. 2005. "Hate Speech and International Criminal Law: The Mugesera Decision by the Supreme Court of Canada." *Journal of International Criminal Justice* 3, no. 5: 1121–33.

Rugenda, Louis Marie. 2008. "Shaming the World at Murambi." *International Justice Tribune*, April 7.

Sewell Jr., William H. 2001. "Space in Contentious Politics." In *Silence and Voice in the Study of Contentious Politics*, edited by Ronald R. Aminzade, Jack A. Goldstone, Doug McAdam, Elizabeth J. Perry, William H. Sewell Jr., Sidney Tarrow, and Charles Tilly, 89–125. New York: Cambridge University Press.

Smith, James M., and Carol Rittner. 2004. "Churches as Memorial Sites: A Photo Essay." In *Genocide in Rwanda: Complicity of the Churches?*, edited by Carol Rittner, John K. Roth, and Wendy Whitworth, 181–205. St. Paul, MN: Paragon.

Supreme Court of Canada. 2005. *Mugesera v. Canada* (Minister of Citizenship and Immigration), [2005] 2 S.C.R. 100, 2005 SCC 40. http://scc.lexum.umontreal.ca/en/2005/2005scc39/2005scc39.html.

Vidal, Claudine. 2001. "Les commémorations du génocide au Rwanda." *Les temps modernes* 613:1–46.

Young, James. 1993. *The Texture of Memory: Holocaust Memorials and Meaning.* New Haven, CT: Yale University Press.

19

Teaching History in Post-Genocide Rwanda

SARAH WARSHAUER FREEDMAN,
HARVEY M. WEINSTEIN, K. L. MURPHY,
AND TIMOTHY LONGMAN

[Hutu extremist] organizers of the [Rwandan] genocide, who had themselves grown up with . . . distortions of history, skillfully exploited misconceptions about who the Tutsi were, where they had come from, and what they had done in the past. From these elements, they fueled the fear and hatred that made genocide imaginable.

Des Forges 1999, 31

History is often a central concern after violent, identity-based conflicts. Citizens of countries that have experienced such devastation often recognize how political leaders distorted and then exploited national history to incite violence. As countries seek social repair, many people believe that a new and more truthful history must be transmitted to the next generation through revised history curricula in schools. In such disparate places as Bosnia and Herzegovina, Colombia, Germany, Guatemala, Japan, Northern Ireland, and Rwanda, the reteaching of history has been expected to lay at least part of the foundation for social reconstruction, a better future, and a lasting peace (Cole and Barsalou 2006; Hodgkin 2006; Cole 2007a, 2007b).

In this chapter, we focus on secondary schools in Rwanda, where we have been working on educational issues since 2001. An initial study by the Human Rights Center at the University of California, Berkeley, asked Rwandan educational stakeholders what they felt was needed to reconstruct their society after the 1994 genocide and wars. Most responded that teaching history was essential to social reconstruction and that they were losing patience with the slow process of official decision making on the issue (Freedman et al. 2004; Weinstein et al. 2007). Stakeholders objected to the fact that a moratorium on teaching history placed by the Ministry of Education immediately after the genocide had remained in effect for over a decade. That study prompted the Ministry to seek assistance in developing materials for teaching history in secondary schools, which, in turn, led to our next project. We explored such questions as: How can material for a history curriculum be developed to avoid propaganda and to facilitate the development of critical thinking skills? What tensions surface for teachers working in an increasingly repressive political climate? What opportunities can encourage and support democratic teaching and debate about multiple perspectives?

Our project revealed tensions related to the government's political goal of teaching history to promote a unified Rwandan identity—a goal that allowed for the transmission of only one official historical narrative. This goal conflicted with another set of official goals for education reform in Rwanda—to learn to evaluate historical sources and evidence through embracing so-called modern, democratic teaching methods that foster skills (such as critical thinking and debate) thought to be essential for successful participation in an increasingly global economy. A further complication resulted from the fact that the official narrative, with its goal to unify Rwanda, denied the modern-day existence of ethnic groups, while the social reality is that ethnic identification remains strong in Rwanda.

Two Dilemmas: What History to Teach and How to Teach It

Most who write about teaching history after ethnic cleansing, genocide, or massive human rights abuses focus on how states deal with the problem of content selection. If nations are "imagined communities" (Anderson 1983), then historical narratives are key to shaping how communities understand themselves. In the aftermath of violent conflict, revising the content of history curricula presents states with an important means of conveying new narratives of the past, which influence the national identity of citizens, particularly those of the next generation.[1] A new collective national identity is often placed in opposition to group identities that were central during violent conflict.[2]

Decisions about what history to teach are based on two contrasting approaches. The first, which has a longer timeline, claims that accurate and sound curriculum can be developed only after historians resolve or at least narrow disputes about politically charged and historically contested events (Emmert and Ingrao 2004; Barkan 2005). The second, more pragmatic approach pushes for new materials to be created in a timely fashion because teaching and learning in schools is ongoing, and perspectives on contested events can be resolved during the materials creation process or left open and be framed for classroom deliberation.[3] For either approach, however, there are few studies evaluating impact. Indeed, determining the influence of history education presents a significant challenge in the context of other societal influences.

Cole and Barsalou (2006) explain that approaches to teaching are as important as content but often receive less attention. They write that "helping history teachers promote critical inquiry may be more urgent than reforming history textbooks" (1). In particular, they suggest that teaching critical thinking and exposing students to multiple historical narratives can promote democratic participation and contribute to the development of a peaceful society. However, the challenges to teaching are inevitably complex, and little is known about how best to prepare teachers to manage them. Even when contested issues are not so emotionally loaded, they are still difficult to teach. Students and teachers bring unofficial histories to the classroom—histories transmitted in the home or in the community—that may well conflict with official histories and with historical evidence (see Wertsch 2000).

The Rwandan History Project and the Official Narrative

Our long-term project on teaching history in Rwanda combined the development of new teaching resources and the promotion of democratic teaching.[4] It included a plan for institutionalizing our work and studies of the effects of our process and its relationship to official political agendas. The project consisted of two phases. The first focused on materials development and was anchored by two workshops. Participants included government officials and other educational stakeholders such as parents, students, and teachers, who took part in the sessions. The second focused on teacher education, materials refinement, and materials elaboration.

The materials development phase centered around two, week-long workshops. During the first workshop, in June 2004, Rwandan educational stake-holders and Rwandan- and U.S.–based academics divided into four small working groups of approximately ten each, balanced as much as possible by ethnicity, geographical region, gender, exposure to the genocide, and experience with history teaching and curriculum development.[5] The working groups held separate meetings during which they developed materials for a specific historical period. Each group chose a controversial historical case that was central to its period, compiled resource materials about the case, and finally created a plan for teaching it, including sample lessons (see MINEDUC 2006). We conducted a supplementary seminar on teaching methods to help the small groups move in similar directions with respect to pedagogy. By the time of the second workshop in June 2005, draft materials were ready, and we focused on testing sample lessons by having a representative of each group facilitate a lesson using the materials. We then began revising materials from each group. These cases were meant to provide a set of models; in future curriculum development, we expected Rwanda's National Curriculum Development Center (NCDC) at the Ministry of Education (MINEDUC) to support the development of other cases to fill out the study of each period, and of full sets of lessons for each case.

The second phase of the project, teacher education, centered around four seminars, each three to five days long, designed to introduce teachers to new ways of teaching associated with the materials and handling the challenging issues they would face in their work. By using Rwandan resources in conjunction with resources in *Facing History and Ourselves: Holocaust and Human Behavior* (Strom 1994), participants were able not only to confront their past directly and wrestle with how to teach it but also to safely make connections— not comparisons—through another historical case: the breakdown of democracy in the Weimar Republic. By studying the sociohistorical context; the rise of a totalitarian state; the role of propaganda, conformity, and obedience in turning people against each other; and stories of courage, compassion, and resistance, participants were able to discuss ideas and events and raise feelings that were too threatening to approach directly. The external case study helped teachers and their students begin to connect out from their history, to not view their history as "exceptional," and to see patterns that contribute not only to better historical thinking, understanding, and interpretation but also to prevention.

To study the process of introducing new materials and ways of teaching history, we conducted evaluations at the end of each workshop and seminar in the form of written questionnaires. For some, we conducted interviews and held focus groups to understand more fully participants' views about the materials development and implementation processes. In addition, the U.S.–based team members produced a final trip report after each workshop and seminar, and we had access to the transcribed interviews and focus groups from the 2001–3 study. To allow for closer study of implementation issues, the first author tape-recorded an entire seminar in June 2006 and interviewed participants about the materials and their implementation. We also interviewed government officials and policymakers, as well as historians and other educators, on their understandings about the history of Rwanda and particularly about the events that led to the genocide.

The Official Historical Narrative

Before describing the project results, we sketch the larger political context for teaching history in contemporary Rwanda since the current government's official narrative of Rwandan history created a backdrop for the tensions that participants experienced as they talked and wrote about teaching history. The official narrative denies the historical validity of ethnicity, leaving no room for any kind of ethnic identification. It also stymies a main goal for teaching history—that students learn to think like historians by using historical evidence to construct narratives (Holt 1990). As it leaves no room for multiple points of view, debate and discussion are discouraged.

The official narrative claims that colonial administrators and missionaries invented ethnicity and promulgated a false belief that the different ethnic groups came to the territory that is now Rwanda in successive, distinct waves of migration. It further asserts that these false teachings set the stage for the genocide, because the post-colonial, radical Hutu government used them to characterize the Hutu as sons of the soil and Tutsi as foreign invaders who persecuted the Hutu, threatened their survival, and therefore did not deserve to live in Rwanda. The perpetrators of the genocide extended this reasoning to argue that the Tutsi did not deserve to live at all. As a correction to these false teachings and to support the political goal of Rwandan unity, the official narrative explains that, before the colonials arrived, Rwandans were a peaceful people who lived together in harmony. Social groupings consisted not of ethnic groups but of fifteen to eighteen clans that cut across ethnic groups. The hope is that, if Rwandans would abandon ethnic categories invented by the Belgians and learn about and identify with this pre-colonial harmony, they would have a positive model for peaceful coexistence and would replace pride in their ethnic identity with pride in their national identity (Longman and Rutagengwa 2004).

Historians agree that the Belgian colonial and radical Hutu post-colonial versions of Rwandan history magnified and racialized the divisions between Hutu and Tutsi, paving the way for violent conflict and eventually making genocide possible (Newbury 1988; Vansina 1998; Newbury and Newbury 2000). At the same time, many historians disagree with much of the current official narrative. Most historians do not characterize Rwanda as a nation-state in pre-colonial times. No idea of a Rwandan national identity was tied to political institutions (Prunier 1995). In addition, recent historiography has argued that clans were not as important as other pre-colonial identities, such as lineage and region (Newbury 1980). Finally, several prominent historians argue that ethnic categories already existed in late pre-colonial times and were even used then to divide the population (Newbury 1988; Vansina 2001).

Developing History Resources

Our project focused on supporting the development of history materials—not a full curriculum but rather teaching resources.[6] The main questions surrounding the official narrative that led to palpable tensions were related to issues of ethnicity and its origins. This tension was foreshadowed in the earlier Berkeley study in that 46 percent of the interviewed education stakeholders expressed beliefs about the origins of ethnicity in Rwanda that were inconsistent with the official narrative. Generally, they believed that ethnicity existed in pre-colonial times (Freedman et al. 2004, 259).[7]

In the history materials that our project produced (MINEDUC 2006), this tension remained evident. The Rwandan writers were unclear in their characterization of whether colonials introduced ethnic categories. When seminar leaders asked participants to reflect in their journals about how they might use materials about earlier identities within Rwandan society with their students, the sensitivity of the topic became clear.[8] A number of the participants voiced insecurity about positioning students as historians and critics on this issue. Although they never explicitly expressed fear, they found a number of excuses to avoid teaching this topic. They said that they were bothered that so little was known and that what was known seemed to raise some questions about the official narrative. They worried that origin stories about the clans seemed to lack factual basis. Their comments reflect a more general, obsessive concern with origin stories and how to deal with them. The stakes seem especially high because the propaganda that helped move the country to genocide included emphasis on who came to Rwanda first and therefore had the most right to be considered Rwandan.

Subtle efforts to include politicized material in the resources created additional tensions. For example, one of the teams created a piece on Felicien Muvara, a Tutsi priest whose promotion to bishop was derailed by false allegations that he had fathered a child. The piece claimed that a leading figure behind that smear campaign was the priest and human rights activist André Sibomana, who was an implacable critic of the current government's human rights abuses up until his death in 1998. The piece also linked Sibomana to Théoneste Bagosora, who had been recently convicted for genocide by the International Criminal Tribunal for Rwanda (ICTR). The U.S.–based team questioned the inclusion of these unproven allegations in a history resource. We also pointed out that Sibomana, who was himself targeted in 1994 for his criticisms of the genocidal government, described in his memoirs how Muvara was "an upright man, with great integrity" and how "a plot was hatched against him" (Sibomana 1999, 11). Weeks later when we read the final draft, the allegations against Sibomana remained. This example illustrates the challenge of developing learning resources in a politically charged environment. It also highlights a challenge for outside consultants. The attack on Sibomana in this case is relatively subtle and indirect. Relinquishing control of the material is a double-edged sword, placing the consultants in the role of evaluating what is propaganda and what is fact, but leaving them without control over what ultimately is included.

Promoting Democratic Teaching

Teaching students to think like historians means that the students must be free to construct their own well-documented historical narratives. Some of the skills that the teachers and their students needed to construct such narratives included the ability to read historical sources critically; the ability to explore an event from multiple points of view, which could lead to competing narratives; and the opportunity to craft and support arguments for discussion and debate (Holt 1990). Since government officials wanted Rwandan citizens to have these tools so as to better compete in the global marketplace but also feared their potential consequences (Freedman et al. 2004), we faced a dilemma. We could introduce tools commonly associated with what we call "democratic teaching," but we would have to be careful about how we handled these tools. Participants remained aware of the political context and the official narrative, and so there were implicit limits to such teaching.

Democratic Teaching

We introduced democratic teaching methods, which were new for the teachers. As in many countries, education in Rwanda has traditionally been teacher-centered, with extensive lecture and little discussion. Democratic teaching methods opened the possibility of thinking of history as multiple and contingent rather than as a single received truth. It moved us away from direct confrontations with highly contested content, such as the topic of ethnicity. It fulfilled the need for students to have space to communicate and for that communication to be open and honest. The teachers accepted the desirability of new ways of teaching that would be more interactive, but many of them expressed concern about the feasibility, given the institutional constraints of large class sizes, the limited availability of teaching materials, and the need to prepare students for traditional examinations.

As we began our July 2006 seminar with the Rwandan educators, we characterized the discipline of history as a process, not a set of facts: "We're not going to look at history like it's a march through time, like this [draws line on board]. We're going to look at a process [laughter over difficulty translating the word 'process' into Kinyarwanda]." The lack of an easy translation for the word "process" indicated the foreignness of the idea. The leader then challenged the idea of a single history by introducing the concept of agency and examining the past from the varied points of view of individuals who made different choices: "We aren't going to look at history as something that just happens to people. We are going to look at history as a series of choices. . . . We'll look at the decision to be a bystander. We will look at the decision to be a perpetrator. We will look at the decision to be a rescuer. And we will look at the decisions of everyday citizens to make a positive difference." The room filled with excitement as participants thought concretely about what they might be able to accomplish by teaching history through the eyes of those who, in similar circumstances, chose to act differently.[9]

The teachers were accustomed to thinking about themselves as transmitters of information for students to memorize to pass examinations. This transmission model was consistent with the government's goal of promoting a single official narrative but not with the more democratic approach we were introducing and that the government also claimed to want. We connected the success of a democratic state with democratic teaching. The seminar leader stressed freedom of speech and freedom of ideas, both in the wider society and in the classroom: "In order for a democracy to be strong, citizens need to exchange ideas. . . . Democracies require public spaces for the exchange of ideas where citizens can try things out with each other. This [seminar] is our civic space. . . . And we have to tell the truth; we come from a difficult past." Still, seminar leaders appreciated the fact that this civic space was necessarily confined in many ways given the complexity of the wider sociopolitical context, and the participants knew this as well.

In Rwanda, issues of safety for free speech are serious, and in some cases free speech may be impossible to guarantee. We emphasized the importance of providing a safe and confidential space for talk on difficult topics in the classroom, talk that could include debate about conflicting points of view. We tried to model the creation of a safe "civic space" for enacting democratic principles, one that was viable within the Rwandan context. Often we used resources that were non-Rwandan and noncontroversial to help the participants understand adolescent development and the concerns of the youth. In doing so, we hoped that teachers would see how to create safe spaces for their students where they could grow into becoming ethical civic thinkers. In thinking about the safety needed for honest communication, the leader emphasized the importance of having rules of confidentiality for classroom talk: "One thing I'm going to ask is that the conversations we have here stay here." As in any context, but especially after violent conflict, each individual has to decide for himself or herself how much to reveal and what can and cannot be said, particularly where freedom of speech is constrained. Also, in the seminars, we consistently offered participants an alternative to public participation, the private space of their journals. The leader explained: "So I ask you two things. To take the risk if you feel you can. Take the chance. And if you're not sure, write it down in your journal. But allow yourself to continue the questioning with yourself. Don't turn that off."

Distancing and Making Connections

With these ideas about democratic teaching in place, we created additional space for thinking through important issues using the technique of distancing. By using the case of the Weimar Republic, the seminar participants examined human motivations, decisions, and responsibilities in violent times by looking at others in similar contexts. Talking through another history proved particularly important in Rwanda since honest and direct discussion of Rwandan history potentially was fraught with danger. We also included a series of activities to frame the concept of identity as more complex than ethnic or national identity, moving beyond Hutu, Tutsi, Twa, Francophone, and Anglophone to such questions as, "Who am I? How do I see myself?" On seeing that people are members of many identity groups and that these groups overlap in varied and complex ways, the teachers interrogated the essentialized categories of ethnicity. We decreased tension by focusing first on the more universal aspects of adolescent identity development rather than more contentious issues such as the group dehumanization underlying the genocide. We then explained how and what parts of students' identities may remain invisible, tailoring our explanation to the Rwandan context: "For a kid it could be because they don't speak the same language. It could be because they are a refugee. Maybe they're an orphan. Maybe their parents have AIDS. Maybe they are very poor." We hoped teachers could distinguish between the experiences that shaped them and those that were shaping and might shape their students.

We then asked the teachers to introduce themselves by contrasting how they see themselves and how others see them, encouraging them to reveal multiple aspects of their identities. This approach prompted the seminar participants to discuss times when aspects of people's identities are invisible, when they see themselves one way but others see them differently. This led to a discussion of stereotyping. Most participants talked and wrote freely, and seemed to feel safe talking about identity in general and about works of fiction and distant historical events, even those that contained themes and illustrated processes that were obviously similar to the Rwandan identity-based violence. As participants shared their thoughts, they were also able to experience what they had in common with those they thought of as "different." The leader then was able to ask participants to ponder, "Why is it that we and they become we versus they?" After reading a series of documents related to Nazi Germany and the Holocaust, the participants began to see how peoples' identities affect their behavior during violent identity-based conflict.[10]

The readings engendered debate about how different people act out different identities and how they do so for complex reasons. Distancing through the Weimar case and through more general discussions of identity took some pressure off the topic of ethnic identity, while the focus on making connections helped the participants move closer to their own context in a way that gave them agency over which connections they felt comfortable drawing. Our goal was to model building a safe community, one bracketed off from the everyday world, where all participants would make commitments to speak honestly and would consider what others said as confidential. The purpose was to move participants from a focus on "facts" to legacies of different choices individuals make in the face of violence. We further hoped to decrease fears that the productive conflicts of opinion associated with learning might erupt into the more violent and destructive conflicts that had plagued the larger society. Distancing allowed for a universalizing of human evil and frailty, and opened a space for imagining a better future.

Political Constraints

The political climate during our research affected how teachers perceived the possibilities of introducing certain issues in the classroom. From the start, teachers were reticent about introducing productive disagreements, such as those that result from thinking from different points of view or from examining contradictory historical narratives. Productive disagreements could stimulate the kinds of conflicts that are integral to critical thinking and that are necessary for learning. In addition to a fear of entering into debates about when varied groups migrated to Rwanda, the teachers expressed a strong need for "truth" about any narratives that entered the classroom. Concerns remained about how to teach the less codified and more controversial aspects of Rwandan history. Across the board, tensions emerged mostly around thinking critically about issues of ethnic identity that were central to the highly contested historical narratives.

Fear of discussing ethnicity in the classroom derived from at least two concerns. First, some teachers accepted the idea promoted by the government that continuing to focus on ethnicity could reignite violent, destructive conflict in Rwanda. This concern remains one of the formidable barriers to restoring the teaching of history. Second, our interviewees and participants were wary of possible negative consequences that might accompany speaking freely about ethnicity. Even in our 2001–3 interviews and focus groups, people said that they talked about ethnicity only when they were with members of their own ethnic group whom they felt they could trust. Two-thirds of our interviewees (67 percent) said, at some point in their interviews, that they felt the topic of ethnicity should be ignored in the schools, while about half (48 percent) said it should be addressed, and 25 percent voiced both points of view (Freedman et al. 2004, 257).[11]

Recent government actions have made Rwandans even more fearful of discussing ethnicity.[12] The government has conducted well-publicized campaigns against the vaguely defined crimes of ethnic "divisionism" and "genocide ideology." Accusations of divisionism and genocide ideology have been used to ban the two most prominent opposition political parties, to crush the only remaining independent human rights organization, and to imprison a number of government critics, including the former president, Pasteur Bizimungu (HRW 2003, 2007; ICG 2002; Reyntjens 2004). In late 2004, MINEDUC dismissed thirty-seven secondary school teachers from their posts and expelled twenty-seven secondary school students on allegations of divisionism and genocide ideology (Front Line 2005, 24–25). Three years later, in 2007, a parliamentary commission was established to investigate genocide ideology in schools, and a March 2008 article in *New Times*, a pro-government newspaper, said that the commission report offered "damning revelations on the extent of genocide ideology in some schools, with some secondary schools registering 97 percent cases of the ideology" (Buyinza and Mutesi 2008). The article reported further that "lawmakers, at one time, insinuated that [the minister of education] could herself be harbouring genocide ideology" because of her inaction on the accusations (ibid.).

This change in the political climate affected our project in two significant ways. First, in the seminars, we saw increasing resistance to discussing ethnicity or identity or to deviating from the government line of unity and reconciliation. Seminar leaders who had been enthusiastic participants in the original process became increasingly hesitant to confront the issues directly. They began to caution against discussing specific areas of fact or interpretation. By the time of our 2007 summer seminar, the Rwandan participants considered ethnicity and stories of origin a "taboo subject." This was reinforced by one of the senior historians who suggested to the U.S. leader that the group was not being "prudent" and that the conversation was approaching genocide ideology. Those familiar with Rwandan history will recognize the way that ethnicity is encoded in the official story. Attempts to highlight this fact or to offer counternarratives that recognize the role of ethnicity in Rwandan history are increasingly not only contested but also criminalized through charges of genocide ideology. Importantly, the U.S. and Rwandan team leaders were aware of and appreciated the changing political climate, and were cautious about how particular resources might be interpreted and potentially misused.

Second, at the policy level, we saw the government beginning to distance itself from the ongoing development of Rwandan history materials while continuing to support the ongoing professional development of Rwandan teachers. In fact, concomitant with the official handover of the created history cases, the minister of education was replaced and the director of NCDC, with whom we had collaborated closely, was also replaced when he was promoted. The new director had no stake in our project, and while giving assurances about further development of the historical cases, he refused to use the allocated funds for printing the training materials; many of our Rwandan colleagues backed away from confronting these changes. The new director ultimately released the funds for printing but began his own project that may or may not incorporate the work of our forty participants.

What do we make of the above changes in support for our project? As we had received nothing but positive feedback about our work over a two-year period, we fear that the Rwandan cases, with their emphasis on openness and individual choice, democratic classrooms, and primary source review, may have become unpalatable for a government increasingly focused on control.

Conclusions

In this study, we saw how the victory of one political side—a group that represents a minority population in the wake of genocide—created a set of tensions that inhibited curricular reform. The inability to discuss issues of ethnic identity, the distortions of a history that the government wishes to tell, the constraints against teaching students how to be critical thinkers, and, above all, the fear of productive conflict have profound implications for the establishment of a progressive history curriculum and a healthy democracy. When one identity group has power and others are subject to that group's policies and practices, history reform becomes an almost impossible task. The danger remains that the party in power, if unopposed, will create a history that structures a civic identity in its own image. If no single party is victorious, each group will struggle for its story to hold sway unless external pressures (as in Bosnia and Herzegovina) or consensus governance (as in South Africa) facilitate curricular transition. In fact, our research suggests that teaching a critical approach to history may be fundamentally at odds with the political effort to re-create the nation as a new, imagined community (Anderson 1983).

Another important conclusion is that external intervention, no matter how well-meaning or thoughtful, will always be subject to the existing political context. Curricular reform is often controversial, regardless of the setting. However, progressive curricular development is more likely in political contexts that support openness and transparency, for example, where mass conflict has ended and a consensus exists that a healthy state is more important than the parochial vision of any one group. This kind of change is possible only where there is rule of law and citizens do not live in fear. Curricular reform must occur thoughtfully and with deliberation as part of a package of post-conflict institutional changes.

The development of a history curriculum after mass violence reflects in microcosm the forces that drove the country's conflict. Political manipulation, ethnic stereotyping and rivalries, economic competition for scarce resources, and the power of collective memory influence how a history curriculum develops in the aftermath of massive violence (Stover and Weinstein 2004; Weinstein and Stover 2004). The inability to discuss issues of ethnic identity, the distortions of a history that the government wishes to tell, the constraints against teaching students how to be critical thinkers, and, above all, the fears of productive conflict have profoundly depressing implications for the establishment of a healthy democracy in Rwanda.

Was this project a failure or a success? An all-or-nothing conclusion would mean falling into the trap that underlies much of international aid. Expectations for concrete, immediate results are often dashed in the developing world, especially in post-conflict transitional periods. The tasks are to institute a process, to introduce possibility, and to create opportunity; we feel that we have accomplished these goals. Educational reform is problematic at best in the Western world, and it is even more so in resource-constrained, politically turbulent societies. However, despite the constraints, we succeeded in building capacity among Rwanda's history educators. After ten years with no history courses taught in secondary schools, our project helped move the country closer to reintroducing the subject into the classroom. Through our project and the publicity surrounding it, the government publicly embraced not only the importance of teaching history but also the adoption of new teaching methodologies. Through our workshops, 40 individuals, most of whom are in positions to influence the future teaching of history and other subjects, were introduced to new types of curriculum and new methods of teaching. An additional 250 teachers have been trained in our seminars on democratic teaching methods, which they can apply regardless of the curriculum that is ultimately implemented in Rwanda's schools. Many of the teachers who have worked with us understand that in any inclusive society, multiple points of view, which are related to the complex identities of its citizens, must find their way into the nation's history.

Notes

This chapter is a condensed and revised version of an article originally published in *Comparative Education Review* 52, no. 4 (November 2008): 663–90 (© 2008 by the University of Chicago Press).

1. The contestation of history as reflected in curriculum design is not limited to post-conflict societies but is also found in pluralistic democracies where advocacy groups based on ethnicity, race, or religion vie for their views to be reflected in what children are taught. A recent example occurred in Texas where conservative members of the Board of Education have mandated changes in history and economics textbooks to reflect a conservative perspective on recent U.S. history. The intrusion of politics defeats the goals of critical thinking wherever it occurs but is more dangerous in countries where massive violence, genocide, or ethnic cleansing has left a divided society filled with enmity and fear. See http://www.examiner.com/x-15870-Populist-Examiner-y2010m3d14-Texas-school-board-revising-curriculum-creating-controversy.

2. The literature on collective memory and identity construction on which our work is grounded is extensive and rich. See, e.g., Halbwachs (1980, 1992); Anderson (1983); Gellner (1983); Connerton (1989); Gillis (1994); Nora and Kritzman (1996); Barahona de Brito et al. (2001); and Bell (2003).

3. In weighing the relative effects of these approaches, one must keep in mind that political goals often determine curricular decisions, regardless of the scholarly record. Such effects are noted by Ann Low-Beer (2001) in her review of the volatile and highly political nature of decisions about textbooks in post-conflict Bosnia and Herzegovina.

4. This project involved collaboration between the Human Rights Center at the University of California, Berkeley; the National University of Rwanda (NUR); and NCDC. Also central to our efforts was a U.S.–based nongovernmental organization (NGO), Facing History and Ourselves (FH), which offers "support to educators and students . . . in a critical examination of history, with particular focus on genocide and mass violence" (http://www.facinghistory.org/campus/reslib.nsf/sub/aboutus/historymission).

5. Participants included officials, whom we interviewed and who interacted with us during the planning and implementation of the project; workshop and seminar leaders; and educational stakeholders such as parents, students, and teachers. The materials development workshops included forty to fifty participants, eight of them U.S.–based consultants and the remainder Rwandan consultants, education officials, and local educational stakeholders. We relied in part on carefully selected participants from our initial study sample (Freedman et al. 2004). One of the Rwandan consultants, a distinguished Rwandan historian, assumed the role of chief writer. Eight of the initial participants emerged as working group leaders, either as writers or as group coordinators to create materials for different periods in Rwandan history. The teacher seminars included from one to two U.S.–based coordinators; two Rwandan coordinators, one each from NUR and NCDC; and two to four other Rwandan leaders. Collectively, the seminars involved 250 teachers from across the country, who together served approximately 30,000 students. All interview or survey data were collected anonymously, and data were kept at Berkeley. All participants both in the curriculum design process and in the subsequent trainings were assured of confidentiality and no records were kept of names of participants.

6. From the start, MINEDUC made clear that only Rwandans would be allowed to write an official version of Rwanda's history or develop an official history curriculum.

7. Importantly, these interviewees were careful to express their belief in the importance of a unified Rwanda. See Eltringham (2004) for an analysis of the occurrence of these narratives among Rwandans living in Europe and those living in Rwanda. He found no disagreement with the official narrative in Rwanda but found consistent disagreement among the Rwandans living in Europe.

8. Journals were used extensively throughout this work to help teachers to "think about their thinking" and to provide another tool for thoughtful, critical reflection and for capturing ideas that might not be safely articulated in the full group.

9. The approach taken here is consistent with the work of Scott Straus (2006), who suggests that the Rwandan genocide was not solely a top-down event with an obedient population; rather, at a local level, individuals made decisions to participate. Such decisions usually reflected some calculation of benefit. While we do not accept his argument fully, we agree that local-level decision making at both an individual and community level is a critical component of ethnic conflict.

10. Readings included an interview with a professor who was a bystander; an interview with a perpetrator, a commandant at a death camp; and a story of rescuers, the people of the French community of Le Chambon who saved Jews.

11. These numbers add up to more than 100 percent because we counted all times a subject voiced an opinion; some subjects voiced different opinions at different times during the interview.

12. While teacher-participants in the training were selected by their schools, no minutes were kept of the discussions nor records of "who said what." As we have noted, participants are well aware of what is acceptable in this discourse.

References

Anderson, Benedict. 1983. *Imagined Communities: Reflections on the Origin and Spread of Nationalism.* London: Verso.

Barahona de Brito, Alexandra, Carmen Gonzalez-Enriquez, and Paloma Aguilar. 2001. *The Politics of Memory: Transitional Justice in Democratizing Societies.* Oxford: Oxford University Press.

Barkan, Elazar. 2005. "Engaging History: Managing Conflict and Reconciliation." *History Workshop Journal* 59, no. 1: 229–36.

Bell, Duncan S. A. 2003. "Mythscapes: Memory, Mythology, and National Identity." *British Journal of Sociology* 54, no. 1: 63–81.

Buyinza, James, and Florence Mutesi. 2008. "Genocide Ideology: Lawmakers Form Another Ad Hoc Commission." *New Times,* March 21.

Cole, Elizabeth, ed. 2007a. *Teaching the Violent Past: History Education and Reconciliation.* Lanham, MD: Rowman and Littlefield.

———. 2007b. "Transitional Justice and the Reform of History Education." *International Journal of Transitional Justice* 1, no. 1: 115–37.

Cole, Elizabeth A., and Judy Barsalou. 2006. "Unite or Divide? The Challenges of Teaching History in Societies Emerging from Violent Conflict." Special Report 163. U.S. Institute of Peace, Washington, DC. June. http://www.usip.org/files/resources/sr163.pdf.

Connerton, Paul. 1989. *How Societies Remember.* Cambridge: Cambridge University Press.

Davis, Madeleine. 2005. "Is Spain Recovering Its Memory? Breaking the Pacto del Olvido." *Human Rights Quarterly* 27, no. 3: 858–80.

Des Forges, Alison. 1999. *Leave None to Tell the Story: Genocide in Rwanda.* New York: Human Rights Watch.

Dierkes, Julian. 2007. "The Trajectory of Reconciliation through History Education in Postunification Germany." In *Teaching the Violent Past: History Education and Reconciliation*, edited by Elizabeth Cole, 31–50. Lanham, MD: Rowman and Littlefield.

Eltringham, Nigel. 2004. *Accounting for Horror: Post-genocide Debates in Rwanda*. London: Pluto.

Emmert, Thomas, and Charles Ingrao. 2004. "Resolving the Yugoslav Controversies: A Scholars' Initiative." *Nationalities Papers* 32, no. 4: 727–30.

Freedman, Sarah Warshauer, Déo Kambanda, Beth Lewis Samuelson, Innocent Mugisha, Immaculée Mukashema, Evode Mukama, Jean Mutabaruka, Harvey M. Weinstein, and Timothy Longman. 2004. "Confronting the Past in Rwandan Schools." In *My Neighbor, My Enemy: Justice and Community in the Aftermath of Mass Atrocity*, edited by Eric Stover and Harvey M. Weinstein, 248–65. Cambridge: Cambridge University Press.

Freedman, Sarah Warshauer, Harvey M. Weinstein, Karen Murphy, and Timothy Longman. 2008. "Teaching History after Identity-based Conflicts: The Rwanda Experience." *Comparative Education Review* 52, no. 4: 663–90.

Front Line. 2005. "Front Line Rwanda: Disappearances, Arrests, Threats, Intimidation and Co-option of Human Rights Defenders 2001–2004." March. http://www.frontlinedefenders.org/files/en/FrontLineRwandaReport.pdf.

Gellner, Ernest. 1983. *Nations and Nationalism*. Ithaca, NY: Cornell University Press.

Gillis, John R., ed. 1994. *Commemorations: The Politics of National Identity*. Princeton, NJ: Princeton University Press.

Halbwachs, Maurice. 1980. *The Collective Memory*. New York: Harper and Row.

———. 1992. *On Collective Memory*. Chicago: University of Chicago Press.

Hodgkin, Marian. 2006. "Reconciliation in Rwanda: Education, History and the State." *Journal of International Affairs* 60, no. 1: 199–211.

Hoepken, Wolfgang. 1999. "War, Memory, and Education in a Fragmented Society: The Case of Yugoslavia." *East European Politics and Societies* 13, no. 1: 190–227.

Holt, Thomas C. 1990. *Thinking Historically: Narrative, Imagination, and Understanding*. New York: College Board.

Human Rights Watch (HRW). 2000. "Rwanda: The Search for Security and Human Rights Abuses." April. http://www.hrw.org/legacy/reports/2000/rwanda/.

———. 2001. "Rwanda: Resolve Disappearances, Assassination." May 4. http://www.hrw.org/english/docs/2001/05/04/rwanda133_txt.htm.

———. 2003. "Preparing for Elections: Tightening Control in the Name of Unity." May 8. http://www.hrw.org/en/node/77843.

———. 2004. "Rwanda: Parliament Seeks to Abolish Rights Group." July 2. http://www.hrw.org/english/docs/2004/07/02/rwanda8996_txt.htm.

———. 2007. "'There Will Be No Trial': Police Killings of Detainees and the Imposition of Collective Punishments." July. http://www.hrw.org/en/reports/2007/07/23/there-will-be-no-trial.

International Crisis Group (ICG). 2002. "Rwanda at the End of the Transition: A

Necessary Political Liberalisation." November 13. http://www.grandslacs.net/doc/2555.pdf.

Ignatieff, Michael. 1998. *The Warrior's Honor: Ethnic War and the Modern Conscience.* New York: Holt.

Longman, Timothy. 2006. "Memory, Justice, and Power in Post-genocide Rwanda." Paper presented at the annual meeting of the American Political Science Association, Philadelphia, August 31.

Longman, Timothy, and Théoneste Rutagengwa. 2004. "Memory, Identity, and Community in Rwanda." In *My Neighbor, My Enemy: Justice and Community in the Aftermath of Mass Atrocity,* edited by Eric Stover and Harvey M. Weinstein, 162–82. Cambridge: Cambridge University Press.

Low-Beer, Ann. 2001. "Politics, School Textbooks and Cultural Identity: The Struggle in Bosnia and Herzegovina." *Paradigm* 2, no. 3: 1–6.

Malkki, Liisa. 1995. *Purity and Exile: Violence, Memory, and National Cosmology among Hutu Refugees in Tanzania.* Chicago: University of Chicago Press.

Ministry of Education (MINEDUC)/University of California. 2006. "The Teaching of History of Rwanda: A Participatory Approach." University of California, Berkeley; National University of Rwanda, Butare; and National Curriculum Development Center, Kigali. Available in French and English at http://hrc.berkeley.edu/rwanda.html.

Naveh, Eyal. 1999. *The Twentieth Century: On the Threshold of Tomorrow* [in Hebrew]. Tel Aviv: Sifre Tel Aviv.

———. 2006. "The Dynamics of Identity Construction in Israel through Education in History." In *Israeli and Palestinian Narratives of Conflict: History's Double Helix,* edited by Robert I. Rotberg, 244–70. Bloomington: Indiana University Press.

Newbury, Catharine. 1988. *The Cohesion of Oppression: Clientship and Ethnicity in Rwanda, 1860–1960.* New York: Columbia University Press.

Newbury, Catharine, and David Newbury. 2000. "Bringing the Peasants Back In: Agrarian Themes in the Construction and Corrosion of Statist Historiography in Rwanda." *American Historical Review* 105, no. 3: 832–77.

Newbury, David. 1980. "The Clans of Rwanda: An Historical Hypothesis." *Africa* 50, no. 4: 389–403.

Nora, Pierre, and Lawrence D. Kritzman, eds. 1996. *Realms of Memory: Rethinking the French Past.* Translated by Arthur Goldhammer. 3 vols. New York: Columbia University Press.

Oglesby, Elizabeth. 2007. "Historical Memory and the Limits of Peace Education: Examining Guatemala's *Memory of Silence* and the Politics of Curriculum Design." In *Teaching the Violent Past: History Education and Reconciliation,* edited by Elizabeth Cole, 175–202. Lanham, MD: Rowman and Littlefield.

Porat, Dan A. 2006. "Who Fired First? Students' Construction of Meaning from One Textbook Account of the Israeli-Arab Conflict." *Curriculum Inquiry* 36, no. 3: 251–71.

Pottier, Johan. 2002. *Re-imagining Rwanda: Conflict, Survival and Disinformation in the Late Twentieth Century.* Cambridge: Cambridge University Press.

Prunier, Gérard. 1995. *The Rwanda Crisis: History of a Genocide, 1959–1994*. London: Hurst.

Republic of Rwanda (RoR). 1999. "The Unity of Rwandans—Before the Colonial Period and Under the Colonial Rule; Under the First Republic." www.grandslacs .net/doc/2379.pdf.

Reyntjens, Filip. 2004. "Rwanda, Ten Years On: From Genocide to Dictatorship." *African Affairs* 103, no. 411: 177–210.

Rwandan Senate. 2006. "Rwanda: Genocide Ideology and Strategies for its Eradication." Kigali, April.

Sibomana, André. 1999. *Hope for Rwanda: Conversations with Laure Guilbert and Hervé Deguine*. Translated by Carina Tertsakian. London: Pluto Press.

Stover, Eric, and Harvey M. Weinstein, eds. 2004. *My Neighbor, My Enemy: Justice and Community in the Aftermath of Mass Atrocity*. Cambridge: Cambridge University Press.

Straus, Scott. 2006. *The Order of Genocide: Race, Power, and War in Rwanda*. Ithaca, NY: Cornell University Press.

Strom, Margot Stern. 1994. *Facing History and Ourselves: Holocaust and Human Behavior*. Boston: Facing History and Ourselves Foundation.

Tawil, Sobhi, and Alexandra Harley, eds. 2004. *Education, Conflict and Social Cohesion: Studies in Comparative Education*. Paris: International Bureau of Education/ UNESCO.

Valls, Rafael. 2007. "The Spanish Civil War and the Franco Dictatorship: The Challenges of Representing a Conflictive Past in Secondary Schools." In *Teaching the Violent Past: History Education and Reconciliation*, edited by Elizabeth Cole, 155–74. Lanham, MD: Rowman and Littlefield.

Vansina, Jan. 1998. "The Politics of History and the Crisis of the Great Lakes." *Africa Today* 45, no. 1: 37–44.

———. 2001. *Antecedents to Modern Rwanda: The Nyiginya Kingdom*. Madison: University of Wisconsin Press.

Weinstein, Harvey M., Sarah Warshauer Freedman, and Holly Hughson. 2007. "School Voices: Challenges Facing Education Systems after Identity-Based Conflicts." *Education, Citizenship and Social Justice* 2, no. 1: 41–71.

Weinstein, Harvey M., and Eric Stover. 2004. "Introduction." In *My Neighbor, My Enemy: Justice and Community in the Aftermath of Mass Atrocity*, edited by Eric Stover and Harvey M. Weinstein, 1–26. Cambridge: Cambridge University Press.

Wertsch, James V. 2000. "Is It Possible to Teach Beliefs, as Well as Knowledge about History?" In *Knowing, Teaching, and Learning History: National and International Perspectives*, edited by Peter N. Stearns, Peter Seixas, and Sam Wineburg, 38–50. New York: New York University Press.

Wolfgram, Mark A. 2006. "Rediscovering Narratives of German Resistance: Opposing the Nazi 'Terror-State.'" *Rethinking History* 10, no. 2: 204–5.

Young Rwandans'
Narratives of the Past
(and Present)

LYNDSAY MCLEAN HILKER

> There are not two worlds—the world of past happenings and the world
> of our present knowledge of those past events—there is only one world,
> and it is the world of present experience.
>
> Oakeshott 1933, quoted in Jackson 2002, 355

Rwanda's past is contested terrain. Most Rwandans are acutely aware of the way history has been—and continues to be—used to legitimate power and justify violence in their country. Competing versions of the past have been a constant feature of the political landscape since the colonial period—and long before—and have been deployed by elites at various moments to justify their actions (Newbury 1998, 7–25). Shortly after taking power in 1994, the Rwandan Patriotic Front (RPF) embarked on a campaign to re-educate Rwandans (and outsiders) about Rwanda's past and the role that ethnicity played in the genocide.[1] To that end, it produced a new historical narrative of the genesis of the groups "Hutu," "Tutsi," and "Twa," and the origins of conflict among them. It argued that the 1994 genocide was the result of a long-standing ideology of ethnic division and anti-Tutsi prejudice, which had permeated all levels of society from the national political arena to school classrooms.

The Rwandan government has worked hard to disseminate its narrative of the past via the largely government-controlled media and *ingando* camps.[2] It has also attempted to limit the exposure of Rwandans to other versions of history. In early 1995, within a year of taking power, the RPF imposed a moratorium on history teaching in schools, arguing that previous history lessons propagated negative stereotypes of Tutsi as foreign enemies and Hutu as the victims of Tutsi injustice (Rutembesa 2002, 83). As of late 2005, when I completed my fieldwork, there had been no history lessons in Rwandan state schools for ten years. Yet—as Haugbolle (2005) has shown in Lebanon, and Trouillot (1997) in Haiti—history is produced in a multiplicity of sites and the dominant metanarratives of the powerful can never totally suppress other voices. Although the "RPF version" of history (Pottier 2002, 109–29) dominates the public sphere in contemporary Rwanda, there are many other diverse narratives of the past that circulate among Rwandans—although mainly in the private sphere.

This chapter examines young people's narratives about the past in contemporary Rwanda. It draws on ethnographic fieldwork conducted in 2004–5 in Kigali among forty-six young people aged fifteen to thirty-five with different social backgrounds and past experiences. It first discusses the politics of history in contemporary Rwanda and how these young people learned about, related to, and talked about the past. It then looks at their explanations for the origins of the groups Hutu, Tutsi, and Twa and the 1994 genocide. It demonstrates that, in contrast to the metanarratives of political elites, there was no strong "ethnic" patterning to young people's narratives. Rather, the way specific individuals related to and accounted for the past varied considerably and was implicitly rooted in their own past experiences and current circumstances. It argues that this diversity is a cause for optimism in contemporary Rwanda and suggests that Rwandans should be given the opportunity to debate the past more openly and critically. Only by recognizing the multiplicity of voices and diversity of experiences of the past will Rwandans break the links between conflict waged through words and conflict waged through violence.

The Politics of History in Contemporary Rwanda

History is very politicized. Each government in power propagates their own version of the past that suits their interests. The history that was taught before the war by Habyarimana's regime is not at all the same history that the RPF tells today.

interview, Bosco, b. 1976 in Rwanda

The Rwandan government has argued that establishing the "truth" about Rwanda's past is essential to "unify" and reconcile Rwandans—an argument that is common after so-called identity-based conflicts where a new collective identity is often promoted to replace the competing group identities of the past (Buckley-Zistel 2009, 32–33; Freedman et al. 2008, 666). Despite this laudable goal, however, the past is inevitably "narrated in a way that secures the new government's position, absolves it from all responsibility for past crimes, and aims to create a society which can be governed according to its intentions" (Buckley-Zistel 2009, 31). In contrast to the version of history that dominated under the previous regime, which emphasized the different origins, characteristics, and history of conflict between the three groups (Rutembesa 2002, 83), the dominant RPF narrative portrays pre-colonial Rwandan society as harmonious and blames Europeans for dividing Rwandans into "ethnic" groups. It claims that the colonial powers then helped the Hutu elite remove the Tutsi elite from power and that the accompanying violence was the beginning of a period of constant persecution that culminated in the 1994 genocide.

This RPF metanarrative has been, and continues to be, contested by academics (e.g., see Newbury 1998; Pottier 2002) and by various counter-narratives—mainly propagated by former elites living in exile.[3] For example, Eltringham has written a detailed analysis of how opposing Rwandan elites in Rwanda and Europe account differently for the past. On the basis of interviews conducted in 1998–99, Eltringham (2004, 178) tentatively identifies two alternative metanarratives that "account for" the 1994 genocide:

"Europe": A Tutsi elite was co-responsible for crystallising ethnic division . . . this division was exploited by a minority of Hutu—a minority that would eventually commit the 1994 genocide.
"Rwanda": Tutsi are victims: of Belgian indirect rule; of Belgian opposition to independence; and of violence orchestrated by a Hutu elite.

While Eltringham avoids attaching ethnic labels to each group, it is clear that the majority of "Europe" exiles were Hutu and the majority of "Rwanda" elites were Tutsi.[4] Other authors more explicitly assert the existence of alternative (pro) Hutu and (pro) Tutsi narratives of Rwandan history (e.g., Mamdani 2001, 267; Newbury 1998, 10; Uvin 2001, 76).

The alternative Hutu and Tutsi versions of history to which these authors refer, however, are the discourses of political elites, not of the wider Rwandan population. There has been very little in-depth research examining how ordinary Rwandans explain the past. The Institut de recherche et de dialogue pour la paix (Institute of Research and Dialogue for Peace, IRDP) in Rwanda has used participatory research methods to explore the perspectives of ordinary Rwandans on the role of history in conflicts in Rwanda and explanations of the genocide (IRDP 2003). This produced a very insightful synthesis, but it is difficult to ascertain which groups of Rwandans expressed which viewpoints. In their study of "popular narratives" of memory in Rwanda, Longman and Rutagengwa (2004, 170) state that "the Tutsi survivors of the genocide held a substantially different view of the genocide than that of others, especially Hutu." They present limited empirical evidence to support this, however, beyond a discussion of the different terms that Hutu and Tutsi used to describe the events of 1994.[5] The rest of this chapter therefore looks at how the young Rwandans I interviewed talked about the past and how this relates to the metanarratives of elites, their own personal circumstances, identity, and experiences.

The Place of the Past in the Lives of Young Rwandans

The oldest of my research participants (i.e., those aged twenty-five or above), who grew up in Rwanda and were already teenagers before the genocide, remember learning history at school before 1994. As might be expected, the history taught was very close to the metanarrative of Eltringham's "Europe" group of pre-1994 elites. With a couple of exceptions, the youngest (i.e., those aged fifteen to twenty-one), who grew up in Rwanda and were too young to go to school before the genocide (or had only done a few years of primary schooling), had received no history lessons at school.[6] Nonetheless, many said they had learned selected elements of Rwandan history from civic education lessons (which began in state schools in the 1990s), the media, their parents, family relations, or members of their community.

Some of my research participants were clearly reluctant to talk about the past. First, some young people expressed a wish to move on from their own and Rwanda's traumatic past and to focus instead on the future. Second, many of my informants were acutely aware of the controversial nature of Rwanda's past and expressed their disillusionment with this. Third, many were fearful of expressing their views about Rwanda's past or relating their own experiences, as they felt this would locate them in terms of their political views and/or ethnic identity, and potentially create problems with others. I quickly found that many young Rwandans avoid engaging in any form of discussion about the past—whether personal or collective—with their peers or even their friends:

Nobody talks about [their past experiences]. Because if you speak to someone about that and he discovers that you aren't of his ethnic group, you become his enemy and we don't want that to happen. So we prefer to avoid talking about that . . . if I tell a Tutsi that my parents were killed by the RPF, he will immediately think that I am Hutu and he knows that the Hutu killed his family. Therefore, I become his enemy straight away. The problem here in Rwanda is that we always generalize. If I am Hutu, I am his enemy. (interview, Théogène, b. 1983 in Rwanda)

Unfortunately, Théogène's fears were not unfounded. Many young Rwandans I interviewed regularly made assumptions about a person's ethnic identity based on what they knew about their personal history. Equally, the views people expressed about the past were often used as shorthand for their "ethnic" identity; that is, if a person was known or believed to be a Hutu (or Tutsi), it was usually assumed he or she held a particular "Hutu" (or "Tutsi") view of the past.

Young People's Narratives of the Origins of Ethnicity

When young people spoke to me about the *meaning* of the groups Hutu, Tutsi, and Twa, this was frequently articulated as a discussion about the *origins* of these groups. This suggests that—as for political elites—the meaning of ethnicity is implicitly linked to the past for many young Rwandans. The most common perspective—particularly dominant among my youngest informants who were small children (under eleven) in 1994—was that the colonial power was responsible for creating ethnicity and fostering ethnic divisions in Rwanda, suggesting that the dominant RPF metanarrative of history has influenced this group:

We learned that before in Rwanda, it was wealth that counted. A Tutsi was someone who was rich and had lots of cows, but the Hutu had fewer cows and the Twa hunted. They lived like that together. Then when the white people arrived . . . [t]hey had to find a way to govern [Rwandans], so they divided them to rule them. They started to categorize people by their physical appearance—like their noses—and they said the Tutsi were the most intelligent and beautiful people. (interview, Consolée, b. 1988 in Rwanda)

Although less frequent, several young people related narratives (or part-narratives) that coincided with elements of the counternarrative propagated by the former regime and more common today among opposition groups outside Rwanda:

[B]efore the colonists arrived . . . the Tutsi ruled the country and the Hutu were often beaten and forced to work as domestic slaves for the Tutsi. . . . When the colonists arrived, they also favored the Tutsi for work and education. But later . . . the colonists started to talk to the Hutu to encourage them to do something as the majority who was treated badly. The Hutu started the insurrection—helped by the colonists—and they won. Then in 1959, 1963, and 1973, they killed Tutsi to avenge the past. That's how conflict began between the two ethnic groups. (interview, Théogène, b. 1983 in Rwanda)

Such narratives were generally most common among the older youth (over eleven in 1994) who grew up in Rwanda and were more likely to have been exposed to this alternative version of history before 1994.

In contrast to the narratives of political elites, however, there was no straightforward correspondence between ethnic identity and the content of the narratives. Although fourteen of the twenty-four people who gave an explanation of the origins of ethnicity that broadly corresponded with the RPF metanarrative identified themselves as Tutsi, the other ten identified themselves as being of Hutu or "mixed" heritage. Equally, while most of the young people who gave an explanation more in line with the dominant counternarrative identified themselves as Hutu or of "mixed" ethnic heritage, this was not exclusively the case. Furthermore, more than half of young people's narratives about the meaning or origins of Rwanda's ethnic groups diverged from these dominant metanarratives at one or more points or included completely different explanations. For example, some young people appeared to mix elements of both metanarratives, weaving them together in more or less coherent ways:

It's said that three tribes arrived in Rwanda at different moments.[7] First, the abatwa, who were potters and good hunters; then the abahutu from central Africa who were cultivators; then four hundred years ago, the Tutsi came from Ethiopia or Somalia and they were pastoralists wealthy in cows. The cow was very special and the Hutu wanted to obtain cows. The only means was to find a patron and give labor in exchange. So, they did this and . . . many Hutu became rich in cows and also became Tutsi. Also, Tutsi who didn't have cows and cultivated became Hutu. So, there was movement between the ethnic groups and they lived like that, but without many problems. (interview, Didier, b. 1980 in Rwanda)

Some young people spoke explicitly about the existence of competing histories of Rwanda and about the manipulation of the past:

In the [*ingando*] camp, they told us that the colonists brought all that to Rwanda, that they tried to divide the Rwandans to rule them . . . but at school we learned something else—that the Tutsi had come from outside to take the country to rule the Hutu and that they had taken the land from Hutu and forced them to work for them . . . and then the Hutu mounted a revolution to end that. (interview, Emmanuel, b. 1981 in Rwanda)

In other cases, young people's accounts seemed to diverge altogether from the two dominant metanarratives. For example, one of my research participants told me that Rwanda's ethnic groups originated from regions called "Tutsi" and "Hutu" in Uganda; another stated that diet was the primary determinant of physical stature, which in turn was used by the colonial powers to categorize Rwandans into different groups.[8]

Narratives of the 1994 Genocide

When young people spoke about the genocide, their narratives were even more diverse. Again, they rarely adhered to either the RPF narrative or counternarrative. In contrast to Eltringham's elites, young people did not tend to preface their explanations of the genocide with carefully crafted narratives about the history of Rwanda's ethnic groups and divisions. Instead, they generally focused on the immediate events preceding and surrounding the genocide, especially on civilian participation in the killing. Their accounts were often nuanced and referred to a combination of factors and circumstances they felt led to the genocide. The factors most commonly cited were: the civil war; the vilification and negative stereotyping of the Tutsi population; the opportunity the genocide provided to pillage; the fact that people were ordered to kill by the authorities; and the role of jealousy and vengeance.

First, almost half of my research participants—mostly, but not exclusively, those who were in Rwanda in the early 1990s—said that the civil war was significant, as it deepened the political crisis and created fear among the wider population.[9] This is largely in line with the dominant counternarrative about the genocide:[10]

[During the war], the RPF took territory very quickly, so Habyarimana and others were afraid of losing power—that's why they said they had to get rid of all Tutsi and started to plan all that . . . (interview, Innocent, b. 1974 in Burundi)

[A]t the beginning people knew nothing. Some of them didn't even know that there were Tutsi outside the country that had fled and were being prevented from returning home . . . but that changed with the news of killings committed by the

RPF in Umutara and Byumba and how they killed. Then there were Tutsi secret meetings in this period, because there were Tutsi who left to fight with the RPF and others that gave information to the RPF. This really influenced people to think that all the Tutsi were their enemies. (interview, Bosco, b. 1976 in Rwanda)

Several young people discussed the impact of the war on social relations in their community, saying that the departure of young Tutsi men (allegedly to join the RPF) lent credence to the extremists' claims that the enemy was not just the RPF, but also Tutsi in their neighborhood. Significantly, fifteen young people—mostly in Rwanda at the time of the genocide—mentioned the belief among the Hutu population in a secret Tutsi plan to take away power, jobs, and property from Hutu or to dominate or even kill them:

I heard that the Tutsi had planned to kill the Hutu and that they had new materials in their houses to do that—like machetes, hoes, spears, and petrol to burn the houses of Hutu. When the Hutu heard that, they decided to kill before being killed. (interview, Baptiste, b. 1986 in Rwanda)

This leads to the second factor cited by almost half of my research participants: the role of the propaganda and negative stereotyping of the Tutsi. In line with the RPF narrative and arguments made by Chrétien et al. (1995) and Des Forges (1999), many young Rwandans talked about the role of local meetings and propaganda in "sensitizing" the population and inciting them to kill:

The war had already begun in 1990 and there were sensitization campaigns in meetings and on the radio RTLM, which everyone listened to. . . . They played on people's fears, saying that the honor of Hutu was threatened; that [the Tutsi] were going to take their property and their lives. There were years of sensitization . . . we learned that Rwanda was the country of the Hutu. [At school] we learned an entire history that justified the domination of Hutu and division. . . . It's also true that there were RPF accomplices among the Tutsi population, but ideas of the Tutsi as malign helped people believe their neighbors all did that in secret as well. The sensitization messages touched something if they pushed people to such a point where they killed people they knew. (interview, Aimé, b. 1974 in Rwanda)

Like Aimé, a number of my informants said that the reason the rumors and propaganda were believable to ordinary Rwandans was because they resonated with what they had already learned about the nature of the Tutsi:

People killed because they learned in history at school that in the past the Tutsi oppressed the Hutu and were cunning and bad. Then the authorities said that the Hutu were going to be dominated again if they didn't kill Tutsi to stop them. (interview, Théogène, b. 1983 in Rwanda)

The third most commonly cited factor that again almost half of my informants said explained people's participation in the genocide was the opportunity it provided to pillage:

People thought they could kill and then occupy or take the property—the houses and field—of others without problem, without condemnation. . . . It was the authorities that thought about killing on the basis of ethnicity, not the population. (interview, Evelyne, b. 1985 in Rwanda)

Beyond this, a third of those interviewed suggested that ordinary Rwandans killed as they were instructed to do so by their leaders and were accustomed to following orders from the authorities, again a message that the RPF propagated in the immediate aftermath of the genocide (see Prunier 1995; Straus 2006). Several of these people—all young men living in Rwanda in 1994—also talked about the role of peer pressure in convincing young men to participate in the killing:[11]

It was well organized. People were incited to do that by the Government. . . . They distributed weapons in the neighborhoods. There were barriers everywhere and all the men of the neighborhood were obliged to go there to kill. If not, you were threatened yourself. Because of that, lots of youth participated and everyone knew that as a youth, you couldn't avoid going to the barrier. You didn't want to be excluded from the group. (interview, Didier, b. 1980 in Rwanda)

Finally, and significantly, a third of young Rwandans mentioned the role of jealousy or vengeance in motivating people to kill others in their neighborhood, factors that have generally been downplayed in both the RPF and counternarratives of the genocide.

There were many cases of vengeance during the genocide. For example, there were two families in our *quartier* [neighborhood] who had a conflict five years before the war. Then during the war, one family went immediately on the first day to kill the other. It was Hutu killing Tutsi, but had nothing to do with ethnicity—that was just the excuse. (interview, Théogène, b. 1983 in Rwanda)

Rwandans are very malicious. . . . If you do well in life, they become very jealous and start to create problems for you or figure how to get something for themselves. In the countryside, people poison others just because they are successful. I think lots of people killed because of this. (interview, Magnifique, b. 1985 in Rwanda)

Again, the most striking finding was that there was no significant ethnic patterning to these narratives. In contrast to Longman and Rutagengwa (2004, 170), I did not find evidence of alternative Hutu and Tutsi explanations of the genocide. I also did not remark the same clear-cut distinction with respect to the terms used to describe the events of 1994. While slightly more young people who identified themselves as Tutsi used the term "genocide" (*itsemba bwoko*) and slightly more people who identified themselves as Hutu or mixed referred to the events as "the war" (*intambara*), young Rwandans of all backgrounds used these terms and sometimes interchanged them from one sentence or conversation to the next.

Explaining Young People's Narratives of the Past (and Present)

The narrator's perspective and predilections shape his [*sic*] choice and use of historical materials. . . . The past we know or experience is always contingent on our own views, our own perspective, above all our own present.

Lowenthal 1985, 216

The critical thing about narratives of the past—whether personal or collective—is that they attempt to legitimate the present as much as they explain the past: "[T]he *past* is a contested place . . . different interpretations of it should be explored . . . because they reveal what actors hold to be *current* disparities" (Eltringham 2004, 148). Accounts of the past are never finished, but continually evolve in response to the needs of the present, in dialogue with others and with our own imagination (Jackson 2002, 15). They are at once less than and more than the past (Lowenthal 1985, 214–19). On the one hand, our narratives are always incomplete as we forget, discard, or block out memories, which are irrelevant, undesirable, or too painful (see Zur 1997, 68). On the other hand, the stories we tell rework the past, rearranging and fusing narratives to make them more comprehensible or bearable (Jackson 2002, 16) or to better explain or justify our current circumstances (Malkki 1995).

This was certainly the case among my research participants who, in their accounts of the past, were implicitly seeking to explain their own past experiences and navigate the everyday politics of their current lives. For those young people who were living in Rwanda in 1994, their stake in Rwanda's past was particularly high. This was sometimes reflected in the detail and complexity of their narratives, which implicitly sought to account for what happened to them or justify their own actions. This is perhaps best illustrated by the case of Gaspard, a young man who had been released from prison the previous year as a "minor."[12] Aware that I would have already learned something of his past from a mutual friend, Gaspard's detailed narrative about his time in prison was designed to evoke both sympathy and admiration:

At the end of the war, my brothers were killed by the RPF and I had to flee to Kibeho camp for displaced persons. In 1995, they came to chase us from the camp and they caught me and put me in prison. They shouldn't have done this as I was thirteen years old and the law said that minors younger than fourteen years old couldn't be put in prison. First, they put me in a *cachot* [commune-level detention center] for four months in horrible conditions without space to sit down or sleep, with almost nothing to eat. Then they transferred me to Nyanza, far from my family where my mother couldn't afford to come and visit me. I suffered a lot there—I was there four years without seeing my parents, without seeing the sun. We had a small piece of ground to sleep on without space to stretch out and there wasn't enough to eat. The older prisoners took advantage of us children who didn't have family to visit us. They offered us food and clothing in return for sex and you know it is very easy to persuade a child who is hungry to accept sex in return for food. I was lucky as I was the *chef des jeunes* and for that, I had the right to two goblets of corn instead of one. I was also lucky to meet adults and teachers who helped me. . . . Instead of doing nothing, I asked them to teach me. . . . I learned seven languages in prison and many other things.

Despite his apparent openness about his experiences in prison, Gaspard evaded opportunities to discuss his own actions in 1994. Instead, he spoke generally about the genocide—although in a way that appeared to shift blame from the Hutus that killed or at least to render their actions more comprehensible:

[The genocide] was authorized by the state. People were told they could kill and take Tutsi's property. Mostly, they were people living in poverty, who would kill if the authorities told them to. They also called Tutsi names like serpents. Hutu were used to seeing Tutsi as animals, even before the genocide. Also there was the war. The RPF attacked and the authorities made people believe that all Tutsi outside and inside the country were the enemy, were in the way and needed to be killed, that all Tutsi were helping the RPF . . . because some Tutsi had sent their sons to fight. The authorities also told people that the RPF had killed their president and Hutu feared they would lose all their privileges and return to a situation of oppression.

In contrast to Gaspard, many young people who grew up outside Rwanda and returned after 1994 appeared to be less concerned about Rwanda's past, and their accounts tended to be less sophisticated, reflective, and intertwined with their personal experiences.

The Perpetuation of Conflict via Talking and Not Talking about the Past?

The narratives discussed in this chapter show that, given their different past experiences and current circumstances, young people in Rwanda today have varying relationships to the past. Although most young people were aware of the sensitive nature of Rwanda's past, their own narratives were far more diverse than those of Eltringham's elites. The RPF metanarrative of history seemed to be the strongest influence on young people's views, but this was often combined with elements of the dominant counternarrative or totally different explanations altogether. This shows that, despite the relatively coercive means used by the current government to impose its own narrative (Buckley-Zistel 2009, 46), young people form their views of the past from a variety of sources. Their narratives of the past are a synthesis of explanations absorbed from different sources and memories of their own firsthand experiences, combined in ways that help them make sense of and justify their current lives and circumstances.

This diversity of narratives should be a cause for optimism. Although, in some cases, it demonstrates that young people are poorly informed about the past, the lack of significant ethnic patterning to their narratives dispels the notion that Rwandans' worldviews and actions are necessarily determined by their ethnic identity. The challenge, however, is that young people rarely talked among themselves about the past—whether personal or collective—and therefore such assumptions remained unchallenged. Although some Rwandans discussed the past in intimate circles, the public domain was dominated by the RPF metanarrative.

There are significant risks attached to the government's attempt to impose a singular version of history on the population. First, and as this research demonstrates, it is not possible to eliminate completely other versions of the past; alternative histories will always continue to circulate in private circles. The danger is, however, that neither these nor the dominant RPF metanarrative will be discussed openly and hence be subjected to critical inquiry and the litmus test of lived experience. This, in turn, leaves the assumption that there are alternative Tutsi and Hutu versions of the past unchallenged and reinforces the "ethnic logic" that persists in contemporary Rwanda (McLean Hilker 2009).

Second, this creates a situation in which competing singular versions of history—the RPF metanarrative or the counternarrative—effectively continue the conflict through discursive means rather than physical violence. As others have shown, there is a critical link between conflict waged through words and that waged through violence: "[A] persistent appeal to absolute history . . . has been a central element in instigating violence and ultimately genocide in Rwanda" (Eltringham 2004, 178). It is for this reason that several authors argue that the Rwandan government needs to explicitly recognize and permit exploration of the multiple histories of contemporary Rwandans in order to break the pattern of manipulation of the past, prevent future violence, and promote dialogue and reconciliation:

[T]o avoid future conflict, instead of glossing over the past and pretending that Rwandans are beyond any conflicts, a more situated version of the past is required in which all members of society may recognize themselves. In order to move towards national unity and reconciliation it is not sufficient to narrate the nation whole—by using the same strategies that were deployed for its division—but to listen to the different stories that emerge from the different population groups and their particular experience as victims, perpetrators, bystanders, or heroes. (Buckley-Zistel 2009, 48; see also Eltringham 2004, 177–79)

In this respect, it is promising that a large number of my research participants stressed the need to recognize everyone's experience of suffering in order to promote reconciliation:

[R]econciliation implies many stages and the first stage must be recognition of the whole truth of what happened in Rwanda. Yes, there was the genocide, but there were many things that happened before and after the genocide that made Rwandans suffer. We must speak about all of this and recognize all the suffering. . . . We have to speak about how the Hutu suffered in the camps in Congo and how they have a complex about this and they have internalized this suffering. We also have to speak about other Rwandans like me who spent years in exile and have also suffered because of that. (interview, Fidèle, b. 1978 in Zaïre)

Notes

A longer version of this chapter can be found in McLean Hilker, "Everyday Ethnicities: Identity and Reconciliation among Youth in Post-genocide Rwanda" (PhD diss., University of Sussex, Brighton, 2009).

1. The RPF effectively dominated the Government of National Unity until it won the 2003 parliamentary and presidential elections (Reyntjens 2004, 177–210).

2. *Ingando* "solidarity" or "reeducation" camps were introduced in 1996 and have been targeted at groups such as ex-prisoners, returnees, demobilized soldiers, and state-funded university students. *Ingando* are military-style camps where participants receive a mix of physical training and civic education lessons about Rwanda (see throughout and especially Thomson, chap. 21, this volume).

3. In practice, a metanarrative might best be described as a collection of overlapping narratives with the same overall sense and components, rather than a singular, uniform narrative.

4. Eltringham's "Europe" group was primarily composed of the pre-1994 political and intellectual elite, which was almost exclusively composed of Hutu. His "Rwanda" group consisted of government officials and pro-government elites, a group that is heavily dominated by Tutsi but includes some Hutu.

5. They say that genocide survivors almost universally invoked the Kinyarwanda term used by the post-1994 government and survivor organizations for "genocide"

(*itsemba bwoko*), whereas Hutu were more likely to refer to "the war" (*intambara*), "the killings" (*ubwicanyi*), "the happenings" (*ibyabaye*), "the tragedy" (*amahono*), or "the massacres" (*itsemba tsemba*).

6. A couple of interviewees had been taught a limited amount of Rwandan history at their private schools, where they learned about less controversial issues like the precolonial secession of kings. Buckley-Zistel (2009, 42–43) also suggests that some children have been taught limited amounts of history at state schools in spite of the ban.

7. It was common for my research participants to preface their response with "it is said that" or "I was taught that," which had the effect of distancing the person from what came next. This suggests an awareness of the problematic nature of the past.

8. This argument was developed in an exhibit organized by the physical anthropologist Hiernaux at the INRS museum in Butare before 1994. The theory that the Tutsi physique had literally been shaped by cattle was formed by the famous chief Kayijuka by the mid-1920s.

9. Straus (2006) argues that the context of war has been underplayed in the literature.

10. It is important to stress that there are variations in the way various opposition groups present the significance of the 1990–94 civil war. For some, this simply provides an important part of the context of fear in which the genocide took place and can help explain why some Hutu participated in the killing. For others, the war is used to deny the genocide. This latter position is clearly both untenable and unacceptable, and none of my research participants ever denied the genocide.

11. See Straus (2006, 143–48) on the role of intra-Hutu coercion.

12. A Presidential Decree in January 2003 led to the release of certain categories of genocide detainees, including those who were minors at the time of the genocide.

References

Buckley-Zistel, Susanne. 2009. "Nation, Narration, Unification? The Politics of History Teaching after the Rwandan Genocide." *Journal of Genocide Research* 11, no. 1: 31–53.

Chrétien, Jean-Pierre, et al. 1995. *Rwanda: Les médias du génocide.* Paris: Karthala.

Des Forges, Alison. 1999. *Leave None to Tell the Story: Genocide in Rwanda.* New York: Human Rights Watch.

Eltringham, Nigel. 2004. *Accounting for Horror: Post-genocide Debates in Rwanda.* London: Pluto Press.

Freedman, Sarah W., Harvey M. Weinstein, K. L. Murphy, and Timothy Longman. 2008. "Teaching History after Identity-based Conflicts: The Rwanda Experience." *Comparative Education Review* 52, no. 4: 663–90.

Haugbolle, Sune. 2005. "Public and Private Memory of the Lebanese Civil War." *Comparative Studies of South Asia, Africa and the Middle East* 25, no. 1: 191–201.

Institut de recherche et de dialogue pour la paix (IRDP). 2003. "Sustaining Peace in Rwanda: Voice of the People." November. http://www.grandslacs.net/doc/3654.pdf.

Jackson, Michael. 2002. *The Politics of Storytelling: Violence, Transgression, and Intersubjectivity.* Copenhagen: Museum Tusculanum Press.

Longman, Timothy, and Théonèste Rutagengwa. 2004. "Memory, Identity, and Community in Rwanda." In *My Neighbor, My Enemy: Justice and Community in the Aftermath of Mass Atrocity,* edited by Eric Stover and Harvey M. Weinstein, 162–82. Cambridge: Cambridge University Press.

Lowenthal, David. 1985. *The Past Is a Foreign Country.* Cambridge: Cambridge University Press.

Malkki, Liisa H. 1995. *Purity and Exile: Violence, Memory and National Cosmology among Hutu Refugees in Tanzania.* Chicago: University of Chicago Press.

Mamdani, Mahmood. 2001. *When Victims Become Killers: Colonialism, Nativism, and the Genocide in Rwanda.* Princeton, NJ: Princeton University Press.

McLean Hilker, Lyndsay. 2009. "Everyday Ethnicities: Identity and Reconciliation among Rwandan Youth." *Journal of Genocide Research* 11, no. 1: 81–100.

Newbury, Catharine. 1998. "Ethnicity and the Politics of History in Rwanda." *Africa Today* 45, no. 1: 7–25.

Pottier, Johan. 2002. *Re-imagining Rwanda: Conflict, Survival and Disinformation in the Late Twentieth Century.* Cambridge: Cambridge University Press.

Prunier, Gérard. 1995. *The Rwanda Crisis: History of a Genocide.* London: Hurst.

Reyntjens, Filip. 2004. "Rwanda, Ten Years On: From Genocide to Dictatorship." *African Affairs* 103, no. 411: 177–210.

Rutembesa, Faustin. 2002. "Le discours sur le peuplement comme instrument de manipulation identitaire." In *Peuplement du Rwanda: Enjeux et Perspectives,* edited by Faustin Rutembesa et al., 73–102. Butare: Editions de l'Université Nationale du Rwanda.

Straus, Scott. 2006. *The Order of Genocide: Race, Power, and War in Rwanda.* Ithaca, NY: Cornell University Press.

Trouillot, Michel-Rolph. 1997. *Silencing the Past: Power and the Production of History.* Boston: Beacon Press.

Uvin, Peter. 2001. "Reading the Rwanda Genocide." *International Studies Review* 3, no. 3: 75–99.

Zur, Judith. 1997. "Reconstructing the Self through Memories of Violence among Mayan Indian War Widows." In *Gender and Catastrophe,* edited by Ronit Lentin, 64–76. London: Zed Books.

21

Reeducation for Reconciliation

Participant Observations on Ingando

SUSAN THOMSON

In the midst of my doctoral fieldwork, the Rwandan government ordered me to undergo "reeducation." I was just
over halfway finished when the executive assistant to the minister of local
government told me that he had to revoke my letter of permission because
my research was "against national unity and reconciliation" and "was not
the kind of research the government needed." The purpose of my 2006 research was to understand the effects of the post-genocide government's policy
of national unity and reconciliation on ordinary peasant Rwandans living
in the southwestern region of the country.[1] My research was ethnographic,
which meant that I spent considerable time in rural areas, consulting ordinary Rwandans about their lives before, during and after the genocide, to
illustrate how they subtly and strategically resist that government policy.[2] In
the government's view, I was "wasting" my time talking to "peasants about
politics" since they are "all liars anyway." Furthermore, I had clearly been
"brainwashed." So, the minister's assistant took my passport "for safekeeping"
and presented me with a list of reeducation activities, including the assign-

ment of a government handler to make sure I stopped talking to peasants; a list of high-ranking government, private sector, and civil society representatives to meet so I could "learn the truth" about the government's policy of national unity and reconciliation; and an order to attend both *gacaca* court proceedings and *ingando* citizenship reeducation camps as a guest of the government.

I knew little about *ingando*, as it is an under-studied aspect of the government's post-genocide reconstruction policy of national unity and reconciliation.[3] I spent a week participating in *ingando* alongside a group of approximately one hundred confessed *génocidaires* who were in the fifth week of their twelve-week reeducation process. All these men had been released from prison following their *gacaca* court appearances, and were required to go through *ingando* reeducation before returning to their home communities. In ordering my reeducation, the Rwandan Patriotic Front (RPF) gave me a frontline look at the tactics and techniques it uses to organize the flow of information and determine what counts as the "truth" in post-genocide Rwanda (see Pottier 2002). In particular, my *ingando* experience offered a behind-the-scenes look at one of the key mechanisms of the RPF's top-down policy of national unity and reconciliation. The purpose of this chapter is to contrast the government's stated goals of *ingando* with its actual effects on its participants. I argue that *ingando* does little to reeducate confessed *génocidaires* on how to reconcile with family, friends, and neighbors. Instead of promoting a sense of national unity and reconciliation, it teaches these men, the majority of whom are ethnic Hutu, to remain silent and not question the RPF's vision for creating peace and security for all Rwandans. For us, *ingando* was an alienating, oppressive, and sometimes humiliating experience that worked hard to silence all forms of dissent—something that may, paradoxically, crystallize and create stronger dissent in the future.

First, I situate *ingando* as a key mechanism within the broader policy of national unity and reconciliation. I then set out the official goals of *ingando* reeducation for genocide suspects to illustrate the extent to which *ingando* teachings are an instrument for consolidating state control—rather than a sincere effort to promote reconciliation among ordinary Rwandans. Specifically, I analyze how those suspects reacted to the version of history that *ingando* taught. The chapter builds on Alison Des Forges's legacy of human rights activism in critiquing and calling to account the oppressive actions of the RPF as it works to exclude a significant portion of the population from political life. It also builds on Alison's academic commitment to including the lived histories of ordinary people.

Situating *Ingando*

The policy of national unity and reconciliation is an ambitious social engineering project that the RPF-led government claims will forge a unified Rwandan identity while fostering reconciliation between genocide survivors and perpetrators. Under this policy, the government reeducates the population on the ethnic unity that existed before colonialism—a time when Tutsi and Hutu lived in "peaceful harmony and worked together for the good of the nation" (NURC 2004, 41, 53). In romanticizing the historical past and presuming that all Hutu need to be reeducated, the policy produces two broad simplifications: all Tutsi (whether they were in Rwanda during the genocide or not) are innocent victims or "survivors" and all Hutu (whether they participated in the genocide or not) are guilty perpetrators. The policing of boundaries of public speech lies at the heart of this national unity and reconciliation. Rwandans—elites and ordinary folk alike—can only speak publicly about ethnicity in state-sanctioned settings like the *ingando* camps, the *gacaca* trials, and during genocide mourning week. Otherwise, the RPF does not allow for public discussion of the violence that individual Rwandans of all ethnicities—Hutu, Tutsi, and Twa—experienced before, during, and after the genocide.

The government promotes national unity and reconciliation in numerous ways. It encourages collective memory of the genocide through memorial sites and mass graves to show the end result of ethnic division. Every year, annual commemorations are held during national mourning week (April 7 to 14) to remind Rwandans of the "pernicious effects of ethnic divisionism" (interview with NURC official, 2006). The government also adopted new national symbols (flag, anthem, and emblem) in 2001 because the existing ones "symbolized the genocide and encouraged an ideology of genocide and divisionism" (ibid.).[4] As part of Rwanda's administrative restructuring in 2006, the government changed place names at all administrative levels (from villages to provinces) to "protect survivors from remembering where their relatives died" (interview with Ministry of Culture official, 2006).[5] In addition, the revised 2003 Constitution criminalized public references to ethnic identity (RoR 2003, art. 33) as well as "ethnic divisionism" and "trivializing the genocide."

The *ingando* camps, then, are but one mechanism for promoting national unity and reconciliation. The government makes an important distinction between *ingando* solidarity camps and *ingando* reeducation camps. Solidarity camps are for politicians, civil society and church leaders, *gacaca* judges, and incoming university students; reeducation camps are for ex-combatants, ex-soldiers, confessed *génocidaires*, released prisoners, prostitutes, and street children. Many of my ordinary Rwandan informants understood the solidarity camps as a form of political indoctrination for those who occupy, or will occupy, leadership positions while they saw re-education camps as a form of social control to keep Hutu out of public life. I received my *ingando* reeducation with confessed *génocidaires* who were about to be released back into their communities. These *ingando* normally run for three months and are designed to "urge them to tell the truth of what they did during the genocide before the *gacaca* courts" and "to prepare them for reintegration back to their communities of origin" (NURC 2006c, 4).

Ingando's Reeducation

Before starting my *ingando* reeducation, I met with the local official responsible for administering the camp. He told me to "pay attention" to the "official goals" of the lessons

because you will quickly learn how we are successfully promoting unity and reconciliation. The lessons you will see are focused on making them [*génocidaires*] understand the importance of telling the truth about what they did during the genocide. Once these Hutu tell the truth, Tutsi survivors can forgive them. We also teach them about the real history of Rwanda because we know corrupt leaders have misled them all these many years; they have been poisoned with ethnic hatred. We teach them that their role in society depends on how they tell their truth.

Following this short speech, the local official assigned me a translator who carried an AK-47, and who held the rank of major in the Rwandan Patriotic Army (RPA). Emile was my escort for the week, and he was responsible for making sure that "I learned what I needed to learn." As I stood up to introduce myself, Emile silenced me, saying that he "knew well who I was" and why I had been ordered to undergo reeducation. Emile turned to salute the local official, promising him that I would be "appropriately reeducated" under his tutelage. As we walked together to the soccer field where the day's lesson was taking place, Emile advised me sternly "to pay attention" and "to keep quiet." I was then taken to the meal hall, where I was introduced to my *ingando* classmates, who were told that I would spend the week with them. Here, we received our final instructions on the government's expectations for our reeducation. As one of the government officials responsible for our reeducation said: "You will not be able to return to your communities without understanding the real causes of the genocide. We will test you on history to make sure you understand.

Remember also that you are former Hutu. We are all Rwandans now and this is the basis of our history lessons."

Following this instruction, we walked single file, with military escort, to the dusty soccer field. In stony silence, everyone sat in their pre-assigned place, sitting cross-legged across the field in three rows of five. I sat in the very back in the fifth row on the instruction of my government-appointed translator. Immediately after taking our seats, another government official strode up to the lectern with a retinue of lecturers. They were introduced as national historians and intellectuals who "have studied Rwandan history and understand the roots of the scourge of genocide well." We received our lessons in two- or three-hour blocks. No questions were allowed; anyone who stretched his legs or began to nod off was jostled back to attention by one of the six armed military escorts who stood guard around the field.

Our history lessons were taught over three days for an approximate total of twenty-four hours of lessons. We received detailed lessons on the root causes of the genocide, notably the "deep-seated and seething ethnic hatred that Hutu have for Tutsi." We were also taught that this hatred that Hutu have for Tutsi is "the root of the Rwandan disease [of genocide]." We were then taught that the path to peace and security was for Hutu to rid themselves of this hatred. We were also taught that ordinary Hutu men caused the genocide because they acted on their hatred for Tutsi. We were then taught how to recognize the signs of trauma and to respect the needs of Tutsi survivors when they exhibit signs of trauma. Lastly, we were taught how to be a "good citizen," which included lessons on respecting the orders of local officials, good hygiene, courtesy to others, and the importance of monocropping for national development. When we were not receiving our history lessons, we were taught how to sow and till the land. We also played a few games of soccer. Throughout the week, the mood was somber. When the men showed signs of exhaustion or boredom, the armed guards appeared to make sure they remained focused on the task at hand. I found the pace grueling, particularly since we were not well fed or rested. There was no downtime. The men around me said that they found the structure of the day to be "no different than being in prison." As Trésor, a former lecturer in chemistry at the National University of Rwanda (NUR), told me during one of our evening meals, "I am a former Hutu. This means I am a source of shame for this government. Prison, gacaca, and ingando are just ways for them to make sure that we don't think for ourselves. The message is that we are not full citizens."

On the first day of our history lessons, some of the men around me made fun of the mzungu (white foreigner) who had to sit so long in the hot sun without eating. They teased me, and some wondered out loud what I must have done to end up at their ingando reeducation camp. When they learned that I was a Canadian researcher who had been sent here to "learn the truth," the teasing stopped and most of the men stepped away from me, perhaps in an attempt to distance themselves from someone who was clearly in hot water with the government.

When my translator went to the toilet, a former physician named Antoine, whom I had sat next to for most of the week, asked me quietly in French to "alert the outside world about how being Hutu is a crime in the new Rwanda." When one of the ever-present armed soldiers who monitored our lesson witnessed this, he strode up to where we were sitting and slammed Antoine's bare feet with the butt of his rifle. He grabbed my arm, pulled me close to him, and then threw me on the ground, pointing to where I was to sit silently for the rest of the lesson. I never saw Antoine again, and my translator did not leave my side after that incident. He immediately took me to the office of the government official responsible for overseeing the *ingando* training, where I was sternly reminded that I was "here to learn; only to listen." If I insisted on speaking to the prisoners, I would be returned to Kigali where "the punishment could be severe." I returned to my spot on the soccer field, duly chastened. I also wondered at this point what might happen to Antoine.

History Lessons

The history lesson that I heard at *ingando* did not vary from the official version of history, which stresses that ethnicity is a fiction created by colonial divide-and-rule policies and manipulated by the post-colonial Hutu regimes (see, e.g., RoR 1999; NURC 2004). At the end of our history lecture on the fifth day of reeducation, I observed more than the usual fatigue on the faces of the men around me. Many seemed despondent and showed little enthusiasm for their usual late afternoon soccer match. I didn't get a chance to speak to any of them given both the language barrier and the constant presence of my translator.

Nonetheless, the ordinary Rwandans I consulted during my research, including a dozen confessed *génocidaires* who had returned to their home communities, shared their views on the new version of history they learned in the *ingando* camps. Many saw this historical narrative as a product of the RPF political elite, something that local officials have to adopt to further their careers.[6] Joseph, a twenty-six-year-old Hutu who graduated from *ingando* in 2002, said: "I don't know if Hutu and Tutsi [peasants] like me were unified before the white man came. That is what they taught us. But does it matter? I want to eat every day and I want to send my children to school. If they tell me whites brought division, then of course I agree."[7] These remarks illustrate how the version of history found in the policy of national unity and reconciliation is the "politically correct" one, and is the one that most ordinary Rwandans parrot in public even if they disagree in private. In promoting a singular version of Rwandan history, the policy of national unity and reconciliation fails to acknowledge the multiplicity of historical interpretations (and individual lived experiences) that constitute Rwandan history.

Lessons in Truth and Reconciliation

Ingando reeducation camps for *génocidaires* do not teach reconciliation. Instead, they mostly teach *génocidaires* to shut up and to stay on the sidelines of public life. During my reeducation, government officials repeatedly told me that Hutu "had a responsibility to tell the truth." Yet many *ingando* graduates I interviewed have said there is no point in telling the actual truth of what they did. Gaston, who graduated from *ingando* in 2004, stated: "Even if I am innocent, I am a former Hutu. In the new Rwanda, this means I must be guilty of killing." By preventing any public discussion outside the acceptable categories of Tutsi survivors and Hutu perpetrators, *ingando* is just another tactic of social control rather than a meaningful effort to unify and reconcile Rwandans. As Vianney, a twenty-five-year-old Tutsi survivor, said:

The Hutu who killed, they know who they are but are they able to tell their truth? No, and I understand why not. If they say anything, they go straight to prison. I understand their problems; I blame this government for its lack of fairness. If we could all just get along in our own way and at our own time, I know we could find some way to co-exist. Reconciliation is never going to happen under this government.

Anselme, the sixteen-year-old nephew of a convicted *génocidaire*, stated: "For adult Hutu like my uncle, *ingando* lessons are just a way for the government to make sure we have no ideas of our own, and to make sure we don't make more genocide for them. It [genocide] could happen because Hutu are no longer welcome here."

Conclusion

As this chapter has shown, *ingando* camps for *génocidaires* simultaneously reveal the strengths and weaknesses of the RPF's reeducation "by announcing the gap between enforcing participation and commanding belief" (Wedeen 1999, 22). The graduates of these *ingando* camps that I met do not believe in the national unity of the re-imagined past or in the reconciliation of a re-engineered future. Rather, they see the camps and their ideological discourse as efforts to exercise social control over adult Hutu men. Instead of being reeducated, these graduates have merely learned new forms of "ritual[ized] dissimulation" (ibid., 82) and strategic compliance.

Notes

I would like to thank Stephen Brown and Villia Jefremovas as well as the editors of this volume for their helpful comments in developing this chapter. I also thank the Canadian Consortium on Human Security, the Faculty of Graduate Studies at Dalhousie University, the International Development Research Centre and the Social Sciences and Humanities Research Council for financial support, my research assistants and translators (all of whom requested anonymity), as well as the individuals who agreed to participate in my research project for making this publication possible.

1. By "ordinary Rwandans," I mean the non-elite and largely peasant citizenry, not members of the political elite who hold formal power or those individuals engaged as agents of the state (police officers, civil servants, military personnel, local officials, etc).

2. Like my dissertation, this chapter is based on research conducted in rural and urban Rwanda between April and October 2006, including interviews with senior government officials and representatives of both the private sector and civil society, as well as thirty-seven life history interviews with ordinary peasant Rwandans resident in South and West provinces. I also collected data through semistructured interviews, participant observation, as well as conversations with more than four hundred ordinary and elite Rwandans resident in both rural and urban settings. Nowhere in the text do I use specific place or community names. This is to respect the confidentiality and anonymity protocols set out in the research design, and to protect the safety of people who participated in my research from possible government backlash. Names used throughout the chapter are pseudonyms.

3. As far as I know, there is only one scholarly publication on *ingando* (Mgbako 2005). A useful nonacademic source is Penal Reform International (PRI) 2004.

4. Several ordinary Rwandans told me that the new anthem is actually an RPF war song that warns Tutsi to protect themselves against "marauding" Hutu. I cannot confirm this as no government official would discuss the lyrics with me. That ordinary people believe that these are the lyrics is nonetheless significant.

5. The restructuring is a part of Rwanda's decentralization policy. The official rationale is to dismantle the highly centralized administrative system that made the genocide possible. In practice, the decentralization policy appears to cover up the deployment of RPF loyalists throughout the lowest levels of the administration (field notes, 2006; see Ingelaere, chap. 3, this volume).

6. Of the forty-six elected and returnee local officials I met during my fieldwork, all but three were known members of the RPF. One said, "You must be a member of the RPF if you are to gain a good [government] position. I joined to provide for my family and have not regretted my decision" (field notes, 2006).

7. I also interviewed Tutsi who were cynical about the official historical narrative. As Aimable, an elderly Tutsi peasant from West province, noted caustically, "Whoever has power are the ones that shape our national history."

References

Mgbako, Chi. 2005. "*Ingando* Solidarity Camps: Reconciliation and Political Indoctrination in Post-Genocide Rwanda." *Harvard Human Rights Journal* 18 (Spring): 201–24.

National Unity and Reconciliation Commission (NURC). 2004. "The Rwandan Conflict: Origin, Development, Exit Strategies." Kigali. http://www.grandslacs.net/doc/3833.pdf.

———. 2006a. "The Ingando Concept and It's [sic] Syllabus Reform." Kigali.

———. 2006b. "The Themes Meant to be Discussed during 'Ingando' Workshop for Leaders." Kigali.

———. 2006c. "The A–Z of Ingando." Kigali.

Penal Reform International (PRI). 2004. "From Camp to Hill: The Reintegration of Released Prisoners." Research Report on the Gacaca 6. London, May. http://www.penalreform.org/files/rep-ga6-2004-released-prisoners-en_0.pdf.

Pottier, Johan. 2002. *Re-Imagining Rwanda: Conflict, Survival and Disinformation in the Late Twentieth Century*. Cambridge: Cambridge University Press.

Republic of Rwanda (RoR). 1999. "The Unity of Rwandans—Before the Colonial Period and Under the Colonial Rule; Under the First Republic." Kigali, August. www.grandslacs.net/doc/2379.pdf.

———. 2003. Constitution. May 26. http://www.mod.gov.rw/IMG/doc/Constitution_of_the_Republic_of_Rda.doc.

Wedeen, Lisa. 1999. *Ambiguities of Domination: Politics, Rhetoric and Symbols in Contemporary Syria*. Chicago: University of Chicago Press.

Part VI

Concluding Observations

Justice and Human Rights for All Rwandans

JOSEPH SEBARENZI

Introduction

Alison Des Forges will always be remembered as a friend of Rwanda, who tirelessly worked for justice and human rights for all. I first met her in 1999 when I was Speaker of the Rwandan Parliament, and she made a courtesy call to my office. She expressed appreciation for the steps parliament was taking, including passage of the law establishing the National Commission for Human Rights (NCHR), and for the efforts that we lawmakers were making to build an independent legislature. After Des Forges left my office, I continued thinking how this woman of modest stature yet keen intelligence was then admired in Rwandan political circles. She was often referred to as a brave woman who had assisted Tutsi refugees in Tanzania in the early 1960s, co-chaired the International Commission of Investigation (1993) that "exposed" human rights violations perpetrated by the Habyarimana regime in the early 1990s, and convinced the international community that large-scale massacres of Tutsi in 1994 were crimes of genocide.[1] Des Forges was considered an ally of the new regime. In fact, she was never an ally of any particular group; rather, her only allegiance was to the human rights cause that she cherished. She later wrote about my departure into exile in 2000 as well as the persecution of Rwandans of all backgrounds, including political leaders and human rights activists. Her integrity and activism earned her a great deal of respect among Rwandans of all ethnic backgrounds.

Owing to the multidisciplinary backgrounds of its contributors, this book fills the gap in the literature on Rwanda's post-conflict reconstruction, particularly in the areas of politics, local and international justice, and human rights. It presents a comprehensive and in-depth analysis of key policies in post-genocide Rwanda, beyond the achievements (albeit shallow) for which President Paul Kagame and his regime are praised. This scholarly work is timely as its completion coincided with concerns surrounding the August 2010 presidential election, in which Kagame took 93 percent of the vote. Had Des Forges been alive, she would have been part of this edited collection, and her voice would have been illuminating. She would have spoken against the assassinations and arrests of political leaders and journalists, against the grenade attacks that hit the capital Kigali, and about the divisions within the RPF's core base.

In this chapter, I discuss how the ruling Rwandan Patriotic Front (RPF) thwarted our efforts to build the rule of law in the late 1990s and the continuing grave consequences—as manifested in the August 2010 presidential elections.

Building the Rule of Law

One of the most difficult decisions I took during my tenure as Speaker of the Rwandan Parliament had to do with the law giving parliament oversight of the executive branch. Parliament had adopted the bill, and the Supreme Court had approved it, but then-president Pasteur Bizimungu insisted this law was not needed. From behind the scenes, then–vice president Kagame and the RPF's leadership opposed the bill, even though RPF representatives in parliament had supported it. This bill provided the cornerstone of good government. Without parliamentary oversight, the executive branch essentially had free rein. If parliament—the representatives of the people—had the power to summon ministers (including the prime minister) and censure them if they failed to demonstrate good governance, the executive branch would have no choice but to strive for efficiency and honesty in running the country. I remember begging the president to sign the oversight bill into law: "I worry that, without it, the country could easily plunge into chaos again." I told him that one reason genocide had occurred was because there were no checks and balances among the branches of government. This law would ensure that ministers would be held accountable. It would show the people that no one is above the law and would foster respect for the government. I continued, "Because this regime is new, we can stop corruption before it worsens—before we get to the point of no return. Individuals are too tempted by money and power. We need to make sure our institutions are stronger than individuals." For Bizimungu, this law would create unnecessary conflicts between the branches of government. I am not sure if Bizimungu believed this or if he was just expressing the views of Kagame, who was the real power. When Bizimungu did not sign the bill, he must have certainly thought his veto would mean the end of it.

Under the constitution in force at the time, the president had ten days to sign a bill into law, after which it was deemed constitutional. After this deadline, if the president did not sign it, the Speaker could. It was dangerous for me to sign a bill into law that had been vetoed by the president. Bizimungu and Kagame could force me out of office. They had done it to the last Speaker, the former prime minister, and other government officials. I considered my options: sign the bill and risk my position, or leave it unsigned and lead a feckless parliament. The best option for the country was definitely to sign the bill. Yet I was advised by friends that I could lose more than my job if I dared to sign a bill that Kagame opposed. After many unsuccessful attempts to have Bizimungu sign the bill, I finally signed it myself on April 14, 1997.

My signature came with a price—though it was far less than what everyone had expected. Kagame refused to meet with me for almost one year. When he eventually received me in his office, I explained why I signed the bill giving parliament the power to oversee government activities. I told him that the only way we could grow stronger was for there to be integrity at all levels of government. I insisted that the only way any regime can succeed and be strong is to instill a culture that respects human rights and enforces good governance. Kagame made me believe at the time that he agreed that more massacres would occur sooner or later without strong institutions and checks and balances. In reality, Kagame never supported the principle of separation of powers. As later became clear, he wanted total control over all public institutions—and even over civil society organizations (as discussed in this volume, in the chapters by Timothy Longman and Paul Gready).

Despite RPF resistance to oversight and to separation of powers, however, lawmakers implemented the new law. We boldly started oversight, though at an initially slow pace. At that time, we had no illusions that lawmakers would be able to exercise any significant oversight over the Ministry of Defence (MINADEF) headed by Kagame. Nevertheless, I had hope that proper oversight over the rest of the ministries would be effective in curbing corruption and ensuring efficiency and human rights. I also hoped that hostility to oversight would subside with time. For a while it seemed the RPF government might eventually embrace the rule of law. Lawmakers were eager to make a difference: enthusiasm was high in parliamentary committees and in plenary sessions as we scrutinized bills initiated by the executive branch, asked tough questions to ministers, and introduced innovative bills. This new working relationship between the executive and the legislature was exciting and promising, but annoying to ministers who were used to a rubber-stamp parliament.

In 1999, however, the RPF proposed the Forum of Political Parties with the obvious intent of weakening parliament's growing independence and momentum. The forum was blatantly unconstitutional: it would have the power to remove any member of parliament at any time even though the constitution stipulated that each lawmaker had the right to act independently of his party's wishes. The RPF would chair the forum, and the RPF's secretary-general would serve as its spokesperson. I tried to have a meeting with Kagame to discuss the forum, but he declined my request. So I wrote a letter to President Bizimungu asking him to prevent the forum. Despite good intentions, he was not able to stop it because the initiative had come from Kagame himself. In disregard of the constitution, the forum was instituted and subsequently removed a number of the nation's best lawmakers.

By the end of 1999, parliament had investigated many cases of corruption and had censured two ministers. The growing power of the legislature ended when the RPF engineered my removal as Speaker. I vividly remember my last meeting with Kagame at his home when he ordered me to resign. As I asked questions, he leaned forward and pointed a finger at me, "If you don't resign, I will get involved." I understood what he meant. I resigned the next day.

My forced resignation saddened many who had seen parliament's efforts as an indication of progress toward the rule of law. However, my family and I were preoccupied with security concerns. I kept receiving news that not only had I lost my job—which I could live with—but that I could lose my life as well. I eventually realized I needed to flee Rwanda. On a Sunday morning, I left my house by sneaking into the back of a truck and hiding amid the furniture to make sure my "bodyguards" did not notice I was gone. Afterward, I rode a motorcycle and then a car to the border, where I crossed by foot into Uganda.

Observers of politics in Rwanda saw my resignation and flight as part of a wider pattern of forced resignations and/or exile of prominent politicians. Yet my case had a unique characteristic: I was the first prominent Tutsi to flee the so-called Tutsi-dominated government.[2] My resignation was part of Kagame's plan to have total control over state institutions, and to clear his way toward the presidency. Before my resignation, Kagame had ordered Chief Justice Jean Mutsinzi, and his two deputies, Paul Ruyenzi and Paul Rutayisire, to resign; they were replaced by RPF loyalists. After my resignation, the prime minister and the president followed in the space of less than three months. Kagame took over the presidency.

In April 2000, Des Forges wrote about my work in parliament. She noted how I had fought "to establish some autonomy for [parliament] and particularly to hold government ministers accountable for alleged corruption, including powerful members of the RPF" (HRW 2000). She added that it was "apparently this commitment to good government which won Sebarenzi approval among ordinary people, Hutu as well as Tutsi" (ibid.). Des Forges also criticized the government for the forced repatriation of the people who had helped me to escape, and for the persecution and exile of journalists who condemned the RPF role in my resignation.[3]

Persecution of the Political Opposition

When Des Forges died in February 2009, preparations for the 2010 presidential election had already begun. Over the next year and a half, Rwanda saw a resurgence of insecurity and a crackdown on political dissidents. These opponents included Bernard Ntaganda, president of the Parti social Imberakuri (PSI); Frank Habineza, president of the Democratic Green Party of Rwanda (DGPR); and Victoire Ingabire, president of the Forces démocratiques unifiées-Inkingi (United Democratic Forces, FDU-Inkingi).

Ingabire returned to Rwanda in January 2010 to run for president. After sixteen years in exile, Ingabire believed, against warnings, that she could mount a constructive opposition. On her arrival, she visited the Gisozi genocide memorial in Kigali and commented in her address that "the Hutu who killed Tutsi must understand that they have to be punished. It is the same for the Tutsi who have killed Hutu." In other words, and as she reiterated a few days later, a genocide was committed by Hutu elements against Tutsi, and war crimes and crimes against humanity were committed by elements within the RPF against Hutu. Like many before her, Ingabire maintains that all perpetrators must be held accountable. This is indeed a matter of justice and fairness. Otherwise, impunity and victor's justice—as discussed in this volume, in the chapters by Victor Peskin and Max Rettig—will continue to hinder the prospects of peace and reconciliation in Rwanda.

What Ingabire said publicly about the RPF is what many Rwandans say privately. With the exception of hardliners on each side, Hutu and Tutsi understand that acknowledgement of each other's suffering and responsibility is essential for sustainable peace and reconciliation. As I have written, "Until we acknowledge all that happened—without minimizing, exaggerating, or equating—we will obstruct reconciliation between the two communities" (Sebarenzi 2009, 228).

If Ingabire can be blamed for asserting that the RPF committed human rights violations, so should the African Panel of Eminent Personalities for stating that it is "persuaded by the evidence that at least some and perhaps many of these charges are true, that such violations took place before, during and after the genocide, and that they have included the period since late 1996 when Rwandan troops began hunting *génocidaires* throughout central Africa" (OAU 2000, 235). Yet this issue remains a highly sensitive topic. It is imperative that Rwandans bring this issue into the open, and deal with it. For "[w]here past human rights violations are ignored and the victims forgotten, there is a cancer in such a society that remains dormant and available for use or abuse by some or other future despotic, nationalistic leader" (Freeman 2006, xi).

Ingabire's discourse caused fury in government circles. She was quickly accused of harboring genocidal ideology and divisionism, and of having contacts with Hutu rebels in the Democratic Republic of Congo (DRC), the Forces démocratiques de libération du Rwanda (Democratic Forces for the Liberation of Rwanda, FDLR). Ingabire was subsequently summoned to the police many times before she was arrested in April 2010 on charges of genocide ideology, divisionism, and collaboration with terrorist groups. Ingabire was released on bail, and, as of September 2010, was awaiting trial. Her political party was not allowed to register, and consequently she was not allowed to run for president.

Another opposition leader, Bernard Ntaganda, endured similar hardships. Ntaganda quit the Parti social démocratie (Social Democratic Party, PSD) and formed the Parti social Imberakuri (PSI) in 2009, because he believed the PSD had become increasingly subservient to the RPF. After some difficulties, the PSI was registered, presumably because Ntaganda was deemed inoffensive to the RPF establishment. His party was welcomed into the Forum of Political Parties. It did not take long, however, before Ntaganda sharply criticized the government on a number of issues, notably through a politically loaded metaphor: "Si leta y'ubumwe, ahubwo ni leta ya bamwe," literally meaning the government is not for all but for some. Since then, the Senate has summoned Ntaganda to explain what he meant by this metaphor on several occasions. He says he meant the RPF was a de facto single party. This may be a half truth; he most certainly intended to convey the widespread perception among Hutu that Rwanda is governed by Tutsi. The truth is that Rwanda is run by an inner circle of Tutsi led by President Kagame. Overall, Tutsi as a group are relatively better off than Hutu, exactly the same way Hutu were under the so-called Hutu-dominated governments. Whatever Ntaganda's intent, his statement fell into what the government calls divisionism and genocide ideology, and exposed him and his party to problems.

Ntaganda alleged that he has received anonymous and threatening telephone calls from operatives working for the ruling party. At some point he hid at undisclosed locations for fear of his life. He often could not obtain government authorization to hold party meetings, and even when he did, the police did not provide protection against disruptions. In March 2010 the attack came from within his party. A faction of his party deposed Ntaganda and elected a new president, who then accused Ntaganda of "divisionism and genocidal ideology." Conflicts like these are not new in Rwanda's politics. President Habyarimana divided political parties in the early 1990s. Under Kagame, political parties that oppose the ruling party, like the Mouvement démocratique républicain (Democratic Republican Movement, MDR), are dealt with by igniting internal strife (HRW 2003). In June, Ntaganda was arrested along with thirty persons as they prepared to protest against the National Electoral Commission (NEC) for failing to allow genuine opponents into the presidential race.[4] Ntaganda was charged with organizing demonstrations without official permission, threatening national security, and divisionism. He was denied bail and, as of September 2010, was awaiting trial.

The reason the RPF vigorously opposed Ingabire's and Ntaganda's bids for the presidency has to do with Kagame's fear of what his fate would be if he lost power. The Tutsi in his entourage have a different worry: voting along ethnic lines would produce a Hutu-dominated government, which would open the possibility of yet another round of ethnic exclusion— or mass violence— against Tutsi. This raises the fundamental issue of power in divided societies, particularly in Rwanda, where the Hutu form an overwhelming majority and the Tutsi a small minority. While Kagame and his entourage's fears are understandable, the repression of Hutu opposition leaders—through the misuse of laws on divisionism and genocide ideology (see the chapter by Lars Waldorf in this volume)—is not a solution. Rwandans should confront this long-standing issue and not pass it on to future generations. The government should stop pretending that Tutsi and Hutu no longer exist, and help devise a power-sharing mechanism that makes all Rwandans feel safe. Rwanda may need to move toward consensus democracy to defuse tensions between its majority and its minority.[5] Otherwise, there is a likelihood of yet more mass violence.

A consensus-based democracy may end violent competition of power between Hutu and Tutsi, but, alone, it would not necessarily achieve peace. Rwanda's woes cannot be reduced to ethnicity. If that were the case, then Frank Habineza—and many other Tutsi—would not be having serious problems with the so-called Tutsi government. Habineza's creation of the DGPR is an indication of growing discontent within the Tutsi community, including genocide survivors and members of the Parti libéral (Liberal Party, PL) (essentially composed of Tutsi).[6] The party was created in 2009, but the government refused to notarize the list of its founding members—a requirement under the law on political parties. This party is particularly troublesome for the RPF. Like Kagame, its key founders grew up in exile and were members of the RPF. The beheading of DGPR's vice president, André Kagwa Rwisereka, in July 2010 was construed as a political assassination intended to suppress the growing disenchantment within Kagame's core base. Conflicts within the RPF core base are also illustrated by the suspension of two independent newspapers (*Umuseso* and *Umuvugizi*) edited by Tutsi who, like Kagame, grew up in exile in Uganda. Both editors subsequently fled the country.

More than anything else, however, the RPF's core base is threatened by divisions within the army. An indication of this is that Lieutenant General Faustin Kayumba Nyamwasa fled on February 26, 2010, after he discovered a plot to arrest him. Kayumba had been one of the key aides to President Kagame. During the guerilla war, Kayumba was second to Kagame in the army. He headed the department of military intelligence until the RPF won the war in 1994. Under the RPF government, he remained very influential in Rwandan politics as deputy chief of the gendarmerie, and then army chief of staff. His popularity within the army appears to have worried Kagame, who sent him for one year of training in the United Kingdom in 2001. On his return to Rwanda in 2002, he nominally served as the coordinator of Rwanda's intelligence services before being appointed ambassador to India. That appointment, like the training in the UK, was a way to remove Kayumba from the army, at a time when many in Rwanda continued to think of him as an alternative to Kagame.

Kayumba's exile added to the growing list of high-ranking soldiers who have either fled or been arrested. Kayumba eventually joined another former close aide to Kagame, Colonel Patrick Karegeya, who had fled to South Africa in 2007. Karegeya was Rwanda's foreign intelligence chief for a decade. After Kayumba's departure into exile, the Government of Rwanda accused him of being behind the grenade attacks of February 19, 2010.[7] More grenade attacks took place in and around Kigali after Kayumba had left. Rwanda's prosecutor general accused Kayumba and Karegeya of "terrorism and creating a terror criminal organization" (*New Times* 2010). The government subsequently issued international arrest warrants against the two officers and asked South Africa to send them back to Rwanda. Lacking an extradition treaty with Rwanda, South Africa rejected the request. After Kayumba spoke out forcefully against President Kagame, he was very nearly assassinated in June 2010 in Johannesburg.[8]

Kayumba, who was seriously wounded in the abdomen, accused Kagame of being behind the shooting. An *Umuvugizi* journalist, Jean-Léonard Rugambage, was gunned down in Kigali in June 2010 after that newspaper published an online article alleging the involvement of senior Rwandan officials in the assassination attempt. The attempted assassination quickly prompted a chilling of relations between South Africa and Rwanda, with South Africa recalling its ambassador from Kigali three days before the presidential elections.

The grenade attacks, the exile and arrests of prominent officers, and the assassination of political leaders and journalists show that the relative peace Rwanda enjoys is fragile. It is a negative peace. A lasting peace depends on Kagame's willingness to allow internal debate and open up political space. The international community that had so far unreservedly praised Kagame reacted to his election with serious worries. For example, the United States expressed its concern "about a series of disturbing events prior to the election, including the suspension of two newspapers, the expulsion of a human rights researcher [from Human Rights Watch (HRW)], the barring of two opposition parties from taking part in the election, and the arrest of journalists" (U.S. Department of State 2010b). Kagame's reaction has been firm and defiant: "Rwandans will not be distracted by such criticism, but will continue along our own path to an increasingly constructive and competitive political environment that takes full account of our history, political culture and evolving circumstances" (Kagame 2010).

Rwanda's donors have urged President Kagame to take steps toward more democratic governance. Yet there is an obstacle to this. Kagame has made so many enemies at home (among Hutu and Tutsi) and abroad that he fears for his future without control over the state. It would therefore be wise for the international community and Kagame's opponents to be mindful of this reality, and to explore ways to handle Kagame's legitimate fears in order to encourage reforms. It would equally be wise for Kagame to drop his belligerent rhetoric, be more humble, and negotiate with his opponents.

Conclusion

Rwanda is increasingly seen not as a nation emerging steadily out of the division of the past but as a country at risk of another cycle of violence. This sad reality is thoroughly examined in this volume. By and large, this book provides insights to policymakers in Rwanda and in the international community on how to prevent another round of mass violence in Rwanda— something Des Forges had done on several occasions. She offered practical recommendations to safeguard human rights for all Rwandans. Many of her recommendations remain valid in contemporary Rwanda. Her death cannot therefore be an excuse for inaction. Rwanda's major donors have a moral obligation to forcefully use their leverage on President Kagame. Rwanda is so dependent on the international community that Kagame would not resist its demands for reforms, especially if his fears and concerns are taken into consideration. International engagement would not only help achieve the peace that Rwandans long for but would also fulfill what Des Forges struggled for over the last two decades: justice and human rights for all Rwandans.

Notes

This chapter reflects the personal opinion of the author.

1. The RPF seemed not to be aware that the Commission's report also mentioned the RPF's attacks against civilians.

2. Other prominent Tutsi subsequently went into exile: Major Gérard Ntashamaje (secretary general in the Ministry of Justice [MINIJUST]), Major Alphonse Furuma (RPF executive committee member), Jean Bosco Rutagengwa (the first president of IBUKA ["Remember"], the main genocide survivors' association), Josué Kayijaho (vice president of IBUKA), Valens Kajeguhakwa (former RPF parliamentarian), Gerald Gahima (former prosecutor general), and Major Théogène Rudasingwa (former RPF secretary general and ambassador to the United States).

3. These journalists included Déogratias Mushayidi, former president of the Rwandan Association of Journalists, and Jason Muhayimana, chief editor of *Imboni*, both of whom fled to Belgium. The persecution of journalists became a pattern, as noted by the U.S. Department of State (2010a): "The government continued to intimidate and arrest independent journalists who expressed views that were deemed critical of the government on sensitive topics."

4. Only President Kagame and three members of parties allied to the RPF were approved to run for president.

5. The political scientist Arendt Lijphart (1984, 23) notes that "consensus democracy is characterized by a decision-making process that takes into account as broad a range of opinions as possible, as opposed to systems where vote-winning majorities can potentially ignore minority opinions." He adds that "in plural societies, majority rule spells majority dictatorship and civil strife rather than democracy" (ibid.). See also Sebarenzi 2009.

6. The PL, like other political parties, remains submissive to the RPF and is required to adhere to the RPF-controlled Forum of Political Parties.

7. Before blaming Kayumba and Karegeya, the Government of Rwanda blamed the FDLR that operates in the eastern DRC. Kayumba has categorically rejected the accusations and has instead hinted that the attacks were perpetrated by persons within the Rwandan government. Some observers alleged that the grenade attacks were carried

out by operatives working for Kagame's inner circle in an effort to demonize Kayumba and to justify the arrest of dissidents, real or perceived. Whoever carried out these attacks—and for whatever reason—should be identified and held accountable.

8. This incident resembles the 1998 assassinations of two high-ranking RPF officials who had fled to Nairobi: Major Théoneste Lizinde and former RPF minister Seth Sendashonga.

References

Amnesty International USA. 2010. "Rwanda: Intimidation of the Opposition Must End." February 18. http://www.amnestyusa.org/document.php?id=ENGPRE 010582010&lang=e.

Economist. 2008. "A Flawed Hero." August 21.

Freeman, Mark. 2006. *Truth Commissions and Procedural Fairness.* Cambridge: Cambridge University Press.

Human Rights Watch (HRW). 2000. "Rwanda: The Search for Security and Human Rights Abuses." April 1. http://www.hrw.org/en/reports/2000/04/01/rwanda-search -security-and-human-rights-abuses.

———. 2003. "Preparing for Elections: Tightening Control in the Name of Unity." May 8. http://www.hrw.org/en/node/77843.

Kagame, Paul. 2010. "Rwanda's Democracy Is Still a Model in Africa." *Financial Times,* August 19.

Lijphart, Arendt. 1984. *Democracies: Patterns of Majoritarian and Consensus Government in Twenty-One Countries.* New Haven, CT: Yale University Press.

New Times. 2010. "Rwanda: Arrest Warrants Issued for Kayumba and Karegeya." April 4.

Organization of African Unity (OAU). 2000. "Rwanda: The Preventable Genocide." Addis Ababa, July 7. http://www.africa-union.org/Official_documents/reports/ Report_rowanda_genocide.pdf.

Sebarenzi, Joseph. 2009. *God Sleeps in Rwanda: A Journey of Transformation.* New York: Simon and Schuster.

U.S. Department of State. 2010a. "Rwanda." *2009 Country Reports on Human Rights Practices.* March 11. http://www.state.gov/g/drl/rls/hrrpt/2009/af/135971.htm.

———. 2010b. "Statement by NSC Spokesman Hammer on Election in Rwanda." August 13. http://www.america.gov/st/texttrans-english/2010/August/20100816112249 suo.3026087.html.

The Dancing Is Still the Same

ALOYS HABIMANA

To understand why Rwanda keeps turning in the wrong direction, we need to seriously consider Einstein's words: "We can't solve problems by using the same kind of thinking we used when we created them." In important ways, the thinking that has underpinned most of the post-genocide regime's policies, institutions, and processes strangely mimics the logic of the pre-genocide regimes. As Rwandans would say, "The dancing is still the same even though the stage has undergone a switch of dancers." The contributors to this volume—most of whom have done extensive field research—show how Rwanda's new leadership opted for a strategy of repression and control that will at best delay national recovery and at worst rekindle intercommunal tensions and violence.

Sadly, Rwandans have never had leaders who truly value them as citizens capable of having a say in their own destiny. It is not rare to hear Rwandan politicians portray the population as an uneducated lot that needs to be shown the way. The elite's tendency to infantilize the masses is nothing but a recipe for disaster. Worse, Rwandan politicians continue treating citizens as objects they can manipulate at whim to serve their parochial interests. The results are the top-down policies so well analyzed in this book.

When Rwandan leaders introduced their "villagization" policy in the late 1990s, what mattered most to them was convincing potential donors that the project was a sound one. The little voices of protest that emerged from the populace were quickly muzzled "à la Rwandaise." Before long, warnings started to pour in from well respected watchdogs that the policy was in fact "uprooting the rural poor." *Gacaca* followed a similar trajectory: although it gained some currency early on as an alternative to failed conventional justice efforts, the government eventually hijacked the process and used it as just another tool of repression. For a country whose recovery hinged on delivering fair and equitable justice to both victims and perpetrators of genocide, the move could not have been more destructive. If any lesson can be learned from this, it is that the politicization of key sectors of national life is antithetical to a genuine spirit of reconstruction.

Of course, the politicization of justice did not start with *gacaca*. Early on, the new leadership felt it could build political capital by manipulating issues of accountability for the Rwandan tragedy. As Victor Peskin's chapter shows, these leaders preached a firm commitment to the fight against impunity while thwarting any probe into their own criminal responsibility at the International Criminal Tribunal for Rwanda (ICTR). This deflecting of responsibility also haunted domestic judicial efforts. For example, references in *gacaca* hearings to the sufferings inflicted on civilians by Rwandan Patriotic Front (RPF) soldiers sometimes led to imprisonment for "genocide denial."

Failure by the ruling elite to assume its share of responsibility has had a number of consequences. For one, it has left the whole judicial process grappling with issues of perception and legitimacy, raising questions about whether genocide suspects properly face the long arm of justice or are subject to political vengeance. It has also resulted in one of the worst types of post-conflict discrimination, leaving some victims to fend for themselves while allowing a select group of perpetrators to walk free as heroes. The concept of equitable justice requires that the state deal seriously with the issue of war crimes perpetrated by former RPF soldiers. Lifting the shroud of impunity that continues to cover these other crimes could be one way of ensuring better ownership of the judicial process; for much as justice needs to be done, it also needs to be seen to be done.

This state of things prompted what became the hallmark of Alison Des Forges's work: advocating for all victims to address the indignity of the crimes and to forge national reconciliation. To ensure justice for all, three goals needed to be pursued: (1) punishment of the guilty, (2) redress for the victims, and (3) rehabilitation of those wrongfully accused. Setting an example for principled activists, Alison pursued those goals unflinchingly. That resolve exposed her to all sorts of misunderstandings and unreasonable attacks. At times, she was labeled an agent of the Rwandan government because she demanded accountability for the genocide. But when she turned to the cover-up of war crimes committed by members of the ruling party, the government treated her as a "divisionist" and eventually banned her from entering Rwanda.

Any savvy observer of Rwanda's genocide proceedings would notice that the judiciary has often been ill-equipped to carry out the task of effectively sorting out individual responsibility for the accused. This problem heightens the risk of wrongful convictions and fuels the mistrust that people have about Rwanda's judicial system. The problem is compounded by disrespect for the presumption of innocence. In the face of all this, Alison did not lose hope. She continued her fight, convinced that Rwanda would one day better its judicial institutions.

Facing the past, no matter how crucial, should not overshadow the equally important obligation for post-conflict leadership to initiate and consolidate future-oriented reforms. Pursuing justice and reconciliation in a viable way is one thing, but creating a social, political, and economic environment capable of sustaining the dividends of that pursuit is another. Yet as this book shows, the Rwandan authorities have not created such an environment. And the way in which governmental policies are implemented is as important as the content of those policies. So, for instance, when the government imposes mono-cropping on farmers, both the gains and sustainability of this reform are called into question.

Turning the page on old ways of conceptualizing political power and leadership is something our leaders need to get up to speed with. The analyses incorporated in this volume have shed light on the areas that call for particular attention for effective national reconstruction to gain some momentum. Clean and shiny cities are a luxury no citizen would complain about, but they are ephemeral assets and could hardly constitute a priority for a society prone to cyclical political turmoil. What would really help Rwanda emerge from the ashes of a violent and discredited past is the building of strong institutions capable of safeguarding the rights and freedoms of all.

Acknowledgments

This volume emerged from conferences in London and Madison, Wisconsin, and we want to acknowledge the critical support of the institutions and individuals that made those conferences and this book possible.

In London, the Institute of Commonwealth Studies and the Human Rights Consortium at the School of Advanced Studies, University of London, funded and hosted the conference "Reconstructing Rwanda: Fifteen Years after Genocide" on March 20, 2009. Kirrily Pells did a wonderful job helping to coordinate and publicize this event. The conference was a moving mix of scholarly conference, Festschrift, and commemoration thanks to the participants: Anne Aghion, An Ansoms, Phil Clark, Nigel Eltringham, Carla Ferstman, Tom Gibson, Paul Gready, Rachel Hayman, Bert Ingelaere, Klaas de Jonge, Kerstin McCourt, Lyndsay McLean Hilker, K. L. Murphy, Venuste Nshimiyimana, Kirrily Pells, Tom Porteous, Max Rettig, Carina Tertsakian, Victoria teVelde, Anneke Van Woudenberg, Don Webster, and Eugenia Zorbas.

In Madison, the African Studies Program, the Global Legal Studies Center, and the Human Rights Initiative provided critical support to the conference "Reconstructing Rwanda: History, Power, and Human Rights" on May 19, 2009. Jennifer Petersen was a terrific coordinator of the latter event. The conference was a moving tribute to Alison Des Forges's life and legacy thanks to the contributions of Roger Des Forges, Lee Ann Fujii, Aloys Habimana, Leslie Haskell, Sharon Hutchinson, Jean-Marie Kamatali, Neil Kodesh, Tim Longman, Catharine Newbury, David Newbury, Victor Peskin, Filip Reyntjens, Thomas Spear, Susan Thomson, Jan Vansina, Michele Wagner, and Crawford Young.

Scott Straus's research for the book was completed with generous support from the Harry Frank Guggenheim Foundation and the Graduate School at the University of Wisconsin–Madison. Lars Waldorf's research for the book was completed with the encouragement of the Centre for Applied Human Rights at the University of York and its director Paul Gready.

We are very grateful to all the authors for their insightful and timely contributions. At the University of Wisconsin Press we owe an enormous debt to Gwen Walker, who attended the entire Madison conference, provided early and sustained encouragement for this book project, and then shepherded us and the manuscript through publication.

We are also grateful to the three anonymous reviewers for their incisive comments. Aliza Luft was an invaluable help in pulling together and copyediting the manuscript. We would also like to thank Angela Bagwell, Sheila McMahon, and Carla Marolt at the UW Press for their efficient handling of the manuscript. Finally, we want to thank Riccardo Gangale for the terrific photo on the cover.

Acknowledgments

Contributors

AN ANSOMS is an assistant at the Institute of Development Policy and Management (IOB) of the University of Antwerp (Belgium), where she focuses on poverty and inequality in the Great Lakes region of Africa. She has published articles on Rwanda in *African Affairs*, *Journal of Modern African Studies*, and other journals. She recently finished her PhD in economics at Antwerp with a dissertation titled "Faces of Rural Poverty in Contemporary Rwanda: Linking Livelihood Profiles and Institutional Processes."

FEDERICO BORELLO is an Italian lawyer who has served with the United Nations and other international agencies and NGOs in Eastern Europe, Africa, Asia, and Latin America. In 1997 he worked for the United Nations High Commissioner for Human Rights (UNHCHR) in Rwanda, where he focused on the justice system and the conditions of prisoners. In 2005 he joined the United Nations Mission in the Democratic Republic of the Congo (MONUC), where he coordinated the justice unit within the human rights division, working on the issue of impunity for serious human rights violations, including sexual violence. He then became the investigations coordinator and legal advisor for the DRC "Mapping Exercise."

NIGEL ELTRINGHAM is a senior lecturer in anthropology at the University of Sussex (UK) and author of *Accounting for Horror: Post-Genocide Debates in Rwanda*.

SARAH WARSHAUER FREEDMAN is a professor of language and literacy, society, and culture at the University of California, Berkeley, in the Graduate School of Education. She is the author of several books, including the collaborative study *Inside City Schools: Investigating Literacy in Multicultural Classrooms*.

PAUL GREADY is the director of the Centre for Applied Human Rights, University of York (UK), and coeditor of the *Journal of Human Rights Practice*. He is the author of *The Era of Transitional Justice: The Aftermath of the Truth and Reconciliation Commission in South Africa and Beyond*.

ALOYS HABIMANA is deputy director of the Africa division of Human Rights Watch (HRW).

RACHEL HAYMAN is a teaching fellow in the Centre of African Studies, School of Social and Political Science, at the University of Edinburgh.

CHRIS HUGGINS is a specialist on the relationships among land rights, violence, and post-conflict development, particularly in Africa, and has consulted for several major organizations. He was the Rwanda researcher for Human Rights Watch (2005–2007) and is currently a PhD candidate at Carleton University, Ottawa. He has published several book chapters, policy reports, and articles on Rwanda, and is coeditor of *From the Ground Up: Land Rights, Conflict and Peace in Sub-Saharan Africa*.

BERT INGELAERE is a researcher at the Institute of Development Policy and Management, University of Antwerp (Belgium). Since 2004, he has conducted more than twenty-five months of anthropological fieldwork in rural Rwanda and Burundi. Previously, he was a researcher for the World Bank in Rwanda and China. He has written several articles and reports on Rwanda and Burundi for such publications as *African Affairs*, *African Studies Review*, *Journal of Modern African Studies*, and *Journal of Eastern African Studies*.

TIMOTHY LONGMAN is director of the African Studies Center at Boston University and author of *Christianity and Genocide in Rwanda*.

LYNDSAY McLEAN HILKER is a postdoctoral research fellow at the University of Sussex (UK). Her PhD dissertation looked at identity and reconciliation among Rwandan youth in Kigali a decade after the 1994 genocide. Her research interests include "identity-based" conflict and violence, reconciliation and peace building, ethnicity, gender, children, and youth. She previously worked for the Department for International Development (DFID) in a number of program and policy positions as well as for the European Council as political assistant to the special envoy for the Great Lakes region.

JENS MEIERHENRICH is a senior lecturer in the Department of International Relations at the London School of Economics and Political Science (LSE). He is the author of *The Legacies of Law: Long-Run Consequences of Legal Development in South Africa, 1652–2000*, which won the American Political Science Association's 2009 Woodrow Wilson Foundation Award.

K. L. MURPHY is the director of international programs at Facing History and Ourselves, an international educational and professional development NGO. She works in a range of countries, including England, where Facing History has an office, and in Northern Ireland, Rwanda, and South Africa, where Facing History has in-depth collaborations. She is also a member of Facing History's research and development team. She is currently working on a Web-based interactive module that explores transitional justice processes in Germany, Northern Ireland, Rwanda, and South Africa.

CATHARINE NEWBURY is a professor of government at Smith College and Five College Professor of Government and African Studies. She is the author of *The Cohesion of Oppression: Clientship and Ethnicity in Rwanda* and has published many articles on Central African political processes. Newbury's research interests include ethnicity and the state in Africa, the politics of peasants and women, and the politics of violence in Francophone Central Africa.

DAVID NEWBURY is Gwendolen Carter Professor of African Studies in the Department of History at Smith College. His latest book is *The Land Beyond the Mists: Essays in Identity and Authority in Precolonial Congo and Rwanda*.

KIRRILY PELLS is a Mellon Sawyer postdoctoral fellow at the Human Rights Consortium, University of London. She has conducted consultancies for CARE International, Save the Children UK, and the British Embassy in Rwanda and is the author of "'No One Ever Listens to Us': Challenging Obstacles to the Participation of Children and Young People in Rwanda," in *A Handbook of Children's Participation: Perspectives from Theory and Practice*.

VICTOR PESKIN is an assistant professor in the School of Politics and Global Studies at Arizona State University. He is the author of *International Justice in Rwanda and the Balkans: Virtual Trials and the Struggle for State Cooperation*.

MAX RETTIG, a former Fulbright Scholar in Rwanda, is currently employed by the U.S. Department of State. His chapter was written before his employment began.

FILIP REYNTJENS is a professor of African law and politics at the University of Antwerp (Belgium). He is the author of many articles and books, including, most recently, *The Great African War: Congo and Regional Geopolitics, 1996–2006*.

KENNETH ROTH has been executive director of Human Rights Watch (HRW) since 1993.

JOSEPH SEBARENZI, a genocide survivor who lost his parents and seven siblings, is the former Speaker of the Rwandan Parliament (1997–2000) and author of *God Sleeps in Rwanda: A Story of Transformation*.

JASON STEARNS was the coordinator of the United Nations Group of Experts on the Congo. He has also worked for Global Rights, the UN peacekeeping operation in the Congo (MONUC), and the International Crisis Group (ICG). He is the author of a forthcoming book on the conflict in Congo and is completing his PhD in political science at Yale University.

SCOTT STRAUS is an associate professor of political science and international studies at the University of Wisconsin–Madison, director of the Human Rights Initiative at UW–Madison, author of *The Order of Genocide: Race, Power, and War in Rwanda*, and coauthor of *Africa's Stalled Development: International Causes and Cures* and *Intimate Enemy: Images and Voices of the Rwandan Genocide*. He has also published articles related to genocide and Rwanda in *World Politics, Politics & Society, Foreign Affairs, Genocide Studies and Prevention*, and *Journal of Genocide Research*.

CARINA TERTSAKIAN is a human rights researcher and campaigner. She has worked for Human Rights Watch (HRW), Amnesty International, and other NGOs. In 1999 she translated, updated, and wrote a postscript for André Sibomana's book *Gardons espoir pour le Rwanda* (Hope for Rwanda). She is the author of *Le Château: The Lives of Prisoners in Rwanda*.

SUSAN M. THOMSON is an assistant professor at Hampshire College. Her dissertation, titled "Resisting Reconciliation: State Power and Everyday Life in Post-Genocide Rwanda," is currently under consideration for publication.

LARS WALDORF is a senior lecturer at the Centre for Applied Human Rights and York Law School, University of York (UK). He ran Human Rights Watch's field office in Rwanda in 2002 and 2003. He has authored numerous chapters, journal articles, and reports on Rwanda and is currently writing a book on Rwanda's community genocide trials (*gacaca*) with generous support from the United States Institute of Peace. He also coedited *Localizing Transitional Justice* and *Disarming the Past: Transitional Justice and Ex-Combatants*.

DON WEBSTER is the lead prosecution counsel for the trial of *Prosecutor v. Karemera et al.*, currently pending before the International Criminal Tribunal for Rwanda (ICTR). He joined the ICTR in 1999 and was initially based in Kigali, Rwanda, as senior legal advisor and head of the legal advisory section. In 2003 he was transferred to the trial section in Arusha, the seat of the tribunal.

HARVEY M. WEINSTEIN, MD, MPH, is a senior research fellow at the Human Rights Center of the University of California, Berkeley, and a clinical professor in the School of Public Health. He was associate director of the Human Rights Center from 1998 to 2005. He is the author of *Psychiatry and the CIA: Victims of Mind Control* and coeditor (with Eric Stover) of *My Neighbor, My Enemy: Justice and Community in the Aftermath of Mass Atrocity*, as well as numerous reports and journal articles. Currently, he is coeditor of the *International Journal of Transitional Justice*.

EUGENIA ZORBAS has worked for the political affairs division of MONUC, the UN peacekeeping mission in DRC, in Goma, and for the United Nations High Commissioner for Refugees (UNHCR) and Human Rights Watch (HRW) in Rwanda. She completed her PhD on reconciliation in post-genocide Rwanda at the London School of Economics. She is currently a policy analyst for the Canadian Department of Foreign Affairs and International Trade and a postdoctoral fellow at the University of Ottawa's Center for International Policy Studies.

Index

Arusha Peace Accords (1993), 32, 236n5

ASF (Avocats sans frontières, Lawyers without Borders), 98n1

assassinations, near-assassinations, and disappearances, 17n7, 30, 32, 33, 34, 35, 50–51, 62–63n27, 90, 190, 344, 350–51, 353n8

authoritarianism and repression: civil society stifled by, 4, 10, 11, 27–31, 89–91; control of elections, 38–41; developmental state trumps democracy, 41–43; donor conditionality and, 125–26; donor support despite, 105–6; freedom of speech suppressed, 36–38; freedom of the press limited, 34–36; international misunderstanding of, 25–26; justification for, 8, 13–14, 50; memorialization as supporting, 292; overview of, 26–27; political parties constrained by, 31–34; techniques of, 10–11

AVEGA-AGAHOZA (Association des veuves du génocide, Association of Genocide Widows), 31

AVP (Association des volontaires de la paix, Association of Volunteers for Peace), 29

Bagosora, Théoneste, 186, 303

Ban Ki-Moon, 163

"Banyamulenge rebellion," 134, 141–42, 154

Barayagwiza, Jean-Bosco, 177

BBC (British Broadcasting Corporation): alleged genocide ideology and divisionism of, 35–36, 48, 53, 54, 56, 59–60, 115n4; donor concern about suppression of, 106

beer, 9, *74*, 228, 234, 277–78

Belgium: colonial governance scheme of, xxxiv; Cour d'Assizes in, xv; Rwandan conflict with, xxix–xxx; Rwandan interests of, 109–10; on Rwandans fighting in DRC, 134; shift in allegiance from Tutsi to Hutu, 50. *See also* Rwanda, colonial regimes (1884–1962)

Bizimungu, Frank, 33

Bizimungu, Pasteur: forced from office and imprisoned, 33, 307; Forum of Political Parties and, 346; Kagame's power

over, 32, 39; oversight bill opposed by, 344–45; *Urugwiro* meetings under, 69

Bizimungu et al. (court case), 186

Bizumuremyi, Bonaventure, 35

Blum, Andrew, 288, 289, 292

boomerang model, 92

Bosnia and Herzegovina: history teaching in, 297, 309, 311n3; War Crimes Chamber in, 164

Boutros-Ghali, Boutros, 137

brick-making, 246

budget (Rwanda): donor aid's importance to, 103–5, *104*, 108, 109, 111–13, 115n1, 121, 128n12, 161; pillaging DRC to bolster, 139–41, 147, 147nn12–13

Bugera, Déogratias, 141

Burundi: desire for buffer zone along border, 146n5; development aid for, *107*; land issues in, 254; Rwanda compared with, 7–8

business community, government and military linked to, 140–41

Busingye, Johnston, 89, 97

Butare Province: local election problems in, 38–39; political preferences in, 190. *See also* Sovu

Butare Six trial, 195, 196–97, 200, 207n2

Byuma, François-Xavier, 30

Byumba Province: local election problems in, 38–39; RPF killings in, 323

CARE International, 37, 48, 53, 91

Carothers, Thomas, 120

Catholic Church: conceptual tools introduced by, xxx–xxxi; court relations with, xxxv; skepticism about reports from, 160; tense relationship with Rwanda, 110. *See also* nuns (Sisters Gertrude and Kisito)

CCOAIB (Conseil de concertation des organisations d'appui aux initiatives de base, Consultative Council of Organizations to Support Grassroots Initiatives), 30, 31

ceceka (keeping silent), 202–3

Centrist Democratic Party, 34

CEPGL (Communauté économique des pays

des Grands Lacs, Economic Community of the Great Lakes Countries), 105
CHC (Congo Holding Company), 141
Child Protection Networks in Rwanda, 85n12
children and youth: active engagement of, 79–80; on ethnicity, 320–22; on genocide, 322–25; identity development of, 305, 306; narratives of past, 317, 319–28; nation-building narrative on, and challenge to, 80–84; in prison, 214, 325–26, 329n12
Chrétien, Jean-Pierre, 323
Christian churches: competition with Catholics, xxxv; leaders of, acceptable to RPF, 28
civil administration: donor aid for, 121; elected officials replaced by central authority appointees, 11, 68–75; as intellectual resource, xxxii; largely corruption free, 105; military and business linked to, 140–41; RPF control of, 32
civil society: government relations with, 87–88, 92–98; inclusion of, 123; RPF control and repression of, 4, 10, 11, 27–31, 89–91
Civil Society Election Observation Mission, 125
civil society organizations: advocacy models of, 92; alleged genocide ideology of, 37–38, 53; blocked or used to locate refugee camps, 137–38; conditions for effectiveness of, 92–98; and *imidugudu* (villagization policy), 230, 231, 236n6; RPF control and repression of, 31, 89–91; security and added numbers as benefits of, 98n7; skepticism about reports from, 160; targeted in genocide, 27. *See also* donor groups and aid funds; human rights organizations; international nongovernmental organizations (INGOs)
Civil Society Platform, 90
CLADHO (Collectif des ligues et associations de défense des droits de l'homme au Rwanda, Collective of Leagues and Associations for the Defense of Human Rights in Rwanda), 29, 31, 90

Clark, Phil, 6, 208n12
Clinton, Bill, xxiv
Clinton Foundation, 6
clothing, modernizing rural life through, 246–47
CMS (Church Missionary Society), xxxv
CNDH (Commission nationale des droits de l'homme, National Human Rights Commission), 81, 89–90
CNDP (Congrès national pour la défense du peuple, National Congress for the Defense of the People), 145, 159, 160, 165–66
Cole, Elizabeth A., 299
collective guilt, xv, 12, 49, 51, 106–7, 215
Collier, Paul, 17n9, 105
COMESA (Common Market for Eastern and Southern Africa), 105
conflict vulnerability assessment, 256
Congolese Army, 112–13, 145, 157
Connerton, Paul, 276, 286, 287, 291, 293
Constitution (2003): children's rights under, 80; ethnic identity referred to in, 333; and the Forum of Political Parties, 34; genocide ideology made illegal by, 37, 51; Tutsi genocide referred to in, 49
Convention on the Rights of the Children (CRC), 80
Corruption Index, 43n10
Côte d'Ivoire, land issues in, 223
Cour d'Assizes (Belgium), xv
court and aristocratic culture (Tutsi): as colonial intermediary, xxxiv; competing factions in, xxxii–xxxiii; external power and relations of, xxxv; land claims in, 255; response of, to Catholic priests, xxx–xxxi; response of, to colonial military forces, xxix–xxx, xxxi–xxxii; words and power in, xxxvi. *See also* Rwanda, colonial regimes (1884–1962); Rwanda, pre-colonial period (up to 1884)
Curic, Vjeko, 30
Cuvelier, Jeroen, 140
Cyiza, Augustin, 30

Dahl, Robert, 43n1
Dallaire, Roméo, xiv

Daniel, Valentine, 269–70

Danish Institute for Human Rights, 98n1

death penalty abolished, 176, 195, 214

decentralization policy: civil-state consultation in, 89, 123; impact of, 11, 68–75; memorialization in context of, 291–92; rationale for, 69, 338n5

de Lacger, Louis, xxxviii*n4*

de Lame, Danielle, 14

De Lorenzo, Mauro, 110

Del Ponte, Carla, 174, 177–78, 179

democracy: assessment of, 122–24; as condition for aid, 124–27; consensus-based, 349–50, 352n5; definition of, 43n1; donors' role in, 119–20; mistrust of Western-style, 123; promoted in Rwanda, 120–22; Rwandan ambassador on, 43n3; teaching linked to, 298, 303–5

democratic transition: absence of, 16, 26–27; aid targeted at encouraging, 119–22; civil society and state relations in, 87–88; civil society-state consultation in, 89, 91–92, 123, 257; civil society stifled in, 4, 10, 11, 27–31, 89–91; developmental state favored over, 41–43; elections controlled in, 38–41; freedom of speech suppressed in, 36–38; freedom of the press limited in, 34–36; international view of, 25–26; land issues in, 223–24; political parties constrained in, 31–34, 347–51

Des Forges, Alison: allegations against, 48, 57, 59–60, 62n21; banned from Rwanda, xxv, 48, 185; dedication of this book to, xiii; "Defeat Is the Only Bad News," xiv, xxviii–xxxvii; as historian and human rights activist, xxiii–xxxviii, 332, 343–44, 355–56; ICTR attorney's encounters with, 184–85; justice sector work of, xiv–xvi, xxiv–xxv, 355–56; proverbs used by, xxxvi, 67, 75; *Leave None to Tell the Story*, xiv–xv, xvi, xxiv, xxvii, 175

Des Forges, Alison, topics discussed by: all victims having chance for redress, 12; domestic trial of RPF officers, 180;

election results, 43n8; *gacaca*, 187, 192; ICTR, 207n5; *imidugudu* (villagization policy), 234, 249n4; land policy, 255, 256, 260; motivation for massacres in DRC, 155; number killed in Rwandan genocide, 17nn1–2; potential for violence, 351–52; propaganda, 323; rewards for *génocidaires*, 228; RPA war crimes, 175; Sebarenzi, 347

development: democracy restricted in favor of, 41–43; *ujamaa* ideology of, 225

development aid: despite concerns of donors, 105–6; donor groups, governance, and democracy in relation to, 119–20; ownership, harmonization, and aid effectiveness, 107, 114, 119; policies designed to attract, 107–9; and Rwanda's "exceptional status," 106–7; status quo in, 113–15; technocratic approach to, 114–15; Western interests in relation to, 109–10

de Zeeuw, Jeroen, 119, 120

DFID (Department for International Development), 96, 98n8

DGPR (Democratic Green Party of Rwanda), 34, 40–41, 347, 349–50

District Development Programs, 232

divisionism: accusations of, 49–50, 53, 90; concept of, 61n9; criminalization of, 37, 61n9, 333; fear of accusations of, 307–8. *See also* freedom of speech; genocide denial; genocide ideology

donor groups and aid funds: alleged genocide ideology of, 53; central role of, in post-conflict recovery, 12; collective guilt of, 106–7, 215; concerns of, 105–6, 351; democracy as condition for, 124–27; democratization targeted in, 119–22; development cooperation program key to, 109–10; domestic politics of, 110–11; election fraud ignored by, 118–19; and "exceptional status" of Rwanda, 106–7; and general budgetary support (GBS), 103–5, *104*, 108, 109, 111–13, 115n1, 121, 128n12, 161; "good enough democracy" for, 127–28; and *imidugudu* (villagization policy), 230, 231, 236n6; influences on donor policy, 17n7; land tenure reform and, 252, 253–54, 258–59; levels of aid from, 103–5, *104, 107*; passive and pliant in face of RPF, 15, 114–15; political reform as viewed by, 25–26, 41–42; praise of, for RPF government, 103; and refusal of aid to DRC, 156; resource pillaging ignored by ("ostrich policy"), 147nn13–14; RPF distrust of, 107–8; RPF attempts to attract, 107–9; Rwanda-DRC wars and, 105, 111–13, 115nn7–8, 126, 159–61; and standards of governance and democracy, 119–20, 122–24. *See also* development aid

DRC (Democratic Republic of the Congo, formerly Zaire): accountability for RPF crimes in, 152–66; anti-Tutsi sentiment and pogroms in, 157, 165–66; as collapsed state, 138–39; cross-border communities of, 166n3; development aid for, *107*, 156; FAR's flight into, 133–34; FDLR based in, 62n25; humanitarian impact of second war on, 157–58; interethnic violence in, 153–54; justice mapping exercise and report on, 161–66; peace agreement, transition, and resurgent violence in, 159; regime change in, 4–5, 132; reluctance to push for accountability, 160–61; roots of Rwandan involvement in, 153–54; RPF massacres in, 5, 17n7, 61n6, 135–37, 154, 156, 161; Rwanda, Burundi, and Uganda's desire for buffer zone in, 146n5; Rwanda's clandestine military activity in, 140–41, 142–46, 147n16, 147n18; Rwanda's exploitation of resources in, 10, 138–41; Rwanda's influence over, 145–46; Rwanda's involvement in Congolese/Zairian politics of, 141–45; standard of success defined by donors for, 110. *See also* Rwanda-DRC wars

EAC (East African Community), 105
Eastern Province: land acquisition by military and officials in, 258–59; land-grabbing in, 255; land sharing mandated in, 257–58; monocropping and planting in rows required in, 247; region of, 261n8

EC (European Commission), aid from, 104, *104*, 121

economic development: achievements in, 105; elite ambitions and rural realities in, 240–48; *imidugudu* (villagization policy) and, 223–35; land reform issues, 252–60; social engineering changes to, 9–10; vision for, 240–41; Western interests limited in, 109–10

"economization of conflict" concept, 147n12, 157

EDPRS (Economic Development and Poverty Reduction Strategy), 81, 85n7, 241, 247. *See also* economic development; poverty reduction

education: achievements in, 105; hopes for, 83

elections: of 1999 (local), 121; of 2001, 118; of 2003, 37–38, 39, 43n8, 72, 118; of 2006, 40, 71–73; "civil disobedience" in, 76n7; development of process for, 121; donor concern about, 105; methods of voting in, 38–39; observers' views of, 124, 125; RPF control and manipulation of, 38–41, 71–73, 118, 352n4. *See also* elections of 2008; elections of 2010; EU EOM (European Union Election Observation Mission)

elections of 2008: donor aid for, 121; donor response to results, 124–25; fraud in, 118; perspective on, 126; results of, 40, *41*

elections of 2010: donor aid for, 121; international concerns about, 351; perspective on, 126; RPF control and manipulation of, 17n7, 34, 38, 40–41, 57–59, 347–51

elite, of Rwanda: agricultural vision of, 243–46; alternative historical narratives of, 318–19; attitudes of, toward peasantry, 242–43, 354; economic reconstruction and poverty reduction goals of, 240–41; failure of, 355; rural term for, 235n2; wealth of, 42, 139–41, 147

"entrepreneurs of insecurity," 147n9

Erlinder, Carl Peter, 58–59, 62–63n27
ESO (External Security Organization, Rwanda), 140
Ethiopia: Hamitic Hypothesis concerning, 293n5; villagization in, 105, 225
ethnicity and ethnic divisions: alternative narratives of, 318–19; banned discussion of, 8, 36–37, 208n9, 270–79, 333; children and youth's views of, 82, 317, 320–22; in colonial rural areas, 227; distrust and, 205; in DRC, 153–54; effects of Rwanda-DRC wars on, 165–66; in elections of 2010, 126–27; emphasis vs. erasure of, 49–50; fabulation in discourse on, 276–78; fear of discussing, 307–8, 309–10, 320; hardening views of, xxxiv; historical context of, 302–3; *imidugudu* (villagization policy) in context of, 235; individuals' re-situation of, 270–73, 274–75; official narrative of, 269–70, 298, 301–2, 309–10, 316–17, 327–28; perceived colonial construction of, 269–70, 272, 273–75, 279–80n5, 301–3, 320–22, 333, 336–37; reeducation about, 333–38; rejection of, 198; relativizing of, 275–76; state restructuring as perpetuating, 73; terms for genocide dependent on, 328–29n5; *Urugwiro* workshops on freedom from, 273–75
EU (European Union): warnings for RPF in DRC, 144
EU EOM (European Union Election Observation Mission): on elections of 2003, 39; on elections of 2008, 40, *41*, 124–25, 126; funding for, 118–19

FAR (Forces armées rwandaises, Rwandan Armed Forces), 133–34, 142
FARDC (Forces armées de la république démocratique du Congo, Armed Forces of the Democratic Republic of the Congo), 144–45
FARG (Fonds d'assistance aux rescapés du génocide, Fund for Assistance to Genocide Survivors), 30–31, 83
FAZ (Forces armées zaïroises, Zairean Armed Forces), 133

FDLR (Forces démocratiques de libération du Rwanda, Democratic Forces for the Liberation of Rwanda): Congolese and RPF operations against, 112–13; Congolese weapons for, 157; instability fostered by, 142, 145, 147n19, 159; realignment of, 165–66; as terrorist organization, 62n25
FDU-Inkingi (Forces démocratiques unifiées-Inkingi, United Democratic Forces), 34, 40–41, 347
FH (Facing History and Ourselves), 311n4
Forum of Political Parties, 33–34, 40, 346, 348, 352n6
Freedom House, 128n7
freedom of speech: democratic teaching linked to, 304–5; donor concern about suspensions of, 106; genocide ideology allegations and, 60; suppression of, 36–38; suppression of discourse and reports, 58–59, 115n3, 163–64, 175, 242; witness testimony problems and, 201–4. *See also* divisionism; genocide denial; genocide ideology
freedom of the press: organizations reporting on, 43n7; repression of, 4, 10, 11, 34–36
FRELIMO (Frente de Libertação de Moçambique, Liberation Front of Mozambique), 14
FRF (Forces républicaines fédéralistes, Federalist Republican Forces), 145
Furuma, Alphonse, 352n2

gacaca (genocide community courts): approach to, 88; characteristics of, 199; civil society and state relations in, 88–89; collective guilt imposed on Hutu in, 12, 49, 51; confessions in, 188–89, 191, 193n2, 201, 215–16; conflicts linked to, 204–6; convicts of, as source of prosecution witnesses, 187–88; Des Forges's criticism of, xv, 187, 192; distrust fostered by, 11, 204–6; donor concern about, 105, 106; historical record distorted in, 186, 189–93; impunity for RPF massacres of Hutu in, 206–7n1; noncompliance with human rights norms, 206–7n1; observation of, 198;

opposition suppressed in, 355; policy implementation vs. interpretation in, 95; PRI's relations with government and, 97; social engineering via, 9; in Sovu, 200–206, 208n12, 208nn8–9; summary of, 91–92; testimony on RPF crimes in, 51–52; witness testimony problems in, 201–4, 213, 218

Gahima, Gerald, 11, 352n2

Gakwandi, Pierre, 33

Garretón, Roberto, 137, 155–56

GDP (gross domestic product), 139, 147n11, 241

gender equality achievements, 105, 115n2

génocidaires: death penalty prohibited for, 176, 195, 214; executions of, 15, 28, 176; as following orders, 322, 324, 326; in *ingando* reeducation camps, 332, 333–38; land as reward for, 228; motivations of, 277; number of, 211–12, 218n1, 219n3; RPF victory over, 13–14. See also *gacaca* (genocide community courts); prisoners

genocide: blanket accusations of, 213; character, scale, and legacy of, 3–4, 13; child victims and perpetrators in, 80; civil society organizations targeted in, 27; civil war implicated in, 322–23, 329nn9–11; collective blind spot created by, 211; collective guilt for, xv, 12, 49, 51, 106–7, 215; Des Forges's attempts to stop, xxiii–xxiv; Des Forges's examination of, xiv–xv, xxvii–xxviii, 343; donor complicity prior to, 127–28; "exceptional status" of Rwanda based on, 106–7; government structure efficient in, 68–69; hate speech and propaganda implicated in, 34–36, 48–49, 53–54, 60n1, 322, 323; historical narrative implicated in, 302–3; impunity for RPF killings of Hutu in aftermath of, 12, 15, 17n2, 51, 173–75, 176, 181, 206–7n1, 355; individual choice in, 304–5, 312n7; intentionalist interpretation of, 8; Interim Government implicated in, 185, 190–92; international community's failure to stop, xxiv; land and property

issues involved in, 227, 228, 255–56, 322, 324; mapping report on potential crimes of, 162–66; media implicated in, 34–36; as motive for Rwanda's war, 159–60; personal jealousy and disputes involved in, 228, 255–56, 322, 324; political nature of, 32, 192; RPF on causes of, 28, 49–50; RPF politicization of, 51; settlement terms of, 13–14; in Sovu, 196–98; terminology for, 49, 324–25, 328–29n5; trivialization of, 59–60; young people's view of factors leading to, 322–25

Genocide Convention, Article IX, 163

genocide credit, 115n5

genocide denial: arrest for, 58–59; evidence of, 50–51; RPF campaign against, 51–52; RPF conflation of genocide ideology and, 49–50. See also divisionism; freedom of speech; genocide ideology

genocide ideology: accusations of and arrests for, 37–38, 56, 62n19; calls for RPF prosecutions labeled as, 174; child accused of, 81; civil groups allegedly harboring, 29–30, 48, 56–57; concept of, 49–50, 53–54, 55, 273–74, 333; donor concerns about allegations of, 126; effects of campaign against, 59–60; fear of accusations of, 307–8; law against, 37, 48, 51–52, 55–56, 58–59, 62nn18–19, 106, 273–74; NGOs allegedly spreading, 88; opposition views demonized as, 11, 12; political parties allegedly promoting, 33, 57–59. See also divisionism; freedom of speech; genocide denial

genocide survivors: definition of, 208n10; investigation of murdered, 53; organizations and funds for, 30–31, 83, 90; RPF harassment of, 30–31; threats against and distrust of, 204–6; witness testimony of, 201–4. See also *gacaca* (genocide community courts); history and memory

geography, mapping and naming, x, xi, 9, 69, 333

Germany: military forces of, xxx, xxxi, xxxiv, xxxv; uniforms from, 138

Gersony Report (1994), 163, 175

Global and Inclusive Accord (2002), 142–43, 158–59, 164

Global IDP Project, 234

Global indictment (*Bagosora and 29 others*), 185–86

GNI (gross national income), 104, *104*

Goldstone, Richard, 174, 175–76

Gourevitch, Philip: on Nyarubuye memorial site, 288–89; refugees stereotyped by, 155; RPA war crimes downplayed by, 175; Rwanda and Kagame praised by, 6, 25–26, 42

governance and state building: assessment of, 122–24; authoritarianism and repression, 25–43; children and youth issues, 79–84; civil society and policymaking, 87–98; decentralization and accountability, 67–75; donors' role in, 119–20; executive branch power in, 344–47; "good enough" democracy as measure, 127–28; instrumentalization of genocide in, 48–60; Joint Governance Assessment's definition of, 123, 128n8; political pluralism and liberalization best after, 16; security, justice, reconciliation and trust, 123. *See also* authoritarianism and repression; democratic transition; government; security

government: civil society engagement with, 87–88, 92–98; Des Forges barred by, xxv, 48, 185; dialogue with vs. criticism of, 125; disadvantages of, 7–8, 17n9; donor aid as conditional on democratic, 124–27; donor aid for accountability program of, 121–22, 123; historical context of, 14–15; ICTR's relationship with, 174–81; reconciliation discourse and fight against negationism of, 49–50

Government of National Unity: political power-sharing in, 32; RPF control of, 32–33, 328n1. *See also* government; RPF

Gowing, Nick, 160

Grands Lacs Metals, 141

Great Lakes region: economic organization for, 105; mining company in, 141; privatization of public space and criminaliza-

tion of states/economies in, 139–40; Rwanda's influence in, 7–8

Gribbin, Robert, 141–42, 146n3, 147n13, 155

Grindle, Merilee S., 128n13

Guyer, Sara, 289, 292

Habineza, Frank, 347, 349–50

Habyarimana, Juvénal: agrarian vision and rural issues under, 227–28, 242–43, 249n2; assassination of, 50–51, 62–63n27, 190; freedom of the press under, 34; human rights violations of, 343; one-party state under, 10; outside support for, 14; political parties under, 32, 349; RPF compared with, 42–43; ties with Hutu in DRC, 154. *See also* MRND; Rwanda, post-colonial, pre-genocide (1962–94)

Hagaruka (women's rights group), 30

Hajabakiga, Patricia, 94

Halbwachs, Maurice, 284

hate speech, 34–36, 48–49, 53–54, 60n1, 322, 323

health sector: coercive policy and fines in, 73–74, *74*; HIV/AIDS and, 80; performance-based plans in, 70, 76n10

Hiernaux, Jean, 329n8

Higgins, Rosalyn, 163

high modernist projects: concepts underlying, 4, 17n10; factors in, 12–13; skepticism about, 230–31; villagization as, 224–26

history and memory: centralization of, 292; controversies over, 283–84, 316–17; current social processes in context of, xxvii–xxviii; explaining present in terms of past, 67–68; fabulation in, 276–78; *gacaca*'s distortion of, 186, 189–93; *ingando* reeducation camps and, 331–38; *lieux de mémoire* (sites of memory) in, 283–93; official narrative of, 12, 298, 301–2, 309–10, 316–17, 327–28, 333; politics of, 318–19; potential of past in, 275, 280n6; present legitimated through narrative of, 325–26; privileged vs.

imidugudu (villagization policy): advantages of, 230, 246; commercialization of agriculture linked to, 244–45; comparison of, 225–26; concept of, 9; context of, 223–24, 226–29, 285; donor concern about, 105, 106; donors' and NGOs' initial involvement with, 230, 231, 236n6; implementation of, 231–32; key elements in, 224–25; law on, 256–57; opposition suppressed, 354–55; peasants' view of, 249n4; problems with, 234–35, 236n9; responses to, 233–35; as security issue, 229–30; terminology for, 69, 235n1. *See also* agriculture; land reform policy

imihigo (performance-based contracts): coercive policy and fines in, 73–74, 74; concept of, 70–71; local officials and central government linked in, 72–73; performance targets of, 247–48

inequalities: economic growth rates as hiding, 10; within and between ethnic groups, 17–18n11; expansion of, 42, 110, 241–42

Ingabire, Victoire, 34, 41; on accountability for Hutu and Tutsi, 347–48; arrest of, 41; death threats against, 34; lawyer of, 58–59; persecution of and accusations against, 57–58, 62n25, 348, 349. *See also* Erlinder, Carl Peter

ingando reeducation camps: concept of, 8, 75n3, 328n2; function of, 279–80n5, 332–34; history lessons in, 274, 322, 335–37; implications of, 337–38; *ingando* solidarity camps distinguished from, 333–34; justification for, 50; official narrative of genocide in, 317; truth and reconciliation lessons in, 337; Ugandan model for, 14

Inkotanyi. *See* RPA

instrumentalization of genocide: background of, 49–50; techniques of, 11–12, 49

Interahamwe militia: incursions into MDR area, 190–91; manipulation of, 140; massacres of, 137; trial of, 186; as witnesses on MRND training, 188–89

International Commission of Investiga-

tion on Human Rights Violations in Rwanda, xiv, 343

international community: alleged divisionism of, 53; collective guilt of, 106–7, 215; distrust of intervention by, 107–8, 114; domestic politics of, 110–11; Kagame praised by, 6, 25–26, 41–42, 110, 344, 351; permissiveness of, 15; political reform as viewed by, 25–26, 41–42; reluctance to challenge Rwanda's wars, 159–61; RPA war crimes downplayed by, 174–75

International Financial Institutions, 147n14

international nongovernmental organizations (INGOs): differences between human rights and development, 88; on massacres of refugees in DRC, 156; rights-based approach of, 93–94; RPF crackdown on, 90–91. *See also* civil society organizations; human rights organizations; *and specific organizations*

IRDP (Institut de recherche et de dialogue pour la paix, Institute of Research and Dialogue for Peace), 76n5, 319

Jackson, Michael, 277, 280n6

Jackson, Stephen, 147n12

Jallow, Hassan: legal duty evaded by, 181; unwillingness to prosecute RPF, 174, 178–81

JGA (Joint Governance Assessment), 114, 122–25

justice sector: debates about, 152; Des Forges's work on, xv–xvi, xxiv–xxv, 355–56; genocide in Sovu and impact of trials on, 194–206; ICTR and *gacaca* relationship, 184–93; ICTR and government relationship, 173–81; lessons of, 206; major players in, 98n1; mechanisms possible in, 166n1; politicization of, 354–56; prison issues, 210–18; rule of law and, 344–47; types of trials in, 194–95

Kabanda, Godfrey, 138

Kabarebe, James, 138, 141, 156

Kabayija, Ephraïm, 146–47n7

Kabera, Assiel, 30
Kabila, Joseph, 142, 165
Kabila, Laurent: AFDL and, 135, 141; goal of, 138; handpicked by Rwanda, 146n4, 156; human rights investigation opposed by, 156; Kagame on, 142; rebel militias supplied by, 157
Kagame, Paul: accusations against, 50–51, 62–63n27; background of, xxv; consolidation of power by, 11, 32–33, 346–47, 348–51; donor-friendly positioning of, 108; influences on, 14; land commission of, 252–53, 257–60; praise for, 6, 25–26, 41–42, 110, 344, 351; press controlled by, 36; reelections of, 17n7, 39, 40–41, 43n8, 126–27; Rusesabagina denounced by, 60n2
Kagame, Paul, topics discussed by: development aid, 115n6, 115n8; ethnicity, 49–50; executive oversight bill, 344–47; foreign interventionism, 114; *imihigo* (performance-based contracts), 71; prisoner releases, 215; RPF in DRC, 134–35, 146n3; Rwandan children, 80, 81; Rwanda's status, 125; work, 243
Kajeguhakwa, Valens, 352n2
Kamanayo, Jean-Baptiste, 198, 199, 200, 206, 207n2
Kambanda, Jean, 186–87, 188, 191
Kamuhanda, Jean de Dieu, 186
Kandt, Richard, xxxi
Kanzenze Bridge memorial site, 287, 290–91, 292
Karaha, Bizima, 142
Karamira, Froduald, 176
Karegeya, Patrick, 11, 148n20, 350
Karemera, Edouard, 185–93
Karemera et al. (court case): background on, 185–87; circular flow of documentation in, 188–89; current status of, 192–93; *gacaca*'s distortion of historical record in, 190–92; potential prosecution witnesses in, 187–88
Kaufman, Zachary, 6
Kayijaho, Josué, 29, 30, 352n2
Kayijuka (chief), 329n8

Kayumba, Christophe, 38
Kayumba Nyamwasa, Faustin, 11, 35, 350–51
Keck, Margaret E., 92
Kenya: land issues in, 223, 254; prosecution for atrocities in, 180
Kibeho internally displaced persons camp, 15, 197, 261n10, 325–26
Kibuye Province, local election problems in, 38–39
Kibwimana, Silas, 190
Kigali (Rwanda): elite lifestyle in, 139–41; grenade attacks in (2010), 344, 350, 351, 352–53n7; Kiyovu Cya Abacyene neighborhood destroyed in, 292–93
Kinzer, Stephen, 6, 25, 26
Kisase, Ngandu, 141
Kumar, Krishna, 119, 120

labor: banning forms of, 246; creating off-farm, 245–46
Lake, Anthony, xxiv
land and property: amount needed for food security, 260n2; conflict dynamics and, 254–56; disputes over, as motive in *gacaca* accusations, 201–2; disputes over, involved in genocide, 227, 228, 255–56, 322, 324; expropriated for *imidugudu* (villagization policy), 233; expropriation law on, 257, 259; indigenous systems of, 260n2; post-conflict land-grabbing, 236n4, 253, 255–56, 258–59; "productive land" specified in law, 249n3; registration of, 252, 253–54, 256, 257, 260, 261n7
LANDNET, 88, 93–94, 96, 98n5
land reform policy: approach to, 252–53; civil society and state relations in, 88–89, 257; context of, 226–29, 254–56, 285; in global South, generally, 253–54; implementation of, 95, 231; land sharing mandated by, 257–58; law on, 249n3, 256–57, 258, 259, 261n9; NGOs and state relations in, 93–94; Presidential Commission's land redistribution, 258–60; summary of, 91–92
Law Punishing Genocide (2003), 51–52, 57

laws: children's rights, 80; divisionism, 37; (ethnic) discrimination and sectarianism, 273; genocide ideology, 37, 48, 51–52, 55–56, 58–59, 62nn18–19, 106, 273–74; human rights, 343; journalism regulations, 36; land and land expropriation, 249n3, 256–57, 258, 259, 261n9; NGOs, 31, 89–90

League of Nations, xxxv

Leave None to Tell the Story (Des Forges), xiv–xv, xvi, xxiv, xxvii, 175

lieux de mémoire (sites of memory): controversies over, 283–84; implications of, 291–93; Kanzenze Bridge site, 287, 290–91, 292; loci or places encoded as, 287; memorials as, 286–87; Nyamata site, 287–90, 292; types of sites, 284, 285–86

LIPRODHOR (Ligue rwandaise pour la promotion et la défense des droits de l'homme, Rwandan League for the Promotion and Defense of Human Rights): alleged genocide ideology of, 37, 52, 53; RPF repression of, 29–30, 90

local government: civil society and policy-making by, 94–95; performance targets for, 247–48; RPF control and manipulation of elections of, 71–73; structure of, 69, *70. See also* decentralization policy; rural areas

Low-Beer, Ann, 311n3

Mai-Mai militia, 157

Manzi, Gérard M., 35

Marysse, Stefaan, 139, 147n14

Masasu, Nindaga, 141

Mazimhaka, Patrick, 142, 147n18

Mbembe, Achille, 139

MDGs (Millennium Development Goals), 85n7, 105, 126

MDR (Mouvement démocratique républicain, Democratic Republican Movement): alleged divisionism and genocide ideology of, 52, 90; attacked, 33, 39; demise of, 61n11; Gitarama dominated by, 190–91; governmental role after accords, 32; internal division fostered by RPF, 349; in Sovu, 196–98

media coverage of Rwanda (print and broadcast): critical turn in 2010, 17n7; donor concern about suppression of, 106; hate speech and propaganda implicated in genocide, 34–36, 48–49, 53–54, 60n1, 322, 323; independent voices punished, 11; official narrative of genocide disseminated in, 317; RPF control and repression of, 4, 5–6, 10, 11, 26, 34–36, 160; RPF persecution of, 347, 352n3

Media High Council, 36

metanarrative: of history and memory, 317, 318–22, 327, 328n3; of national identity, 79–80, 82

Mgbako, Chi, 279–80n5, 338n3

MIGEPROF (Ministry of Gender and Promotion of Child and Family Rights), 80–81

military tribunals, 195

Millennium Challenge Corporation, 122, 125

MINADEF (Ministry of Defence), 345. *See also* RPA

MINAGRI (Ministry of Agriculture and Animal Resources), 241, 244–45. *See also* agriculture; MINITERE

MINECOFIN (Ministry of Finance and Economic Planning), 241. *See also* EDPRS

MINEDUC (Ministry of Education), 298, 307–9, 311n6. *See also* NCDC

MINIJUST (Ministry of Justice), 187–88

Ministry of Foreign Affairs, 53–54

Ministry of Internal Security, 93

MINITERE (Ministry of Land): on civil discourse, 257; on commercialization of agriculture and *imidugudu* (villagization policy), 244–45; DFID pilot project with, 98n8; interviews of officials from, 241; LANDNET and, 93–94, 96, 98n5; on villagization advantages, 230. See also *imidugudu* (villagization policy); MINAGRI

Mironko, Charles, 277

Misago, Augustin, 28

Misser, François, 134

Mobutu Sese Seko, 4, 135, 138, 146n5, 153

modernization: democratic teaching as, 298, 303–5; memorialization in relation to, 290. *See also* high modernist projects

MONUC (Mission des Nations Unies en république démocratique du Congo, United Nations Mission in the Democratic Republic of the Congo), 142, 143, 147n16, 157–58

Moreno-Ocampo, Luis, 179–80

MoU (Memorandum of Understanding, UK-Rwanda), 109

Moyo, Dambisa, 115n6

Mozambique: revolutionary movement in, 14; villagization in, 225

MRND (Mouvement républicain national pour la démocratie et le développement, National Republican Movement for Democracy and Development), 10, 188–91. See also *Karemera et al.* (court case)

MSF (Médecins sans frontières, Doctors without Borders), 137, 166n4

Mugesera, Antoine, 31

Mugesera, Léon, 291, 293n5

Mugisha, Furaha, 35

Muhayimana, Jason, 352n3

Mujawamariya, Monique, xxiv

Mukezamfura, Alfred, 34

Mukiza, Mustafa, 158

multiparty system, 123

Munyango, Gaston, 138

Munyarubuga, Gratien, 33

Muramba, Anastase, 31

Murigande, Charles, 143

Musevini, Yoweri, 141

Mushayidi, Déogratias, 58, 62n25, 63n29, 352n3

Mushikiwabo, Louise, 50, 56, 62n20, 62n26

Musoni, James, 242

Mutebutsi, Jules, 143, 144

Mutsinzi, Jean, 346

Muvara, Felicien, 303

National Assembly, 32–33, 40, 115n2

National Commission for the Fight against Genocide, 61n8, 292

National Land Commission, 261n12

National Land Policy, 254

national mourning week (April 7–14), 333

National Policy on Orphans and Vulnerable Children, 80

National Prisons Service, 214

National Strategic Plan, 80

National Summit for Children and Young People, 80–84

national unity and reconciliation ideology: children's challenge to rhetoric of, 81, 82, 84; goals of, 8, 333; official narrative in, 298, 301–2, 309–10, 316–17, 327–28; perceived historical unity and restoration of, 269–70, 272, 273–75, 279–80n5, 301–3; research of Susan Thomson allegedly against, 331–32

National University of Rwanda (NUR), 311nn4–5

NCDC (National Curriculum Development Center), 300, 308–9, 311nn4–5

NCHR (National Commission for Human Rights), 343

Ndahiro, Tom, 52

Ndombasi, Yerodia, 159

Ndung'u Commission (Kenya), 254

NEC (National Election Commission), 40, 126, 128n11, 349

negationism. *See* genocide denial

Netherlands: aid for Rwanda cut by, 111, 112–13, 115n8, 125, 126, 128n12, 145, 160; Rwanda's "exceptional status" in policy of, 106–7

Ngarambe, François, 291

Ngirabatware, Augustin, 186

Ngirumpatse, Matthieu, 185–93

Ngoga, Martin, 58, 61n9

Niyitegeka, Eliezer, 186

Nkubito, Alphonse-Marie, 29, 32

Nkunda, Laurent: arrest of, 165; civilians massacred by, 112, 142–43, 144–45; militia of, 159; Rwandan support for, 160

Nkurunziza, Jackson (alias Jack Nziza), 138

NLTRP (National Land Tenure Reform Programme), 257, 260

Nora, Pierre, 285–86

Norwegian Center for Human Rights, 39
NPA (Norwegian People's Aid), 48, 53, 91
NRM (National Resistance Movement), 14
Nsabimana, Sylvain, 196
Nsanzabaganwa, Richard, 29
Ntaganda, Bernard, 57–58, 62n25, 347, 348–49
Ntakirutinka, Charles, 33
Ntashamaje, Gérard, 352n2
Ntezimana, Emmanuel, xxxviii*n4*
nuns (Sisters Gertrude and Kisito): actions of, 196–97; conditional release of, 207n7; trial of, 195, 200, 207n3
NUR (National University of Rwanda), 311nn4–5
NURC (National Unity and Reconciliation Commission), 84n6, 89–90, 208n9
Nuremberg trials, 173, 186
Nyamata memorial site, 287–90, 292
Nyarubuye memorial site, 288–89
Nzirorera, Joseph, 185–93

official development assistance (ODA) levels, 104, *104*, *107*
Organic Land Law (2005), 256–57, 258, 261n9
Organisation for Economic Co-operation and Development (OECD), 126

Paris, Roland, 16
Paris Principles on Aid Effectiveness (2005), 108, 113–14
Parliament: attempt to build rule of law in, 344–47; donor technical assistance for, 122; genocide ideology commission of, 53, 54–55, 90, 307–8; Standing Committee on Unity, Human Rights, and the Fight Against Genocide, 57–58
Party for Progress and Concord, 40
Pax Christi, 37
PDR-Ubuyanja (Parti pour la démocratie et le renouveau-Ubuyanja, Party for Democratic Renewal-Ubuyanja), 33
peasants: collectivization rejected by, 249n4; elite attitudes toward, 242–43, 354; government dismissiveness toward, 226; history invoked by, 67–68; modernizing

life for, 246–47; monocropping and crop specialization policies imposed on, 243–46, 247, 252, 260n1; radicalism of, 227–28, 235–36n3; reluctance to discuss policy, 249n5; resistance to national unity and reconciliation ideology, 331; response to Catholic priests, xxx–xxxii; risk aversion vs. profit maximization choice of, 225; social engineering and implications for future, 247–48; term used by, for those in power (*abaryi*), 235n2; worsening conditions for, 242. See also *imidugudu* (villagization policy); *ingando* reeducation camps; land reform policy; poverty; rural areas
"performance legitimation" strategy, 41
Pierre-Prosper, Richard, 179
PL (Parti libéral, Liberal Party), 32, 33–34, 40, *41*, 350, 352n6
policy and policymaking: aid dependence and, 103–15; children's rights in, 80; civil society groups utilized to implement, 31; civil society-state consultation over, 89, 91–92, 123, 257; peasants' reluctance to discuss, 249n5; performance targets in, 247–48; prisons, 214, 215–17; RPF donor-friendly, 107–9
political parties and participation: alleged genocide ideology of, 33, 57–59; constraints on, 4, 31–34, 71–72; Forum of Political Parties as control mechanism, 33–34, 40, 346, 352n6; keys to, 27; persecution of opposition, 347–51
politics: court conflicts reflected in, xxxii–xxxiii; donor-friendly, 107–9; external power influences on, xxxv; forced resignations and exiles, 346–47, 352n2; of history, 318–19; impact of, on history curriculum, 303, 307–9, 311n3; persecution of opposition, 347–51; regional divisions in, xxxiii–xxxiv; repression of opposition, 10, 11, 57–59, 347–51; words and power in, xxxvi. See also authoritarianism and repression; elections
Pomfret, John, 138
post-conflict recovery/post-genocide reconstruction: approach to, 3–5, 344; critical

issues in, 13–17; democratization and donors in, 119–22; findings and themes in present volume, 10–13; implications of findings on, 13–17; land reform key to, 253–54; new thinking needed in, 354–56; objectives in present volume, 5–8; peace vs. justice in, 152; periodization of, 120–21; Rwanda as critical case in, 7–8; talking vs. not talking about past in, 326–28; teaching history in, 297–99, 309–10. *See also* civil society; democratic transition; government; national unity and reconciliation ideology; reconstruction and development policy; social engineering

Pottier, Johan, 5–6, 26, 95, 244

poverty: alternative approach to, 248; elite view of, 243; expansion of, 42, 110, 241–42; food insecurity, 252, 255, 260n3; measurement of general well-being and, 246–47

poverty reduction: limits of, 242; monocropping and crop specialization policies aimed at, 243–46, 247, 252, 260n1; off-farm employment aimed at, 245–46; Rwanda's vision for, 240–41

Power, Samantha, 175

Presidential Commission on Land in Eastern Province: context of, 257–58; land redistribution by, 252–53; members of, 258–59; skepticism about, 259–60

PRI (Penal Reform International): approach to, 88; crisis in, 96, 97; on *gacaca*, 199; on *ingando* reeducation camps, 338n3; prison computerization developed by, 219n8; role of, 98n1; training provided by, 93

prisoners: legacy of prison time for, 217–18; number and background of, 212, 214, 218–19n2; as potential prosecution witnesses, 187–88; release of, 210–11, 214, 215–17, 329n12; youth in, 214, 325–26, 329n12

prisons: computerization in, 214, 219n8; conditions in, 211–14, 326; fear of returning to, 217–18; government's management of, 214, 215–17

Profemme Twese Hamwe (women's organization), 28, 31, 90

Prosecutor v. Karemera et al. See Karemera et al. (court case)

proverbs: *igiti kigororwa kikiri gito/* "a stick can be straightened while it is still young," 80, 84n6; *induru ntirwana n'ingoma/* "the drum is greater than the shout," 67–68, 75; on rulers and the ruled, 76n11; *umwana ni umutware/* "a child is king," 80, 84n3; *utazi umukungu yima umwana/* "if you give a child opportunities . . . ," 82, 85n10

provinces: local election problems in, 38–39; redrawn boundaries and renaming of, 9, 69, 333

PRSP (Poverty Reduction Strategy Paper), 91, 245. *See also* EDPRS

PSD (Parti social démocratie, Social Democratic Party), 32, 33–34, 40, 41, 348

PSI (Parti social Imberakuri, Imberakuri Social Party), 347, 348

public sector, performance-based financing in, 70

Radio Rwanda, 35–36

RCD (Rassemblement Congolais pour la Démocratie, Congolese Rally for Democracy), 140–41, 142, 143, 157, 159

RCN Justice and Démocratie, 98n1

RDF (Rwanda Defense Forces). *See* RPA

reconciliation and trust: destruction of, 211–12; as factor in community, 195, 202; as factor in governance and state building, 123; fight against negationism/genocide denial and, 49–50; *ingando* reeducation lessons in, 337; limits to, 205–6, 307–8; memorialization linked to, 291–93; truth as factor in, 318–19

reconstruction and development policy: donor-friendly orientation of, 107–9; framing of, 4; overview of, 241–42; replacement of Kanzenze Bridge as symbol of, 291; re-teaching of history in, 297–98. *See also* development; donor groups and aid funds

reeducation. See *ingando* reeducation camps

refugee camps: "administrative closure" of, 146n1; distribution of humanitarian aid used by rebels to locate, 137–38; Hutu killed at internal, 15, 197, 261n10, 325–26; repatriation avenues for, 146–47n7; RPA attacks on, 5, 17n7, 61n6, 134, 135–37; Rwandan refugee-warriors in, 133–34; stereotypes of inhabitants of, 155

regionalism in Rwanda: crop specialization and land-use consolidation in, 260; and genocide, 192; political divisions of, xxxiii–xxxiv; redrawing maps to eliminate, 9, 69

Rekeraho, Emmanuel: actions of, 196–97; interview of, 198; testimony on nuns, 195; on training youth, 207n3; trial of, 199, 200, 206, 207n2

religious organizations: alleged genocide ideology of, 37–38, 53; co-opted or intimidated by RPF, 28

RISD (Rwanda Initiative for Sustainable Development), 233, 235, 236n7

Roman Catholic Church. *See* Catholic Church

Rose, Laurel, 236n4

RPA (Rwandan Patriotic Army, later Rwanda Defense Forces, RDF): attempts to stop FAR, 133; distribution of humanitarian aid used by, to locate refugees, 137–38; DRC pillaged to fund, 139–40; government and business linked to, 140–41; growing divisions in, 350–51; humanitarian aid blocked by, 137–38; Hutu killed after genocide, 12, 15, 17n2, 51, 173–75, 176, 181, 206–7n1, 355; mapping report on, 162–66; massacres perpetrated in DRC, 5, 17n7, 61n6, 134, 135–37, 154–55, 157, 159, 165, 166n4; origins of, 115n3; recruitment in Congo, 153–54; reports on movements of, 147n16; as "soldiers without borders," 147n10

RPF (Rwandan Patriotic Front): ambitions of, 4–5; centralized control over rural areas, 11, 68–75; characteristic tactics of, 132–33; civil society organizations co-opted or intimidated by, 27–31;

commemorative policies of, 289–90, 292, 333; donor-friendly policies of, 107–9; historical narrative of, 298, 301–2, 309–10, 316–19; impunity for massacres by (victor's justice), 12, 15, 16, 17n2, 51, 173–75, 176, 181, 206–7n1, 355; indigenous terminology of, 75n3; international status of, as rescuer, 174; justification of, for social engineering, 8, 13–14, 50; land acquisition by, 258–59; membership required in, 339n6; military victory of, 13–15; potential genocide charges against, 347–48; praise for, 6, 25–26, 41–42, 103, 344; quiet (or off-screen) diplomacy preferred by, 93–94; "territorial reform" under, 69–70

RSF (Reporters sans frontières, Reporters without Borders), 11, 43n7

RTLM (Radio télévision libre des Mille Collines), 35, 53–54, 323

Rubibi, Joseph, 141

Rudasingwa, Théogène, 11, 352n2

Rugambage, Jean-Léonard, 35, 351

Rukimbika, Manassé, 141

rule of law, 344–47

rural areas: alternative approach to, 248; coercive policy and fines in, 73–74, *74*; elections manipulated in, 71–73; elite goals vs. realities of, 240–48; ethnic stratification in, 227; government restructuring in, 10–11, 69–71, *70*; land issues central to, 223–24, 228, 236n4; monocropping and crop specialization policies in, 243–46, 247, 252, 260n1; percentage of population in, 223–24; perspective from, 67–68; Presidential Commission's land redistribution in, 258–60; responses of, to *imidugudu* (villagization policy), 233–35; social engineering and implications for future of, 247–48

Rusatira, Léonidas, xv

Rusesabagina, Paul, 60n2

Rutagengwa, Jean Bosco, 31, 352n2

Rutagengwa, Théonèste, 319, 324

Rutaremera, Tito, 52, 292

Rutayisire, Paul, 346

Ruyenzi, Paul, 346

Rwabugiri (Kigeri IV), xxxii

Rwanda, colonial regimes (1884–1962): allegiance with Tutsi vs. Hutu in, 50; anti-Tutsi violence in, 255, 279n4; competing forms of external power, xxxv; confrontation of court, colonial power, and common people in, xxix–xxxiii; Des Forges's dissertation on, xiv, xxviii–xxxvii; dual administration (court and Belgians) in, xxxiv, xxxviii*n*6; education policy in, 231; forced cultivation in, 244; land claims in, 255; migrations under, 153; northern societies incorporated by, xxxiii–xxxiv; rural production in, 226–27. *See also* court and aristocratic culture (Tutsi)

Rwanda, post-colonial, pre-genocide (1962–94): agrarian vision of, 242–43, 244, 249n2; civil society expansion in, 27; clientist associational sector in, 88–89; freedom of the press in, 34; historical narrative of, 321; human rights violations in, 343; land claims in, 255; one-party state of, 10, 32, 34, 42–43; rural radicalism in, 227–28, 235–36n3; social structure in, 68–69; stability and order in, 7

Rwanda, post-genocide (1994–): as army with a state, 147n10; concerns and questions about, 3–5, 7, 92; critical issues for, 13–17; desire of, for buffer zone along border, 146n5; as "fit for children," 79, 81, 84; land issues facing, 228–29; new symbols of, 333, 338n4; new thinking needed in, 354–56; response of, to mapping report, 162–64; scholarship on, 5–8; violence potential in, 351–52

Rwanda, pre-colonial period (up to 1884): central statist tradition of, 14–15; drum as symbol in, 67, 75; fabulated memory of, 277–78; perceived unity and now restoration of, 269–70, 272, 273–75, 279–80n5, 301–3, 320–22, 333, 336–37

Rwanda-DRC wars: accountability for RPF crimes in, 152–66; Congolese proxy in (2008), 112; Congolese resources sought in, 138–41; distribution of humanitarian aid used to locate refugees during, 137–38; donors' responses to, 105, 111–13, 115nn7–8, 126; genocide references in Rwandan rhetoric on, 107; identifying refugee camp areas in, 146–47n7; mapping exercise and report concerning, 161–66; massacres in, 5, 17n7, 61n6, 134, 135–37, 147n8, 154–55, 157, 159, 165, 166n4; pursuit of refugees in, 132–34; regime changes sought in, 134–35; roots of, 153–54; RPF troop withdrawal in (2002), 128n10; Rwandan clandestine military activity in and influence over DRC, 140–41, 142–46, 147n16, 147n18; summaries of first (1996–97) and second (1998–2003), 4–5, 154–58; wealth made in, 139–41, 147, 147nn12–13; Western acceptance of Rwanda's rationale in, 141–42, 159–60

Rwanda Metals, 141

Rwandan Civil War (1990–94): continuation in DRC, 132–34; demands for democracy in, 120; as factor in genocide, 322–23, 329nn9–11; implications of RPF victory in, 13–14

Rwigema, Pierre-Celestin, 33, 61n10

Rwisereka, André Kagwa, 34, 350

schools: alleged genocide ideology of, 37, 54–55; civic education in, 319; democratic teaching in, 303–5; distancing technique in, 305–6; historical materials (curricula) development for, 299–300, 302–3; history teaching halted in, 51, 298, 317; history teaching limited in, 329n6; journals as tool in, 311n8; official historical narrative in, 298–303; political constraints on, 307–10; studies of, 297–98; talking vs. not talking about past in, 326–28; teacher education and preparation for, 300–301; what and how to teach history in, 298–99

Scott, James: on high modernist projects, 4, 12–13, 17n10, 224–26, 233; on "weapons of the weak," 236n8 security: community conflicts underlying, 204–6; as core issue in governance, 123; effects of Rwanda-DRC wars on, 165–66; as rationale for *imidugudu* (villagization policy), 229–30; as rationale for war, 132–33, 141–42

Senate, 40, 54, 62n22

Sendashonga, Seth, 32

Serufuli, Eugène, 140

Sezibera, Richard, 144

Shivji, Issa, 223

Short, Clare, 159–60

Sibomana, André, 28, 29, 30, 51, 303

Sikkink, Kathryn, 92

Simba, Aloys, 195, 196, 200, 207n2

Singapore, as economic model, 10, 42, 105

slavery of children, reports of, 81

SNJG (Service national des juridictions gacaca, National Service of Gacaca Jurisdictions), 91, 95, 97

social engineering: ambitions of, 4–5; arenas of, 8–10; implications for future, 248; justification for, 8, 13, 50; models for, 14; performance targets in, 247–48

society: personal jealousy and disputes in, 228, 255–56, 322, 324; pre-genocide structure of, 68–69

SOMIGL (Société minière des Grands Lacs, Great Lakes Mining Company), 141

South Africa: extradition of Nyamwasa refused by, 350–51; history teaching in, 309; land issues in, 223, 254; revolutionary movement in, 14

Soviet Union, collectivization in, 225–26

Sovu: conflicts linked to *gacaca* in, 204–6; *gacaca* trials in, 200–204, 208n12, 208nn8–9; genocide and its legacy in, 196–98; international, transnational, and military trials largely ignored in, 199–200; judicial context of, 195–96; surveys of, 207n4, 208n9

Strategic Plan for Agricultural Transformation, 243

Sudan, prosecution for atrocities in, 180

Sweden, aid for Rwanda cut by, 112–13, 115nn7–8, 126, 128n12, 145, 160

Tanzania, villagization in, 9, 105, 224–26, 256

Theunis, Guy, xv

TIG (Travaux d'intérêt général), 214, 215, 219n15

Tokyo military tribunals, 173

Transitional National Assembly, 32–33

Transparency International, Corruption Index, 43n10

Trócaire, 48, 53, 88, 91

trust. *See* reconciliation and trust

truth: about ethnicity, 273–74; *ingando* reeducation lessons in, 337; uncertainty about, 201

Tutsi: anthropological theory about, 329n8; Catholic priests and, xxxi; ethnicity re-situated by, 270–73, 274–75; growing dissatisfaction with RPF among, 349–50; increased security hazards for, 165–66; key rural positions held by, 73; number killed, 14, 17n1; RPF accusations against critics among, 52; vilification and stereotypes of, 322, 323; violence against in 1959, 255, 279n4; young people's narratives about, 320–22. *See also* genocide

Tutsi elite: agricultural vision of, 243–46; attitudes toward peasantry, 242–43, 354; economic reconstruction and poverty reduction goals of, 240–41; exiled leaders of, 346–47, 352n2; migration to Congo, 153; number of, 279n3; RPF support from, 15; in rural areas, 227; wealth of, 42, 139–41, 147

Tutsi refugee returnees: civil society organizations of, 27–28; land sharing of, 257–58; placement locations for, 229–31, 236n5, 261n8; power concentrated among minority of, 37

Twa: perspectives on, 272–73; young people's narratives about, 320–22

Twagiramungu, Faustin, 32, 39, 52, 56, 115n3

Twizeyimana, Albert-Baudoin, 246

ubudehe (community development planning), 74

Uganda: constraints on children of, 85n9, 85n11; desire for buffer zone along border, 146n5; development aid for, *107*, 161; incursions of, into DRC, 132; "Movement" system of, 10; revolutionary movement in, 14; RPF assistance from, 13; Rwanda compared with, 8

ujamaa ideology, 225

Umoja Wetu ("Our Unity"), 145

Umuco (periodical), 35

umudugudu. See *imidugudu* (villagization policy)

umuganda (community work), 42, 74, 75n3, 227

Umurabyo (periodical), 35

umuryango (family lineage), 10

Umuseso (periodical), 35, 52, 53, 350

Umuvugizi (periodical), 35, 350, 351

UNDP (United Nations Development Programme), 10, 110, 121–22, 240

UN Group of Experts: on RPF in DRC, 144, 145, 147n19, 148n20, 165; on RPF killings in 1994, 175, 181

UNHCHR (United Nations High Commissioner for Human Rights): mapping exercise and report for, 161–66; massacres of refugees investigated by, 155–56; on RPA massacres in DRC, 5, 61n6, 136

UNHCR (United Nations High Commissioner for Refugees): on humanitarian aid and refugees, 138; on *imidugudu* (villagization policy), 235; on land sharing, 258; on refugee repatriation by air, 146–47n7; report on RPF killings of Hutu (not released), 175; Zairian refugee camps of, 133–34

UNITA (*União Nacional para a Independência Total de Angola*, Union for the Total Independence of Angola), 146n5

United Kingdom: aid cut in response to Rwanda-DRC wars, 111–13; aid from, 104, *104*, *107*; attempts to extradite genocide suspects to Rwanda from, 62n23; domestic politics and RPF support in, 110–11; domestic prosecution option advocated by, 179–80; forced to cede territory to Belgians and court, xxxv; government accountability pro-

gram of, 121–22; investigation of RPA war crimes undermined by, 177–78; land reform program aided by, 257; MoU (Memorandum of Understanding) with Rwanda, 109; warnings for RPF in DRC, 144

United Nations: attempt of, to suppress evidence of RPF killings, xvi; report on lack of accountability for RPF crimes in DRC, 152; on RPF's income from Congo, 139–40

United Nations Security Council: arms embargo on Rwanda lifted, 134; ICTR mandate and deadlines, 175, 179; investigation of RPA war crimes undermined by, 178; report on resource pillaging for, 140–41; report on RPA attacks on refugee camps for, 135–38; RPF ordered out of DRC by, 144, 148n20; on Rwandan refugee-warriors, 133

United Nations Trusteeship Council, 227

United States: aid from, 104, *104*; concerns about Rwanda of, 351; contestation of history in, 310n1; domestic politics and RPF support in, 110–11; domestic prosecution option advocated by, 179–80; failure of, to stop genocide, xxiv; investigation of RPA war crimes undermined by, 177–78; warnings for RPF in DRC, 144

UN peacekeeping force. *See* MONUC

Urugwiro meetings, 69, 89, 273–75, 280n5

USAID (U.S. Agency for International Development), 68–69, 94, 125, 256

Uvin, Peter, 109, 110, 114

Vansina, Jan, 277, 280n7

villagization. See *imidugudu* (villagization policy)

Vision 2020, 81, 83, 85n7, 89, 243, 245

VOA (Voice of America), 36, 48, 53, 54, 115n4

war crimes of RPA: accountability for, in DRC, 152–66, 347–48; Del Ponte's "special investigations" of, 177–78, 179; domestic trial of, 180–81; downplayed,

war crimes of RPA (*continued*)
174–75; genocide distinguished from, 61n7; Goldstone's characterization of, 176; impunity for Hutu killed in 1994, 12, 15, 17n2, 51, 173–75, 176, 181, 206–7n1, 355; impunity for Hutu refugees killed in DRC, 5, 17n7, 61n6, 134, 135–37, 138, 154–55, 156, 161; impunity for northwest Rwanda and DRC killings, 12, 15; Jallow's unwillingness to prosecute, 178–81; organized and disciplined, 175; raised in Sovu research surveys, 202–3; suppression of discourse and reports on, 58–59, 115n3, 163–64, 175

war crimes tribunals: approaches of, 173–74; first person convicted of genocide in, 190

Warren, Rick, 26
Wolpe, Howard, 160
women: agricultural labor of, 235–36n3; land registration issues and, 254; organizations of, 28, 30, 31, 90
World Bank: aid from, 104, *104*; rural study halted by, 242; Rwanda praised by, 42–43; on smallholders' importance, 245; World Development Report of, 114

Yugoslavia tribunals, 173, 176, 179, 180

Zaire. *See* DRC
Zakaria, Fareed, 6
Zimbabwe, land issues in, 223

Critical Human Rights